Trio: A Book Of Stories,
Plays, and Poems

# TRIO

## A Book of Stories, Plays, and Poems

*Edited by* HAROLD P. SIMONSON

*University of Puget Sound*

Harper & Row, Publishers

*New York and Evanston*

# Acknowledgments

Sherwood Anderson, "Death in the Woods," published in *American Mercury*, 1926; and *Horses and Men, 1933*, by Liveright. Copyright © 1926 by Eleanor Anderson. Reprinted by permission of Harold Ober Associates Incorporated.

W. H. Auden, "Musée des Beaux Arts," "September 1, 1939." Copyright 1940 by W. H. Auden. Reprinted from *The Collected Poetry of W. H. Auden* by permission of Random House, Inc.

John Cheever, "The Enormous Radio." Permission the author; Copr. © 1947 The New Yorker Magazine, Inc.

Anton Chekhov, "The Cherry Orchard," from *The Portable Chekhov* translated by Avrahm Yarmolinsky. Copyright 1947 by The Viking Press, Inc. and reprinted by their permission.

T. S. Eliot, "The Love Song of J. Alfred Prufrock" from *Collected Poems 1909–1935* by T. S. Eliot, copyright, 1936, by Harcourt, Brace and Company, Inc. and reprinted with their permission. By permission also of Faber and Faber Ltd.

William Faulkner, "That Evening Sun." Copyright 1931 and renewed 1958 by William Faulkner. Reprinted from *Collected Stories of William Faulkner* by permission of Random House, Inc.

Emily Dickinson, "Success Is Counted Sweetest," "Safe in Their Alabaster Chambers," "I Like a Look of Agony," "Because I Could Not Stop for Death," "A Narrow Fellow in the Grass," "The Bustle in a House," "Immortal is an Ample Word," "Apparently with No Surprise," reprinted by permission of the publishers from Thomas H. Johnson, Editor, *The Poems of Emily Dickinson*. Cambridge, Mass.: The Belknap Press of Harvard University Press, Copyright 1951, 1955 by The President and Fellows of Harvard College.

Robert Frost, "Reluctance," "After Apple-Picking," "Out, Out—," "Fire

v

and Ice," "Stopping by Woods on a Snowy Evening," "Desert Places," from *Complete Poems of Robert Frost.* Copyright, 1916, 1921, 1923, 1930, 1949, by Henry Holt and Company, Inc. Copyright, 1936, 1944, 1951, by Robert Frost. By permission of Holt, Rinehart and Winston, Inc.

James Joyce, "A Little Cloud," from *Dubliners* by James Joyce. Reprinted by permission of The Viking Press, Inc.

A. E. Housman, "Loveliest Of Trees," "With Rue My Heart Is Laden," "Terence, This Is Stupid Stuff," "The Chestnut Casts His Flambeaux," from *Complete Poems* by A. E. Housman. Copyright, 1940, © 1959 by Henry Holt and Company, Inc. By permission of Holt, Rinehart and Winston, Inc., and by the Society of Authors as the literary representative of the Trustees of the Estate of the late A. E. Housman, and Messrs. Jonathan Cape, Ltd., publishers of A. E. Housman's *Collected Poems.*

Franz Kafka, "A Hunger Artist," reprinted from *The Penal Colony* by Franz Kafka by permission of Schocken Books, Inc., N. Y. Copyright 1948 by Schocken Books Inc., N. Y. Translated by Willa and Edwin Muir.

D. H. Lawrence, "The Shades of Spring," from *The Prussian Officer* by D. H. Lawrence. Reprinted by permission of The Viking Press, Inc.

Archibald MacLeish, "Ars Poetica," from *Collected Poems of Archibald MacLeish 1917–1952,* copyright 1952 by Houghton Mifflin Company. Reprinted by permission.

Theodore Roethke, "Open House," from *Open House,* by Theodore Roethke. Copyright 1941 by Theodore Roethke. "Dolor," from *The Lost Son and Other Poems,* by Theodore Roethke. Copyright 1947 by Theodore Roethke. Both selections reprinted by permission of Doubleday & Company, Inc.

Jean-Paul Sartre, "The Wall," from *Bedside Book of Famous French Stories,* ed. by Belle Becker and Robert N. Linscott. Copyright 1945 by Random House, Inc. Reprinted by permission.

Dylan Thomas, "The Force That Through The Green Fuse Drives The Flower," "A Refusal To Mourn," "And Death Shall Have No Dominion," "Do Not Go Gentle Into That Good Night," from *The Collected Poems of Dylan Thomas.* Copyright 1952, 1953 by Dylan Thomas. Reprinted by permission of New Directions and J. M. Dent & Sons, Ltd.

Leo Tolstoy, *The Death of Iván Ilých* from *Iván Ilých and Hadji Murád, and Other Stories,* translated by Aylmer Maud and published by Oxford University Press as part of the World's Classics series. Reprinted by permission of the Publisher.

William Butler Yeats, "The Lake Isle Of Innisfree," "The Magi," "The Second Coming," "Leda And The Swan," "Sailing To Byzantium" from *The Collected Poems of W. B. Yeats,* copyright, 1906, 1924, 1928, 1944 by The Macmillan Company. Reprinted by permission of The Macmillan Company, Mrs. William Butler Yeats, A. P. Watt & Son, Macmillan and Co. Ltd., London, and The Macmillan Company of Canada Limited.

To Eric, Greta, and Peter

# Contents

## POETRY

# Preface

Several principles have guided the compilation of this book. Perhaps most obvious is that the collection is not a large one. If a student spends considerable time during a semester studying a single story, play, or poem, then large sections of a more extensive anthology necessarily remain untouched. Fewer works encourage closer analysis, not frantic skimming. This collection is limited enough to promote close and thorough reading. On the other hand, its twelve short stories, two novelettes, two plays, and fifty-eight poems contain sufficient material for introductory courses in literature or humanities, or for a one-quarter or one-semester literary study so common now as part of Freshman English programs. The selections are representative of the three main genres and include a wide range of styles, techniques, and themes.

The editor hopes that a careful reading of these pieces will sharpen the student's perceptions and broaden his sensibilities by introducing him to aspects of human life of which he is perhaps only dimly aware. The stories loosely follow a thematic sequence leading from youthful illusion to knowledge, then to death, recapitulated in the two novelettes. The plays, introducing students to two masterpieces heralding modern realism, explore strange new worlds of mind and culture where, with Ibsen, beliefs become "ghosts of belief" and where, with Chekhov, the symbolic cherry disappears. The poems, with gem-like intensity, compel the reader to participate freely and privately in the experience which the poet has concentrated much like sunlight under a magnifying glass. Some Elizabethan and seventeenth-century poetry is included, but emphasis favors poetry of the last one hundred years.

Biographical notes on each author appear at the end.

For assistance in preparing this book I am grateful to the English

Department faculty of the University of Puget Sound and to Miss Janet Grimes; to my father whose influence extends far more deeply than he realizes; and to my wife, Carolyn.

HAROLD P. SIMONSON

*Tacoma, Washington*
*June, 1961*

# Fiction

SHORT STORIES

Joseph Conrad · William Faulkner
Stephen Crane · D. H. Lawrence
James Joyce · John Cheever
Nathaniel Hawthorne · Edgar Allan Poe
Franz Kafka · Herman Melville
Jean-Paul Sartre · Sherwood Anderson

NOVELETTES

Henry James
Leo Tolstoy

# Youth

## JOSEPH CONRAD

THIS could have occurred nowhere but in England, where men and sea interpenetrate, so to speak—the sea entering into the life of most men, and the men knowing something or everything about the sea, in the way of amusement, of travel, or of bread-winning.

We were sitting round a mahogany table that reflected the bottle, the claret-glasses, and our faces as we leaned on our elbows. There was a director of companies, an accountant, a lawyer, Marlow, and myself. The director had been a *Conway* boy, the accountant had served four years at sea, the lawyer—a fine crusted Tory, High Churchman, the best of old fellows, the soul of honour—had been chief officer in the P. & O. service in the good old days when mailboats were square-rigged at least on two masts, and used to come down the China Sea before a fair monsoon with stun'sails set alow and aloft. We all began life in the merchant service. Between the five of us there was the strong bond of the sea, and also the fellowship of the craft, which no amount of enthusiasm for yachting, cruising, and so on can give, since one is only the amusement of life and the other is life itself.

Marlow (at least I think that is how he spelt his name) told the story, or rather the chronicle, of a voyage:—

"Yes, I have seen a little of the Eastern seas; but what I remember best is my first voyage there. You fellows know there are those voyages that seem ordered for the illustration of life, that might stand for a symbol of existence. You fight, work, sweat, nearly kill yourself, sometimes do kill yourself, trying to accomplish something—and you can't. Not from any fault of yours. You simply can do nothing, neither great nor little—not a thing in the world—not even marry an old maid, or get a wretched 600-ton cargo of coal to its port of destination.

3

"It was altogether a memorable affair. It was my first voyage to the East, and my first voyage as second mate; it was also my skipper's first command. You'll admit it was time. He was sixty if a day; a little man, with a broad, not very straight back, with bowed shoulders and one leg more bandy than the other, he had that queer twisted-about appearance you see so often in men who work in the fields. He had a nut-cracker face—chin and nose trying to come together over a sunken mouth—and it was framed in iron-gray fluffy hair, that looked like a chin-strap of cotton-wool sprinkled with coal-dust. And he had blue eyes in that old face of his, which were amazingly like a boy's, with that candid expression some quite common men preserve to the end of their days by a rare internal gift of simplicity of heart and rectitude of soul. What induced him to accept me was a wonder. I had come out of a crack Australian clipper, where I had been third officer, and he seemed to have a prejudice against crack clippers as aristocratic and high-toned. He said to me, 'You know, in this ship you will have to work.' I said I had to work in every ship I had ever been in. 'Ah, but this is different, and you gentlemen out of them big ships; . . . but there! I dare say you will do. Join tomorrow.'

"I joined tomorrow. It was twenty-two years ago; and I was just twenty. How time passes! It was one of the happiest days of my life. Fancy! Second mate for the first time—a really responsible officer! I wouldn't have thrown up my new billet for a fortune. The mate looked me over carefully. He was also an old chap, but of another stamp. He had a Roman nose, a snow-white, long beard, and his name was Mahon, but he insisted that it should be pronounced Mann. He was well connected; yet there was something wrong with his luck, and he had never got on.

"As to the captain, he had been for years in coasters, then in the Mediterranean, and last in the West Indian trade. He had never been round the Capes. He could just write a kind of sketchy hand, and didn't care for writing at all. Both were thorough good seamen of course, and between those two old chaps I felt like a small boy between two grandfathers.

"The ship also was old. Her name was the *Judea*. Queer name, isn't it? She belonged to a man Wilmer, Wilcox—some name like that; but he has been bankrupt and dead these twenty years or more, and his name don't matter. She had been laid up in Shadwell basin for ever so long. You may imagine her state. She was all rust, dust, grime—

soot aloft, dirt on deck. To me it was like coming out of a palace into a ruined cottage. She was about 400 tons, had a primitive windlass, wooden latches to the doors, not a bit of brass about her, and a big square stern. There was on it, below her name in big letters, a lot of scrollwork, with the gilt off, and some sort of a coat of arms, with the motto 'Do or Die' underneath. I remember it took my fancy immensely. There was a touch of romance in it, something that made me love the old thing—something that appealed to my youth!

"We left London in ballast—sand ballast—to load a cargo of coal in a northern port for Bankok! I thrilled. I had been six years at sea, but had only seen Melbourne and Sydney, very good places, charming places in their way—but Bankok!

"We worked out of the Thames under canvas, with a North Sea pilot on board. His name was Jermyn, and he dodged all day long about the galley drying his handkerchief before the stove. Apparently he never slept. He was a dismal man, with a perpetual tear sparkling at the end of his nose, who either had been in trouble, or was in trouble, or expected to be in trouble—couldn't be happy unless something went wrong. He mistrusted my youth, my common-sense, and my seamanship, and made a point of showing it in a hundred little ways. I dare say he was right. It seems to me I knew very little then, and I know not much more now; but I cherish a hate for that Jermyn to this day.

"We were a week working up as far as Yarmouth Roads, and then we got into a gale—the famous October gale of twenty-two years ago. It was wind, lightning, sleet, snow, and a terrific sea. We were flying light, and you may imagine how bad it was when I tell you we had smashed bulwarks and a flooded deck. On the second night she shifted her ballast into the lee bow, and by that time we had been blown off somewhere on the Dogger Bank. There was nothing for it but go below with shovels and try to right her, and there we were in that vast hold, gloomy like a cavern, the tallow dips stuck and flickering on the beams, the gale howling above, the ship tossing about like mad on her side; there we all were, Jermyn, the captain, everyone, hardly able to keep our feet, engaged on that gravedigger's work, and trying to toss shovelfuls of wet sand up to windward. At every tumble of the ship you could see vaguely in the dim light men falling down with a great flourish of shovels. One of the ship's boys (we had two), impressed by the weirdness of the scene, wept as if his heart would break.

We could hear him blubbering somewhere in the shadows.

"On the third day the gale died out, and by and by a north-country tug picked us up. We took sixteen days in all to get from London to the Tyne! When we got into dock we had lost our turn for loading, and they hauled us off to a tier where we remained for a month. Mrs. Beard (the captain's name was Beard) came from Colchester to see the old man. She lived on board. The crew of runners had left, and there remained only the officers, one boy and the steward, a mulatto who answered to the name of Abraham. Mrs. Beard was an old woman, with a face all wrinkled and ruddy like a winter apple, and the figure of a young girl. She caught sight of me once, sewing on a button, and insisted on having my shirts to repair. This was something different from the captains' wives I had known on board crack clippers. When I brought her the shirts, she said: 'And the socks? They want mending, I am sure, and John's—Captain Beard's—things are all in order now. I would be glad of something to do.' Bless the old woman. She overhauled my outfit for me, and meantime I read for the first time *Sartor Resartus* and Burnaby's *Ride to Khiva*. I didn't understand much of the first then; but I remember I preferred the soldier to the philosopher at the time; a preference which life has only confirmed. One was a man, and the other was either more—or less. However, they are both dead and Mrs. Beard is dead, and youth, strength, genius, thoughts, achievements, simple hearts—all die. . . . No matter.

"They loaded us at last. We shipped a crew. Eight able seamen and two boys. We hauled off one evening to the buoys at the dock-gates, ready to go out, and with a fair prospect of beginning the voyage next day. Mrs. Beard was to start for home by a late train. When the ship was fast we went to tea. We sat rather silent through the meal—Mahon, the old couple, and I. I finished first, and slipped away for a smoke, my cabin being in a deck-house just against the poop. It was high water, blowing fresh with a drizzle; the double dock-gates were opened, and the steam-colliers were going in and out in the darkness with their lights burning bright, a great plashing of propellers, rattling of winches, and a lot of hailing on the pierheads. I watched the procession of head-lights gliding low in the night, when suddenly a red gleam flashed at me, vanished, came into view again, and remained. The fore-end of a steamer loomed up close. I shouted down the cabin, 'Come up, quick!' and then heard a startled voice saying afar in the dark, 'Stop her, sir.' A bell jingled. Another voice cried warningly, 'We are going right into that barque, sir.' The answer to this was a gruff 'All right,' and the next thing was a heavy crash as the steamer struck a glancing blow with the bluff of her bow about our fore-rigging. There was a moment of confusion, yelling, and running about. Steam roared. Then somebody was heard saying, 'All clear, sir.' . . . 'Are you all right?' asked the gruff voice. I had jumped forward to see the damage, and hailed back, 'I think so.' 'Easy astern,' said the gruff voice. A bell jingled. 'What steamer is that?' screamed Mahon. By that time she was no more to us than a bulky shadow manoeuvring a little way off. They shouted at us some name—a woman's name, Miranda or Melissa—or some such thing. 'This means another month in this beastly hole,' said Mahon to me, as we peered with lamps about the splintered bulwarks and broken braces. 'But where's the captain?'

"We had not heard or seen anything of him all that time. We went aft to look. A doleful voice arose hailing somewhere in the middle of the dock, '*Judea* ahoy!' . . . How the devil did he get there? . . . 'Hallo!' we shouted. 'I am adrift in our boat without oars,' he cried. A belated waterman offered his services, and Mahon struck a bargain with him for half-a-crown to tow our skipper alongside; but it was Mrs. Beard that came up the ladder first. They had been floating about the dock in that mizzly cold rain for nearly an hour. I was never so surprised in my life.

"It appears that when he heard my shout 'Come up' he understood at once what was the matter, caught up his wife, ran on deck, and across, and down into our boat, which was fast to the ladder. Not bad for a sixty-year-old. Just imagine that old fellow saving heroically in his arms that old woman—the woman of his life. He set her down on a thwart, and was ready to climb back on board when the painter came adrift somehow, and away they went together. Of course in the confusion we did not hear him shouting. He looked abashed. She said cheerfully, 'I suppose it does not matter my losing the train now?' 'No, Jenny—you go below and get warm,' he growled. Then to us: 'A sailor has no business with a wife—I say. There I was, out of the ship. Well, no harm done this time. Let's go and look at what that fool of a steamer smashed.'

"It wasn't much, but it delayed us three weeks. At the end of that time, the captain being engaged with his agents, I carried Mrs. Beard's bag to the railway-station and put her all comfy into a third-class carriage. She lowered the window to say, 'You are a good young man. If you see John—Captain Beard—without his muffler at night, just remind him from me to keep his throat well wrapped up.' 'Certainly, Mrs. Beard,' I said. 'You are a good young man; I noticed how attentive you are to John—to Captain—' The train pulled out suddenly; I took my cap off to the old woman: I never saw her again. . . . Pass the bottle.

"We went to sea next day. When we made that start for Bankok we had been already three months out of London. We had expected to be a fortnight or so—at the outside.

"It was January, and the weather was beautiful—the beautiful sunny winter weather that has more charm than in the summer-time, because it is unexpected, and crisp, and you know it won't, it can't, last long. It's like a windfall, like a godsend, like an unexpected piece of luck.

"It lasted all down the North Sea, all down Channel; and it lasted till we were three hundred miles or so to the westward of the Lizards: then the wind went round to the sou'west and began to pipe up. In two days it blew a gale. The *Judea,* hove to, wallowed on the Atlantic like an old candlebox. It blew day after day: it blew with spite, without interval, without mercy, without rest. The world was nothing but an immensity of great foaming waves rushing at us, under a sky low enough to touch with the hand and dirty like a smoked ceiling. In the stormy space surrounding us there was as much flying spray as air. Day after day and night after night there was nothing round the ship but the howl of the wind, the tumult of the sea, the noise of water pouring over her deck. There was no rest for her and no rest for us. She tossed, she pitched, she stood on her head, she sat on her tail, she rolled, she groaned, and we had to hold on while on deck and cling to our bunks when below, in a constant effort of body and worry of mind.

"One night Mahon spoke through the small window of my berth. It opened right into my very bed, and I was lying there sleepless, in my boots, feeling as though I had not slept for years, and could not if I tried. He said excitedly—

" 'You got the sounding-rod in here, Marlow? I can't get the pumps to suck. By God! it's no child's play.'

"I gave him the sounding-rod and lay down again, trying to think of various things—but I thought only of the pumps. When I came on deck they were still at it, and my watch relieved at the pumps. By the light of the lantern brought on deck to examine the sounding-rod I caught a glimpse of their weary, serious faces. We pumped all night, all day, all the week—watch and watch. She was working herself loose, and leaked badly—not enough to drown us at once, but enough to kill us with the work at the pumps. And while we pumped the ship was going from us piecemeal: the bulwarks went, the stanchions were torn out, the ventilators smashed, the cabin-door burst in. There was not a dry spot in the ship. She was being gutted bit by bit. The long-boat changed, as if by magic, into matchwood where she stood in her gripes. I had lashed her myself, and was rather proud of my handi-work, which had withstood so long the malice of the sea. And we pumped. And there was no break in the weather. The sea was white like a sheet of foam, like a caldron of boiling milk; there was not a break in the clouds, no—not the size of a man's hand—no, not for so much as ten seconds. There was for us no sky, there were for us no stars, no sun, no universe—nothing but angry clouds and an infuriated sea. We pumped watch and watch, for dear life; and it seemed to last for months, for years, for all eternity, as though we had been dead and gone to a hell for sailors. We forgot the day of the week, the name of the month, what year it was, and whether we had ever been ashore. The sails blew away, she lay broadside on under a weather-cloth, the ocean poured over her, and we did not care. We turned those handles, and had the eyes of idiots. As soon as we had crawled on deck I used to take a round turn with a rope about the men, the pumps, and the mainmast, and we turned, we turned incessantly, with the water to our waists, to our necks, over our heads. It was all one. We had forgotten how it felt to be dry.

"And there was somewhere in me the thought: By Jove! this is the deuce of an adventure—something you read about; and it is my first voyage as second mate—and I am only twenty—and here I am lasting it out as well as any of these men, and keeping my chaps up to the mark. I was pleased. I would not have given up the experience for worlds. I had moments of exultation. Whenever the old dismantled craft pitched heavily with her counter high in the air, she seemed to me to throw up, like an appeal, like a defiance, like a cry to the clouds without mercy, the words written on her stern: '*Judea,* London. Do or Die.'

"O youth! The strength of it, the faith of it, the imagination of it! To me she was not an old rattle-trap carting about the world a lot of coal for a freight—to me she was the endeavour, the test, the trial of life. I think of her with pleasure, with affection, with regret—as you would think of someone dead you have loved. I shall never forget her. . . . Pass the bottle.

"One night when tied to the mast, as I explained, we were pumping on, deafened with the wind, and without spirit enough in us to wish ourselves dead, a heavy sea crashed aboard and swept clean over us. As soon as I got my breath I shouted, as in duty bound, 'Keep on, boys!' when suddenly I felt something hard floating on deck strike the calf of my leg. I made a grab at it and missed. It was so dark we could not see each other's faces within a foot—you understand.

"After that thump the ship kept quiet for a while, and the thing, whatever it was, struck my leg again. This time I caught it—and it was a saucepan. At first, being stupid with fatigue and thinking of nothing but the pumps, I did not understand what I had in my hand. Suddenly it dawned upon me, and I shouted, 'Boys, the house on deck is gone. Leave this, and let's look for the cook.'

"There was a deck-house forward, which contained the galley, the cook's berth, and the quarters of the crew. As we had expected for days to see it swept away, the hands had been ordered to sleep in the cabin—the only safe place in the ship. The steward, Abraham, however, persisted in clinging to his berth, stupidly, like a mule—from sheer fright I believe, like an animal that won't leave a stable falling in an earthquake. So we went to look for him. It was chancing death, since once out of our lashings we were as exposed as if on a raft. But we went. The house was shattered as if a shell had exploded inside. Most of it had gone overboard—stove, men's quarters, and their property, all was gone; but two posts, holding a portion of the bulkhead to which Abraham's bunk was attached, remained as if by a miracle. We groped in the ruins and came upon this, and there he was, sitting in his bunk, surrounded by foam and wreckage, jabbering cheerfully to himself. He was out of his mind; completely and for ever mad, with this sudden shock coming upon the fag-end of his endurance. We snatched him up, lugged him aft, and pitched him head-first down the cabin companion. You understand there was no time to carry him down with infinite precautions and wait to see how he got on. Those below would pick him up at the bottom of the stairs all right. We were in a hurry to go back to the pumps. That business could not wait. A bad leak is an inhuman thing.

"One would think that the sole purpose of that fiendish gale had been to make a lunatic of that poor devil of a mulatto. It eased before morning, and next day the sky cleared, and as the sea went down the leak took up. When it came to bending a fresh set of sails the crew demanded to put back—and really there was nothing else to do. Boats gone, decks swept clean, cabin gutted, men without a stitch but what they stood in, stores spoiled, ship strained. We put her head for home, and—would you believe it? The wind came east right in our teeth. It blew fresh, it blew continuously. We had to beat up every inch of the way, but she did not leak so badly, the water keeping comparatively smooth. Two hours' pumping in every four is no joke—but it kept her afloat as far as Falmouth.

"The good people there live on casualties of the sea, and no doubt were glad to see us. A hungry crowd of shipwrights sharpened their chisels at the sight of that carcass of a ship. And, by Jove! they had pretty pickings off us before they were done. I fancy the owner was already in a tight place. There were delays. Then it was decided to take part of the cargo out and caulk her topsides. This was done, the repairs finished, cargo reshipped; a new crew came on board, and we went out—for Bankok. At the end of a week we were back again. The crew said they weren't going to Bankok—a hundred and fifty days' passage—in a something hooker that wanted pumping eight hours out of the twenty-four; and the nautical papers inserted again the little paragraph: 'Judea. Barque. Tyne to Bankok; coals; put back to Falmouth leaky and with crew refusing duty.'

"There were more delays—more tinkering. The owner came down for a day, and said she was as right as a little fiddle. Poor old Captain Beard looked like the ghost of a Geordie skipper—through the worry and humiliation of it. Remember he was sixty, and it was his first command. Mahon said it was a foolish business, and would end badly. I loved the ship more than ever, and wanted awfully to get to Bankok. To Bankok! Magic name, blessed name. Mesopotamia wasn't a patch on it. Remember I was twenty, and it was my first second-mate's billet, and the East was waiting for me.

"We went out and anchored in the outer roads with a fresh crew—the third. She leaked worse than ever. It was as if those confounded shipwrights had actually made a hole in her. This time we did not even go outside. The crew simply refused to man the windlass.

"They towed us back to the inner harbour, and we became a fixture, a feature, an institution of the place. People pointed us out to visitors as 'That 'ere barque that's going to Bankok—has been here six months —put back three times.' On holidays the small boys pulling about in boats would hail, '*Judea,* ahoy!' and if a head showed above the rail shouted, 'Where you bound to?—Bankok?' and jeered. We were only three on board. The poor old skipper mooned in the cabin. Mahon undertook the cooking, and unexpectedly developed all a Frenchman's genius for preparing nice little messes. I looked languidly after the rigging. We became citizens of Falmouth. Every shopkeeper knew us. At the barber's or tobacconist's they asked familiarly, 'Do you think you will ever get to Bankok?' Meantime the owner, the underwriters, and the charterers squabbled amongst themselves in London, and our pay went on. . . . Pass the bottle.

"It was horrid. Morally it was worse than pumping for life. It seemed as though we had been forgotten by the world, belonged to nobody, would get nowhere; it seemed that, as if bewitched, we would have to live for ever and ever in that inner harbour, a derision and a byword to generations of long-shore loafers and dishonest boatmen. I obtained three months' pay and a five days' leave, and made a rush for London. It took me a day to get there and pretty well another to come back—but three months' pay went all the same. I don't know what I did with it. I went to a music-hall, I believe, lunched, dined, and supped in a swell place in Regent Street, and was back to time, with nothing but a complete set of Byron's works and a new railway rug to show for three months' work. The boatman who pulled me off to the ship said: 'Hallo! I thought you had left the old thing. *She* will never get to Bankok.' 'That's all *you* know about it,' I said scornfully—but I didn't like that prophecy at all.

"Suddenly a man, some kind of agent to somebody, appeared with full powers. He had grog-blossoms all over his face, an indomitable energy, and was a jolly soul. We leaped into life again. A hulk came alongside, took our cargo, and then we went into dry dock to get our copper stripped. No wonder she leaked. The poor thing, strained beyond endurance by the gale, had, as if in disgust, spat out all the oakum of her lower seams. She was recaulked, new coppered, and made as tight as a bottle. We went back to the hulk and reshipped our cargo.

"Then, on a fine moonlight night, all the rats left the ship.

"We had been infested with them. They had destroyed our sails, consumed more stores than the crew, affably shared our beds and our dangers, and now, when the ship was made seaworthy, concluded to clear out. I called Mahon to enjoy the spectacle. Rat after rat appeared on our rail, took a last look over his shoulder, and leaped with a hollow thud into the empty hulk. We tried to count them, but soon lost the tale. Mahon said: 'Well, well! don't talk to me about the intelligence of rats. They ought to have left before, when we had that narrow squeak from foundering. There you have the proof how silly is the superstition about them. They leave a good ship for an old rotten hulk, where there is nothing to eat, too, the fools! . . . I don't believe they know what is safe or what is good for them, any more than you or I.'

"And after some more talk we agreed that the wisdom of rats had been grossly overrated, being in fact no greater than that of men.

"The story of the ship was known, by this, all up the Channel from Land's End to the Forelands, and we could get no crew on the south coast. They sent us one all complete from Liverpool, and we left once more—for Bankok.

"We had fair breezes, smooth water right into the tropics, and the old *Judea* lumbered along in the sunshine. When she went eight knots everything cracked aloft, and we tied our caps to our heads; but mostly she strolled on at the rate of three miles an hour. What could you expect? She was tired—that old ship. Her youth was where mine is—where yours is—you fellows who listen to this yarn; and what friend would throw your years and weariness in your face? We didn't grumble at her. To us aft, at least, it seemed as though we had been born in her, reared in her, had lived in her for ages, had never known any other ship. I would just as soon have abused the old village church at home for not being a cathedral.

"And for me there was also my youth to make me patient. There was all the East before me, and all life, and the thought that I had been tried in that ship and had come out pretty well. And I thought of men of old who, centuries ago, went that road in ships that sailed no better, to the land of palms, and spices, and yellow sands, and of brown nations ruled by kings more cruel than Nero the Roman, and more splendid than Solomon the Jew. The old bark lumbered on, heavy with her age and the burden of her cargo, while I lived the life of youth in ignorance and hope. She lumbered on through an interminable procession of days; and the fresh gilding flashed back at the setting sun, seemed to cry out over the darkening sea the words painted on her stern, '*Judea*, London. Do or Die.'

"Then we entered the Indian Ocean and steered northerly for Java Head. The winds were light. Weeks slipped by. She crawled on, do or die, and people at home began to think of posting us as overdue.

"One Saturday evening, I being off duty, the men asked me to give them an extra bucket of water or so—for washing clothes. As I did not wish to screw on the fresh-water pump so late, I went forward whistling, and with a key in my hand to unlock the forepeak scuttle, intending to serve the water out of a spare tank we kept there.

"The smell down below was as unexpected as it was frightful. One would have thought hundreds of paraffin-lamps had been flaring and smoking in that hole for days. I was glad to get out. The man with me coughed and said, 'Funny smell, sir.' I answered negligently, 'It's good for the health they say,' and walked aft.

"The first thing I did was to put my head down the square of the mid-ship ventilator. As I lifted the lid a visible breath, something like a thin fog, a puff of faint haze, rose from the opening. The ascending air was hot, and had a heavy, sooty, paraffiny smell. I gave one sniff, and put down the lid gently. It was no use choking myself. The cargo was on fire.

"Next day she began to smoke in earnest. You see it was to be expected, for though the coal was of a safe kind, that cargo had been so handled, so broken up with handling, that it looked more like smithy coal than anything else. Then it had been wetted—more than once. It rained all the time we were taking it back from the hulk, and now with this long passage it got heated, and there was another case of spontaneous combustion.

"The captain called us into the cabin. He had a chart spread on the table, and looked unhappy. He said, 'The coast of West Australia is near, but I mean to proceed to our destination. It is the hurricane month, too; but we will just keep her head for Bankok, and fight the fire. No more putting back anywhere, if we all get roasted. We will try first to stifle this 'ere damned combustion by want of air.'

"We tried. We battened down everything, and still she smoked. The smoke kept coming out through imperceptible crevices; it forced itself through bulkheads and covers; it oozed here and there and everywhere in slender threads, in an invisible film, in an incomprehensible manner. It made its way into the cabin, into the forecastle; it poisoned the sheltered places on the deck, it could be sniffed as high as the mainyard. It was clear that if the smoke came out the air came in.

This was disheartening. This combustion refused to be stifled.

"We resolved to try water, and took the hatches off. Enormous volumes of smoke, whitish, yellowish, thick, greasy, misty, choking, ascended as high as the trucks. All hands cleared out aft. Then the poisonous cloud blew away, and we went back to work in a smoke that was no thicker now than that of an ordinary factory chimney.

"We rigged the force-pump, got the hose along, and by and by it burst. Well, it was as old as the ship—a prehistoric hose, and past repair. Then we pumped with the feeble head-pump, drew water with buckets, and in this way managed in time to pour lots of Indian Ocean into the main hatch. The bright stream flashed in sunshine, fell into a layer of white crawling smoke, and vanished on the black surface of coal. Steam ascended mingling with the smoke. We poured salt water as into a barrel without a bottom. It was our fate to pump in that ship, to pump out of her, to pump into her; and after keeping water out of her to save ourselves from being drowned, we frantically poured water into her to save ourselves from being burnt.

"And she crawled on, do or die, in the serene weather. The sky was a miracle of purity, a miracle of azure. The sea was polished, was blue, was pellucid, was sparkling like a precious stone, extending on all sides, all round to the horizon—as if the whole terrestrial globe had been one jewel, one colossal sapphire, a single gem fashioned into a planet. And on the lustre of the great calm waters the *Judea* glided imperceptibly, enveloped in languid and unclean vapours, in a lazy cloud that drifted to leeward, light and slow; a pestiferous cloud defiling the splendour of sea and sky.

"All this time of course we saw no fire. The cargo smouldered at the bottom somewhere. Once Mahon, as we were working side by side, said to me with a queer smile: 'Now, if she only would spring a tidy leak—like that time when we first left the Channel—it would put a stopper on this fire. Wouldn't it?' I remarked irrelevantly, 'Do you remember the rats?'

"We fought the fire and sailed the ship too as carefully as though nothing had been the matter. The steward cooked and attended on us. Of the other twelve men, eight worked while four rested. Everyone took his turn, captain included. There was equality, and if not exactly fraternity, then a deal of good feeling. Sometimes a man, as he dashed a bucketful of water down the hatchway, would yell out, 'Hurrah for Bankok!' and the rest laughed. But generally we were taciturn and serious—and thirsty. Oh! how thirsty! And we had to be careful with the water. Strict allowance. The ship smoked, the sun blazed. . . . Pass the bottle.

"We tried everything. We even made an attempt to dig down to the fire. No good, of course. No man could remain more than a minute below. Mahon, who went first, fainted there, and the man who went to fetch him out did likewise. We lugged them out on deck. Then I leaped down to show how easily it could be done. They had learned wisdom by that time, and contented themselves by fishing for me with a chain-hook tied to a broom-handle, I believe. I did not offer to go and fetch up my shovel, which was left down below.

"Things began to look bad. We put the long-boat into the water. The second boat was ready to swing out. We had also another, a 14-foot thing, on davits aft, where it was quite safe.

"Then, behold, the smoke suddenly decreased. We redoubled our efforts to flood the bottom of the ship. In two days there was no smoke at all. Everybody was on the broad grin. This was on a Friday. On Saturday no work, but sailing the ship of course, was done. The men washed their clothes and their faces for the first time in a fortnight, and had a special dinner given them. They spoke of spontaneous combustion with contempt, and implied *they* were the boys to put out combustions. Somehow we all felt as though we each had inherited a large fortune. But a beastly smell of burning hung about the ship. Captain Beard had hollow eyes and sunken cheeks. I had never noticed so much before how twisted and bowed he was. He and Mahon prowled soberly about hatches and ventilators, sniffing. It struck me suddenly poor Mahon was a very, very old chap. As to me, I was as pleased and proud as though I had helped to win a great naval battle. O! Youth!

"The night was fine. In the morning a homeward-bound ship passed us hull down—the first we had seen for months; but we were nearing the land at last, Java Head being about 190 miles off, and nearly due north.

"Next day it was my watch on deck from eight to twelve. At breakfast the captain observed, 'It's wonderful how that smell hangs about the cabin.' About ten, the mate being on the poop, I stepped down on the main-deck for a moment. The carpenter's bench stood abaft the mainmast: I leaned against it sucking at my pipe, and the carpenter, a young chap, came to talk to me. He remarked, 'I think we have done

very well, haven't we?' and then I perceived with annoyance the fool
was trying to tilt the bench. I said curtly, 'Don't, Chips,' and immediately became aware of a queer sensation, of an absurd delusion,—I
seemed somehow to be in the air. I heard all round me like a pent-up
breath release—as if a thousand giants simultaneously had said Phoo!
—and felt a dull concussion which made my ribs ache suddenly. No
doubt about it—I was in the air, and my body was describing a short
parabola. But short as it was, I had the time to think several thoughts
in, as far as I can remember, the following order: 'This can't be the
carpenter—What is it?—Some accident—Submarine volcano?—Coals,
gas!—By Jove! we are being blown up—Everybody's dead—I am falling into the after-hatch—I see fire in it.'

"The coal-dust suspended in the air of the hold had glowed dull-red
at the moment of the explosion. In the twinkling of an eye, in an
infinitesimal fraction of a second since the first tilt of the bench, I
was sprawling full length on the cargo. I picked myself up and
scrambled out. It was quick like a rebound. The deck was a wilderness
of smashed timber, lying crosswise like trees in a wood after a hurricane; an immense curtain of soiled rags waved gently before me—it
was the mainsail blown to strips. I thought, The masts will be top-
pling over directly; and to get out of the way bolted on all-fours towards the poop-ladder. The first person I saw was Mahon, with eyes
like saucers, his mouth open, and the long white hair standing straight
on end round his head like a silver halo. He was just about to go
down when the sight of the main-deck stirring, heaving up, and
changing into splinters before his eyes, petrified him on the top step.
I stared at him in unbelief, and he stared at me with a queer kind of
shocked curiosity. I did not know that I had no hair, no eyebrows, no
eyelashes, that my young moustache was burnt off, that my face was
black, one cheek laid open, my nose cut, and my chin bleeding. I had
lost my cap, one of my slippers, and my shirt was torn to rags. Of all
this I was not aware. I was amazed to see the ship still afloat, the
poop-deck whole—and, most of all, to see anybody alive. Also the
peace of the sky and the serenity of the sea were distinctly surprising.
I suppose I expected to see them convulsed with horror. . . . Pass the
bottle.

"There was a voice hailing the ship from somewhere—in the air, in
the sky—I couldn't tell. Presently I saw the captain—and he was mad.
He asked eagerly, 'Where's the cabin-table?' and to hear such a ques-

tion was a frightful shock. I had just been blown up, you understand, and vibrated with that experience,—I wasn't quite sure whether I was alive. Mahon began to stamp with both feet and yelled at him, 'Good God! don't you see the deck's blown out of her?' I found my voice, and stammered out as if conscious of some gross neglect of duty, 'I don't know where the cabin-table is.' It was like an absurd dream.

"Do you know what he wanted next? Well, he wanted to trim the yards. Very placidly, and as if lost in thought, he insisted on having the foreyard squared. 'I don't know if there's anybody alive,' said Mahon, almost tearfully. 'Surely,' he said, gently, 'there will be enough left to square the foreyard.'

"The old chap, it seems, was in his own berth winding up the chronometers, when the shock sent him spinning. Immediately it occurred to him—as he said afterwards—that the ship had struck something, and he ran out into the cabin. There, he saw, the cabin-table had vanished somewhere. The deck being blown up, it had fallen down into the lazarette of course. Where we had our breakfast that morning he saw only a great hole in the floor. This appeared to him so awfully mysterious, and impressed him so immensely, that what he saw and heard after he got on deck were mere trifles in comparison. And, mark, he noticed directly the wheel deserted and his barque off her course—and his only thought was to get that miserable, stripped, undecked, smouldering shell of a ship back again with her head pointing at her port of destination. Bankok! That's what he was after. I tell you this quiet, bowed, bandy-legged, almost deformed little man was immense in the singleness of his idea and in his placid ignorance of our agitation. He motioned us forward with a commanding gesture, and went to take the wheel himself.

"Yes; that was the first thing we did—trim the yards of that wreck! No one was killed, or even disabled, but everyone was more or less hurt. You should have seen them! Some were in rags, with black faces, like coal-heavers, like sweeps, and had bullet heads that seemed closely cropped, but were in fact singed to the skin. Others, of the watch below, awakened by being shot out from their collapsing bunks, shivered incessantly, and kept on groaning even as we went about our work. But they all worked. That crew of Liverpool hard cases had in them the right stuff. It's my experience they always have. It is the sea that gives it—the vastness, the loneliness surrounding their dark stolid souls. Ah! Well! we stumbled, we crept, we fell, we barked our shins on the wreckage, we hauled. The masts stood, but we did not know how much they might be charred down below. It was nearly calm, but a long swell ran from the west and made her roll. They might go at any moment. We looked at them with apprehension. One could not foresee which way they would fall.

"Then we retreated aft and looked about us. The deck was a tangle of planks on edge, of planks on end, of splinters, of ruined woodwork. The masts rose from that chaos like big trees above a matted undergrowth. The interstices of that mass of wreckage were full of something whitish, sluggish, stirring—of something that was like a greasy fog. The smoke of the invisible fire was coming up again, was trailing, like a poisonous thick mist in some valley choked with dead wood. Already lazy wisps were beginning to curl upwards amongst the mass of splinters. Here and there a piece of timber, stuck upright, resembled a post. Half of a fife-rail had been shot through the foresail, and the sky made a patch of glorious blue in the ignobly soiled canvas. A portion of several boards holding together had fallen across the rail, and one end protruded overboard, like a gangway leading upon nothing, like a gangway leading over the deep sea, leading to death—as if inviting us to walk the plank at once and be done with our ridiculous troubles. And still the air, the sky—a ghost, something invisible was hailing the ship.

"Someone had the sense to look over, and there was the helmsman, who had impulsively jumped overboard, anxious to come back. He yelled and swam lustily like a merman, keeping up with the ship. We threw him a rope, and presently he stood amongst us streaming with water and very crestfallen. The captain had surrendered the wheel, and apart, elbow on rail and chin in hand, gazed at the sea wistfully. We asked ourselves, What next? I thought, Now, this is something like. This is great. I wonder what will happen. O youth!

"Suddenly Mahon sighted a steamer far astern. Captain Beard said, 'We may do something with her yet.' We hoisted two flags, which said in the international language of the sea, 'On fire. Want immediate assistance.' The steamer grew bigger rapidly, and by and by spoke with two flags on her foremast, 'I am coming to your assistance.'

"In half an hour she was abreast, to windward, within hail, and rolling slightly, with her engines stopped. We lost our composure, and yelled all together with excitement, 'We've been blown up.' A man in a white helmet, on the bridge, cried, 'Yes! All right! All right!' and he nodded his head, and smiled, and made soothing motions with his hand as though at a lot of frightened children. One of the boats dropped in the water, and walked towards us upon the sea with her long oars. Four Calashes pulled a swinging stroke. This was my first sight of Malay seamen. I've known them since, but what struck me was their unconcern: they came alongside, and even the bowman standing up and holding to our main-chains with the boat-hook did not deign to lift his head for a glance. I thought people who had been blown up deserved more attention.

"A little man, dry like a chip and agile like a monkey, clambered up. It was the mate of the steamer. He gave one look, and cried, 'Oh, boys—you had better quit.'

"We were silent. He talked apart with the captain for a time,—seemed to argue with him. Then they went away together to the steamer.

"When our skipper came back we learned that the steamer was the *Somerville,* Captain Nash, from West Australia to Singapore via Batavia with mails, and that the agreement was she should tow us to Anjer or Batavia, if possible, where we could extinguish the fire by scuttling, and then proceed on our voyage—to Bankok! The old man seemed excited. 'We will do it yet,' he said to Mahon, fiercely. He shook his first at the sky. Nobody else said a word.

"At noon the steamer began to tow. She went ahead slim and high, and what was left of the *Judea* followed at the end of seventy fathom of tow-rope,—followed her swiftly like a cloud of smoke with mast-heads protruding above. We went aloft to furl the sails. We coughed on the yards, and were careful about the bunts. Do you see the lot of us there, putting a neat furl on the sails of that ship doomed to arrive nowhere? There was not a man who didn't think that at any moment the masts would topple over.

From aloft we could not see the ship for smoke, and they worked carefully, passing the gaskets with even turns. 'Harbour furl—aloft there!' cried Mahon from below.

"You understand this? I don't think one of those chaps expected to get down in the usual way. When we did I heard them saying to each other, 'Well, I thought we would come down overboard, in a lump —sticks and all—blame me if I didn't.' 'That's what I was thinking to myself,' would answer wearily another battered and bandaged scarecrow. And, mind, these were men without the drilled-in habit of obedience. To an onlooker they would be a lot of profane scallywags without a redeeming point. What made them do it—what made them obey me when I, thinking consciously how fine it was, made them drop the bunt of the foresail twice to try and do it better? What? They had no professional reputation—no examples, no praise. It wasn't a sense of duty; they all knew well enough how to shirk, and laze, and dodge—when they had a mind to it—and mostly they had. Was it the two pounds ten a month that sent them there? They didn't think their pay half good enough. No; it was something in them, something inborn and subtle and everlasting. I don't say positively that the crew of a French or German merchantman wouldn't have done it, but I doubt whether it would have been done in the same way. There was a completeness in it, something solid like a principle, and masterful like an instinct—a disclosure of something secret—of that hidden something, that gift of good or evil that makes racial difference, that shapes the fate of nations.

"It was that night at ten that, for the first time since we had been fighting it, we saw the fire. The speed of the towing had fanned the smouldering destruction. A blue gleam appeared forward, shining below the wreck of the deck. It wavered in patches, it seemed to stir and creep like the light of a glowworm. I saw it first, and told Mahon. 'Then the game's up,' he said. 'We had better stop this towing, or she will burst out suddenly fore and aft before we can clear out.' We set up a yell; rang bells to attract their attention; they towed on. At last Mahon and I had to crawl forward and cut the rope with an axe. There was no time to cast off the lashings. Red tongues could be seen licking the wilderness of splinters under our feet as we made our way back to the poop.

"Of course they very soon found out in the steamer that the rope was gone. She gave a loud blast of her whistle, her lights were seen sweeping in a wide circle, she came up ranging close alongside, and stopped. We were all in a tight group on the poop looking at her. Every man had saved a little bundle or a bag. Suddenly a conical flame with a twisted top shot up forward and threw upon the black sea a circle of light, with the two vessels side by side and heaving gently in its centre. Captain Beard had been sitting on the gratings still and mute for hours, but now he rose slowly and advanced in front of us, to the mizzen-shrouds. Captain Nash hailed: 'Come along! Look sharp. I have mail-bags on board. I will take you and your boats to Singapore.'

" 'Thank you! No!' said our skipper. 'We must see the last of the ship.'

" 'I can't stand by any longer,' shouted the other. 'Mails—you know.'

" 'Ay, ay! We are all right.'

" 'Very well! I'll report you in Singapore. . . . Good-bye!'

"He waved his hand. Our men dropped their bundles quietly. The steamer moved ahead, and passing out of the circle of light, vanished at once from our sight, dazzled by the fire which burned fiercely. And then I knew that I would see the East first as commander of a small boat. I thought it fine; and the fidelity to the old ship was fine. We should see the last of her. Oh, the glamour of youth! Oh, the fire of it, more dazzling than the flames of the burning ship, throwing a magic light on the wide earth, leaping audaciously to the sky, presently to be quenched by time, more cruel, more pitiless, more bitter than the sea—and like the flames of the burning ship surrounded by an impenetrable night.

"The old man warned us in his gentle and inflexible way that it was part of our duty to save for the underwriters as much as we could of the ship's gear. Accordingly we went to work aft, while she blazed forward to give us plenty of light. We lugged out a lot of rubbish. What didn't we save? An old barometer fixed with an absurd quantity of screws nearly cost me my life: a sudden rush of smoke came upon me, and I just got away in time. There were various stores, bolts of canvas, coils of rope; the poop looked like a marine bazaar, and the boats were lumbered to the gunwales. One would have thought the old man wanted to take as much as he could of his first command with him. He was very, very quiet, but off his balance evidently. Would you believe it? He wanted to take a length of old stream-cable and a kedge-anchor with him in the long-boat. We said, 'Ay, ay, sir,' deferentially, and on the quiet let the things slip overboard. The heavy medicine-chest went that way, two bags of green coffee, tins of paint —fancy, paint!—a whole lot of things. Then I was ordered with two hands into the boats to make a stowage and get them ready against the time it would be proper for us to leave the ship.

"We put everything straight, stepped the long-boat's mast for our skipper, who was to take charge of her, and I was not sorry to sit down for a moment. My face felt raw, every limb ached as if broken, I was aware of all my ribs, and would have sworn to a twist in the backbone. The boats, fast astern, lay in a deep shadow, and all around I could see the circle of the sea lighted by the fire. A gigantic flame arose forward straight and clear. It flared fierce, with noises like the whirr of wings, with rumbles as of thunder. There were cracks, detonations, and from the cone of flame the sparks flew upwards, as man is born to trouble, to leaky ships, and to ships that burn.

"What bothered me was that the ship, lying broadside to the swell and to such wind as there was—a mere breath—the boats would not keep astern where they were safe, but persisted, in a pig-headed way boats have, in getting under the counter and then swinging alongside. They were knocking about dangerously and coming near the flame, while the ship rolled on them, and, of course, there was always the danger of the masts going over the side in any moment. I and my two boat-keepers kept them off as best we could, with oars and boat-hooks; but to be constantly at it became exasperating, since there was no reason why we should not leave at once. We could not see those on board, nor could we imagine what caused the delay. The boat-keepers were swearing feebly, and I had not only my share of the work but also had to keep at it two men who showed a constant inclination to lay themselves down and let things slide.

"At last I hailed, 'On deck there,' and someone looked over. 'We're ready here,' I said. The head disappeared, and very soon popped up again. 'The captain says, All right, sir, and to keep the boats well clear of the ship.'

"Half an hour passed. Suddenly there was a frightful racket, rattle, clanking of chain, hiss of water, and millions of sparks flew up into the shivering column of smoke that stood leaning slightly above the ship. The cat-heads had burned away, and the two red-hot anchors had gone to the bottom, tearing out after them two hundred fathom of red-hot chain. The ship trembled, the mass of flame swayed as if ready to collapse, and the fore top-gallant-mast fell. It darted down like an arrow of fire, shot under, and instantly leaping up within an oar's-length of the boats, floated quietly, very black on the luminous sea. I hailed the deck again. After some time a man in an unexpectedly cheerful but also muffled tone, as though he had been trying to speak with his mouth shut, informed me, 'Coming directly, sir,' and vanished.

For a long time I heard nothing but the whirr and roar of the fire.
There were also whistling sounds. The boats jumped, tugged at the
painters, ran at each other playfully, knocked their sides together, or,
do what we would, swung in a bunch against the ship's side. I couldn't
stand it any longer, and swarming up a rope, clambered aboard over
the stern.

"It was as bright as day. Coming up like this, the sheet of fire facing
me was a terrifying sight, and the heat seemed hardly bearable at first.
On a settee cushion dragged out of the cabin Captain Beard, his legs
drawn up and one arm under his head, slept with the light playing
on him. Do you know what the rest were busy about? They were
sitting on deck right aft, round an open case, eating bread and cheese
and drinking bottled stout.

"On the background of flames twisting in fierce tongues above their
heads they seemed at home like salamanders, and looked like a band
of desperate pirates. The fire sparkled in the whites of their eyes,
gleamed on patches of white skin seen through the torn shirts. Each
had the marks as of a battle about him—bandaged heads, tied-up arms,
a strip of dirty rag around a knee—and each man had a bottle between
his legs and a chunk of cheese in his hand. Mahon got up. With his
handsome and disreputable head, his hooked profile, his long white
beard, and with an uncorked bottle in his hand, he resembled one of
those reckless sea-robbers of old making merry amidst violence and
disaster. 'The last meal on board,' he explained solemnly. 'We had
nothing to eat all day, and it was no use leaving all this.' He flourished
the bottle and indicated the sleeping skipper. 'He said he couldn't
swallow anything, so I got him to lie down,' he went on; and as I
stared, 'I don't know whether you are aware, young fellow, the man
had no sleep to speak of for days—and there will be dam' little sleep
in the boats.' 'There will be no boats by-and-by if you fool about much
longer,' I said indignantly. I walked up to the skipper and shook him
by the shoulder. At last he opened his eyes, but did not move. 'Time
to leave her, sir,' I said quietly.

"He got up painfully, looked at the flames, at the sea sparkling
round the ship, and black, black as ink farther away; he looked at the
stars shining dim through a thin veil of smoke in a sky black, black
as Erebus.

" 'Youngest first,' he said.

"And the ordinary seaman, wiping his mouth with the back of his hand, got up, clambered over the taffrail, and vanished. Others followed. One, on the point of going over, stopped short to drain his bottle, and with a great swing of his arm flung it at the fire. 'Take this!' he cried.

"The skipper lingered disconsolately, and we left him to commune alone for a while with his first command. Then I went up again and brought him away at last. It was time. The ironwork on the poop was hot to the touch.

"Then the painter of the long-boat was cut, and the three boats, tied together, drifted clear of the ship. It was just sixteen hours after the explosion when we abandoned her. Mahon had charge of the second boat, and I had the smallest—the 14-foot thing. The long-boat would have taken the lot of us; but the skipper said we must save as much property as we could—for the underwriters—and so I got my first command. I had two men with me, a bag of biscuits, a few tins of meat, and a breaker of water. I was ordered to keep close to the long-boat, that in case of bad weather we might be taken into her.

"And do you know what I thought? I thought I would part company as soon as I could. I wanted to have my first command all to myself. I wasn't going to sail in a squadron if there were a chance for independent cruising. I would make land by myself. I would beat the other boats. Youth! All youth! The silly, charming, beautiful youth.

"But we did not make a start at once. We must see the last of the ship. And so the boats drifted about that night, heaving and setting on the swell. The men dozed, waked, sighed, groaned. I looked at the burning ship.

"Between the darkness of earth and heaven she was burning fiercely upon a disc of purple sea shot by the blood-red play of gleams; upon a disc of water glittering and sinister. A high, clear flame, an immense black smoke poured continuously at the sky. She burned furiously; mournful and imposing like a funeral pile kindled in the night, surrounded by the sea, watched over by the stars. A magnificent death had come like a grace, like a gift, like a reward to that old ship at the end of her laborious days. The surrender of her weary ghost to the keeping of stars and sea was stirring like the sight of a glorious triumph. The masts fell just before daybreak, and for a moment there was a burst and turmoil of sparks that seemed to fill with flying fire the night patient and watchful, the vast night lying silent upon the sea. At daylight she was only a charred shell, floating still under a cloud of smoke and bearing a glowing mass of coal within.

"Then the oars were got out, and the boats forming in a line moved round her remains as if in procession—the long-boat leading. As we pulled across her stern a slim dart of fire shot out viciously at us, and suddenly she went down, head first, in a great hiss of steam. The unconsumed stern was the last to sink; but the paint had gone, had cracked, had peeled off, and there were no letters, there was no word, no stubborn device that was like her soul, to flash at the rising sun her creed and her name.

"We made our way north. A breeze sprang up, and about noon all the boats came together for the last time. I had no mast or sail in mine, but I made a mast out of a spare oar and hoisted a boat-awning for a sail, with a boat-hook for a yard. She was certainly over-masted, but I had the satisfaction of knowing that with the wind aft I could beat the other two. I had to wait for them. Then we all had a look at the captain's chart, and, after a sociable meal of hard bread and water, got our last instructions. These were simple: steer north, and keep together as much as possible. 'Be careful with that jury-rig, Marlow,' said the captain; and Mahon, as I sailed proudly past his boat, wrinkled his curved nose and hailed, 'You will sail that ship of yours under water, if you don't look out, young fellow.' He was a malicious old man—and may the deep sea where he sleeps now rock him gently, rock him tenderly to the end of time!

"Before sunset a thick rain-squall passed over the two boats, which were far astern, and that was the last I saw of them for a time. Next day I sat steering my cockle-shell—my first command—with nothing but water and sky around me. I did sight in the afternoon the upper sails of a ship far away, but said nothing, and my men did not notice her. You see I was afraid she might be homeward bound, and I had no mind to turn back from the portals of the East. I was steering for Java—another blessed name—like Bankok, you know. I steered many days.

"I need not tell you what it is to be knocking about in an open boat. I remember nights and days of calm, and we pulled, we pulled, and the boat seemed to stand still, as if bewitched within the circle of the sea horizon. I remember the heat, the deluge of rain-squalls that kept us baling for dear life (but filled our water-cask), and I remember sixteen hours on end with a mouth dry as a cinder and a steering-oar

over the stern to keep my first command head on to a breaking sea.
I did not know how good a man I was till then. I remember the drawn
faces, the dejected figures of my two men, and I remember my youth
and the feeling that will never come back any more—the feeling that
I could last for ever, outlast the sea, the earth, and all men; the de-
ceitful feeling that lures us on to joys, to perils, to love, to vain effort
—to death; the triumphant conviction of strength, the heat of life in
the handful of dust, the glow in the heart that with every year grows
dim, grows cold, grows small, and expires—and expires, too soon, too
soon—before life itself.

"And this is how I see the East. I have seen its secret places and
have looked into its very soul; but now I see it always from a small
boat, a high outline of mountains, blue and afar in the morning; like
faint mist at noon; a jagged wall of purple at sunset. I have the feel
of the oar in my hand, the vision of a scorching blue sea in my eyes.
And I see a bay, a wide bay, smooth as glass and polished like ice,
shimmering in the dark. A red light burns far off upon the gloom of
the land, and the night is soft and warm. We drag at the oars with
aching arms, and suddenly a puff of wind, a puff faint and tepid and
laden with strange odours of blossoms, of aromatic wood, comes out
of the still night—the first sign of the East on my face. That I can
never forget. It was impalpable and enslaving, like a charm, like a
whispered promise of mysterious delight.

"We had been pulling this finishing spell for eleven hours. Two
pulled, and he whose turn it was to rest sat at the tiller. We had made
out the red light in that bay and steered for it, guessing it must mark
some small coasting port. We passed two vessels, outlandish and high-
sterned, sleeping at anchor, and, approaching the light, now very dim,
ran the boat's nose against the end of a jutting wharf. We were blind
with fatigue. My men dropped the oars and fell off the thwarts as if
dead. I made fast to a pile. A current rippled softly. The scented obscurity of the shore was grouped into vast masses, a density of colossal
clumps of vegetation, probably—mute and fantastic shapes. And at
their foot the semicircle of a beach gleamed faintly, like an illusion.
There was not a light, not a stir, not a sound. The mysterious East
faced me, perfumed like a flower, silent like death, dark like a grave.

"And I sat weary beyond expression, exulting like a conqueror,
sleepless and entranced as if before a profound, a fateful enigma.

"A splashing of oars, a measured dip reverberating on the level of water, intensified by the silence of the shore into loud claps, made me jump up. A boat, a European boat, was coming in. I invoked the name of the dead; I hailed: *Judea* ahoy! A thin shout answered.

"It was the captain. I had beaten the flagship by three hours, and I was glad to hear the old man's voice again, tremulous and tired. 'Is it you, Marlow?' 'Mind the end of that jetty, sir,' I cried.

"He approached cautiously, and brought up with the deep-sea lead-line which we had saved—for the underwriters. I eased my painter and fell alongside. He sat, a broken figure at the stern, wet with dew, his hands clasped in his lap. His men were asleep already. 'I had a terrible time of it,' he murmured. 'Mahon is behind—not very far.' We conversed in whispers, in low whispers, as if afraid to wake up the land. Guns, thunder, earthquakes would not have awakened the men just then.

"Looking round as we talked, I saw away at sea a bright light travelling in the night. 'There's a steamer passing the bay,' I said. She was not passing, she was entering, and she even came close and anchored. 'I wish,' said the old man, 'you would find out whether she is English. Perhaps they could give us a passage somewhere.' He seemed nervously anxious. So by dint of punching and kicking I started one of my men into a state of somnambulism, and giving him an oar, took another and pulled towards the lights of the steamer.

"There was a murmur of voices in her, metallic hollow clangs of the engine-room, footsteps on the deck. Her ports shone, round like dilated eyes. Shapes moved about, and there was a shadowy man high up on the bridge. He heard my oars.

"And then, before I could open my lips, the East spoke to me, but it was in a Western voice. A torrent of words was poured into the enigmatical, the fateful silence; outlandish, angry words, mixed with words and even whole sentences of good English, less strange but even more surprising. The voice swore and cursed violently; it riddled the solemn peace of the bay by a volley of abuse. It began by calling me Pig, and from that went crescendo into unmentionable adjectives —in English. The man up there raged aloud in two languages, and with a sincerity in his fury that almost convinced me I had, in some way, sinned against the harmony of the universe. I could hardly see him, but began to think he would work himself into a fit.

"Suddenly he ceased, and I could hear him snorting and blowing like a porpoise. I said—

" 'What steamer is this, pray?'

" 'Eh? What's this? And who are you?'

" 'Castaway crew of an English barque burnt at sea. We came here tonight. I am the second mate. The captain is in the long-boat, and wishes to know if you would give us a passage somewhere.'

" 'Oh, my goodness! I say. . . . This is the *Celestial* from Singapore on her return trip. I'll arrange with your captain in the morning, . . . and, . . . I say, . . . did you hear me just now?'

" 'I should think the whole bay heard you.'

" 'I thought you were a shore-boat. Now, look here—this infernal lazy scoundrel of a caretaker has gone to sleep again—curse him. The light is out, and I nearly ran foul of the end of this damned jetty. This is the third time he plays me this trick. Now, I ask you, can anybody stand this kind of thing? It's enough to drive a man out of his mind. I'll report him. . . . I'll get the Assistant Resident to give him the sack, by . . . ! See—there's no light. It's out, isn't it! I take you to witness the light's out. There should be a light, you know. A red light on the—'

" 'There was a light,' I said, mildly.

" 'But it's out, man! What's the use of talking like this? You can see for yourself it's out—don't you? If you had to take a valuable steamer along this God-forsaken coast you would want a light, too. I'll kick him from end to end of his miserable wharf. You'll see if I don't. I will—'

" 'So I may tell my captain you'll take us?' I broke in.

" 'Yes, I'll take you. Good-night,' he said, brusquely.

"I pulled back, made fast again to the jetty, and then went to sleep at last. I had faced the silence of the East. I had heard some of its language. But when I opened my eyes again the silence was as complete as though it had never been broken. I was lying in a flood of light, and the sky had never looked so far, so high, before. I opened my eyes and lay without moving.

"And then I saw the men of the East—they were looking at me. The whole length of the jetty was full of people. I saw brown, bronze, yellow faces, the black eyes, the glitter, the colour of an Eastern crowd. And all these beings stared without a murmur, without a sigh, without a movement. They stared down at the boats, at the sleeping men who at night had come to them from the sea. Nothing moved. The fronds of palms stood still against the sky. Not a branch stirred along the shore, and the brown roofs of hidden houses peeped through the green foliage, through the big leaves that hung shining and still like leaves forged of heavy metal. This was the East of the ancient navigators, so old, so mysterious, resplendent and sombre, living and unchanged, full of danger and promise. And these were the men. I sat up suddenly. A wave of movement passed through the crowd from end to end, passed along the heads, swayed the bodies, ran along the jetty like a ripple on the water, like a breath of wind on a field—and all was still again. I see it now—the wide sweep of the bay, the glittering sands, the wealth of green infinite and varied, the sea blue like the sea of a dream, the crowd of attentive faces, the blaze of vivid colour—the water reflecting it all, the curve of the shore, the jetty, the high-sterned outlandish craft floating still, and the three boats with the tired men from the West sleeping, unconscious of the land and the people and of the violence of sunshine. They slept thrown across the thwarts, curled on bottom-boards, in the careless attitudes of death. The head of the old skipper, leaning back in the stern of the long-boat, had fallen on his breast, and he looked as though he would never wake. Farther out old Mahon's face was upturned to the sky, with the long white beard spread out on his breast, as though he had been shot where he sat at the tiller; and a man, all in a heap in the bows of the boat, slept with both arms embracing the stem-head and with his cheek laid on the gunwale. The East looked at them without a sound.

"I have known its fascination since; I have seen the mysterious shores, the still water, the lands of brown nations, where a stealthy Nemesis lies in wait, pursues, overtakes so many of the conquering race, who are proud of their wisdom, of their knowledge, of their strength. But for me all the East is contained in that vision of my youth. It is all in that moment when I opened my young eyes on it. I came upon it from a tussle with the sea—and I was young—and I saw it looking at me. And this is all that is left of it! Only a moment; a moment of strength, of romance, of glamour—of youth! . . . A flick of sunshine upon a strange shore, the time to remember, the time for a sigh, and—good-bye!—Night—Good-bye . . . !"

He drank.

"Ah! The good old time—the good old time. Youth and the sea. Glamour and the sea! The good, strong sea, the salt, bitter sea, that could whisper to you and roar at you and knock your breath out of you."

He drank again.

"By all that's wonderful it is the sea, I believe, the sea itself—or is it youth alone? Who can tell? But you here—you all had something out of life: money, love—whatever one gets on shore—and, tell me, wasn't that the best time, that time when we were young at sea; young and had nothing, on the sea that gives nothing, except hard knocks— and sometimes a chance to feel your strength—that only—what you all regret?"

And we all nodded at him: the man of finance, the man of accounts, the man of law, we all nodded at him over the polished table that like a still sheet of brown water reflected our faces, lined, wrinkled; our faces marked by toil, by deceptions, by success, by love; our weary eyes looking still, looking always, looking anxiously for something out of life, that while it is expected is already gone—had passed unseen, in a sigh, in a flash—together with the youth, with the strength, with the romance of illusions.

# That Evening Sun

## WILLIAM FAULKNER

### I

MONDAY is no different from any other weekday in Jefferson now. The streets are paved now, and the telephone and electric companies are cutting down more and more of the shade trees—the water oaks, the maples and locusts and elms—to make room for iron poles bearing clusters of bloated and ghostly and bloodless grapes, and we have a city laundry which makes the rounds on Monday morning, gathering the bundles of clothes into bright-colored, specially-made motor cars: the soiled wearing of a whole week now flees apparitionlike behind alert and irritable electric horns, with a long diminishing noise of rubber and asphalt like tearing silk, and even the Negro women who still take in white people's washing after the old custom, fetch and deliver it in automobiles.

But fifteen years ago, on Monday morning the quiet, dusty, shady streets would be full of Negro women with, balanced on their steady, turbaned heads, bundles of clothes tied up in sheets, almost as large as cotton bales, carried so without touch of hand between the kitchen door of the white house and the blackened washpot beside a cabin door in Negro Hollow.

Nancy would set her bundle on the top of her head, then upon the bundle in turn she would set the black straw sailor hat which she wore winter and summer. She was tall, with a high, sad face sunken a little where her teeth were missing. Sometimes we would go a part of the way down the lane and across the pasture with her, to watch the balanced bundle and the hat that never bobbed nor wavered, even when she walked down into the ditch and up the other side and stooped through the fence. She would go down on her hands and knees and crawl through the gap, her head rigid, uptilted, the bundle steady as a rock or a balloon, and rise to her feet again and go on.

Sometimes the husbands of the washing women would fetch and deliver the clothes, but Jesus never did that for Nancy, even before father told him to stay away from our house, even when Dilsey was sick and Nancy would come to cook for us.

And then about half the time we'd have to go down the lane to Nancy's cabin and tell her to come on and cook breakfast. We would stop at the ditch, because father told us to not have anything to do with Jesus—he was a short black man, with a razor scar down his face—and we would throw rocks at Nancy's house until she came to the door, leaning her head around it without any clothes on.

"What yawl mean, chunking my house?" Nancy said. "What you little devils mean?"

"Father says for you to come on and get breakfast," Caddy said. "Father says it's over a half an hour now, and you've got to come this minute."

"I aint studying no breakfast," Nancy said. "I going to get my sleep out."

"I bet you're drunk," Jason said. "Father says you're drunk. Are you drunk, Nancy?"

"Who says I is?" Nancy said. "I got to get my sleep out. I aint studying no breakfast."

So after a while we quit chunking the cabin and went back home. When she finally came, it was too late for me to go to school. So we thought it was whisky until that day they arrested her again and they were taking her to jail and they passed Mr. Stovall. He was the cashier in the bank and a deacon in the Baptist church, and Nancy began to say:

"When you going to pay me, white man? When you going to pay me, white man? It's been three times now since you paid me a cent—" Mr Stovall knocked her down, but she kept on saying, "When you going to pay me, white man? It's been three times now since—" until Mr Stovall kicked her in the mouth with his heel and the marshal caught Mr Stovall back, and Nancy lying in the street, laughing. She turned her head and spat out some blood and teeth and said, "It's been three times now since he paid me a cent."

That was how she lost her teeth, and all that day they told about

Nancy and Mr Stovall, and all that night the ones that passed the jail could hear Nancy singing and yelling. They could see her hands holding to the window bars, and a lot of them stopped along the fence, listening to her and to the jailer trying to make her stop. She didn't shut up until almost daylight, when the jailer began to hear a bumping and a scraping upstairs and he went up there and found Nancy hanging from the window bar. He said that it was cocaine and not whisky, because no nigger would try to commit suicide unless he was full of cocaine, because a nigger full of cocaine wasn't a nigger any longer.

The jailer cut her down and revived her; then he beat her, whipped her. She had hung herself with her dress. She had fixed it all right, but when they arrested her she didn't have on anything except a dress and so she didn't have anything to tie her hands with and she couldn't make her hands let go of the window ledge. So the jailer heard the noise and ran up there and found Nancy hanging from the window, stark naked, her belly already swelling out a little, like a little balloon.

When Dilsey was sick in her cabin and Nancy was cooking for us, we could see her apron swelling out; that was before father told Jesus to stay away from the house. Jesus was in the kitchen, sitting behind the stove, with his razor scar on his black face like a piece of dirty string. He said it was a watermelon that Nancy had under her dress.

"It never come off your vine, though," Nancy said.

"Off of what vine?" Caddy said.

"I can cut down the vine it did come off of," Jesus said.

"What makes you want to talk like that before these chillen?" Nancy said. "Whyn't you go on to work? You done et. You want Mr Jason to catch you hanging around his kitchen, talking that way before these chillen?"

"Talking what way?" Caddy said. "What vine?"

"I cant hang around white man's kitchen," Jesus said. "But white man can hang around mine. White man can come in my house, but I cant stop him. When white man want to come in my house, I aint got no house. I cant stop him, but he cant kick me outen it. He cant do that."

Dilsey was still sick in her cabin. Father told Jesus to stay off our place. Dilsey was still sick. It was a long time. We were in the library after supper.

"Isn't Nancy through in the kitchen yet?" mother said. "It seems to me that she has had plenty of time to have finished the dishes."

"Let Quentin go and see," father said. "Go and see if Nancy is through, Quentin. Tell her she can go on home."

I went to the kitchen. Nancy was through. The dishes were put away and the fire was out. Nancy was sitting in a chair, close to the cold stove. She looked at me.

"Mother wants to know if you are through," I said.

"Yes," Nancy said. She looked at me. "I done finished." She looked at me.

"What is it?" I said. "What is it?"

"I aint nothing but a nigger," Nancy said. "It aint none of my fault."

She looked at me, sitting in the chair before the cold stove, the sailor hat on her head. I went back to the library. It was the cold stove and all, when you think of a kitchen being warm and busy and cheerful. And with a cold stove and the dishes all put away, and no-body wanting to eat at that hour.

"Is she through?" mother said.

"Yessum," I said.

"What is she doing?" mother said.

"She's not doing anything. She's through."

"I'll go and see," father said.

"Maybe she's waiting for Jesus to come and take her home," Caddy said.

"Jesus is gone," I said. Nancy told us how one morning she woke up and Jesus was gone.

"He quit me," Nancy said. "Done gone to Memphis, I reckon. Dodging them city *po*-lice for a while, I reckon."

"And a good riddance," father said. "I hope he stays there."

"Nancy's scaired of the dark," Jason said.

"So are you," Caddy said.

"I'm not," Jason said.

"Scairy cat," Caddy said.

"I'm not," Jason said.

"You, Candace!" mother said. Father came back.

"I am going to walk down the lane with Nancy," he said. "She says that Jesus is back."

"Has she seen him?" mother said.

"No. Some Negro sent her word that he was back in town. I wont be long."

"You'll leave me alone, to take Nancy home?" mother said. "Is her safety more precious to you than mine?"

"I wont be long," father said.

"You'll leave these children unprotected, with that Negro about?"

"I'm going too," Caddy said. "Let me go, Father."

"What would he do with them, if he were unfortunate enough to have them?" father said.

"I want to go, too," Jason said.

"Jason!" mother said. She was speaking to father. You could tell that by the way she said the name. Like she believed that all day father had been trying to think of doing the thing she wouldn't like the most, and that she knew all the time that after a while he would think of it. I stayed quiet, because father and I both knew that mother would want him to make me stay with her if she just thought of it in time. So father didn't look at me. I was the oldest. I was nine and Caddy was seven and Jason was five.

"Nonsense," father said. "We wont be long."

Nancy had her hat on. We came to the lane. "Jesus always been good to me," Nancy said. "Whenever he had two dollars, one of them was mine." We walked in the lane. "If I can just get through the lane," Nancy said, "I be all right then."

The lane was always dark. "This is where Jason got scared on Hallowe'en," Caddy said.

"I didn't," Jason said.

"Cant Aunt Rachel do anything with him?" father said. Aunt Rachel was old. She lived in a cabin beyond Nancy's, by herself. She had white hair and she smoked a pipe in the door, all day long; she didn't work any more. They said she was Jesus' mother. Sometimes she said she was and sometimes she said she wasn't any kin to Jesus.

"Yes, you did," Caddy said. "You were scairder than Frony. You were scairder than T.P. even. Scairder than niggers."

"Cant nobody do nothing with him," Nancy said. "He say I done woke up the devil in him and aint but one thing going to lay it down again."

"Well, he's gone now," father said. "There's nothing for you to be afraid of now. And if you'd just let white men alone."

"Let what white men alone?" Caddy said. "How let them alone?"

"He aint gone nowhere," Nancy said. "I can feel him. I can feel him now, in this lane. He hearing us talk, every word, hid somewhere, waiting. I aint seen him, and I aint going to see him again but once more, with that razor in his mouth. That razor on that string down his back, inside his shirt. And then I aint going to be even surprised."

"I wasn't scaired," Jason said.

"If you'd behave yourself, you'd have kept out of this," father said. "But it's all right now. He's probably in St. Louis now. Probably got another wife by now and forgot all about you."

"If he has, I better not find out about it," Nancy said. "I'd stand there right over them, and every time he wropped her, I'd cut that arm off. I'd cut his head off and I'd slit her belly and I'd shove—"

"Hush," father said.

"Slit whose belly, Nancy?" Caddy said.

"I wasn't scaired," Jason said. "I'd walk right down this lane by myself."

"Yah," Caddy said. "You wouldn't dare to put your foot down in it if we were not here too."

## II

Dilsey was still sick, so we took Nancy home every night until mother said, "How much longer is this going on? I to be left alone in this big house while you take home a frightened Negro?"

We fixed a pallet in the kitchen for Nancy. One night we waked up, hearing the sound. It was not singing and it was not crying, coming up the dark stairs. There was a light in mother's room and we heard father going down the hall, down the back stairs, and Caddy and I went into the hall. The floor was cold. Our toes curled away from it while we listened to the sound. It was like singing and it wasn't like singing, like the sounds that Negroes make.

Then it stopped and we heard father going down the back stairs, and we went to the head of the stairs. Then the sound began again, in the stairway, not loud, and we could see Nancy's eyes halfway up the stairs, against the wall. They looked like cat's eyes do, like a big cat against the wall, watching us. When we came down the steps to where she was, she quit making the sound again, and we stood there until father came back up from the kitchen, with his pistol in his hand. He went back down with Nancy and they came back with Nancy's pallet.

We spread the pallet in our room. After the light in mother's room went off, we could see Nancy's eyes again. "Nancy," Caddy whispered, "are you asleep, Nancy?"

Nancy whispered something. It was oh or no, I dont know which. Like nobody had made it, like it came from nowhere and went nowhere, until it was like Nancy was not there at all; that I had looked so hard at her eyes on the stairs that they had got printed on my eyeballs, like the sun does when you have closed your eyes and there is no sun. "Jesus," Nancy whispered. "Jesus."

"Was it Jesus?" Caddy said. "Did he try to come into the kitchen?"

"Jesus," Nancy said. Like this: Jeeeeeeeeeeeeeeeesus, until the sound went out, like a match or a candle does.

"It's the other Jesus she means," I said.

"Can you see us, Nancy?" Caddy whispered. "Can you see our eyes too?"

"I aint nothing but a nigger," Nancy said. "God knows. God knows."

"What did you see down there in the kitchen?" Caddy whispered. "What tried to get in?"

"God knows," Nancy said. We could see her eyes. "God knows."

Dilsey got well. She cooked dinner. "You'd better stay in bed a day or two longer," father said.

"What for?" Dilsey said. "If I had been a day later, this place would be to rack and ruin. Get on out of here now, and let me get my kitchen straight again."

Dilsey cooked supper too. And that night, just before dark, Nancy came into the kitchen.

"How do you know he's back?" Dilsey said. "You aint seen him."

"Jesus is a nigger," Jason said.

"I can feel him," Nancy said. "I can feel him laying yonder in the ditch."

"Tonight?" Dilsey said. "Is he there tonight?"

"Dilsey's a nigger too," Jason said.

"You try to eat something," Dilsey said.

"I dont want nothing," Nancy said.

"I aint a nigger," Jason said.

"Drink some coffee," Dilsey said. She poured a cup of coffee for Nancy. "Do you know he's out there tonight? How come you know it's tonight?"

"I know," Nancy said. "He's there, waiting. I know. I done lived with him too long. I know what he is fixing to do fore he know it himself."

"Drink some coffee," Dilsey said. Nancy held the cup to her mouth and blew into the cup. Her mouth pursed out like a spreading adder's, like a rubber mouth, like she had blown all the color out of her lips with blowing the coffee.

"I aint a nigger," Jason said. "Are you a nigger, Nancy?"

"I hellborn, child," Nancy said. "I wont be nothing soon. I going back where I come from soon."

## III

She began to drink the coffee. While she was drinking, holding the cup in both hands, she began to make the sound again. She made the sound into the cup and the coffee sploshed out onto her hands and her dress. Her eyes looked at us and she sat there, her elbows on her knees, holding the cup in both hands, looking at us across the wet cup, making the sound. "Look at Nancy," Jason said. "Nancy cant cook for us now. Dilsey's got well now."

"You hush up," Dilsey said. Nancy held the cup in both hands, looking at us, making the sound, like there were two of them: one looking at us and the other making the sound. "Whyn't you let Mr Jason telefoam the marshal?" Dilsey said. Nancy stopped then, holding the cup in her long brown hands. She tried to drink some coffee again, but it sploshed out of the cup, onto her hands and her dress, and she put the cup down. Jason watched her.

"I cant swallow it," Nancy said. "I swallows but it wont go down me."

"You go down to the cabin," Dilsey said. "Frony will fix you a pallet and I'll be there soon."

"Wont no nigger stop him," Nancy said.

"I aint a nigger," Jason said. "Am I, Dilsey?"

"I reckon not," Dilsey said. She looked at Nancy. "I dont reckon so. What you going to do, then?"

Nancy looked at us. Her eyes went fast, like she was afraid there wasn't time to look, without hardly moving at all. She looked at us, at all three of us at one time. "You member that night I stayed in yawls' room?" she said. She told about how we waked up early the next morning, and played. We had to play quiet, on her pallet, until father woke up and it was time to get breakfast. "Go and ask your maw to let me stay here tonight," Nancy said. "I wont need no pallet. We can play some more."

Caddy asked mother. Jason went too. "I cant have Negroes sleeping in the bedrooms," mother said. Jason cried. He cried until mother said he couldn't have any dessert for three days if he didn't stop. Then Jason said he would stop if Dilsey would make a chocolate cake. Father was there.

"Why dont you do something about it?" mother said. "What do we have officers for?"

"Why is Nancy afraid of Jesus?" Caddy said. "Are you afraid of father, mother?"

"What could the officers do?" father said. "If Nancy hasn't seen him, how could the officers find him?"

"Then why is she afraid?" mother said.

"She says he is there. She says she knows he is there tonight."

"Yet we pay taxes," mother said. "I must wait here alone in this big house while you take a Negro woman home."

"You know that I am not lying outside with a razor," father said.

"I'll stop if Dilsey will make a chocolate cake," Jason said. Mother told us to go out and father said he didn't know if Jason would get a chocolate cake or not, but he knew what Jason was going to get in about a minute. We went back to the kitchen and told Nancy.

"Father said for you to go home and lock the door, and you'll be all right," Caddy said. "All right from what, Nancy? Is Jesus mad at you?" Nancy was holding the coffee cup in her hands again, her elbows on her knees and her hands holding the cup between her knees. She was looking into the cup. "What have you done that made Jesus mad?" Caddy said. Nancy let the cup go. It didn't break on the floor, but the coffee spilled out, and Nancy sat there with her hands still making the shape of the cup. She began to make the sound again, not loud. Not singing and not unsinging. We watched her.

"Here," Dilsey said. "You quit that, now. You get aholt of yourself. You wait here. I going to get Versh to walk home with you." Dilsey went out.

We looked at Nancy. Her shoulders kept shaking, but she quit making the sound. We watched her. "What's Jesus going to do to you?" Caddy said. "He went away."

Nancy looked at us. "We had fun that night I stayed in yawls' room, didn't we?"

"I didn't," Jason said. "I didn't have any fun."

"You were asleep in mother's room," Caddy said. "You were not there."

"Let's go down to my house and have some more fun," Nancy said.

"Mother wont let us," I said. "It's too late now."

"Don't bother her," Nancy said. "We can tell her in the morning. She wont mind."

"She wouldn't let us," I said.

"Dont ask her now," Nancy said. "Dont bother her now."

"She didn't say we couldn't go," Caddy said.

"We didn't ask," I said.

"If you go, I'll tell," Jason said.

"We'll have fun," Nancy said. "They won't mind, just to my house. I been working for yawl a long time. They won't mind."

"I'm not afraid to go," Caddy said. "Jason is the one that's afraid. He'll tell."

"I'm not," Jason said.

"Yes, you are," Caddy said. "You'll tell."

"I won't tell," Jason said. "I'm not afraid."

"Jason ain't afraid to go with me," Nancy said. "Is you, Jason?"

"Jason is going to tell," Caddy said. The lane was dark. We passed the pasture gate. "I bet if something was to jump out from behind that gate, Jason would holler."

"I wouldn't," Jason said. We walked down the lane. Nancy was talking loud.

"What are you talking so loud for, Nancy?" Caddy said.

"Who; me?" Nancy said. "Listen at Quentin and Caddy and Jason saying I'm talking loud."

"You talk like there was five of us here," Caddy said. "You talk like father was here too."

"Who; me talking loud, Mr. Jason?" Nancy said.

"Nancy called Jason 'Mister,'" Caddy said.

"Listen how Caddy and Quentin and Jason talk," Nancy said.

"We're not talking loud," Caddy said. "You're the one that's talking like father—"

"Hush," Nancy said; "hush, Mr. Jason."

"Nancy called Jason 'Mister' aguh—"

"Hush," Nancy said. She was talking loud when we crossed the ditch and stooped through the fence where she used to stoop through with the clothes on her head. Then we came to her house. We were going fast then. She opened the door. The smell of the house was like the lamp and the smell of Nancy was like the wick, like they were waiting for one another to begin to smell. She lit the lamp and closed the door and put the bar up. Then she quit talking loud, looking at us.

"What're we going to do?" Caddy said.

"What do yawl want to do?" Nancy said.

"You said we would have some fun," Caddy said.

There was something about Nancy's house; something you could smell besides Nancy and the house. Jason smelled it, even. "I don't want to stay here," he said. "I want to go home."

"Go home, then," Caddy said.

"I don't want to go by myself," Jason said.

"We're going to have some fun," Nancy said.

"How?" Caddy said.

Nancy stood by the door. She was looking at us, only it was like she had emptied her eyes, like she had quit using them. "What do you want to do?" she said.

"Tell us a story," Caddy said. "Can you tell a story?"

"Yes," Nancy said.

"Tell it," Caddy said. We looked at Nancy. "You don't know any stories."

"Yes," Nancy said. "Yes, I do."

She came and sat in a chair before the hearth. There was a little fire there. Nancy built it up, when it was already hot inside. She built a good blaze. She told a story. She talked like her eyes looked, like her eyes watching us and her voice talking to us did not belong to her. Like she was living somewhere else, waiting somewhere else. She was outside the cabin. Her voice was inside and the shape of her, the Nancy that could stoop under a barbed wire fence with a bundle of clothes balanced on her head as though without weight, like a balloon, was there. But that was all. "And so this here queen come walking up to the ditch, where that bad man was hiding. She was walking up to the ditch, and she say, 'If I can just get past this here ditch,' was what she say. . . ."

"What ditch?" Caddy said. "A ditch like that one out there? Why did a queen want to go into a ditch?"

"To get to her house," Nancy said. She looked at us. "She had to cross the ditch to get into her house quick and bar the door."

"Why did she want to go home and bar the door?" Caddy said.


## IV


Nancy looked at us. She quit talking. She looked at us. Jason's legs stuck straight out of his pants where he sat on Nancy's lap. "I don't think that's a good story," he said. "I want to go home."

"Maybe we had better," Caddy said. She got up from the floor. "I bet they are looking for us right now." She went toward the door.

"No," Nancy said. "Don't open it." She got up quick and passed Caddy. She didn't touch the door, the wooden bar.

"Why not?" Caddy said.

"Come back to the lamp," Nancy said. "We'll have fun. You don't have to go."

"We ought to go," Caddy said. "Unless we have a lot of fun." She and Nancy came back to the fire, the lamp.

"I want to go home," Jason said. "I'm going to tell."

"I know another story," Nancy said. She stood close to the lamp. She looked at Caddy, like when your eyes look up at a stick balanced on your nose. She had to look down to see Caddy, but her eyes looked like that, like when you are balancing a stick.

"I won't listen to it," Jason said. "I'll bang on the floor."

"It's a good one," Nancy said. "It's better than the other one."

"What's it about?" Caddy said. Nancy was standing by the lamp. Her hand was on the lamp, against the light, long and brown.

"Your hand is on that hot globe," Caddy said. "Don't it feel hot to your hand?"

Nancy looked at her hand on the lamp chimney. She took her hand away, slow. She stood there, looking at Caddy, wringing her long hand as though it were tied to her wrist with a string.

"Let's do something else," Caddy said.

"I want to go home," Jason said.

"I got some popcorn," Nancy said. She looked at Caddy and then at Jason and then at me and then at Caddy again. "I got some popcorn."

"I don't like popcorn," Jason said. "I'd rather have candy."

Nancy looked at Jason. "You can hold the popper." She was still wringing her hand; it was long and limp and brown.

"All right," Jason said. "I'll stay a while if I can do that. Caddy can't hold it. I'll want to go home again if Caddy holds the popper."

Nancy built up the fire. "Look at Nancy putting her hands in the fire," Caddy said. "What's the matter with you, Nancy?"

"I got popcorn," Nancy said. "I got some." She took the popper from under the bed. It was broken. Jason began to cry.

"Now we can't have any popcorn," he said.

"We ought to go home, anyway," Caddy said. "Come on, Quentin."

"Wait," Nancy said; "wait. I can fix it. Don't you want to help me fix it?"

"I don't think I want any," Caddy said. "It's too late now."

"You help me, Jason," Nancy said. "Don't you want to help me?"

"No," Jason said. "I want to go home."

"Hush," Nancy said; "hush. Watch. Watch me. I can fix it so Jason can hold it and pop the corn." She got a piece of wire and fixed the popper.

"It won't hold good," Caddy said.

"Yes, it will," Nancy said. "Yawl watch. Yawl help me shell some corn."

The popcorn was under the bed too. We shelled it into the popper and Nancy helped Jason hold the popper over the fire.

"It's not popping," Jason said. "I want to go home."

"You wait," Nancy said. "It'll begin to pop. We'll have fun then." She was sitting close to the fire. The lamp was turned up so high it was beginning to smoke.

"Why don't you turn it down some?" I said.

"It's all right," Nancy said. "I'll clean it. Yawl wait. The popcorn will start in a minute."

"I don't believe it's going to start," Caddy said. "We ought to start home, anyway. They'll be worried."

"No," Nancy said. "It's going to pop. Dilsey will tell um yawl with me. I been working for yawl long time. They won't mind if yawl at my house. You wait, now. It'll start popping any minute now."

Then Jason got some smoke in his eyes and he began to cry. He dropped the popper into the fire. Nancy got a wet rag and wiped Jason's face, but he didn't stop crying.

"Hush," she said. "Hush." But he didn't hush. Caddy took the popper out of the fire.

"It's burned up," she said. "You'll have to get some more popcorn, Nancy."

"Did you put all of it in?" Nancy said.

"Yes," Caddy said. Nancy looked at Caddy. Then she took the popper and opened it and poured the cinders into her apron and began to sort the grains, her hands long and brown, and we watching her.

"Haven't you got any more?" Caddy said.

"Yes," Nancy said; "yes. Look. This here ain't burnt. All we need to do is—"

"I want to go home," Jason said. "I'm going to tell."

"Hush," Caddy said. We all listened. Nancy's head was already turned toward the barred door, her eyes filled with red lamplight. "Somebody is coming," Caddy said.

Then Nancy began to make that sound again, not loud, sitting there above the fire, her long hands dangling between her knees; all of a sudden water began to come out on her face in big drops, running down her face, carrying in each one a little turning ball of firelight like a spark until it dropped off her chin. "She's not crying." I said.

"I ain't crying," Nancy said. Her eyes were closed. "I ain't crying. Who is it?"

"I don't know," Caddy said. She went to the door and looked out. "We've got to go now," she said. "Here comes father."

"I'm going to tell," Jason said. "Yawl made me come."

The water still ran down Nancy's face. She turned in her chair. "Listen. Tell him. Tell him we going to have fun. Tell him I take good care of yawl until in the morning. Tell him to let me come home with yawl and sleep on the floor. Tell him I won't need no pallet. We'll have fun. You remember last time how we had so much fun?"

"I didn't have fun," Jason said. "You hurt me. You put smoke in my eyes. I'm going to tell."

## V

Father came in. He looked at us. Nancy did not get up.

"Tell him," she said.

"Caddy made us come down here," Jason said. "I didn't want to."

Father came to the fire. Nancy looked up at him. "Can't you go to

Aunt Rachel's and stay?" he said. Nancy looked up at father, her hands between her knees. "He's not here," father said. "I would have seen him. There's not a soul in sight."

"He in the ditch," Nancy said. "He waiting in the ditch yonder."

"Nonsense," father said. He looked at Nancy. "Do you know he's there?"

"I got the sign," Nancy said.

"What sign?"

"I got it. It was on the table when I come in. It was a hog-bone, with blood meat still on it, laying by the lamp. He's out there. When yawl walk out that door, I gone."

"Gone where, Nancy?" Caddy said.

"I'm not a tattletale," Jason said.

"Nonsense," father said.

"He out there," Nancy said. "He looking through that window this minute, waiting for yawl to go. Then I gone."

"Nonsense," father said. "Lock up your house and we'll take you on to Aunt Rachel's."

" 'Twont do no good," Nancy said. She didn't look at father now, but he looked down at her, at her long, limp, moving hands. "Putting it off wont do no good."

"Then what do you want to do?" father said.

"I don't know," Nancy said. "I can't do nothing. Just put it off. And that don't do no good. I reckon it belong to me. I reckon what I going to get ain't no more than mine."

"Get what?" Caddy said. "What's yours?"

"Nothing," father said. "You all must get to bed."

"Caddy made me come," Jason said.

"Go on to Aunt Rachel's," father said.

"It won't do no good," Nancy said. She sat before the fire, her elbows on her knees, her long hands between her knees. "When even your own kitchen wouldn't do no good. When even if I was sleeping on the floor in the room with your chillen, and the next morning there I am, and blood—"

"Hush," father said. "Lock the door and put out the lamp and go to bed."

"I scared of the dark," Nancy said. "I scared for it to happen in the dark."

"You mean you're going to sit right here with the lamp lighted?" father said. Then Nancy began to make the sound again, sitting before the fire, her long hands between her knees. "Ah, damnation," father said. "Come along, chillen. It's past bedtime."

"When yawl go home, I gone," Nancy said. She talked quieter now, and her face looked quiet, like her hands. "Anyway, I got my coffin money saved up with Mr. Lovelady." Mr. Lovelady was a short, dirty man who collected the Negro insurance, coming around to the cabins or the kitchens every Saturday morning, to collect fifteen cents. He and his wife lived at the hotel. One morning his wife committed suicide. They had a child, a little girl. He and the child went away. After a week or two he came back alone. We would see him going along the lanes and the back streets on Saturday mornings.

"Nonsense," father said. "You'll be the first thing I'll see in the kitchen tomorrow morning."

"You'll see what you'll see, I reckon," Nancy said. "But it will take the Lord to say what that will be."

## VI

We left her sitting before the fire.

"Come and put the bar up," father said. But she didn't move. She didn't look at us again, sitting quietly there between the lamp and the fire. From some distance down the lane we could look back and see her through the open door.

"What, Father?" Caddy said. "What's going to happen?"

"Nothing," father said. Jason was on father's back, so Jason was the tallest of all of us. We went down into the ditch. I looked at it, quiet. I couldn't see much where the moonlight and the shadows tangled.

"If Jesus is hid here, he can see us, cant he?" Caddy said.

"He's not there," father said. "He went away a long time ago."

"You made me come," Jason said, high; against the sky it looked like father had two heads, a little one and a big one. "I didn't want to."

We went up out of the ditch. We could still see Nancy's house and the open door, but we couldn't see Nancy now, sitting before the fire with the door open, because she was tired. "I just done got tired," she said. "I just a nigger. It ain't no fault of mine."

But we could hear her, because she began just after we came up out of the ditch, the sound that was not singing and not unsinging. "Who will do our washing now, Father?" I said.

"I'm not a nigger," Jason said, high and close above father's head.

"You're worse," Caddy said, "you are a tattletale. If something was to jump out, you'd be scairder than a nigger."

"I wouldn't," Jason said.

"You'd cry," Caddy said.

"Caddy," father said.

"I wouldn't!" Jason said.

"Scairy cat," Caddy said.

"Candace!" father said.

# The Open Boat

*A Tale intended to be after the Fact:*
*Being the Experience of Four Men*
*from the Sunk Steamer* Commodore

## STEPHEN CRANE

### I

NONE of them knew the colour of the sky. Their eyes glanced level, and were fastened upon the waves that swept toward them. These waves were of the hue of slate, save for the tops, which were of foaming white, and all of the men knew the colours of the sea. The horizon narrowed and widened, and dipped and rose, and at all times its edge was jagged with waves that seemed thrust up in points like rocks.

Many a man ought to have a bathtub larger than the boat which here rode upon the sea. These waves were most wrongfully and barbarously abrupt and tall, and each froth-top was a problem in small-boat navigation.

The cook squatted in the bottom, and looked with both eyes at the six inches of gunwale which separated him from the ocean. His sleeves were rolled over his fat forearms, and the two flaps of his unbuttoned vest dangled as he bent to bail out the boat. Often he said, "Gawd! that was a narrow clip." As he remarked it he invariably gazed eastward over the broken sea.

The oiler, steering with one of the two oars in the boat, sometimes raised himself suddenly to keep clear of the water that swirled in over the stern. It was a thin little oar, and it seemed often ready to snap.

The correspondent, pulling at the other oar, watched the waves and wondered why he was there.

The injured captain, lying in the bow, was at this time buried in that profound dejection and indifference which come, temporarily at least, to even the bravest and most enduring when, willy-nilly, the firm fails, the army loses, the ship goes down. The mind of the master of a vessel is rooted deep in the timbers of her, though he command for a day or a decade; and this captain had on him the stern impression of a scene in the greys of dawn of seven turned faces, and later a stump of a topmast with a white ball on it, that slashed to and fro at the waves, went low and lower, and down. Thereafter there was something strange in his voice. Although steady, it was deep with mourning, and of a quality beyond oration or tears.

"Keep 'er a little more south, Billie," said he.

"A little more south, sir," said the oiler in the stern.

A seat in this boat was not unlike a seat upon a bucking broncho, and by the same token a broncho is not much smaller. The craft pranced and reared and plunged like an animal. As each wave came, and she rose for it, she seemed like a horse making at a fence outrageously high. The manner of her scramble over these walls of water is a mystic thing, and, moreover, at the top of them were ordinarily these problems in white water, the foam racing down from the summit of each wave requiring a new leap, and a leap from the air. Then, after scornfully bumping a crest, she would slide and race and splash down a long incline, and arrive bobbing and nodding in front of the next menace.

A singular disadvantage of the sea lies in the fact that after successfully surmounting one wave you discover that there is another behind it just as important and just as nervously anxious to do something effective in the way of swamping boats. In a ten-foot dinghy one can get an idea of the resources of the sea in the line of waves that is not probable to the average experience which is never at sea in a dinghy. As each slaty wall of water approached, it shut all else from the view of the men in the boat, and it was not difficult to imagine that this particular wave was the final outburst of the ocean, the last effort of the grim water. There was a terrible grace in the move of the waves, and they came in silence, save for the snarling of the crests.

In the wan light the faces of the men must have been grey. Their eyes must have glinted in strange ways as they gazed steadily astern. Viewed from a balcony, the whole thing would doubtless have been weirdly picturesque. But the men in the boat had no time to see it, and if they had had leisure, there were other things to occupy their minds. The sun swung steadily up the sky, and they knew it was broad day because the colour of the sea changed from slate to emerald green streaked with amber lights, and the foam was like tumbling snow. The process of the breaking day was unknown to them. They were aware only of this effect upon the colour of the waves that rolled toward them.

In disjointed sentences the cook and the correspondent argued as to the difference between a life-saving station and a house of refuge. The cook had said: "There's a house of refuge just north of the Mosquito Inlet Light, and as soon as they see us they'll come off in their boat and pick us up."

"As soon as who see us?" said the correspondent.

"The crew," said the cook.

"Houses of refuge don't have crews," said the correspondent. "As I understand them, they are only places where clothes and grub are stored for the benefit of shipwrecked people. They don't carry crews."

"Oh, yes, they do," said the cook.

"No, they don't," said the correspondent.

"Well, we're not there yet, anyhow," said the oiler, in the stern.

"Well," said the cook, "perhaps it's not a house of refuge that I'm thinking of as being near Mosquito Inlet Light; perhaps it's a life-saving station."

"We're not there yet," said the oiler in the stern.

## II

As the boat bounced from the top of each wave the wind tore through the hair of the hatless men, and as the craft plopped her stern down again the spray slashed past them. The crest of each of these waves was a hill, from the top of which the men surveyed for a moment a broad tumultuous expanse, shining and wind-riven. It was probably splendid, it was probably glorious, this play of the free sea, wild with lights of emerald and white and amber.

"Bully good thing it's an on-shore wind," said the cook. "If not, where would we be? Wouldn't have a show."

"That's right," said the correspondent.

The busy oiler nodded his assent.

Then the captain, in the bow, chuckled in a way that expressed humour, contempt, tragedy, all in one. "Do you think we've got much of a show now, boys?" said he.

Whereupon the three were silent, save for a trifle of hemming and hawing. To express any particular optimism at this time they felt to be childish and stupid, but they all doubtless possessed this sense of the situation in their minds. A young man thinks doggedly at such times. On the other hand, the ethics of their condition was decidedly against any open suggestion of hopelessness. So they were silent.

"Oh, well," said the captain, soothing his children, "we'll get ashore all right."

But there was that in his tone which made them think; so the oiler quoth, "Yes! if this wind holds."

The cook was bailing. "Yes! if we don't catch hell in the surf."

Canton-flannel gulls flew near and far. Sometimes they sat down on the sea, near patches of brown seaweed that rolled over the waves with a movement like carpets on a line in a gale. The birds sat comfortably in groups, and they were envied by some in the dinghy, for the wrath of the sea was no more to them than it was to a covey of prairie chickens a thousand miles inland. Often they came very close and stared at the men with black bead-like eyes. At these times they were uncanny and sinister in their unblinking scrutiny, and the men hooted angrily at them, telling them to be gone. One came, and evidently decided to alight on the top of the captain's head. The bird flew parallel to the boat and did not circle, but made short sidelong jumps in the air in chicken-fashion. His black eyes were wistfully fixed upon the captain's head. "Ugly brute," said the oiler to the bird. "You look as if you were made with a jackknife." The cook and the correspondent swore darkly at the creature. The captain naturally wished to knock it away with the end of the heavy painter, but he did not dare do it, because anything resembling an emphatic gesture would have capsized this freighted boat; and so, with his open hand, the captain gently and carefully waved the gull away. After it had been discouraged from the pursuit the captain breathed easier on account of his hair, and others breathed easier because the bird struck their minds at this time as being somehow gruesome and ominous.

In the meantime the oiler and the correspondent rowed. And also they rowed. They sat together in the same seat, and each rowed an oar. Then the oiler took both oars; then the correspondent took both oars; then the oiler; then the correspondent. They rowed and they rowed. The very ticklish part of the business was when the time came for the reclining one in the stern to take his turn at the oars. By the very last star of truth, it is easier to steal eggs from under a hen than it was to change seats in the dinghy. First the man in the stern slid his hand along the thwart and moved with care, as if he were of Sèvres. Then the man in the rowing-seat slid his hand along the other thwart. It was all done with the most extraordinary care. As the two sidled past each other, the whole party kept watchful eyes on the coming wave, and the captain cried: "Look out, now! Steady, there!"

The brown mats of seaweed that appeared from time to time were like islands, bits of earth. They were traveling, apparently, neither one way nor the other. They were, to all intents, stationary. They informed the men in the boat that it was making progress slowly toward the land.

The captain, rearing cautiously in the bow after the dinghy soared on a great swell, said that he had seen the lighthouse at Mosquito Inlet. Presently the cook remarked that he had seen it. The correspondent was at the oars then, and for some reason he too wished to look at the lighthouse; but his back was toward the far shore, and the waves were important, and for some time he could not seize an opportunity to turn his head. But at last there came a wave more gentle than the others, and when at the crest of it he swiftly scoured the western horizon.

"See it?" said the captain.

"No," said the correspondent, slowly; "I didn't see anything."

"Look again," said the captain. He pointed. "It's exactly in that direction."

At the top of another wave the correspondent did as he was bid, and this time his eyes chanced on a small, still thing on the edge of the swaying horizon. It was precisely like the point of a pin. It took an anxious eye to find a lighthouse so tiny.

"Think we'll make it, Captain?"

"If this wind holds and the boat don't swamp, we can't do much else," said the captain.

The little boat, lifted by each towering sea and splashed viciously by the crests, made progress that in the absence of seaweed was not apparent to those in her. She seemed just a wee thing wallowing, miraculously top up, at the mercy of five oceans. Occasionally a great spread of water, like white flames, swarmed into her.

"Bail her, cook," said the captain, serenely.

"All right, Captain," said the cheerful cook.

## III

It would be difficult to describe the subtle brotherhood of men that was here established on the seas. No one said that it was so. No one mentioned it. But it dwelt in the boat, and each man felt it warm him. They were a captain, an oiler, a cook, and a correspondent, and they were friends—friends in a more curiously iron-bound degree than may be common. The hurt captain, lying against the water-jar in the bow, spoke always in a low voice and calmly; but he could never command a more ready and swiftly obedient crew than the motley three of the dinghy. It was more than a mere recognition of what was best for the common safety. There was surely in it a quality that was personal and heart-felt. And after this devotion to the commander of the boat, there was this comradeship, that the correspondent, for instance, who had been taught to be cynical of men, knew even at the time was the best experience of his life. But no one said that it was so. No one mentioned it.

"I wish we had a sail," remarked the captain. "We might try my overcoat on the end of an oar, and give you two boys a chance to rest." So the cook and the correspondent held the mast and spread wide the overcoat; the oiler steered; and the little boat made good way with her new rig. Sometimes the oiler had to scull sharply to keep a sea from breaking into the boat, but otherwise sailing was a success.

Meanwhile the lighthouse had been growing slowly larger. It had now almost assumed colour, and appeared like a little grey shadow on the sky. The man at the oars could not be prevented from turning his head rather often to try for a glimpse of this little grey shadow.

At last, from the top of each wave, the men in the tossing boat could see land. Even as the lighthouse was an upright shadow on the sky, this land seemed but a long black shadow on the sea. It certainly was thinner than paper. "We must be about opposite New Smyrna," said the cook, who had coasted this shore often in schooners. "Captain, by the way, I believe they abandoned that life-saving station there about a year ago."

"Did they?" said the captain.

The wind slowly died away. The cook and the correspondent were not now obliged to slave in order to hold high the oar. But the waves continued their old impetuous swooping at the dinghy, and the little craft, no longer under way, struggled woundily over them. The oiler or the correspondent took the oars again.

Shipwrecks are *àpropos* of nothing. If men could only train for them and have them occur when the men had reached pink condition, there would be less drowning at sea. Of the four in the dinghy none had slept any time worth mentioning for two days and two nights previous to embarking in the dinghy, and in the excitement of clambering about the deck of a foundering ship they had also forgotten to eat heartily.

For these reasons, and for others, neither the oiler nor the correspondent was fond of rowing at this time. The correspondent wondered ingenuously how in the name of all that was sane could there be people who thought it amusing to row a boat. It was not an amusement; it was a diabolical punishment, and even a genius of mental aberrations could never conclude that it was anything but a horror to the muscles and a crime against the back. He mentioned to the boat in general how the amusement of rowing struck him, and the weary-faced oiler smiled in full sympathy. Previously to the foundering, by the way, the oiler had worked a double watch in the engine-room of the ship.

"Take her easy now, boys," said the captain. "Don't spend yourselves. If we have to run a surf you'll need all your strength, because we'll sure have to swim for it. Take your time."

Slowly the land arose from the sea. From a black line it became a line of black and line of white—trees and sand. Finally the captain said that he could make out a house on the shore. "That's the house of refuge, sure," said the cook. "They'll see us before long, and come out after us."

The distant lighthouse reared high. "The keeper ought to be able to make us out now, if he's looking through a glass," said the captain. "He'll notify the life-saving people."

"None of those other boats could have got ashore to give word of this wreck," said the oiler, in a low voice, "else the life-boat would be out hunting us."

Slowly and beautifully the land loomed out of the sea. The wind came again. It had veered from the north-east to the south-east. Finally a new sound struck the ears of the men in the boat. It was the low thunder of the surf on the shore. "We'll never be able to make the lighthouse now," said the captain. "Swing her head a little more north, Billie."

"A little more north, sir," said the oiler.

Whereupon the little boat turned her nose once more down the wind, and all but the oarsman watched the shore grow. Under the influence of this expansion doubt and direful apprehension were leaving the minds of the men. The management of the boat was still most absorbing, but it could not prevent a quiet cheerfulness. In an hour, perhaps, they would be ashore.

Their backbones had become thoroughly used to balancing in the boat, and they now rode this wild colt of a dinghy like circus men. The correspondent thought that he had been drenched to the skin, but happening to feel in the top pocket of his coat, he found therein eight cigars. Four of them were soaked with sea-water; four were perfectly scatheless. After a search, somebody produced three dry matches; and thereupon the four waifs rode impudently in their little boat and, with an assurance of an impending rescue shining in their eyes, puffed at the big cigars, and judged well and ill of all men. Everybody took a drink of water.

## IV

"Cook," remarked the captain, "there don't seem to be any signs of life about your house of refuge."

"No," replied the cook. "Funny they don't see us!"

A broad stretch of lowly coast lay before the eyes of the men. It was of low dunes topped with dark vegetation. The roar of the surf was plain, and sometimes they could see the white lip of a wave as it spun up the beach. A tiny house was blocked out black upon the sky. Southward, the slim lighthouse lifted its little grey length.

Tide, wind, and waves were swinging the dinghy northward. "Funny they don't see us," said the men.

The surf's roar was here dulled, but its tone was nevertheless thunderous and mighty. As the boat swam over the great rollers the men sat listening to this roar. "We'll swamp sure," said everybody.

It is fair to say here that there was not a life-saving station within twenty miles in either direction; but the men did not know this fact, and in consequence they made dark and opprobrious remarks concerning the eyesight of the nation's life-savers. Four scowling men sat in the dinghy and surpassed records in the invention of epithets.

"Funny they don't see us."

The light-heartedness of a former time had completely faded. To their sharpened minds it was easy to conjure pictures of all kinds of incompetency and blindness and, indeed, cowardice. There was the shore of the populous land, and it was bitter and bitter to them that from it came no sign.

"Well," said the captain, ultimately, "I suppose we'll have to make a try for ourselves. If we stay out here too long, we'll none of us have strength left to swim after the boat swamps."

And so the oiler, who was at the oars, turned the boat straight for the shore. There was a sudden tightening of muscles. There was some thinking.

"If we don't all get ashore," said the captain—"if we don't all get ashore, I suppose you fellows know where to send news of my finish?"

They then briefly exchanged some addresses and admonitions. As for the reflections of the men, there was a great deal of rage in them. Perchance they might be formulated thus: "If I am going to be drowned—if I am going to be drowned—if I am going to be drowned, why, in the name of the seven mad gods who rule the sea, was I allowed to come thus far and contemplate sand and trees? Was I brought here merely to have my nose dragged away as I was about to nibble the sacred cheese of life? It is preposterous. If this old ninny-woman, Fate, cannot do better than this, she should be deprived of the management of men's fortunes. She is an old hen who knows not her intention. If she has decided to drown me, why did she not do it in the beginning and save me all this trouble? The whole affair is absurd.—But no; she cannot mean to drown me. She dare not drown me. She cannot drown me. Not after all this work." Afterward the man might have had an impulse to shake his fist at the clouds. "Just you drown me, now, and then hear what I call you!"

The billows that came at this time were more formidable. They seemed always just about to break and roll over the little boat in a turmoil of foam. There was a preparatory and long growl in the speech of them. No mind unused to the sea would have concluded that the dinghy could ascend these sheer heights in time. The shore was still afar. The oiler was a wily surfman. "Boys," he said swiftly, "she won't

live three minutes more, and we're too far out to swim. Shall I take
her to sea again, Captain?"

"Yes; go ahead!" said the captain.

This oiler, by a series of quick miracles and fast and steady oarsman-
ship, turned the boat in the middle of the surf and took her safely to
sea again.

There was a considerable silence as the boat bumped over the furrowed sea to deeper water. Then somebody in gloom spoke: "Well,
anyhow, they must have seen us from the shore by now."

The gulls went in slanting flight up the wind toward the grey,
desolate east. A squall, marked by dingy clouds and clouds brick-red
like smoke from a burning building, appeared from the south-east.

"What do you think of those life-saving people? Ain't they peaches?"

"Funny they haven't seen us."

"Maybe they think we're out here for sport! Maybe they think we're
fishin'. Maybe they think we're damned fools."

It was a long afternoon. A changed tide tried to force them southward, but wind and wave said northward. Far ahead, where coast-line,
sea, and sky formed their mighty angle, there were little dots which
seemed to indicate a city on the shore.

"St. Augustine?"

The captain shook his head. "Too near Mosquito Inlet."

And the oiler rowed, and then the correspondent rowed; then the
oiler rowed. It was a weary business. The human back can become the
seat of more aches and pains than are registered in books for the
composite anatomy of a regiment. It is a limited area, but it can become the theatre of innumerable muscular conflicts, tangles, wrenches,
knots, and other comforts.

"Did you ever like to row, Billie?" asked the correspondent.

"No," said the oiler; "hang it!"

When one exchanged the rowing-seat for a place in the bottom of
the boat, he suffered a bodily depression that caused him to be careless
of everything save an obligation to wiggle one finger. There was
cold sea-water swashing to and fro in the boat, and he lay in it. His
head, pillowed on a thwart, was within an inch of the swirl of a wave-
crest, and sometimes a particularly obstreperous sea came inboard and
drenched him once more. But these matters did not annoy him. It is
almost certain that if the boat had capsized he would have tumbled

comfortably out upon the ocean as if he felt sure that it was a great soft mattress.

"Look! There's a man on the shore!"

"Where?"

"There! See 'im? See 'im?"

"Yes, sure! He's walking along."

"Now he's stopped. Look! He's facing us!"

"He's waving at us!"

"So he is! By thunder!"

"Ah, now we're all right! Now we're all right! There'll be a boat out here for us in half an hour."

"He's going on. He's running. He's going up to that house there."

The remote beach seemed lower than the sea, and it required a searching glance to discern the little black figure. The captain saw a floating stick, and they rowed to it. A bath towel was by some weird chance in the boat, and, tying this on the stick, the captain waved it. The oarsman did not dare turn his head, so he was obliged to ask questions.

"What's he doing now?"

"He's standing still again. He's looking, I think.—There he goes again—toward the house.—Now he's stopped again."

"Is he waving at us?"

"No, not now; he was, though."

"Look! There comes another man!"

"He's running."

"Look at him go, would you!"

"Why, he's on a bicycle. Now he's met the other man. They're both waving at us. Look!"

"There comes something up the beach."

"What the devil is that thing?"

"Why, it looks like a boat."

"Why, certainly, it's a boat."

"No; it's on wheels."

"Yes, so it is. Well, that must be the life-boat. They drag them along shore on a wagon."

"That's the life-boat, sure."

"No, by God, it's—it's an omnibus."

"I tell you it's a life-boat."

"It is not! It's an omnibus. I can see it plain. See? One of these big hotel omnibuses."

"By thunder, you're right. It's an omnibus, sure as fate. What do you suppose they are doing with an omnibus? Maybe they are going around collecting the life-crew, hey?"

"That's it, likely. Look! There's a fellow waving a little black flag. He's standing on the steps of the omnibus. There come those other two fellows. Now they're all talking together. Look at the fellow with the flag. Maybe he ain't waving it!"

"That ain't a flag, is it? That's his coat. Why, certainly, that's his coat."

"So it is; it's his coat. He's taken it off and is waving it around his head. But would you look at him swing it!"

"Oh, say, there isn't any life-saving station there. That's just a winter-resort hotel omnibus that has brought over some of the boarders to see us drown."

"What's that idiot with the coat mean? What's he signaling, anyhow?"

"It looks as if he were trying to tell us to go north. There must be a life-saving station up there."

"No; he thinks we're fishing. Just giving us a merry hand. See? Ah, there, Willie!"

"Well, I wish I could make something out of those signals. What do you suppose he means?"

"He don't mean anything; he's just playing."

"Well, if he'd just signal us to try the surf again, or to go to sea and wait, or go north, or go south, or go to hell, there would be some reason in it. But look at him! He just stands there and keeps his coat revolving like a wheel. The ass!"

"There come more people."

"Now there's quite a mob. Look! Isn't that a boat?"

"Where? Oh, I see where you mean. No, that's no boat."

"That fellow is still waving his coat."

"He must think we like to see him do that. Why don't he quit it? It don't mean anything."

"I don't know. I think he is trying to make us go north. It must be that there's a life-saving station there somewhere."

"Say, he ain't tired yet. Look at 'im wave!"

"Wonder how long he can keep that up. He's been revolving his coat ever since he caught sight of us. He's an idiot. Why aren't they getting men to bring a boat out? A fishing-boat—one of those big yawls—could come out here all right. Why don't he do something?"

"Oh, it's all right now."

"They'll have a boat out here for us in less than no time, now that they've seen us."

A faint yellow tone came into the sky over the low land. The shadows on the sea slowly deepened. The wind bore coldness with it, and the men began to shiver.

"Holy smoke!" said one, allowing his voice to express his impious mood, "if we keep on monkeying out here! If we've got to flounder out here all night!"

"Oh, we'll never have to stay here all night! Don't you worry. They've seen us now, and it won't be long before they'll come chasing out after us."

The shore grew dusky. The man waving a coat blended gradually into this gloom, and it swallowed in the same manner the omnibus and the group of people. The spray, when it dashed uproariously over the side, made the voyagers shrink and swear like men who were being branded.

"I'd like to catch the chump who waved the coat. I feel like socking him one, just for luck."

"Why? What did he do?"

"Oh, nothing, but then he seemed so damned cheerful."

In the meantime the oiler rowed, and then the correspondent rowed, and then the oiler rowed. Grey-faced and bowed forward, they mechanically, turn by turn, plied the leaden oars. The form of the lighthouse had vanished from the southern horizon, but finally a pale star appeared, just lifting from the sea. The streaked saffron in the west passed before the all-merging darkness, and the sea to the east was black. The land had vanished, and was expressed only by the low and drear thunder of the surf.

"If I am going to be drowned—if I am going to be drowned—if I am going to be drowned, why, in the name of the seven mad gods who rule the sea, was I allowed to come thus far and contemplate sand and trees? Was I brought here merely to have my nose dragged away as I was about to nibble the sacred cheese of life?"

The patient captain, drooped over the water-jar, was sometimes obliged to speak to the oarsman.

"Keep her head up! Keep her head up!"

"Keep her head up, sir." The voices were weary and low.

This was surely a quiet evening. All save the oarsman lay heavily and listlessly in the boat's bottom. As for him, his eyes were just capable of noting the tall black waves that swept forward in a most sinister silence, save for an occasional subdued growl of a crest.

The cook's head was on a thwart, and he looked without interest at the water under his nose. He was deep in other scenes. Finally he spoke. "Billie," he murmured, dreamfully, "what kind of pie do you like best?"

## V

"Pie!" said the oiler and the correspondent, agitatedly, "Don't talk about those things, blast you!"

"Well," said the cook, "I was just thinking about ham sandwiches and—"

A night on the sea in an open boat is a long night. As darkness settled finally, the shine of the light, lifting from the sea in the south, changed to full gold. On the northern horizon a new light appeared, a small bluish gleam on the edge of the waters. These two lights were the furniture of the world. Otherwise there was nothing but waves.

Two men huddled in the stern, and distances were so magnificent in the dinghy that the rower was enabled to keep his feet partly warm by thrusting them under his companions. Their legs indeed extended far under the rowing-seat until they touched the feet of the captain forward. Sometimes, despite the efforts of the tired oarsman, a wave came piling into the boat, an icy wave of the night, and the chilling water soaked them anew. They would twist their bodies for a moment and groan, and sleep the dead sleep once more, while the water in the boat gurgled about them as the craft rocked.

The plan of the oiler and the correspondent was for one to row until he lost the ability, and then arouse the other from his sea-water couch in the bottom of the boat.

The oiler plied the oars until his head drooped forward and the overpowering sleep blinded him; and he rowed yet afterward. Then he touched a man in the bottom of the boat, and called his name. "Will you spell me for a little while?" he said, meekly.

"Sure, Billie," said the correspondent, awaking and dragging himself to a sitting position. They exchanged places carefully, and the oiler, cuddling down in the seawater at the cook's side, seemed to go to sleep instantly.

The particular violence of the sea had ceased. The waves came without snarling. The obligation of the man at the oars was to keep the boat headed so that the tilt of the rollers would not capsize her, and to preserve her from filling when the crests rushed past. The black waves were silent and hard to be seen in the darkness. Often one was almost upon the boat before the oarsman was aware.

In a low voice the correspondent addressed the captain. He was not sure that the captain was awake, although this iron man seemed to be always awake. "Captain, shall I keep her making for that light north, sir?"

The same steady voice answered him. "Yes. Keep it about two points off the port bow."

The cook had tied a life-belt around himself in order to get even the warmth which this clumsy cork contrivance could donate, and he seemed almost stove-like when a rower, whose teeth invariably chattered wildly as soon as he ceased his labour, dropped down to sleep.

The correspondent, as he rowed, looked down at the two men sleeping underfoot. The cook's arm was around the oiler's shoulders, and, with their fragmentary clothing and haggard faces, they were the babes of the sea—a grotesque rendering of the old babes in the wood.

Later he must have grown stupid at his work, for suddenly there was a growling of water, and a crest came with a roar and a swash into the boat, and it was a wonder that it did not set the cook afloat in his life-belt. The cook continued to sleep, but the oiler sat up, blinking his eyes and shaking with the new cold.

"Oh, I'm awful sorry, Billie," said the correspondent, contritely.

"That's all right, old boy," said the oiler, and lay down again and was asleep.

Presently it seemed that even the captain dozed, and the correspondent thought that he was the one man afloat on all the oceans. The wind had a voice as it came over the waves, and it was sadder than the end.

There was a long, loud swishing astern of the boat, and a gleaming trail of phosphorescence, like blue flame, was furrowed on the black waters. It might have been made by a monstrous knife.

Then there came a stillness, while the correspondent breathed with open mouth and looked at the sea.

Suddenly there was another swish and another long flash of bluish light, and this time it was alongside the boat, and might almost have been reached with an oar. The correspondent saw an enormous fin speed like a shadow through the water, hurling the crystalline spray and leaving the long glowing trail.

The correspondent looked over his shoulder at the captain. His face was hidden, and he seemed to be asleep. He looked at the babes of the sea. They certainly were asleep. So, being bereft of sympathy, he leaned a little way to one side and swore softly into the sea.

But the thing did not then leave the vicinity of the boat. Ahead or astern, on one side or the other, at intervals long or short, fled the long sparkling streak, and there was to be heard the *whirroo* of the dark fin. The speed and power of the thing was greatly to be admired. It cut the water like a gigantic and keen projectile.

The presence of this biding thing did not affect the man with the same horror that it would if he had been a picnicker. He simply looked at the sea dully and swore in an undertone.

Nevertheless, it is true that he did not wish to be alone with the thing. He wished one of his companions to awake by chance and keep him company with it. But the captain hung motionless over the water-jar, and the oiler and the cook in the bottom of the boat were plunged in slumber.

## VI

"If I am going to be drowned—if I am going to be drowned—if I am going to be drowned, why, in the name of the seven mad gods who rule the sea, was I allowed to come thus far and contemplate sand and trees?"

During this dismal night, it may be remarked that a man would conclude that it was really the intention of the seven mad gods to drown him, despite the abominable injustice of it. For it was certainly an abominable injustice to drown a man who had worked so hard, so hard. The man felt it would be a crime most unnatural. Other people had drowned at sea since galleys swarmed with painted sails, but still—

When it occurs to a man that nature does not regard him as important, and that she feels she would not maim the universe by disposing of him, he at first wishes to throw bricks at the temple, and he hates deeply the fact that there are no bricks and no temples. Any visible expression of nature would surely be pelleted with his jeers.

Then, if there be no tangible thing to hoot, he feels, perhaps, the desire to confront a personification and indulge in pleas, bowed to one knee, and with hands supplicant, saying, "Yes, but I love myself."

A high cold star on a winter's night is the word he feels that she says to him. Thereafter he knows the pathos of his situation.

The men in the dinghy had not discussed these matters, but each had, no doubt, reflected upon them in silence and according to his mind. There was seldom any expression upon their faces save the general one of complete weariness. Speech was devoted to the business of the boat.

To chime the notes of his emotion, a verse mysteriously entered the correspondent's head. He had even forgotten that he had forgotten this verse, but it suddenly was in his mind.

*A soldier of the Legion lay dying in Algiers;*
*There was lack of woman's nursing, there was dearth of woman's tears;*
*But a comrade stood beside him, and he took that comrade's hand,*
*And he said, "I never more shall see my own, my native land."*

In his childhood the correspondent had been made acquainted with the fact that a soldier of the Legion lay dying in Algiers, but he had never regarded the fact as important. Myriads of his school-fellows had informed him of the soldier's plight, but the dinning had naturally ended by making him perfectly indifferent. He had never considered it his affair that a soldier of the Legion lay dying in Algiers, nor had it appeared to him as a matter for sorrow. It was less to him than the breaking of a pencil's point.

Now, however, it quaintly came to him as a human, living thing. It was no longer merely a picture of a few throes in the breast of a poet, meanwhile drinking tea and warming his feet at the grate; it was an actuality—stern, mournful, and fine.

The correspondent plainly saw the soldier. He lay on the sand with his feet out straight and still. While his pale left hand was upon his chest in an attempt to thwart the going of his life, the blood came between his fingers. In the far Algerian distance, a city of low square forms was set against a sky that was faint with the last sunset hues. The correspondent, plying the oars and dreaming of the slow and slower movements of the lips of the soldier, was moved by a profound and perfectly impersonal comprehension. He was sorry for the soldier of the Legion who lay dying in Algiers.

The thing which had followed the boat and waited had evidently grown bored at the delay. There was no longer to be heard the slash of the cut-water, and there was no longer the flame of the long trail. The light in the north still glimmered, but it was apparently no nearer to the boat. Sometimes the boom of the surf rang in the correspondent's ears, and he turned the craft seaward then and rowed harder. Southward, some one had evidently built a watch-fire on the beach. It was too low and too far to be seen, but it made a shimmering, rose-ate reflection upon the bluff in back of it, and this could be discerned from the boat. The wind came stronger, and sometimes a wave suddenly raged out like a mountain cat, and there was to be seen the sheen and sparkle of a broken crest.

The captain, in the bow, moved on his water-jar and sat erect. "Pretty long night," he observed to the correspondent. He looked at the shore. "Those life-saving people take their time."

"Did you see that shark playing around?"

"Yes, I saw him. He was a big fellow, all right."

"Wish I had known you were awake."

Later the correspondent spoke into the bottom of the boat. "Billie!" There was a slow and gradual disentanglement. "Billie, will you spell me?"

"Sure," said the oiler.

As soon as the correspondent touched the cold, comfortable sea-water in the bottom of the boat and had huddled close to the cook's life-belt he was deep in sleep, despite the fact that his teeth played all the popular airs. This sleep was so good to him that it was but a moment before he heard a voice call his name in a tone that demonstrated the last stages of exhaustion. "Will you spell me?"

"Sure, Billie."

The light in the north had mysteriously vanished, but the correspondent took his course from the wide-awake captain.

Later in the night they took the boat farther out to sea, and the captain directed the cook to take one oar at the stern and keep the boat facing the seas. He was to call out if he should hear the thunder of the surf. This plan enabled the oiler and the correspondent to get respite together. "We'll give those boys a chance to get into shape again," said the captain. They curled down and, after a few preliminary chatterings and trembles, slept once more the dead sleep. Neither knew they had bequeathed to the cook the company of another shark, or perhaps the same shark.

As the boat caroused on the waves, spray occasionally bumped over the side and gave them a fresh soaking, but this had no power to break their repose. The ominous slash of the wind and the water affected them as it would have affected mummies.

"Boys," said the cook, with the notes of every reluctance in his voice, "she's drifted in pretty close. I guess one of you had better take her to sea again." The correspondent, aroused, heard the crash of the toppled crests.

As he was rowing, the captain gave him some whisky-and-water, and this steadied the chills out of him. "If I ever get ashore and anybody shows me even a photograph of an oar—"

At last there was a short conversation.

"Billie!—Billie, will you spell me?"

"Sure," said the oiler.

## VII

When the correspondent again opened his eyes, the sea and the sky were each of the grey hue of the dawning. Later, carmine and gold was painted upon the waters. The morning appeared finally, in its splendour, with a sky of pure blue, and the sunlight flamed on the tips of the waves.

On the distant dunes were set many little black cottages, and a tall white windmill reared above them. No man, nor dog, nor bicycle appeared on the beach. The cottages might have formed a deserted village.

The voyagers scanned the shore. A conference was held in the boat.

"Well," said the captain, "if no help is coming, we might better try a run through the surf right away. If we stay out here much longer we will be too weak to do anything for ourselves at all." The others silently acquiesced in this reasoning. The boat was headed for the beach. The correspondent wondered if none ever ascended the tall wind-tower, and if then they never looked seaward. This tower was a giant, standing with its back to the plight of the ants. It represented in a degree, to the correspondent, the serenity of nature amid the struggles of the individual—nature in the wind, and nature in the vision of men. She did not seem cruel to him then, nor beneficent, nor treacherous, nor wise. But she was indifferent, flatly indifferent. It is, perhaps, plausible that a man in this situation, impressed with the unconcern of the universe, should see the innumerable flaws of his life, and have them taste wickedly in his mind, and wish for another chance. A distinction between right and wrong seems absurdly clear to him, then, in this new ignorance of the grave-edge, and he understands that if he were given another opportunity he would mend his conduct and his words, and be better and brighter during an introduction or at a tea.

"Now, boys," said the captain, "she is going to swamp sure. All we can do is to work her in as far as possible, and then when she swamps, pile out and scramble for the beach. Keep cool now, and don't jump until she swamps sure."

The oiler took the oars. Over his shoulders he scanned the surf. "Captain," he said, "I think I'd better bring her about and keep her head-on to the seas and back her in."

"All right, Billie," said the captain. "Back her in." The oiler swung the boat then, and, seated in the stern, the cook and the correspondent were obliged to look over their shoulders to contemplate the lonely and indifferent shore.

The monstrous inshore rollers heaved the boat high until the men were again enabled to see the white sheets of water scudding up the slanted beach. "We won't get in very close," said the captain. Each time a man could wrest his attention from the rollers, he turned his glance toward the shore, and in the expression of the eyes during this contemplation there was a singular quality. The correspondent, observing the others, knew that they were not afraid, but the full meaning of their glances was shrouded.

As for himself, he was too tired to grapple fundamentally with the fact. He tried to coerce his mind into thinking of it, but the mind was dominated at this time by the muscles, and the muscles said they did not care. It merely occurred to him that if he should drown it would be a shame.

There were no hurried words, no pallor, no plain agitation. The men simply looked at the shore. "Now, remember to get well clear of the boat when you jump," said the captain.

Seaward the crest of a roller suddenly fell with a thunderous crash, and the long white comber came roaring down upon the boat.

"Steady now," said the captain. The men were silent. They turned their eyes from the shore to the comber and waited. The boat slid up the incline, leaped at the furious top, bounced over it, and swung down the long back of the wave. Some water had been shipped, and the cook bailed it out.

But the next crest crashed also. The tumbling, boiling flood of white water caught the boat and whirled it almost perpendicular. Water swarmed in from all sides. The correspondent had his hands on the gunwale at this time, and when the water entered at that place he swiftly withdrew his fingers, as if he objected to wetting them.

The little boat, drunken with this weight of water, reeled and snuggled deeper into the sea.

"Bail her out, cook! Bail her out!" said the captain.

"All right, Captain," said the cook.

"Now, boys, the next one will do for us sure," said the oiler. "Mind to jump clear of the boat."

The third wave moved forward, huge, furious, implacable. It fairly swallowed the dinghy, and almost simultaneously the men tumbled into the sea. A piece of life-belt had lain in the bottom of the boat, and as the correspondent went overboard he held this to his chest with his left hand.

The January water was icy, and he reflected immediately that it was colder than he had expected to find it off the coast of Florida. This appeared to his dazed mind as a fact important enough to be noted at the time. The coldness of the water was sad; it was tragic. This fact was somehow mixed and confused with his opinion of his own situation, so that it seemed almost a proper reason for tears. The water was cold.

When he came to the surface he was conscious of little but the noisy water. Afterward he saw his companions in the sea. The oiler was ahead in the race. He was swimming strongly and rapidly. Off to the correspondent's left, the cook's great white and corked back bulged out of the water; and in the rear the captain was hanging with his one good hand to the keel of the overturned dinghy.

There is a certain immovable quality to a shore, and the correspondent wondered at it amid the confusion of the sea.

It seemed also very attractive; but the correspondent knew that it was a long journey, and he paddled leisurely. The piece of life-preserver lay under him, and sometimes he whirled down the incline of a wave as if he were on a hand-sled.

But finally he arrived at a place in the sea where travel was beset with difficulty. He did not pause swimming to inquire what manner of current had caught him, but there his progress ceased. The shore was set before him like a bit of scenery on a stage, and he looked at it and understood with his eyes each detail of it.

As the cook passed, much farther to the left, the captain was calling to him. "Turn over on your back, cook! Turn over on your back and use the oar."

"All right, sir." The cook turned on his back, and, paddling with an oar, went ahead as if he were a canoe.

Presently the boat also passed to the left of the correspondent, with the captain clinging with one hand to the keel. He would have appeared like a man raising himself to look over a board fence if it were not for the extraordinary gymnastics of the boat. The correspondent marvelled that the captain could still hold to it.

They passed on nearer to the shore—the oiler, the cook, the captain —and following them went the water-jar, bouncing gaily over the seas.

The correspondent remained in the grip of this strange new enemy —a current. The shore, with its white slope of sand and its green bluff topped with little silent cottages, was spread like a picture before him. It was very near to him then, but he was impressed as one who, in a gallery, looks at a scene from Brittany or Algiers.

He thought: "I am going to drown? Can it be possible? Can it be possible? Can it be possible?" Perhaps an individual must consider his own death to be the final phenomenon of nature.

But later a wave perhaps whirled him out of this small deadly current, for he found suddenly that he could again make progress toward the shore. Later still he was aware that the captain, clinging with one hand to the keel of the dinghy, had his face turned away from the shore and toward him, and was calling his name. "Come to the boat! Come to the boat!"

In his struggle to reach the captain and the boat, he reflected that when one gets properly wearied drowning must really be a comfortable arrangement—a cessation of hostilities accompanied by a large degree of relief; and he was glad of it, for the main thing in his mind for some moments had been horror of the temporary agony. He did not wish to be hurt.

Presently he saw a man running along the shore. He was undressing with most remarkable speed. Coat, trousers, shirt, everything flew magically off him.

"Come to the boat!" called the captain.

"All right, Captain." As the correspondent paddled, he saw the captain let himself down to bottom and leave the boat. Then the correspondent performed his one little marvel of the voyage. A large wave caught him and flung him with ease and supreme speed completely over the boat and far beyond it. It struck him even then as an event in gymnastics and a true miracle of the sea. An overturned boat in the surf is not a plaything to a swimming man.

The correspondent arrived in water that reached only to his waist, but his condition did not enable him to stand for more than a moment. Each wave knocked him into a heap, and the undertow pulled at him.

Then he saw the man who had been running and undressing, and undressing and running, come bounding into the water. He dragged ashore the cook, and then waded toward the captain; but the captain waved him away and sent him to the correspondent. He was naked— naked as a tree in winter; but a halo was about his head, and he shone like a saint. He gave a strong pull, and a long drag, and a bully heave at the correspondent's hand. The correspondent, schooled in the minor formulae, said, "Thanks, old man." But suddenly the man cried, "What's that?" He pointed a swift finger. The correspondent said, "Go."

In the shallows, face downward, lay the oiler. His forehead touched sand that was periodically, between each wave, clear of the sea.

The correspondent did not know all that transpired afterward. When he achieved safe ground he fell, striking the sand with each particular part of his body. It was as if he had dropped from a roof, but the thud was grateful to him.

It seemed that instantly the beach was populated with men with blankets, clothes, and flasks, and women with coffee-pots and all the remedies sacred to their minds. The welcome of the land to the men from the sea was warm and generous; but a still and dripping shape was carried slowly up the beach, and the land's welcome for it could only be the different and sinister hospitality of the grave.

When it came night, the white waves paced to and fro in the moonlight, and the wind brought the sound of the great sea's voice to the men on the shore, and they felt that they could then be interpreters.

# The Shades of Spring

## D. H. LAWRENCE

### I

It was a mile nearer through the wood. Mechanically, Syson turned up by the forge and lifted the field-gate. The blacksmith and his mate stood still, watching the trespasser. But Syson looked too much a gentleman to be accosted. They let him go on in silence across the small field to the wood.

There was not the least difference between this morning and those of bright springs, six or eight years back. White and sandy-gold fowls still scratched round the gate, littering the earth and the field with feathers and scratched-up rubbish. Between the two thick holly bushes in the wood-hedge was the hidden gap, whose fence one climbed to get into the wood; the bars were scored just the same by the keeper's boots. He was back in the eternal.

Syson was extraordinarily glad. Like an uneasy spirit he had returned to the country of his past, and he found it waiting for him, unaltered. The hazel still spread glad little hands downwards, the bluebells here were still wan and few, among the lush grass and in shade of the bushes.

The path through the wood, on the very brow of a slope, ran winding easily for a time. All around were twiggy oaks, just issuing their gold, and floor spaces diapered with woodruff, with patches of dog-mercury and tufts of hyacinth. Two fallen trees still lay across the track. Syson jolted down a steep, rough slope, and came again upon the open land, this time looking north as through a great window in the wood. He stayed to gaze over the level fields of the hill-top, at the village which strewed the bare upland as if it had tumbled off the passing waggons of industry, and been forsaken. There was a stiff, modern, grey little church, and block and rows of red dwellings lying at random; at the back, the twinkling headstocks of the pit, and the looming pit-hill. All was naked and out-of-doors, not a tree! It was quite unaltered.

Syson turned, satisfied, to follow the path that sheered downhill into the wood. He was curiously elated, feeling himself back in an enduring vision. He started. A keeper was standing a few yards in front, barring the way.

"Where might you be going this road, sir?" asked the man. The tone of his question had a challenging twang. Syson looked at the fellow with an impersonal, observant gaze. It was a young man of four or five-and-twenty, ruddy and well favoured. His dark blue eyes now stared aggressively at the intruder. His black moustache, very thick, was cropped short over a small, rather soft mouth. In every other respect the fellow was manly and good-looking. He stood just above middle height; the strong forward thrust of his chest, and the perfect ease of his erect, self-sufficient body, gave one the feeling that he was taut with animal life, like the thick jet of a fountain balanced in itself. He stood with the butt of his gun on the ground, looking uncertainly and questioningly at Syson. The dark, restless eyes of the trespasser, examining the man and penetrating into him without heeding his office, troubled the keeper and made him flush.

"Where is Naylor? Have you got his job?" Syson asked.

"You're not from the House, are you?" inquired the keeper. It could not be, since everyone was away.

"No, I'm not from the House," the other replied. It seemed to amuse him.

"Then might I ask where you were making for?" said the keeper, nettled.

"Where I am making for?" Syson repeated. "I am going to Willey-Water Farm."

"This isn't the road."

"I think so. Down this path, past the well, and out by the white gate."

"But that's not the public road."

"I suppose not. I used to come so often, in Naylor's time, I had forgotten. Where is he, by the way?"

"Crippled with rheumatism," the keeper answered reluctantly.

"Is he?" Syson exclaimed in pain.

"And who might you be?" asked the keeper, with a new intonation.

"John Adderley Syson; I used to live in Cordy Lane."

"Used to court Hilda Millership?"

Syson's eyes opened with a pained smile. He nodded. There was an awkward silence.

"And you—who are you?" asked Syson.

"Arthur Pilbeam—Naylor's my uncle," said the other.

"You live here in Nuttall?"

"I'm lodgin' at my uncle's—at Naylor's."

"I see!"

"Did you say you was goin' down to Willey-Water?" asked the keeper.

"Yes."

There was a pause of some moments, before the keeper blurted: "*I'm* courtin' Hilda Millership."

The young fellow looked at the intruder with a stubborn defiance, almost pathetic. Syson opened new eyes.

"Are you?" he said, astonished. The keeper flushed dark.

"She and me are keeping company," he said.

"I didn't know!" said Syson. The other man waited uncomfortably.

"What, is the thing settled?" asked the intruder.

"How, settled?" retorted the other sulkily.

"Are you going to get married soon, and all that?"

The keeper stared in silence for some moments, impotent.

"I suppose so," he said, full of resentment.

"Ah!" Syson watched closely.

"I'm married myself," he added, after a time.

"You are?" said the other incredulously.

Syson laughed in his brilliant, unhappy way.

"This last fifteen months," he said.

The keeper gazed at him with wide, wondering eyes, apparently thinking back, and trying to make things out.

"Why, didn't you know?" asked Syson.

"No, I didn't," said the other sulkily.

There was silence for a moment.

"Ah well!" said Syson, "I will go on. I suppose I may." The keeper stood in silent opposition. The two men hesitated in the open, grassy space, set round with small sheaves of sturdy bluebells; a little open platform on the brow of the hill. Syson took a few indecisive steps forward, then stopped.

"I say, how beautiful!" he cried.

He had come in full view of the downslope. The wide path ran from his feet like a river, and it was full of bluebells, save for a green winding thread down the center, where the keeper walked. Like a stream the path opened into azure shallows at the levels, and there were pools of bluebells, with still the green thread winding through, like a thin current of ice-water through blue lakes. And from under the twig-purple of the bushes swam the shadowed blue, as if the flowers lay in flood water over the woodland.

"Ah, isn't it lovely!" Syson exclaimed; this was his past, the country he had abandoned, and it hurt him to see it so beautiful. Wood-pigeons cooed overhead, and the air was full of the brightness of birds singing.

"If you're married, what do you keep writing to her for, and sending her poetry books and things?" asked the keeper. Syson stared at him, taken aback and humiliated. Then he began to smile.

"Well," he said, "I did not know about you. . ."

Again the keeper flushed darkly.

"But if you are married—" he charged.

"I am," answered the other cynically.

Then, looking down the blue beautiful path, Syson felt his own humiliation. "What right *have* I to hang on to her?" he thought, bitterly self-contemptuous.

"She knows I'm married and all that," he said.

"But you keep sending her books," challenged the keeper.

Syson, silenced, looked at the other man quizzically, half pitying. Then he turned.

"Good day," he said, and was gone. Now everything irritated him: the two sallows, one all gold and perfume and murmur, one silver-green and bristly, reminded him that here he had taught her about pollination. What a fool he was! What god-forsaken folly it all was!

"Ah well," he said to himself; "the poor devil seems to have a grudge against me. I'll do my best for him." He grinned to himself, in a very bad temper.

## II

The farm was less than a hundred yards from the wood's edge. The wall of trees formed the fourth side to the open quadrangle. The house faced the wood. With tangled emotions, Syson noted the plum blossom falling on the profuse, coloured primroses, which he himself had brought here and set. How they had increased! There were thick tufts of scarlet, and pink, and pale purple primroses under the plum trees. He saw somebody glance at him through the kitchen window, heard men's voices.

The door opened suddenly: very womanly she had grown! He felt himself going pale.

"You?—Addy!" she exclaimed, and stood motionless.

"Who?" called the farmer's voice. Men's low voices answered. Those low voices, curious and almost jeering, roused the tormented spirit in the visitor. Smiling brilliantly at her, he waited.

"Myself—why not?" he said.

The flush burned very deep on her cheek and throat.

"We are just finishing dinner," she said.

"Then I will stay outside." He made a motion to show that he would sit on the red earthenware pipkin that stood near the door among the daffodils, and contained the drinking water.

"Oh no, come in," she said hurriedly. He followed her. In the door-way, he glanced swiftly over the family, and bowed. Every one was confused. The farmer, his wife, and the four sons sat at the coarsely laid dinnertable, the men with arms bare to the elbows.

"I am sorry I come at lunch-time," said Syson.

"Hello, Addy!" said the farmer, assuming the old form of address, but his tone cold. "How are you?"

And he shook hands.

"Shall you have a bit?" he invited the young visitor, but taking for granted the offer would be refused. He assumed that Syson was become too refined to eat so roughly. The young man winced at the imputation.

"Have you had any dinner?" asked the daughter.

"No," replied Syson. "It is too early. I shall be back at half-past one."

"You call it lunch, don't you?" asked the eldest son, almost ironical. He had once been an intimate friend of this young man.

"We'll give Addy something when we've finished," said the mother, an invalid, deprecating.

"No—don't trouble. I don't want to give you any trouble," said Syson.

"You could allus live on fresh air an' scenery," laughed the youngest son, a lad of nineteen.

Syson went round the buildings, and into the orchard at the back of the house, where daffodils all along the hedgerow swung like yellow, ruffled birds on their perches. He loved the place extraordinarily, the hills ranging round, with bear-skin woods covering their giant shoulders, and small red farms like brooches clasping their garments; the blue streak of water in the valley, the bareness of the home pasture, the sound of myriad-threaded bird-singing, which went mostly unheard. To his last day, he would dream of this place, when he felt the sun on his face or saw the small handfuls of snow between the winter twigs, or smelt the coming of spring.

Hilda was very womanly. In her presence he felt constrained. She was twenty-nine, as he was, but she seemed to him much older. He felt foolish, almost unreal, beside her. She was so static. As he was fingering some shed plum blossom on a low bough, she came to the back door to shake the tablecloth. Fowls raced from the stackyard, birds rustled from the trees. Her dark hair was gathered up in a coil like a crown on her head. She was very straight, distant in her bearing. As she folded the cloth, she looked away over the hills.

Presently Syson returned indoors. She had prepared eggs and curd cheese, stewed gooseberries and cream.

"Since you will dine tonight," she said, "I have only given you a light lunch."

"It is awfully nice," he said. "You keep a real idyllic atmosphere—your belt of straw and ivy buds."

Still they hurt each other.

He was uneasy before her. Her brief, sure speech, her distant bearing, were unfamiliar to him. He admired again her grey-black eyebrows, and her lashes. Their eyes met. He saw, in the beautiful grey and black of her glance, tears and a strange light, and at the back of all, calm acceptance of herself, and triumph over him.

He felt himself shrinking. With an effort he kept up the ironic manner.

She sent him into the parlour while she washed the dishes. The long low room was refurnished from the Abbey sale, with chairs upholstered in claret-coloured rep, many years old, and an oval table of polished walnut, and another piano, handsome, though still antique. In spite of the strangeness, he was pleased. Opening a high cupboard let into the thickness of the wall, he found it full of his books, his old lesson-books, and volumes of verse he had sent her, English and German. The daffodils in the white window-bottoms shone across the room, he could almost feel their rays. The old glamour caught him again. His youthful water-colours on the wall no longer made him grin; he remembered how fervently he had tried to paint for her, twelve years before.

She entered, wiping a dish, and he saw again the bright, kernel-white beauty of her arms.

"You are quite splendid here," he said, and their eyes met.

"Do you like it?" she asked. It was the old, low, husky tone of intimacy. He felt a quick change beginning in his blood. It was the old, delicious sublimation, the thinning, almost the vaporizing of himself, as if his spirit were to be liberated.

"Aye," he nodded, smiling at her like a boy again. She bowed her head.

"This was the countess's chair," she said in low tones. "I found her scissors down here between the padding."

"Did you? Where are they?"

Quickly, with a lilt in her movement, she fetched her workbasket, and together they examined the long-shanked old scissors.

"I knew you could use them," she said, laughing, as he fitted his fingers into the round loops of the countess's scissors.

"I knew you could use them," she said, with certainty. He looked at his fingers, and at the scissors. She meant his fingers were fine enough for the small-looped scissors.

"That is something to be said for me," he laughed, putting the scissors aside. She turned to the window. He noticed the fine, fair down on her cheek and her upper lip, and her soft, white neck, like the throat of a nettle flower, and her fore-arms, bright as newly blanched kernels. He was looking at her with new eyes, and she was a different person to him. He did not know her. But he could regard her objectively now.

"Shall we go out awhile?" she asked.

"Yes!" he answered. But the predominant emotion, that troubled the excitement and perplexity of his heart, was fear, fear of that which he saw. There was about her the same manner, the same intonation in her voice, now as then, but she was not what he had known her to be. He knew quite well what she had been for him. And gradually he was realizing that she was something quite other, and always had been.

She put no covering on her head, merely took off her apron, saying, "We will go by the larches." As they passed the old orchard, she called him in to show him a blue-tit's nest in one of the apple trees, and a sycock's in the hedge. He rather wondered at her surety, at a certain hardness like arrogance hidden under her humility.

"Look at the apple buds," she said, and he then perceived myriads of little scarlet balls among the drooping boughs. Watching his face, her eyes went hard. She saw the scales were fallen from him, and at last he was going to see her as she was. It was the thing she had most dreaded in the past, and most needed, for her soul's sake. Now he was going to see her as she was. He would not love her, and he would know he never could love her. The old illusion gone, they were strangers, crude and entire. But he would give her her due—she would have her due from him.

She was brilliant as he had not known her. She showed him nests: a jenny wren's in a low bush.

"See this jinty's!" she exclaimed.

He was surprised to hear her use the local name. She reached carefully through the thorns, and put her finger in the nest's round door.

"Five!" she said. "Tiny little things."

She showed him nests of robins, and chaffinches, and linnets, and buntings; of a wagtail beside the water.

"And if we go down, nearer the lake, I will show you a kingfisher's. . . ."

"Among the young fir trees," she said, "there's a throstle's or a blackie's on nearly every bough, every ledge. The first day, when I had seen them all, I felt as if I mustn't go in the wood. It seemed a city of birds: and in the morning, hearing them all, I thought of the noisy early markets. I was afraid to go in my own wood."

She was using the language they had both of them invented. Now it was all her own. He had done with it. She did not mind his silence, but was always dominant, letting him see her wood. As they came along a marshy path where forget-me-nots were opening in a rich blue drift: "We know all the birds, but there are many flowers we can't find out," she said. It was half an appeal to him, who had known the names of things.

She looked dreamily across the open fields that slept in the sun.

"I have a lover as well, you know," she said, with assurance, yet dropping again almost into the intimate tone.

This woke in him the spirit to fight her.

"I think I met him. He is good-looking—also in Arcady."

Without answering, she turned into a dark path that led up-hill, where the trees and undergrowth were very thick.

"They did well," she said at length, "to have various altars to various gods, in old days."

"Ah yes!" he agreed. "To whom is the new one?"

"There are no old ones," she said. "I was always looking for this."

"And whose is it?" he asked.

"I don't know," she looking full at him.

"I'm very glad for your sake," he said, "that you are satisfied."

"Aye—but the man doesn't matter so much," she said. There was a pause.

"No!" he exclaimed, astonished, yet recognizing her as her real self.

"It is one's self that matters," she said. "Whether one is being one's own self and serving one's own God."

There was silence, during which he pondered. The path was almost flowerless, gloomy. At the side, his heels sank into soft clay.

### III

"I," she said, very slowly, "I was married the same night as you."

He looked at her.

"Not legally, of course," she replied. "But—actually."

"To the keeper?" he said, not knowing what else to say.

She turned to him.

"You thought I could not?" she said. But the flush was deep in her cheek and throat, for all her assurance.

Still he would not say anything.

"You see"—she was making an effort to explain—"I had to understand also."

"And what does it amount to, this *understanding?*" he asked.

"A very great deal—does it not to you?" she replied. "One is free."

"And you are not disappointed?"

"Far from it!" Her tone was deep and sincere.

"You love him?"

"Yes, I love him."

"Good!" he said.

This silenced her for a while.

"Here, among his things, I love him," she said.

His conceit would not let him be silent.

"It needs this setting?" he asked.

"It does," she cried. "You were always making me to be not myself."

He laughed shortly.

"But is it a matter of surroundings?" he said. He had considered her all spirit.

"I am like a plant," she replied. "I can only grow in my own soil."

They came to a place where the undergrowth shrank away, leaving a bare, brown space, pillared with the brick-red and purplish trunks of pine trees. On the fringe, hung the sombre green of elder trees, with flat flowers in bud, and below were bright, unfurling pennons of fern. In the midst of the bare space stood a keeper's log hut. Pheasant-coops were lying about, some occupied by a clucking hen, some empty.

Hilda walked over the brown pine-needles to the hut, took a key from among the eaves, and opened the door. It was a bare wooden place with a carpenter's bench and form, carpenter's tools, an axe, snares, traps, some skins pegged down, everything in order. Hilda closed the door. Syson examined the weird flat coats of wild animals, that were pegged down to be cured. She turned some knotch in the side wall, and disclosed a second, small apartment.

"How romantic!" said Syson.

"Yes. He is very curious—he has some of a wild animal's cunning—in a nice sense—and he is inventive, and thoughtful—but not beyond a certain point."

She pulled back a dark green curtain. The apartment was occupied almost entirely by a large couch of heather and bracken, on which was an ample rabbit-skin rug. On the floor were patchwork rugs of cat-skin, and a red calf-skin, while hanging from the wall were other furs. Hilda took down one which she put on. It was a cloak of rabbit-skin and of white fur, with a hood, apparently of the skins of stoats. She laughed at Syson from out of this barbaric mantle, saying:

"What do you think of it?"

"Ah—! I congratulate you on your man," he replied.

"And look!" she said.

In a little jar on a shelf were some sprays, frail and white, of the first honeysuckle.

"They will scent the place at night," she said.

He looked round curiously.

"Where does he come short, then?" he asked. She gazed at him for a few moments. Then, turning aside:

"The stars aren't the same with him," she said. "You could make them flash and quiver, and the forget-me-nots come up at me like phosphorescence. You could make things *wonderful*. I have it out—it is true. But I have them all for myself, now."

He laughed, saying:

"After all, stars and forget-me-nots are only luxuries. You ought to make poetry."

"Aye," she assented. "But I have them all now."

Again he laughed bitterly at her.

She turned swiftly. He was leaning against the small window of the tiny, obscure room and was watching her, who stood in the doorway, still cloaked in her mantle. His cap was removed, so she saw his face and head distinctly in the dim room. His black, straight, glossy hair was brushed clean back from his brow. His black eyes were watching her, and his face, that was clear and cream, and perfectly smooth, was flickering.

"We are very different," she said bitterly.

Again he laughed.

"I see you disapprove of me," he said.

"I disapprove of what you have become," she said.

"You think we might"—he glanced at the hut—"have been like this —you and I?"

She shook her head.

"You! No; never! You plucked a thing and looked at it till you had found out all you wanted to know about it, then you threw it away," she said.

"Did I?" he asked. "And could your way never have been my way? I suppose not."

"Why should it?" she said. "I am a separate being."

"But surely two people sometimes go the same way," he said.

"You took me away from myself," she said.

He knew he had mistaken her, had taken her for something she was not. That was his fault, not hers.

"And did you always know?" he asked.

"No—you never let me know. You bullied me. I couldn't help myself. I was glad when you left me, really."

"I know you were," he said. But his face went paler, almost deathly luminous.

"Yet," he said, "it was you who sent me the way I have gone."

"I!" she exclaimed, in pride.

"You *would* have me take the Grammar School scholarship—and you would have me foster poor little Botell's fervent attachment to me, till he couldn't live without me—and because Botell was rich and influential. You triumphed in the wine-merchant's offer to send me to Cambridge, to befriend his only child. You wanted me to rise in the world. And all the time you were sending me away from you—every new success of mine put a separation between us, and more for you than for me. You never wanted to come with me: you wanted just to send me to see what it was like. I believe you even wanted me to marry a lady. You wanted to triumph over society in me."

"And I am responsible," she said, with sarcasm.

"I distinguished myself to satisfy you," he replied.

"Ah!" she cried, "you always wanted change, change, like a child."

"Very well! And I am a success, and I know it, and I do some good work. But—I thought you were different. What right have you to a man?"

"What do you want?" she said, looking at him with wide, fearful eyes.

He looked back at her, his eyes pointed, like weapons.

"Why, nothing," he laughed shortly.

There was a rattling at the outer latch, and the keeper entered. The woman glanced round, but remained standing, fur-cloaked, in the inner doorway. Syson did not move.

The other man entered, saw, and turned away without speaking. The two also were silent.

Pilbeam attended to his skins.

"I must go," said Syson.

"Yes," she replied.

"Then I give you 'To our vast and varying fortunes.'" He lifted his hand in pledge.

"'To our vast and varying fortunes,'" she answered gravely, and speaking in cold tones.

"Arthur!" she said.

The keeper pretended not to hear. Syson, watching keenly, began to smile. The woman drew herself up.

"Arthur!" she said again, with a curious upward inflection, which warned the two men that her soul was trembling on a dangerous crisis.

The keeper slowly put down his tool and came to her.

"Yes," he said.

"I wanted to introduce you," she said, trembling.

"I've met him a'ready," said the keeper.

"Have you? It is Addy, Mr. Syson, whom you know about.—This is Arthur, Mr. Pilbeam," she added, turning to Syson. The latter held out his hand to the keeper, and they shook hands in silence.

"I'm glad to have met you," said Syson. "We drop our correspondence, Hilda?"

"Why need we?" she asked.

The two men stood at a loss.

"*Is* there no need?" said Syson.

Still she was silent.

"It is as you will," she said.

They went all three together down the gloomy path.

" 'Qu'il était bleu, le ciel, et grand l'espoir,' " quoted Syson, not knowing what to say.

"What do you mean?" she said. "Besides, *we* can't walk in *our* wild oats—we never sowed any."

Syson looked at her. He was startled to see his young love, his nun, his Botticelli angel, so revealed. It was he who had been the fool. He and she were more separate than any two strangers could be. She only wanted to keep up a correspondence with him—and he, of course, wanted it kept up, so that he could write to her, like Dante to some Beatrice who had never existed save in the man's own brain.

At the bottom of the path she left him. He went along with the keeper, towards the open, towards the gate that closed on the wood. The two men walked almost like friends. They did not broach the subject of their thoughts.

Instead of going straight to the high-road gate, Syson went along the wood's edge, where the brook spread out in a little bog, and under the alder trees, among the reeds, great yellow stools and bosses of marigolds shone. Threads of brown water trickled by, touched with gold from the flowers. Suddenly there was a blue flash in the air, as a kingfisher passed.

Syson was extraordinarily moved. He climbed the bank to the gorse bushes, whose sparks of blossom had not yet gathered into a flame. Lying on the dry brown turf, he discovered sprigs of tiny purple milk-wort and pink spots of lousewort. What a wonderful world it was—marvellous, forever new. He felt as if it were underground, like the fields of monotone hell, notwithstanding. Inside his breast was a pain like a wound. He remembered the poem of William Morris, where in the Chapel of Lyonesse a knight lay wounded, with the truncheon of a spear deep in his breast, lying always as dead, yet did not die, while day after day the coloured sunlight dipped from the painted window across the chancel, and passed away. He knew now it never had been true, that which was between him and her, not for a moment. The truth had stood apart all the time.

Syson turned over. The air was full of the sound of larks, as if the sunshine above were condensing and falling in a shower. Amid this bright sound, voices sounded small and distinct.

"But if he's married, an' quite willing to drop it off, what has ter against it?" said the man's voice.

"I don't want to talk about it now. I want to be alone."

Syson looked through the bushes. Hilda was standing in the wood, near the gate. The man was in the field, loitering by the hedge, and playing with the bees as they settled on the white bramble flowers.

There was silence for a while, in which Syson imagined her will among the brightness of the larks. Suddenly the keeper exclaimed "Ah!" and swore. He was gripping at the sleeve of his coat, near the shoulder. Then he pulled off his jacket, threw it on the ground, and absorbedly rolled up his shirt sleeve right to the shoulder.

"Ah!" he said vindictively, as he picked out the bee and flung it away. He twisted his fine, bright arm, peering awkwardly over his shoulder.

"What is it?" asked Hilda.

"A bee—crawled up my sleeve," he answered.

"Come here to me," she said.

The keeper went to her, like a sulky boy. She took his arm in her hands.

"Here it is—and the sting left in—poor bee!"

She picked out the sting, put her mouth to his arm, and sucked away the drop of poison. As she looked at the red mark her mouth had made, and at his arm, she said, laughing:

"That is the reddest kiss you will ever have."

When Syson next looked up, at the sound of voices, he saw in the shadow the keeper with his mouth on the throat of his beloved, whose head was thrown back, and whose hair had fallen, so that one rough rope of dark brown hair hung across his bare arm.

"No," the woman answered. "I am not upset because he's gone. You won't understand. . . ."

Syson could not distinguish what the man said. Hilda replied, clear and distinct:

"You know I love you. He has gone quite out of my life—don't trouble about him. . . ." He kissed her, murmuring. She laughed hollowly.

"Yes," she said, indulgent. "We will be married, we will be married. But not just yet." He spoke to her again. Syson heard nothing for a time. Then she said:

"You must go home, now, dear—you will get no sleep."

Again was heard the murmur of the keeper's voice, troubled by fear and passion.

"But why should we be married at once?" she said. "What more would you have, by being married? It is most beautiful as it is."

At last he pulled on his coat and departed. She stood at the gate, not watching him, but looking over the sunny country.

When at last she had gone, Syson also departed, going back to town.

# A Little Cloud

## JAMES JOYCE

EIGHT years before he had seen his friend off at the North Wall and wished him godspeed. Gallaher had got on. You could tell that at once by his travelled air, his well-cut tweed suit, and fearless accent. Few fellows had talents like his and fewer still could remain unspoiled by such success. Gallaher's heart was in the right place and he had deserved to win. It was something to have a friend like that.

Little Chandler's thoughts ever since lunchtime had been of his meeting with Gallaher, of Gallaher's invitation and of the great city London where Gallaher lived. He was called Little Chandler because, though he was but slightly under the average stature, he gave one the idea of being a little man. His hands were white and small, his frame was fragile, his voice was quiet and his manners were refined. He took the greatest care of his fair silken hair and moustache and used perfume discreetly on his handkerchief. The half-moons of his nails were perfect and when he smiled you caught a glimpse of a row of childish white teeth.

As he sat at his desk in the King's Inns he thought what changes those eight years had brought. The friend whom he had known under a shabby and necessitous guise had become a brilliant figure on the London Press. He turned often from his tiresome writing to gaze out of the office window. The glow of a late autumn sunset covered the grass plots and walks. It cast a shower of kindly golden dust on the untidy nurses and decrepit old men who drowsed on the benches; it flickered upon all the moving figures—on the children who ran screaming along the gravel paths and on everyone who passed through the gardens. He watched the scene and thought of life; and (as always happened when he thought of life) he became sad. A gentle melancholy took possession of him. He felt how useless it was to struggle against fortune, this being the burden of wisdom which the ages had bequeathed to him.

He remembered the books of poetry upon his shelves at home. He had bought them in his bachelor days and many an evening, as he sat in the little room off the hall, he had been tempted to take one down from the bookshelf and read out something to his wife. But shyness had always held him back; and so the books had remained on their shelves. At times he repeated lines to himself and this consoled him.

When his hour had struck he stood up and took leave of his desk and of his fellow-clerks punctiliously. He emerged from under the feudal arch of the King's Inns, a neat modest figure, and walked swiftly down Henrietta Street. The golden sunset was waning and the air had grown sharp. A horde of grimy children populated the street. They stood or ran in the roadway or crawled up the steps before the gaping doors or squatted like mice upon the thresholds. Little Chandler gave them no thought. He picked his way deftly through all that minute vermin-like life and under the shadow of the gaunt spectral mansions in which the old nobility of Dublin had roystered. No memory of the past touched him for his mind was full of a present joy.

He had never been in Corless's but he knew the value of the name. He knew that people went there after the theatre to eat oysters and drink liqueurs; and he had heard that the waiters there spoke French and German. Walking swiftly by at night he had seen cabs drawn up before the door and richly dressed ladies, escorted by cavaliers, alight and enter quickly. They wore noisy dresses and many wraps. Their faces were powdered and they caught up their dresses, when they touched earth, like alarmed Atalantas. He had always passed without turning his head to look. It was his habit to walk swiftly in the street even by day and whenever he found himself in the city late at night he hurried on his way apprehensively and excitedly. Sometimes, however, he courted the causes of his fear. He chose the darkest and narrowest streets and, as he walked boldly forward, the silence that was spread about his footsteps troubled him, the wandering, silent figures troubled him; and at times a sound of low fugitive laughter made him tremble like a leaf.

He turned to the right towards Capel Street. Ignatius Gallaher on the London Press! Who would have thought it possible eight years before? Still, now that he reviewed the past, Little Chandler could remember many signs of future greatness in his friend. People used to say that Ignatius Gallaher was wild. Of course, he did mix with a rakish set of fellows at that time, drank freely and borrowed money on all sides. In the end he had got mixed up in some shady affair, some money transaction: at least, that was one version of his flight. But nobody denied him talent. There was always a certain . . . something in Ignatius Gallaher that impressed you in spite of yourself. Even when he was out at elbows and at his wits' end for money he kept up a bold face. Little Chandler remembered (and the rememberance brought a slight flush of pride to his cheek) one of Ignatius Gallaher's sayings when he was in a tight corner:

"Half time now, boys," he used to say light-heartedly. "Where's my considering cap?"

That was Ignatius Gallaher all out; and, damn it, you couldn't but admire him for it.

Little Chandler quickened his pace. For the first time in his life he felt himself superior to the people he passed. For the first time his soul revolted against the dull inelegance of Capel Street. There was no doubt about it: if you wanted to succeed you had to go away. You could do nothing in Dublin. As he crossed Grattan Bridge he looked down the river towards the lower quays and pitied the poor stunted houses. They seemed to him a band of tramps, huddled together along the river-banks, their old coats covered with dust and soot, stupefied by the panorama of sunset and waiting for the first chill of night to bid them arise, shake themselves and begone. He wondered whether he could write a poem to express his idea. Perhaps Gallaher might be able to get it into some London paper for him. Could he write something original? He was not sure what idea he wished to express but the thought that a poetic moment had touched him took life within him like an infant hope. He stepped onward bravely.

Every step brought him nearer to London, farther from his own sober inartistic life. A light began to tremble on the horizon of his mind. He was not so old—thirty-two. His temperament might be said to be just at the point of maturity. There were so many different moods and impressions that he wished to express in verse. He felt them within him. He tried to weigh his soul to see if it was a poet's soul. Melancholy was the dominant note of his temperament, he thought, but it was a melancholy tempered by recurrences of faith and resignation and simple joy. If he could give expression to it in a book of poems perhaps men would listen. He would never be popular: he saw that. He could not sway the crowd but he might appeal to a little circle of kindred minds. The English critics, perhaps, would recognize him as one of the Celtic school by reason of the melancholy tone of his poems; besides that, he would put in allusions. He began to invent sentences and phrases from the notice which his book would get. *"Mr. Chandler has the gift of easy and graceful verse."* . . . *"A wistful sadness pervades these poems."* . . . *"The Celtic note."* It was a pity his name was not more Irish-looking. Perhaps it would be better to insert his mother's name before the surname: Thomas Malone Chandler, or better still: T. Malone Chandler. He would speak to Gallaher about it.

He pursued his revery so ardently that he passed his street and had to turn back. As he came near Corless's his former agitation began to overmaster him and he halted before the door in indecision. Finally he opened the door and entered.

The light and noise of the bar held him at the doorways for a few moments. He looked about him, but his sight was confused by the shining of many red and green wine-glasses. The bar seemed to him to be full of people and he felt that the people were observing him curiously. He glanced quickly to the right and left (frowning slightly to make his errand appear serious), but when his sight cleared a little he saw that nobody had turned to look at him: and there, sure enough, was Ignatius Gallaher leaning with his back against the counter and his feet planted far apart.

"Hallo, Tommy, old hero, here you are! What is it to be? What will you have? I'm taking whisky: better stuff than we get across the water. Soda? Lithia? No mineral? I'm the same. Spoils the flavour. . . . Here, *garçon,* bring us two halves of malt whisky, like a good fellow. . . . Well, and how have you been pulling along since I saw you last? Dear God, how old we're getting! Do you see any signs of aging in me—eh, what? A little gray and thin on the top—what?"

Ignatius Gallaher took off his hat and displayed a large closely cropped head. His face was heavy, pale and clean-shaven. His eyes, which were of bluish slate-colour, relieved his unhealthy pallor and shone out plainly above the vivid orange tie he wore. Between these rival features the lips appeared very long and shapeless and colourless. He bent his head and felt with two sympathetic fingers the thin hair at the crown. Little Chandler shook his head as a denial. Ignatius Gallaher put on his hat again.

"It pulls you down," he said, "Press life. Always hurry and scurry, looking for copy and sometimes not finding it: and then, always to have something new in your stuff. Damn proofs and printers, I say, for a few days. I'm deuced glad, I can tell you, to get back to the old country. Does a fellow good, a bit of a holiday. I feel a ton better since I landed again in dear dirty Dublin. . . . Here you are, Tommy. Water? Say when."

Little Chandler allowed his whisky to be very much diluted.

"You don't know what's good for you, my boy," said Ignatius Gallaher. "I drink mine neat."

"I drink very little as a rule," said Little Chandler modestly. "An odd half-one or so when I meet any of the old crowd: that's all."

"Ah, well," said Ignatius Gallaher, cheerfully, "here's to us and to old times and old acquaintance."

They clinked glasses and drank the toast.

"I met some of the old gang to-day," said Ignatius Gallaher. "O'Hara seems to be in a bad way. What's he doing?"

"Nothing," said Little Chandler. "He's gone to the dogs."

"But Hogan has a good sit, hasn't he?"

"Yes; he's in the Land Commission."

"I met him one night in London and he seemed to be very flush. . . . Poor O'Hara! Boose, I suppose?"

"Other things, too," said Little Chandler shortly.

Ignatius Gallaher laughed.

"Tommy," he said, "I see you haven't changed an atom. You're the very same serious person that used to lecture me on Sunday mornings when I had a sore head and a fur on my tongue. You'd want to knock about a bit in the world. Have you never been anywhere even for a trip?"

"I've been to the Isle of Man," said Little Chandler.

Ignatius Gallaher laughed.

"The Isle of Man!" he said. "Go to London or Paris: Paris, for choice. That'd do you good."

"Have you seen Paris?"

"I should think I have! I've knocked about there a little."

"And is it really so beautiful as they say?" asked Little Chandler.

He sipped a little of his drink while Ignatius Gallaher finished his boldly.

"Beautiful?" said Ignatius Gallaher, pausing on the word and on the flavour of his drink. "It's not so beautiful, you know. Of course, it is beautiful. . . . But it's the life of Paris; that's the thing. Ah, there's no city like Paris for gaiety, movement, excitement. . . ."

Little Chandler finished his whisky and, after some trouble, succeeded in catching the barman's eye. He ordered the same again.

"I've been to the Moulin Rouge," Ignatius Gallaher continued when the barman had removed their glasses, "and I've been to all the Bohemian cafes. Hot stuff! Not for a pious chap like you, Tommy."

Little Chandler said nothing until the barman returned with two glasses: then he touched his friend's glass lightly and reciprocated the former toast. He was beginning to feel somewhat disillusioned. Gallaher's accent and way of expressing himself did not please him. There was something vulgar in his friend which he had not observed before. But perhaps it was only the result of living in London amid the bustle and competition of the Press. The old personal charm was still there under this new gaudy manner. And, after all, Gallaher had lived, he had seen the world. Little Chandler looked at his friend enviously.

"Everything in Paris is gay," said Ignatius Gallaher. "They believe in enjoying life—and don't you think they're right? If you want to enjoy yourself properly you must go to Paris. And, mind you, they've a great feeling for the Irish there. When they heard I was from Ireland they were ready to eat me, man."

Little Chandler took four or five sips from his glass.

"Tell me," he said, "is it true that Paris is so . . . immoral as they say?"

Ignatius Gallaher made a catholic gesture with his right arm.

"Every place is immoral," he said. "Of course you do find spicy bits in Paris. Go to one of the students' balls, for instance. That's lively, if you like, when the *cocottes* begin to let themselves loose. You know what they are, I suppose?"

"I've heard of them," said Little Chandler.

Ignatius Gallaher drank off his whisky and shook his head.

"Ah," he said, "you may say what you like. There's no woman like the Parisienne—for style, for go."

"Then it is an immoral city," said Little Chandler, with timid insistence—"I mean, compared with London or Dublin?"

"London!" said Ignatius Gallaher. "It's six of one and half-a-dozen of the other. You ask Hogan, my boy. I showed him a bit about London when he was over there. He'd open your eye. . . . I say, Tommy, don't make punch of that whisky: liquor up."

"No, really. . . ."

"O, come on, another one won't do you any harm. What is it? The same again, I suppose?"

"Well . . . all right."

*"François,* the same again. . . . Will you smoke, Tommy?"

Ignatius Gallaher produced his cigar-case. The two friends lit their cigars and puffed at them in silence until their drinks were served.

"I'll tell you my opinion," said Ignatius Gallaher, emerging after some time from the clouds of smoke in which he had taken refuge, "it's a rum world. Talk of immorality! I've heard of cases—what am I saying?—I've known them: cases of . . . immorality. . . ."

Ignatius Gallaher puffed thoughtfully at his cigar and then, in a calm historian's tone, he proceeded to sketch for his friend some pictures of the corruption which was rife abroad. He summarised the vices of many capitals and seemed inclined to award the palm to Berlin. Some things he could not vouch for (his friends had told him), but of others he had had personal experience. He spared neither rank nor caste. He revealed many of the secrets of religious houses on the Continent and described some of the practices which were fashionable in high society and ended by telling, with details, a story about an English duchess—a story which he knew to be true. Little Chandler was astonished.

"Ah, well," said Ignatius Gallaher, "here we are in old jog-along Dublin where nothing is known of such things."

"How dull you must find it," said Little Chandler, "after all the other places you've seen!"

"Well," said Ignatius Gallaher, "it's a relaxation to come over here, you know. And, after all, it's the old country, as they say, isn't it? You can't help having a certain feeling for it. That's human nature. . . . But tell me something about yourself. Hogan told me you had . . . tasted the joys of connubial bliss. Two years ago, wasn't it?"

Little Chandler blushed and smiled.

"Yes," he said. "I was married last May twelve months."

"I hope it's not too late in the day to offer my best wishes," said

Ignatius Gallaher. "I didn't know your address or I'd have done so at the time."

He extended his hand, which Little Chandler took.

"Well, Tommy," he said, "I wish you and yours every joy in life, old chap, and tons of money, and may you never die till I shoot you. And that's the wish of a sincere friend, an old friend. You know that?"

"I know that," said Little Chandler.

"Any youngsters?" said Ignatius Gallaher.

Little Chandler blushed again.

"We have one child," he said.

"Son or daughter?"

"A little boy."

Ignatius Gallaher slapped his friend sonorously on the back.

"Bravo," he said, "I wouldn't doubt, Tommy."

Little Chandler smiled, looked confusedly at his glass and bit his lower lip with three childishly white front teeth.

"I hope you'll spend an evening with us," he said, "before you go back. My wife will be delighted to meet you. We can have a little music and—"

"Thanks awfully, old chap," said Ignatius Gallaher, "I'm sorry we didn't meet earlier. But I must leave to-morrow night."

"To-night, perhaps . . . ?"

"I'm awfully sorry, old man. You see I'm over here with another fellow, clever young chap he is too, and we arranged to go to a little card party. Only for that. . . ."

"O, in that case. . . ."

"But who knows?" said Ignatius Gallaher considerately. "Next year I may take a little skip over here now that I've broken the ice. It's only a pleasure deferred."

"Very well," said Little Chandler, "the next time you come we must have an evening together. That's agreed now, isn't it?"

"Yes, that's agreed," said Ignatius Gallaher. "Next year if I come, *parole d' honneur.*"

"And to clinch the bargain," said Little Chandler, "we'll just have one more now."

Ignatius Gallaher took out a large gold watch and looked at it.

"Is it to be the last?" he said. "Because you know, I have an a.p."

"O, yes, positively," said Little Chandler.

"Very well, then," said Ignatius Gallaher, "let us have another one as a *deoc an doruis*—that's good vernacular for a small whisky, I believe."

Little Chandler ordered the drinks. The blush which had risen to his face a few moments before was establishing itself. A trifle made him blush at any time: and now he felt warm and excited. Three small whiskies had gone to his head and Gallaher's strong cigar had confused his mind, for he was a delicate and abstinent person. The adventure of meeting Gallaher after eight years, of finding himself with Gallaher in Corless's surrounded by lights and noise, of listening to Gallaher's stories and of sharing for a brief space Gallaher's vagrant and triumphant life, upset the equipoise of his sensitive nature. He felt acutely the contrast between his own life and his friend's, and it seemed to him unjust. Gallaher was his inferior in birth and education. He was sure that he could do something better than his friend had ever done, or could ever do, something higher than mere tawdry journalism if he only got the chance. What was it that stood in his way? His unfortunate timidity! He wished to vindicate himself in some way, to assert his manhood. He saw behind Gallaher's refusal of his invitation. Gallaher was only patronising him by his friendliness just as he was patronising Ireland by his visit.

The barman brought their drinks. Little Chandler pushed one glass towards his friend and took up the other boldly.

"Who knows?" he said, as they lifted their glasses. "When you come next year I may have the pleasure of wishing long life and happiness to Mr. and Mrs. Ignatius Gallaher."

Ignatius Gallaher in the act of drinking closed one eye expressively over the rim of his glass. When he had drunk he smacked his lips decisively, set down his glass and said:

"No blooming fear of that, my boy. I'm going to have my fling first and see a bit of life and the world before I put my head in the sack—if I ever do."

"Some day you will," said Little Chandler calmly.

Ignatius Gallaher turned his orange tie and slate-blue eyes full upon his friend.

"You think so?" he said.

"You'll put your head in the sack," repeated Little Chandler stoutly, "like everyone else if you can find the girl."

He had slightly emphasised his tone and he was aware that he had betrayed himself; but, though the colour had heightened in his cheek, he did not flinch from his friend's gaze. Ignatius Gallaher watched him for a few moments and then said:

"If ever it occurs, you may bet your bottom dollar there'll be no mooning and spooning about it. I mean to marry money. She'll have a good fat account at the bank or she won't do for me."

Little Chandler shook his head.

"Why, man alive," said Ignatius Gallaher, vehemently, "do you know what it is? I've only to say the word and to-morrow I can have the woman and the cash. You don't believe it? Well, I know it. There are hundreds—what am I saying?—thousands of rich Germans and Jews, rotten with money, that'd only be too glad. . . . You wait a while, my boy. See if I don't play my cards properly. When I go about a thing I mean business, I tell you. You just wait."

He tossed his glass to his mouth, finished his drink and laughed loudly. Then he looked thoughtfully before him and said in a calmer tone:

"But I'm in no hurry. They can wait. I don't fancy tying myself up to one woman, you know."

He imitated with his mouth the act of tasting and made a wry face.

"Must get a bit stale, I should think," he said.

. . . . . . . . . . . .

Little Chandler sat in the room off the hall, holding a child in his arms. To save money they kept no servant but Annie's young sister Monica came for an hour or so in the morning and an hour or so in the evening to help. But Monica had gone home long ago. It was a quarter to nine. Little Chandler had come home late for tea and, moreover, he had forgotten to bring Annie home the parcel of coffee from Bewley's. Of course she was in a bad humour and gave him short answers. She said she would do without any tea but when it came near the time at which the shop at the corner closed she decided to go out herself for a quarter of a pound of tea and two pounds of sugar. She put the sleeping child deftly in his arms and said:

"Here. Don't waken him."

A little lamp with a white china shade stood upon the table and its light fell over a photograph which was enclosed in a frame of crumpled horn. It was Annie's photograph. Little Chandler looked at it, pausing at the thin tight lips. She wore the pale blue summer blouse which he had brought her home as a present one Saturday. It cost him ten and elevenpence; but what an agony of nervousness it had cost him! How he had suffered that day, waiting at the shop door until the shop was empty, standing at the counter and trying to appear at his ease while the girl piled ladies' blouses before him, paying at the desk and forgetting to take up the odd penny of his change, being called back by the cashier, and finally, striving to hide his blushes as he left the shop by examining the parcel to see if it was securely tied. When he brought the blouse home Annie kissed him and said it was very pretty and stylish; but when she heard the price she threw the blouse on the table and said it was a regular swindle to charge ten and elevenpence for it. At first she wanted to take it back but when she tried it on she was delighted with it, especially with the make of the sleeves, and kissed him and said he was very good to think of her.

Hm! . . .

He looked coldly into the eyes of the photograph and they answered coldly. Certainly they were pretty and the face itself was pretty. But he found something mean in it. Why was it so unconscious and lady-like? The composure of the eyes irritated him. They repelled him and defied him: there was no passion in them, no rapture. He thought of what Gallaher had said about rich Jewesses. Those dark Oriental eyes, he thought, how full they are of passion, of voluptuous longing! . . . Why had he married the eyes in the photograph?

He caught himself up at the question and glanced nervously round the room. He found something mean in the pretty furniture which he had bought for his house on the hire system. Annie had chosen it herself and it reminded him of her. It too was prim and pretty. A dull resentment against his life awoke within him. Could he not escape from his little house? Was it too late for him to try to live bravely like Gallaher? Could he go to London? There was the furniture still to be paid for. If he could only write a book and get it published, that might open the way for him.

A volume of Byron's poems lay before him on the table. He opened it cautiously with his left hand lest he should waken the child and began to read the first poem in the book:

> *Hushed are the winds and still the evening gloom,*
> *Not e'en a Zephyr wanders through the grove,*
> *Whilst I return to view my Margaret's tomb*
> *And scatter flowers on the dust I love.*

He paused. He felt the rhythm of the verse about him in the room.

How melancholy it was! Could he, too, write like that, express the melancholy of his soul in verse? There were so many things he wanted to describe: his sensation of a few hours before on Grattan Bridge, for example. If he could get back again into that mood. . . .

The child awoke and began to cry. He turned from the page and tried to hush it: but it would not be hushed. He began to rock it to and fro in his arms but its wailing cry grew keener. He rocked it faster while his eyes began to read the second stanza:

> *Within this narrow cell reclines her clay,*
> *That clay where once. . . .*

It was useless. He couldn't read. He couldn't do anything. The wailing of the child pierced the drum of his ear. It was useless, useless! He was a prisoner for life. His arms trembled with anger and suddenly bending to the child's face he shouted:

"Stop!"

The child stopped for an instant, had a spasm of fright and began to scream. He jumped up from his chair and walked hastily up and down the room with the child in his arms. It began to sob piteously, losing its breath for four or five seconds, and then bursting out anew. The thin walls of the room echoed the sound. He tried to soothe it but it sobbed more convulsively. He looked at the contracted and quivering face of the child and began to be alarmed. He counted seven sobs without a break between them and caught the child to his breast in fright. If it died! . . .

The door was burst open and a young woman ran in, panting.

"What is it? What is it?" she cried.

The child, hearing its mother's voice, broke out into a paroxysm of sobbing.

"It's nothing, Annie . . . it's nothing. . . . He began to cry. . . ."

She flung her parcels on the floor and snatched the child from him.

"What have you done to him?" she cried, glaring into his face.

Little Chandler sustained for one moment the gaze of her eyes and his heart closed together as he met the hatred in them. He began to stammer:

"It's nothing. . . . He . . . he began to cry. . . . I couldn't . . . I didn't do anything. . . . What?"

Giving no heed to him she began to walk up and down the room, clasping the child tightly in her arms and murmuring:

"My little man! My little mannie! Was 'ou frightened, love? . . .
There now, love! There now! . . . Lambabaun! Mamma's little lamb
of the world! . . . There now!"

Little Chandler felt his cheeks suffused with shame and he stood
back out of the lamplight. He listened while the paroxysm of the
child's sobbing grew less and less; and tears of remorse started to his
eyes.

# The Enormous Radio

## JOHN CHEEVER

Jim and Irene Westcott were the kind of people who seem to strike that satisfactory average of income, endeavor, and respectability that is reached by the statistical reports in college alumni bulletins. They were the parents of two young children, they had been married nine years, they lived on the twelfth floor of an apartment house near Sutton Place, they went to the theatre on an average of 10.3 times a year, and they hoped someday to live in Westchester. Irene Westcott was a pleasant, rather plain girl with soft brown hair and a wide, fine forehead upon which nothing at all had been written, and in the cold weather she wore a coat of fitch skins dyed to resemble mink. You could not say that Jim Westcott looked younger than he was, but you could at least say of him that he seemed to feel younger. He wore his graying hair cut very short, he dressed in the kind of clothes his class had worn at Andover, and his manner was earnest, vehement, and intentionally naïve. The Westcotts differed from their friends, their classmates, and their neighbors only in an interest they shared in serious music. They went to a great many concerts—although they seldom mentioned this to anyone—and they spent a good deal of time listening to music on the radio.

Their radio was an old instrument, sensitive, unpredictable, and beyond repair. Neither of them understood the mechanics of radio—or of any of the other appliances that surrounded them—and when the instrument faltered, Jim would strike the side of the cabinet with his hand. This sometimes helped. One Sunday afternoon, in the middle of a Schubert quartet, the music faded away altogether. Jim struck the cabinet repeatedly, but there was no response; the Schubert was

Permission the author; Copr. © 1947 The New Yorker Magazine, Inc.

lost to them forever. He promised to buy Irene a new radio, and on Monday when he came home from work he told her that he had got one. He refused to describe it, and said it would be a surprise for her when it came.

The radio was delivered at the kitchen door the following afternoon, and with the assistance of her maid and the handyman Irene uncrated it and brought it into the living room. She was struck at once with the physical ugliness of the large gumwood cabinet. Irene was proud of her living room, she had chosen its furnishings and colors as carefully as she chose her clothes, and now it seemed to her that the new radio stood among her intimate possessions like an aggressive intruder. She was confounded by the number of dials and switches on the instrument panel, and she studied them thoroughly before she put the plug into a wall socket and turned the radio on. The dials flooded with a malevolent green light, and in the distance she heard the music of a piano quintet. The quintet was in the distance for only an instant; it bore down upon her with a speed greater than light and filled the apartment with the noise of music amplified so mightily that it knocked a china ornament from a table to the floor. She rushed to the instrument and reduced the volume. The violent forces that were snared in the ugly gumwood cabinet made her uneasy. Her children came home from school then, and she took them to the Park. It was not until later in the afternoon that she was able to return to the radio.

The maid had given the children their suppers and was supervising their baths when Irene turned on the radio, reduced the volume, and sat down to listen to a Mozart quintet that she knew and enjoyed. The music came through clearly. The new instrument had a much purer tone, she thought, than the old one. She decided that tone was most important and that she could conceal the cabinet behind a sofa. But as soon as she had made her peace with the radio, the interference began. A crackling sound like the noise of a burning powder fuse began to accompany the singing of the strings. Beyond the music, there was a rustling that reminded Irene unpleasantly of the sea, and as the quintet progressed, these noises were joined by many others. She tried all the dials and switches but nothing dimmed the interference, and she sat down, disappointed and bewildered, and tried to trace the flight of the melody. The elevator shaft in her building ran beside the living-room wall, and it was the noise of the elevator that gave her a clue to the character of the static. The rattling of the elevator cables and the opening and closing of the elevator doors were reproduced in her loud-speaker, and, realizing that the radio was sensitive to electrical currents of all sorts, she began to discern through the Mozart the ringing of telephone bells, the dialing of phones, and the lamentation of a vacuum cleaner. By listening more carefully, she was able to distinguish doorbells, elevator bells, electric razors, and Waring mixers, whose sounds had been picked up from the apartments that surrounded hers and transmitted through her loudspeaker. The powerful and ugly instrument, with its mistaken sensitivity to discord, was more than she could hope to master, so she turned the thing off and went into the nursery to see her children.

When Jim Westcott came home that night, he went to the radio confidently and worked the controls. He had the same sort of experience Irene had had. A man was speaking on the station Jim had chosen, and his voice swung instantly from the distance into a force so powerful that it shook the apartment. Jim turned the volume control and reduced the voice. Then, a minute or two later, the interference began. The ringing of telephones and doorbells set in, joined by the rasp of the elevator doors and the whir of cooking appliances. The character of the noise had changed since Irene had tried the radio earlier; the last of the electric razors was being unplugged, the vacuum cleaners had all been returned to their closets, and the static reflected that change in pace that overtakes the city after the sun goes down. He fiddled wih the knobs but couldn't get rid of the noises, so he turned the radio off and told Irene that in the morning he'd call the people who had sold it to him and give them hell.

The following afternoon, when Irene returned to her apartment from a luncheon date, the maid told her that a man had come and fixed the radio. Irene went into the living room before she took off her hat or her furs and tried the instrument. From the loudspeaker came a recording of the "Missouri Waltz." It reminded her of the thin, scratchy music from an old-fashioned phonograph that she sometimes heard across the lake where she spent her summers. She waited until the waltz had finished, expecting an explanation of the recording, but there was none. The music was followed by silence, and then the plaintive and scratchy record was repeated. She turned the dial and got a satisfactory burst of Caucasian music—the thump of bare feet in the dust and the rattle of coin jewelry—but in the background she could hear the ringing of bells and a confusion of voices. Her children came home from school then, and she turned off the radio and went to the nursery.

When Jim came home that night, he was tired, and he took a bath and changed his clothes. Then he joined Irene in the living room. He had just turned on the radio when the maid announced dinner, so he left it on, and he and Irene went to the table.

Jim was too tired to make even a pretense of sociability, and there was nothing about the dinner to hold Irene's interest, so her attention wandered from the food to the deposits of silver polish on the candlesticks and from there to the music in the other room. She listened for a few moments to a Chopin prelude and then was surprised to hear a man's voice break in. "For Christ's sake, Kathy," he said, "do you always have to play the piano when I get home?" The music stopped abruptly. "It's the only chance I have," a woman said. "I'm at the office all day." "So am I," the man said. He added something obscene about an upright piano, and slammed a door. The passionate and melancholy music began again.

"Did you hear that?" Irene asked.

"What?" Jim was eating his dessert.

"The radio. A man said something while the music was still going on—something dirty."

"It's probably a play."

"I don't think it *is* a play," Irene said.

They left the table and took their coffee into the living room. Irene asked Jim to try another station. He turned the knob. "Have you seen my garters?" a man asked. "Button me up," a woman said. "Have you seen my garters?" the man said again. "Just button me up and I'll find your garters," the woman said. Jim shifted to another station. "I wish you wouldn't leave apple cores in the ashtrays," a man said. "I hate the smell."

"This is strange," Jim said.

"Isn't it?" Irene said.

Jim turned the knob again. " 'On the coast of Coromandel where the early pumpkins blow,' " a woman with a pronounced English accent said, " 'in the middle of the woods lived the Yonghy-Bonghy-Bò. Two old chairs, and half a candle, one old jug without a handle. . . .' "

"My God!" Irene cried. "That's the Sweeneys' nurse."

" 'These were all his worldly goods,' " the British voice continued.

"Turn that thing off," Irene said. "Maybe they can hear *us.*" Jim switched the radio off. "That was Miss Armstrong, the Sweeneys' nurse," Irene said. "She must be reading to the little girl. They live in 17-B. I've talked with Miss Armstrong in the Park. I know her voice very well. We must be getting other people's apartments."

"That's impossible," Jim said.

"Well, that was the Sweeneys' nurse," Irene said hotly. "I know her voice. I know it very well. I'm wondering if they can hear us."

Jim turned the switch. First from a distance and then nearer, nearer, as if borne on the wind, came the pure accents of the Sweeneys' nurse again: " *'Lady Jingly! Lady Jingly!'* " she said, " *'Sitting where the pumpkins blow, will you come and be my wife, said the Yonghy-Bonghy-Bò. . . .'* "

Jim went over to the radio and said "Hello" loudly into the speaker.

" *'I am tired of living singly,'* " the nurse went on, " *'on this coast so wild and shingly, I'm a-weary of my life; if you'll come and be my wife, quite serene would be my life. . . .'* "

"I guess she can't hear us," Irene said. "Try something else."

Jim turned to another station, and the living room was filled with the uproar of a cocktail party that had overshot its mark. Someone was playing the piano and singing the Whiffenpoof Song, and the voices that surrounded the piano were vehement and happy. "Eat some more sandwiches," a woman shrieked. There were screams of laughter and a dish of some sort crashed to the floor.

"Those must be the Fullers, in 11-E," Irene said. "I knew they were giving a party this afternoon. I saw her in the liquor store. Isn't this too divine? Try something else. See if you can get those people in 18-C."

The Westcotts overheard that evening a monologue on salmon fishing in Canada, a bridge game, running comments on home movies of what had apparently been a fortnight at Sea Island, and a bitter family quarrel about an overdraft at the bank. They turned off their radio at midnight and went to bed, weak with laughter. Sometime in the night, their son began to call for a glass of water and Irene got one and took it to his room. It was very early. All the lights in the neighborhood were extinguished, and from the boy's window she could see the empty street. She went into the living room and tried the radio. There was some faint coughing, a moan, and then a man spoke. "Are you all right, darling?" he asked. "Yes," a woman said wearily. "Yes, I'm all right, I guess," and then she added with great feeling, "but, you know, Charlie, I don't feel like myself any more. Sometimes there are about fifteen or twenty minutes in the week when I feel like myself. I don't like to go to another doctor, because the doctor's bills are so awful already, but I just don't feel like myself, Charlie. I just never feel like myself." They were not young, Irene thought. She guessed from the timbre of their voices that they were middle-aged. The restrained melancholy of the dialogue and the draft from the bedroom window made her shiver, and she went back to bed.

The following morning, Irene cooked breakfast for the family—the maid didn't come up from her room in the basement until ten—braided her daughter's hair, and waited at the door until her children and her husband had been carried away in the elevator. Then she went into the living room and tried the radio. "I don't want to go to school," a child screamed. "I hate school. I won't go to school. I hate school." "You will go to school," an enraged woman said. "We paid eight hundred dollars to get you into that school and you'll go if it kills you." The next number on the dial produced the worn record of the "Missouri Waltz." Irene shifted the control and invaded the privacy of several breakfast tables. She overheard demonstrations of indigestion, carnal love, abysmal vanity, faith, and despair. Irene's life was nearly as simple and sheltered as it appeared to be, and the forthright and sometimes brutal language that came from the loudspeaker that morning astonished and troubled her. She continued to listen until her maid came in. Then she turned off the radio quickly, since this insight, she realized, was a furtive one.

Irene had a luncheon date with a friend that day, and she left her apartment at a little after twelve. There were a number of women in the elevator when it stopped at her floor. She stared at their handsome and impassive faces, their furs, and the cloth flowers in their hats. Which one of them had been to Sea Island, she wondered. Which one had overdrawn her bank account? The elevator stopped at the tenth floor and a woman with a pair of Skye terriers joined them. Her hair was rigged high on her head and she wore a mink cape. She was humming the "Missouri Waltz."

Irene had two Martinis at lunch, and she looked searchingly at her friend and wondered what her secrets were. They had intended to go shopping after lunch, but Irene excused herself and went home. She told the maid that she was not to be disturbed; then she went into the living room, closed the doors, and switched on the radio. She heard, in the course of the afternoon, the halting conversation of a woman entertaining her aunt, the hysterical conclusion of a luncheon party, and a hostess briefing her maid about some cocktail guests. "Don't give the best Scotch to anyone who hasn't white hair," the hostess said. "See if you can get rid of that liver paste before you pass those hot things, and could you lend me five dollars? I want to tip the elevator man."

As the afternoon waned, the conversations increased in intensity. From where Irene sat, she could see the open sky above the East River. There were hundreds of clouds in the sky, as though the south wind had broken the winter into pieces and were blowing it north, and on her radio she could hear the arrival of cocktail guests and the return of children and businessmen from their schools and offices. "I found a good-sized diamond on the bathroom floor this morning," a woman said. "It must have fallen out of that bracelet Mrs. Dunston was wearing last night." "We'll sell it," a man said. "Take it down to the jeweller on Madison Avenue and sell it. Mrs. Dunston won't know the difference, and we could use a couple of hundred bucks. . . ." "'Oranges and lemons, say the bells of St. Clement's,'" the Sweeneys' nurse sang. "'Half-pence and farthings, say the bells of St. Martin's. When will you pay me? say the bells at old Bailey. . . .'" "It's not a hat," a woman cried, and at her back roared a cocktail party. "It's not a hat, it's a love affair. That's what Walter Florell said. He said it's not a hat, it's a love affair," and then, in a lower voice, the same woman added, "Talk to somebody, for Christ's sake, honey, talk to somebody. If she catches you standing here not talking to anybody, she'll take us off her invitation list, and I love these parties."

The Westcotts were going out for dinner that night, and when Jim came home, Irene was dressing. She seemed sad and vague, and he brought her a drink. They were dining with friends in the neighborhood, and they walked to where they were going. The sky was broad and filled with light. It was one of those splendid spring evenings that excite memory and desire, and the air that touched their hands and faces felt very soft. A Salvation Army band was on the corner playing "Jesus Is Sweeter." Irene drew on her husband's arm and held him there for a minute, to hear the music. "They're really such nice people, aren't they?" she said. "They have such nice faces. Actually, they're so much nicer than a lot of the people we know." She took a bill from her purse and walked over and dropped it into the tambourine. There was in her face, when she returned to her husband, a look of radiant melancholy that he was not familiar with. And her conduct at the dinner party that night seemed strange to him, too. She interrupted her hostess rudely and stared at the people across the table from her with an intensity for which she would have punished her children.

It was still mild when they walked home from the party, and Irene looked up at the spring stars. " 'How far that little candle throws its beams,' " she exclaimed. " 'So shines a good deed in a naughty world.' " She waited that night until Jim had fallen asleep, and then went into the living room and turned on the radio.

Jim came home at about six the next night. Emma, the maid, let him in, and he had taken off his hat and was taking off his coat when Irene ran into the hall. Her face was shining with tears and her hair was disordered. "Go up to 16-C, Jim!" she screamed. "Don't take off your coat. Go up to 16-C. Mr. Osborn's beating his wife. They've been quarrelling since four o'clock, and now he's hitting her. Go up there and stop him."

From the radio in the living room, Jim heard screams, obscenities, and thuds. "You know you don't have to listen to this sort of thing," he said. He strode into the living room and turned the switch. "It's indecent," he said. "It's like looking in windows. You know you don't have to listen to this sort of thing. You can turn it off."

"Oh, it's so horrible, it's so dreadful," Irene was sobbing. "I've been listening all day, and it's so depressing."

"Well, if it's so depressing, why do you listen to it? I bought this damned radio to give you some pleasure," he said. "I paid a great deal of money for it. I thought it might make you happy. I wanted to make you happy."

"Don't, don't, don't, don't quarrel with me," she moaned, and laid her head on his shoulder. "All the others have been quarrelling all day. Everybody's been quarrelling. They're all worried about money. Mrs. Hutchinson's mother is dying of cancer in Florida and they don't have enough money. And some woman in this building is having an affair with the handyman—with that hideous handyman. It's too disgusting. And Mrs. Melville has heart trouble and Mr. Hendricks is going to lose his job in April and Mrs. Hendricks is horrid about the whole thing, and that girl who plays the 'Missouri Waltz' is a whore, a common whore, and the elevator man has tuberculosis and Mr. Osborn has been beating Mrs. Osborn." She wailed, she trembled with grief and checked the stream of tears down her face with the heel of her palm.

"Well, why do you have to listen?" Jim asked again. "Why do you have to listen to this stuff if it makes you so miserable?"

"Oh, don't, don't, don't," she cried. "Life is too terrible, too sordid and awful. But we've never been like that, have we, darling? Have we? I mean we've always been good and decent and loving to one another, haven't we? And we have two children, two beautiful children. Our lives aren't sordid, are they, darling? Are they?" She flung her arms around his neck and drew his face down to hers. "We're happy, aren't we, darling? We are happy, aren't we?"

"Of course we're happy," he said tiredly. He began to surrender his resentment. "Of course we're happy. I'll have that damned radio fixed or taken away tomorrow." He stroked her soft hair. "My poor girl," he said.

"You love me, don't you?" she asked. "And we're not hypercritical or worried about money or dishonest, are we?"

"No, darling," he said.

A man came in the morning and fixed the radio. Irene turned it on cautiously and was happy to hear a California-wine commercial and a recording of Beethoven's Ninth Symphony, including Schiller's "Ode to Joy." She kept the radio on all day and nothing untoward came from the speaker.

A Spanish suite was being played when Jim came home. "Is everything all right?" he asked. His face was pale, she thought. They had some cocktails and went in to dinner to the "Anvil Chorus" from "Il Trovatore." This was followed by Debussy's "La Mer."

"I paid the bill for the radio today," Jim said. "It cost four hundred dollars. I hope you'll get some enjoyment out of it."

"Oh, I'm sure I will," Irene said.

"Four hundred dollars is a good deal more than I can afford," he went on. "I wanted to get something that you'd enjoy. It's the last extravagance we'll be able to indulge in this year. I see that you haven't paid your clothing bills yet. I saw them on your dressing table." He looked directly at her. "Why did you tell me you'd paid them? Why did you lie to me?"

"I just didn't want you to worry, Jim," she said. She drank some water. "I'll be able to pay my bills out of this month's allowance. There were the slipcovers last month, and that party."

"You've got to learn to handle the money I give you a little more intelligently, Irene," he said. "You've got to understand that we won't have as much money this year as we had last. I had a very sobering talk with Mitchell today. No one is buying anything. We're spending all our time promoting issues, and you know how long that takes. I'm not getting any younger, you know. I'm thirty-seven. My hair will be gray next year. I haven't done as well as I'd hoped to do. And I don't suppose things will get any better."

"Yes, dear," she said.

"We've got to start cutting down," Jim said. "We've got to think of the children. To be perfectly frank with you, I worry about money a great deal. I'm not at all sure of the future. No one is. If anything should happen to me, there's the insurance, but that wouldn't go very far today. I've worked awfully hard to give you and the children a comfortable life," he said bitterly. "I don't like to see all of my energies, all of my youth, wasted in fur coats and radios and slipcovers and—"

"Please, Jim," she said. "Please. They'll hear us."

"*Who'll hear us?* Emma can't hear us."

"The radio."

"Oh, I'm sick!" he shouted. "I'm sick to death of your apprehensiveness. The radio can't hear us. Nobody can hear us. And what if they can hear us? Who cares?"

Irene got up from the table and went into the living room. Jim went to the door and shouted at her from there. "Why are you so Christly all of a sudden? What's turned you overnight into a convent girl? You stole your mother's jewelry before they probated her will. You never gave your sister a cent of that money that was intended for her —not even when she needed it. You made Grace Howland's life miserable, and where was all your piety and your virtue when you went to that abortionist? I'll never forget how cool you were. You packed your bag and went off to have that child murdered as if you were going to Nassau. If you'd had any reasons, if you'd had any good reasons—"

Irene stood for a minute before the hideous cabinet, disgraced and sickened, but she held her hand on the switch before she extinguished the music and the voices, hoping that the instrument might speak to her kindly, that she might hear the Sweeneys' nurse. Jim continued to shout at her from the door. The voice on the radio was suave and noncommittal. "An early-morning railroad disaster in Tokyo," the loudspeaker said, "killed twenty-nine people. A fire in a Catholic hospital near Buffalo for the care of blind children was extinguished early this morning by nuns. The temperature is forty-seven. The humidity is eighty-nine."

# Young Goodman Brown

## NATHANIEL HAWTHORNE

Young Goodman Brown came forth at sunset into the street at Salem village; but put his head back, after crossing the threshold, to exchange a parting kiss with his young wife. And Faith, as the wife was aptly named, thrust her own pretty head into the street, letting the wind play with the pink ribbons of her cap while she called to Goodman Brown.

"Dearest heart," whispered she, softly and rather sadly, when her lips were close to his ear, "prithee put off your journey until sunrise and sleep in your own bed to-night. A lone woman is troubled with such dreams and such thoughts that she's afeard of herself sometimes. Pray tarry with me this night, dear husband, of all nights in the year."

"My love and my Faith," replied young Goodman Brown, "of all nights in the year, this one night must I tarry away from thee. My journey, as thou callest it, forth and back again, must needs be done 'twixt now and sunrise. What, my sweet, pretty wife, dost thou doubt me already, and we but three months married?"

"Then God bless you!" said Faith, with the pink ribbons; "and may you find all well when you come back."

"Amen!" cried Goodman Brown. "Say thy prayers, dear Faith, and go to bed at dusk, and no harm will come to thee."

So they parted; and the young man pursued his way until, being about to turn the corner by the meeting-house, he looked back and saw the head of Faith still peeping after him with a melancholy air, in spite of her pink ribbons.

"Poor little Faith!" thought he, for his heart smote him. "What a wretch am I to leave her on such an errand! She talks of dreams, too. Methought as she spoke there was trouble in her face, as if a dream had warned her what work is to be done to-night. But no, no; 't would kill her to think it. Well, she's a blessed angel on earth; and after this one night I'll cling to her skirts and follow her to heaven."

With this excellent resolve for the future, Goodman Brown felt himself justified in making more haste on his present evil purpose. He had taken a dreary road, darkened by all the gloomiest trees of the forest, which barely stood aside to let the narrow path creep through, and closed immediately behind. It was all as lonely as could be; and there is this peculiarity in such a solitude, that the traveller knows not who may be concealed by the innumerable trunks and the thick boughs overhead; so that with lonely footsteps he may yet be passing through an unseen multitude.

"There may be a devilish Indian behind every tree," said Goodman Brown to himself; and he glanced fearfully behind him as he added, "What if the devil himself should be at my very elbow!"

His head being turned back, he passed a crook of the road, and, looking forward again, beheld the figure of a man, in grave and decent attire, seated at the foot of an old tree. He arose at Goodman Brown's approach and walked onward side by side with him.

"You are late, Goodman Brown," said he. "The clock of the Old South was striking as I came through Boston, and that is full fifteen minutes agone."

"Faith kept me back a while," replied the young man, with a tremor in his voice, caused by the sudden appearance of his companion, though not wholly unexpected.

It was now deep dusk in the forest, and deepest in that part of it where these two were journeying. As nearly as could be discerned, the second traveller was about fifty years old, apparently in the same rank of life as Goodman Brown, and bearing a considerable resemblance to him, though perhaps more in expression than features. Still they might have been taken for father and son. And yet, though the elder person was as simply clad as the younger, and as simple in manner too, he had an indescribable air of one who knew the world, and who would not have felt abashed at the governor's dinner table or in King William's court, were it possible that his affairs should call him thither. But the only thing about him that could be fixed upon as remarkable was his staff, which bore the likeness of a great black snake, so curiously wrought that it might almost be seen to twist and wriggle itself like a living serpent. This, of course, must have been an ocular deception, assisted by the uncertain light.

"Come, Goodman Brown," cried his fellow-traveller, "this is a dull pace for the beginning of a journey. Take my staff, if you are so soon weary."

"Friend," said the other, exchanging his slow pace for a full stop, "having kept covenant by meeting thee here, it is my purpose now to return whence I came. I have scruples touching the matter thou wot'st of."

"Sayest thou so?" replied he of the serpent, smiling apart. "Let us walk on, nevertheless, reasoning as we go; and if I convince thee not thou shalt turn back. We are but a little way in the forest yet."

"Too far! too far!" exclaimed the goodman, unconsciously resuming his walk. "My father never went into the woods on such an errand, nor his father before him. We have been a race of honest men and good Christians since the days of the martyrs; and shall I be the first of the name of Brown that ever took this path and kept"—

"Such company, thou wouldst say," observed the elder person, interpreting his pause. "Well said, Goodman Brown! I have been as well acquainted with your family as with ever a one among the Puritans; and that's no trifle to say. I helped your grandfather, the constable, when he lashed the Quaker woman so smartly through the streets of Salem; and it was I that brought your father a pitch-pine knot, kindled at my own hearth, to set fire to an Indian village, in King Philip's war. They were my good friends, both; and many a pleasant walk have we had along this path, and returned merrily after midnight. I would fain be friends with you for their sake."

"If it be as thou sayest," replied Goodman Brown, "I marvel they never spoke of these matters; or, verily, I marvel not, seeing that the least rumor of the sort would have driven them from New England. We are a people of prayer, and good works to boot, and abide no such wickedness."

"Wickedness or not," said the traveller with the twisted staff, "I have a very general acquaintance here in New England. The deacons of many a church have drunk the communion wine with me; the selectmen of divers towns make me their chairman; and a majority of the Great and General Court are firm supporters of my interest. The governor and I, too—But these are state secrets."

"Can this be so?" cried Goodman Brown, with a stare of amazement at his undisturbed companion. "Howbeit, I have nothing to do with the governor and council; they have their own ways, and are no rule for a simple husbandman like me. But, were I to go on with thee, how should I meet the eye of that good old man, our minister, at Salem village? Oh, his voice would make me tremble both Sabbath day and lecture day."

Thus far the elder traveller had listened with due gravity; but now burst into a fit of irrepressible mirth, shaking himself so violently that his snake-like staff actually seemed to wriggle in sympathy.

"Ha! ha! ha!" shouted he again and again; then composing himself, "Well, go on, Goodman Brown, go on; but, prithee, don't kill me with laughing."

"Well, then, to end the matter at once," said Goodman Brown, considerably nettled, "there is my wife, Faith. It would break her dear little heart; and I'd rather break my own."

"Nay, if that be the case," answered the other, "e'en go thy ways, Goodman Brown. I would not for twenty old women like the one hobbling before us that Faith should come to any harm."

As he spoke he pointed his staff at a female figure on the path, in whom Goodman Brown recognized a very pious and exemplary dame, who had taught him his catechism in youth, and was still his moral and spiritual adviser, jointly with the minister and Deacon Gookin.

"A marvel, truly, that Goody Cloyse should be so far in the wilderness at nightfall," said he. "But with your leave, friend, I shall take a cut through the woods until we have left this Christian woman behind. Being a stranger to you, she might ask whom I was consorting with and whither I was going."

"Be it so," said his fellow-traveller. "Betake you the woods, and let me keep the path."

Accordingly the young man turned aside, but took care to watch his companion, who advanced softly along the road until he had come within a staff's length of the old dame. She, meanwhile, was making the best of her way, with singular speed for so aged a woman, and mumbling some indistinct words—a prayer, doubtless—as she went. The traveller put forth his staff and touched her withered neck with what seemed the serpent's tail.

"The devil!" screamed the pious old lady.

"Then Goody Cloyse knows her old friend?" observed the traveller, confronting her and leaning on his writhing stick.

"Ah, forsooth, and is it your worship indeed?" cried the good dame.
"Yea, truly is it, and in the very image of my old gossip, Goodman
Brown, the grandfather of the silly fellow that now is. But—would
your worship believe it?—my broomstick hath strangely disappeared,
stolen, as I suspect, by that unhanged witch, Goody Cory, and that,
too, when I was all anointed with the juice of smallage, and cinquefoil,
and wolf's bane"—

"Mingled with fine wheat and the fat of a new-born babe," said
the shape of old Goodman Brown.

"Ah, your worship knows the recipe," cried the old lady, cackling
aloud. "So, as I was saying, being all ready for the meeting, and no
horse to ride on, I made up my mind to foot it; for they tell me there
is a nice young man to be taken into communion to-night. But now
your good worship will lend me your arm, and we shall be there in
a twinkling."

"That can hardly be," answered her friend. "I may not spare you
my arm, Goody Cloyse; but here is my staff, if you will."

So saying, he threw it down at her feet, where, perhaps, it assumed
life, being one of the rods which its owner had formerly lent to the
Egyptian magi. Of this fact, however, Goodman Brown could not
take cognizance. He had cast up his eyes in astonishment, and, looking down again, beheld neither Goody Cloyse nor the serpentine staff,
but his fellow-traveller alone, who waited for him as calmly as if
nothing had happened.

"That old woman taught me my catechism," said the young man;
and there was a world of meaning in this simple comment.

They continued to walk onward, while the elder traveller exhorted
his companion to make good speed and persevere in the path, dis-
coursing so aptly that his arguments seemed rather to spring up in the
bosom of his auditor than to be suggested by himself. As they went,
he plucked a branch of maple to serve for a walking stick, and began
to strip it of the twigs and little boughs, which were wet with evening
dew. The moment his fingers touched them they became strangely
withered and dried up as with a week's sunshine. Thus the pair proceeded, at a good free pace, until suddenly, in a gloomy hollow of the
road, Goodman Brown sat himself down on the stump of a tree and
refused to go any farther.

"Friend," said he, stubbornly, "my mind is made up. Not another step will I budge on this errand. What if a wretched old woman do choose to go to the devil when I thought she was going to heaven: is that any reason why I should quit my dear Faith and go after her?"

"You will think better of this by and by," said his acquaintance, composedly. "Sit here and rest yourself a while; and when you feel like moving again, there is my staff to help you along."

Without more words, he threw his companion the maple stick, and was as speedily out of sight as if he had vanished into the deepening gloom. The young man sat a few moments by the roadside, applauding himself greatly, and thinking with how clear a conscience he should meet the minister in his morning walk, nor shrink from the eye of good old Deacon Gookin. And what calm sleep would be his that very night, which was to have been spent so wickedly, but so purely and sweetly now, in the arms of Faith! Amidst these pleasant and praiseworthy meditations, Goodman Brown heard the tramp of horses along the road, and deemed it advisable to conceal himself within the verge of the forest, conscious of the guilty purpose that had brought him thither, though now so happily turned from it.

On came the hoof tramps and the voices of the riders, two grave old voices, conversing soberly as they drew near. These mingled sounds appeared to pass along the road, within a few yards of the young man's hiding-place; but, owing doubtless to the depth of the gloom at that particular spot, neither the travellers nor their steeds were visible. Though their figures brushed the small boughs by the wayside, it could not be seen that they intercepted, even for a moment, the faint gleam from the strip of bright sky athwart which they must have passed. Goodman Brown alternately crouched and stood on tiptoe, pulling aside the branches and thrusting forth his head as far as he durst without discerning so much as a shadow. It vexed him the more because he could have sworn, were such a thing possible, that he recognized the voices of the minister and Deacon Gookin, jogging along quietly, as they were wont to do, when bound to some ordination or ecclesiastical council. While yet within hearing, one of the riders stopped to pluck a switch.

"Of the two, reverend sir," said the voice like the deacon's, "I had rather miss an ordination dinner than to-night's meeting. They tell me that some of our community are to be here from Falmouth and beyond, and others from Connecticut and Rhode Island, besides several of the Indian powwows, who, after their fashion, know almost as much deviltry as the best of us. Moreover, there is a goodly young woman to be taken into communion."

"Mighty well, Deacon Gookin!" replied the solemn old tones of the minister. "Spur up, or we shall be late. Nothing can be done, you know, until I get on the ground."

The hoofs clattered again; and the voices, talking so strangely in the empty air, passed on through the forest, where no church had ever been gathered or solitary Christian prayed. Whither, then, could these holy men be journeying so deep into the heathen wilderness? Young Goodman Brown caught hold of a tree for support, being ready to sink down on the ground, faint and overburdened with the heavy sickness of his heart. He looked up to the sky, doubting whether there really was a heaven above him. Yet there was the blue arch, and the stars brightening in it.

"With heaven above and Faith below, I will yet stand firm against the devil!" cried Goodman Brown.

While he still gazed upward into the deep arch of the firmament and had lifted his hands to pray, a cloud, though no wind was stirring, hurried across the zenith and hid the brightening stars. The blue sky was still visible, except directly overhead, where this black mass of cloud was sweeping swiftly northward. Aloft in the air, as if from the depths of the cloud, came a confused and doubtful sound of voices. Once the listener fancied that he could distinguish the accents of towns-people of his own, men and women, both pious and ungodly, many of whom he had met at the communion table, and had seen others rioting at the tavern. The next moment, so indistinct were the sounds, he doubted whether he had heard aught but the murmur of the old forest, whispering without a wind. Then came a stronger swell of those familiar tones, heard daily in the sunshine at Salem village, but never until now from a cloud of night. There was one voice, of a young woman, uttering lamentations, yet with an uncertain sorrow, and entreating for some favor, which, perhaps, it would grieve her to obtain; and all the unseen multitude, both saints and sinners, seemed to encourage her onward.

"Faith!" shouted Goodman Brown, in a voice of agony and desperation; and the echoes of the forest mocked him, crying, "Faith! Faith!" as if bewildered wretches were seeking her all through the wilderness.

The cry of grief, rage, and terror was yet piercing the night when the unhappy husband held his breath for a response. There was a scream, drowned immediately in a louder murmur of voices, fading into far-off laughter, as the dark cloud swept away, leaving the clear and silent sky above Goodman Brown. But something fluttered lightly down through the air and caught on the branch of a tree. The young man seized it, and beheld a pink ribbon.

"My Faith is gone!" cried he, after one stupefied moment. "There is no good on earth; and sin is but a name. Come, devil; for to thee is this world given."

And, maddened with despair, so that he laughed loud and long, did Goodman Brown grasp his staff and set forth again, at such a rate that he seemed to fly along the forest path rather than to walk or run. The road grew wilder and drearier and more faintly traced, and vanished at length, leaving him in the heart of the dark wilderness, still rushing onward with the instinct that guides mortal man to evil. The whole forest was peopled with frightful sounds—the creaking of the trees, the howling of wild beasts, and the yell of Indians; while sometimes the wind tolled like a distant church bell, and sometimes gave a broad roar around the traveller, as if all Nature were laughing him to scorn. But he was himself the chief horror of the scene, and shrank not from its other horrors.

"Ha! ha! ha!" roared Goodman Brown when the wind laughed at him. "Let us hear which will laugh loudest. Think not to frighten me with your deviltry. Come witch, come wizard, come Indian powwow, come devil himself, and here comes Goodman Brown. You may as well fear him as he fear you."

In truth, all through the haunted forest there could be nothing more frightful than the figure of Goodman Brown. On he flew among the black pines, brandishing his staff with frenzied gestures, now giving vent to an inspiration of horrid blasphemy, and now shouting forth such laughter as set all the echoes of the forest laughing like demons around him. The fiend in his own shape is less hideous than when he rages in the breast of man. Thus sped the demoniac on his course, until, quivering among the trees, he saw a red light before him, as when the felled trunks and branches of a clearing have been set on fire, and throw up their lurid blaze against the sky, at the hour of midnight. He paused, in a lull of the tempest that had driven him onward, and heard the swell of what seemed a hymn, rolling solemnly from a distance with the weight of many voices. He knew the tune; it was a familiar one in the choir of the village meeting-house. The verse died heavily away, and was lengthened by a chorus, not of human voices, but of all the sounds of the benighted wilderness pealing in awful harmony together. Goodman Brown cried out, and his cry was lost to his own ear by its unison with the cry of the desert.

In the interval of silence he stole forward until the light glared full upon his eyes. At one extremity of an open space, hemmed in by the dark wall of the forest, rose a rock, bearing some rude natural resemblance either to an altar or a pulpit, and surrounded by four blazing pines, their tops aflame, their stems untouched, like candles at an evening meeting. The mass of foliage that had overgrown the summit of the rock was all on fire, blazing high into the night and fitfully illuminating the whole field. Each pendent twig and leafy festoon was in a blaze. As the red light arose and fell, a numerous congregation alternately shone forth, then disappeared in shadow, and again grew, as it were, out of the darkness, peopling the heart of the solitary woods at once.

"A grave and dark-clad company," quoth Goodman Brown.

In truth they were such. Among them, quivering to and fro between gloom and splendor, appeared faces that would be seen next day at the council board of the province, and others which, Sabbath after Sabbath, looked devoutly heavenward, and benignantly over the crowded pews, from the holiest pulpits in the land. Some affirm that the lady of the governor was there. At least there were high dames well known to her, and wives of honored husbands, and widows, a great multitude, and ancient maidens, all of excellent repute, and fair young girls, who trembled lest their mothers should espy them. Either the sudden gleam of light flashing over the obscure field bedazzled Goodman Brown, or he recognized a score of the church members of Salem village famous for their especial sanctity. Good old Deacon Gookin had arrived, and waited at the skirts of that venerable saint, his revered pastor. But, irreverently consorting with these grave, reputable, and pious people, there were men of dissolute lives and women of spotted fame, wretches given over to all mean and filthy vice, and suspected even of horrid crimes. It was strange to see that the good shrank not from the wicked, nor were the sinners abashed by the saints. Scattered also among their pale-faced enemies were the Indian priests, or powwows, who had often scared their native forest with more hideous incantations than any known to English witchcraft.

"But where is Faith?" thought Goodman Brown; and, as hope came into his heart, he trembled.

Another verse of the hymn arose, a slow and mournful strain, such as the pious love, but joined to words which expressed all that our nature can conceive of sin, and darkly hinted at far more. Unfathomable to mere mortals is the lore of fiends. Verse after verse was sung; and still the chorus of the desert swelled between like the deepest tone of a mighty organ; and with the final peal of that dreadful anthem there came a sound, as if the roaring wind, the rushing streams, the howling beasts, and every other voice of the unconcerted wilderness were mingling and according with the voice of guilty man in homage to the prince of all. The four blazing pines threw up a loftier flame, and obscurely discovered shapes and visages of horror on the smoke wreaths above the impious assembly. At the same moment the fire on the rock shot redly forth and formed a glowing arch above its base, where now appeared a figure. With reverence be it spoken, the figure bore no slight similitude, both in garb and manner, to some grave divine of the New England churches.

"Bring forth the converts!" cried a voice that echoed through the field and rolled into the forest.

At the word, Goodman Brown stepped forth from the shadow of the trees and approached the congregation, with whom he felt a loathful brotherhood by the sympathy of all that was wicked in his heart. He could have well-nigh sworn that the shape of his own dead father beckoned him to advance, looking downward from a smoke wreath, while a woman, with dim features of despair, threw out her hand to warn him back. Was it his mother? But he had no power to retreat one step, nor to resist, even in thought, when the minister and good old Deacon Gookin seized his arms and led him to the blazing rock. Thither came also the slender form of a veiled female, led between Goody Cloyse, that pious teacher of the catechism, and Martha Carrier, who had received the devil's promise to be queen of hell. A rampant hag was she. And there stood the proselytes beneath the canopy of fire.

"Welcome, my children," said the dark figure, "to the communion of your race. Ye have found thus young your nature and your destiny. My children, look behind you!"

They turned; and flashing forth, as it were, in a sheet of flame, the fiend worshippers were seen; the smile of welcome gleamed darkly on every visage.

"There," resumed the sable form, "are all whom ye have reverenced from youth. Ye deemed them holier than yourselves, and shrank from your own sin, contrasting it with their lives of righteousness and prayerful asperations heavenward. Yet here are they all in my worshipping assembly. This night it shall be granted you to know their secret deeds: how hoary-bearded elders of the church have whispered wanton words to the young maids of their households; how many a woman, eager for widows' weeds, has given her husband a drink at bedtime and let him sleep his last sleep in her bosom; how beardless youths have made haste to inherit their fathers' wealth; and how fair damsels —blush not, sweet ones—have dug little graves in the garden, and bidden me, the sole guest, to an infant's funeral. By the sympathy of your human hearts for sin ye shall scent out all the places—whether in church, bed-chamber, street, field, or forest—where crime has been committed, and shall exult to behold the whole earth one stain of guilt, one mighty blood spot. Far more than this. It shall be yours to penetrate, in every bosom, the deep mystery of sin, the fountain of all wicked arts, and which inexhaustibly supplies more evil impulses than human power—than my power at its utmost—can make manifest in deeds. And now, my children, look upon each other."

They did so; and, by the blaze of the hell-kindled torches, the wretched man beheld his Faith, and the wife her husband, trembling before that unhallowed altar.

"Lo, there ye stand, my children," said the figure, in a deep and solemn tone, almost sad with its despairing awfulness, as if his once angelic nature could yet mourn for our miserable race. "Depending upon one another's hearts, ye had still hoped that virtue were not all a dream. Now are ye undeceived. Evil is the nature of mankind. Evil must be your only happiness. Welcome again, my children, to the communion of your race."

"Welcome," repeated the field worshippers, in one cry of despair and triumph.

And there they stood, the only pair, as it seemed, who were yet hesitating on the verge of wickedness in this dark world. A basin was hollowed, naturally, in the rock. Did it contain water, reddened by the lurid light? or was it blood? or, perchance, a liquid flame? Herein did the shape of evil dip his hand and prepare to lay the mark of baptism upon their foreheads, that they might be partakers of the mystery of sin, more conscious of the secret guilt of others, both in deed and thought, than they could now be of their own. The husband cast one look at his pale wife, and Faith at him. What polluted wretches would the next glance show them to each other, shuddering alike at what they disclosed and what they saw!

"Faith! Faith!" cried the husband, "look up to heaven, and resist the wicked one."

Whether Faith obeyed he knew not. Hardly had he spoken when he found himself amid calm night and solitude, listening to a roar of the wind which died heavily away through the forest. He staggered against the rock, and felt it chill and damp; while a hanging twig, that had been all on fire, besprinkled his cheek with the coldest dew.

The next morning young Goodman Brown came slowly into the street of Salem village, staring around him like a bewildered man. The good old minister was taking a walk along the graveyard to get an appetite for breakfast and meditate his sermon, and bestowed a blessing, as he passed, on Goodman Brown. He shrank from the venerable saint as if to avoid an anathema. Old Deacon Gookin was at domestic worship, and the holy words of his prayer were heard through the open window. "What God doth the wizard pray to?" quoth Goodman Brown. Goody Cloyse, that excellent old Christian, stood in the early sunshine at her own lattice, catechizing a little girl who had brought her a pint of morning's milk. Goodman Brown snatched away the child as from the grasp of the fiend himself. Turning the corner by the meeting-house, he spied the head of Faith, with the pink ribbons, gazing anxiously forth, and bursting into such joy at sight of him that she skipped along the street and almost kissed her husband before the whole village. But Goodman Brown looked sternly and sadly into her face, and passed on without a greeting.

Had Goodman Brown fallen asleep in the forest and only dreamed a wild dream of a witch-meeting?

Be it so if you will; but, alas! it was a dream of evil omen for young Goodman Brown. A stern, a sad, a darkly meditative, a distrustful, if not a desperate man did he become from the night of that fearful dream. On the Sabbath day, when the congregation were singing a holy psalm, he could not listen because an anthem of sin rushed loudly upon his ear and drowned all the blessed strain. When the minister spoke from the pulpit with power and fervid eloquence, and, with his hand on the open Bible, of the sacred truths of our religion, and of saint-like lives and triumphant deaths, and of future bliss or misery unutterable, then did Goodman Brown turn pale, dreading lest the roof should thunder down upon the gray blasphemer and his hearers. Often, awaking suddenly at midnight, he shrank from the bosom of Faith; and at morning or eventide, when the family knelt down at prayer, he scowled and muttered to himself, and gazed sternly at his wife, and turned away. And when he had lived long, and was borne to his grave a hoary corpse, followed by Faith, an aged woman, and children and grandchildren, a goodly procession, besides neighbors not a few, they carved no hopeful verse upon his tombstone, for his dying hour was gloom.

# The Fall of the House of Usher

EDGAR ALLAN POE

*Son coeur est un luth suspendu;*
*Sitôt qu'on le touche il résonne.*[1]
*De Béranger*

DURING the whole of a dull, dark, and soundless day in the autumn of the year, when the clouds hung oppressively low in the heavens, I had been passing alone, on horseback, through a singularly dreary tract of country; and at length found myself, as the shades of the evening drew on, within view of the melancholy House of Usher. I know not how it was—but, with the first glimpse of the building, a sense of insufferable gloom pervaded my spirit. I say insufferable; for the feeling was unrelieved by any of that half-pleasurable, because poetic, sentiment, with which the mind usually receives even the sternest natural images of the desolate or terrible. I looked upon the scene before me—upon the mere house, and the simple landscape features of the domain—upon the bleak walls—upon the vacant eye-like windows—upon a few rank sedges—and upon a few white trunks of decayed trees—with an utter depression of soul which I can compare to no earthly sensation more properly than to the after-dream of the reveller upon opium—the bitter lapse into everyday life—the hideous dropping off of the veil. There was an iciness, a sinking, a sickening of the heart—an unredeemed dreariness of thought which no goading

---

[1] His heart is a suspended lute;
As soon as one touches it, it responds.

of the imagination could torture into aught of the sublime. What was it—I paused to think—what was it that so unnerved me in the contemplation of the House of Usher? It was a mystery all insoluble; nor could I grapple with the shadowy fancies that crowded upon me as I pondered. I was forced to fall back upon the unsatisfactory conclusion, that while, beyond doubt, there *are* combinations of very simple natural objects which have the power of thus affecting us, still the analysis of this power lies among considerations beyond our depth. It was possible, I reflected, that a mere different arrangement of the particulars of the scene, of the details of the picture, would be sufficient to modify, or perhaps to annihilate its capacity for sorrowful impression; and, acting upon this idea, I reined my horse to the precipitous brink of a black and lurid tarn that lay in unruffled lustre by the dwelling, and gazed down—but with a shudder even more thrilling than before—upon the remodelled and inverted images of the gray sedge, and the ghastly tree-stems, and the vacant and eye-like windows.

Nevertheless, in this mansion of gloom I now proposed to myself a sojourn of some weeks. Its proprietor, Roderick Usher, had been one of my boon companions in boyhood; but many years had elapsed since our last meeting. A letter, however, had lately reached me in a distant part of the country—a letter from him—which, in its wildly importunate nature, had admitted of no other than a personal reply. The MS. gave evidence of nervous agitation. The writer spoke of acute bodily illness—of a mental disorder which oppressed him—and of an earnest desire to see me, as his best, and indeed his only personal friend, with a view of attempting, by the cheerfulness of my society, some alleviation of his malady. It was the manner in which all this, and much more, was said—it was the apparent *heart* that went with his request—which allowed me no room for hesitation; and I accordingly obeyed forthwith what I still considered a very singular summons.

Although, as boys, we had been even intimate associates, yet I really knew little of my friend. His reserve had been always excessive and habitual. I was aware, however, that his very ancient family had been noted, time out of mind, for a peculiar sensibility of temperament, displaying itself, through long ages, in many works of exalted art, and manifested, of late, in repeated deeds of munificent yet unobtrusive charity, as well as in a passionate devotion to the intricacies, perhaps even more than to the orthodox and easily recognizable beauties, of musical science. I had learned, too, the very remarkable fact, that the stem of the Usher race, all time-honored as it was, had put forth, at no period, any enduring branch; in other words, that the entire family lay in the direct line of descent, and had always, with very trifling and very temporary variation, so lain. It was this deficiency, I considered, while running over in thought the perfect keeping of the character of the premises with the accredited character of the people, and while speculating upon the possible influence which the one, in the long lapse of centuries, might have exercised upon the other—it was this deficiency, perhaps, of collateral issue, and the consequent undeviating transmission, from sire to son, of the patrimony with the name, which had, at length, so identified the two as to merge the original title of the estate in the quaint and equivocal appellation of the "House of Usher"—an appellation which seemed to include, in the minds of the peasantry who used it, both the family and the family mansion.

I have said that the sole effect of my somewhat childish experiment —that of looking down within the tarn—had been to deepen the first singular impression. There can be no doubt that the consciousness of the rapid increase of my superstition—for why should I not so term it?—served mainly to accelerate the increase itself. Such, I have long known, is the paradoxical law of all sentiments having terror as a basis. And it might have been for this reason only, that, when I again uplifted my eyes to the house itself, from its image in the pool, there grew in my mind a strange fancy—a fancy so ridiculous, indeed, that I but mention it to show the vivid force of the sensations which oppressed me. I had so worked upon my imagination as really to believe that about the whole mansion and domain there hung an atmosphere peculiar to themselves and their immediate vicinity—an atmosphere which had no affinity with the air of heaven, but which had reeked up from the decayed trees, and the gray wall, and the silent tarn—a pestilent and mystic vapor, dull sluggish, faintly discernible, and leaden-hued.

Shaking off from my spirit what *must* have been a dream, I scanned more narrowly the real aspect of the building. Its principal feature seemed to be that of an excessive antiquity. The discoloration of ages had been great. Minute fungi overspread the whole exterior, hanging in a fine tangled web-work from the eaves. Yet all this was apart from any extraordinary dilapidation. No portion of the masonry had fallen; and there appeared to be a wild inconsistency between its still perfect adaptation of parts, and the crumbling condition of the individual stones. In this there was much that reminded me of the specious totality of old wood-work which has rotted for long years in some neglected fault, with no disturbance from the breath of the external air. Beyond this indication of extensive decay, however, the fabric gave little token of instability. Perhaps the eye of a scrutinizing observer might have discovered a barely perceptible fissure, which, extending from the roof of the building in front, made its way down the wall in a zigzag direction, until it became lost in the sullen waters of the tarn.

Noticing these things, I rode over a short causeway to the house. A servant in waiting took my horse, and I entered the Gothic archway of the hall. A valet, of stealthy step, thence conducted me, in silence, through many dark and intricate passages in my progress to the *studio* of his master. Much that I encountered on the way contributed, I know not how, to heighten the vague sentiments of which I have already spoken. While the objects around me—while the carvings of the ceilings, the sombre tapestries of the walls, the ebon blackness of the floors, and the phantasmagoric armorial trophies which rattled as I strode, were but matters to which, or to such as which, I had been accustomed from my infancy—while I hesitated not to acknowledge how familiar was all this—I still wondered to find how unfamiliar were the fancies which ordinary images were stirring up. On one of the staircases, I met the physician of the family. His countenance, I thought, wore a mingled expression of low cunning and perplexity. He accosted me with trepidation and passed on. The valet now threw open a door and ushered me into the presence of his master.

The room in which I found myself was very large and lofty. The windows were long, narrow, and pointed, and at so vast a distance from the black oaken floor as to be altogether inaccessible from within. Feeble gleams of encrimsoned light made their way through the trellissed panes, and served to render sufficiently distinct the more prominent objects of the chamber, or the recesses of the vaulted and fretted ceiling. Dark draperies hung upon the walls. The general furniture was profuse, comfortless, antique, and tattered. Many books and musical instruments lay scattered about, but failed to give any vitality to the scene. I felt that I breathed an atmosphere of sorrow. An air of stern, deep, and irredeemable gloom hung over and pervaded all.

Upon my entrance, Usher arose from a sofa on which he had been lying at full length, and greeted me with a vivacious warmth which had much in it, I at first thought, of an overdone cordiality—of the constrained effort of the *ennuyé* man of the world. A glance, however, at his countenance, convinced me of his perfect sincerity. We sat down; and for some moments, while he spoke not, I gazed upon him with a feeling half of pity, half of awe. Surely, man had never before so terribly altered, in so brief a period, as had Roderick Usher! It was with difficulty that I could bring myself to admit the identity of the wan being before me with the companion of my early boyhood. Yet the character of his face had been at all times remarkable. A cadaverousness of complexion; an eye large, liquid, and luminous beyond comparison; lips somewhat thin and very pallid, but of a surpassingly beautiful curve; a nose of a delicate Hebrew model, but with a breadth of nostril unusual in similar formations; a finely moulded chin, speaking, in its want of prominence, of a want of moral energy; hair of a more than web-like softness and tenuity; these features, with an inordinate expansion above the regions of the temple, made up altogether a countenance not easily to be forgotten. And now in the mere exaggeration of the prevailing character of these features, and of the expression they were wont to convey, lay so much of change that I doubted to whom I spoke. The now ghastly pallor of the skin, and the now miraculous lustre of the eye, above all things startled and even awed me. The silken hair, too, had been suffered to grow all unheeded, and as, in its wild gossamer texture, it floated rather than fell about the face, I could not, even with effort, connect its Arabesque expression with any idea of simple humanity.

In the manner of my friend I was at once struck with an incoherence—an inconsistency; and I soon found this to arise from a series of feeble and futile struggles to overcome an habitual trepidancy—an excessive nervous agitation. For something of this nature I had indeed been prepared, no less by his letter, than by reminiscences of certain boyish traits, and by conclusions deduced from his peculiar physical conformation and temperament. His action was alternately vivacious and sullen. His voice varied rapidly from a tremulous indecision (when the animal spirits seemed utterly in abeyance) to that species of energetic concision—that abrupt, weighty, unhurried, and hollow-sounding enunciation—that leaden, self-balanced, and perfectly modulated guttural utterance, which may be observed in the lost drunkard, or the irreclaimable eater of opium, during the periods of his most intense excitement.

It was thus that he spoke of the object of my visit, of his earnest desire to see me, and of the solace he expected me to afford him. He entered, at some length, into what he conceived to be the nature of his malady. It was, he said, a constitutional and a family evil, and one for which he despaired to find a remedy—a mere nervous affection, he immediately added, which would undoubtedly soon pass off. It displayed itself in a host of unnatural sensations. Some of these, as he detailed them, interested and bewildered me; although, perhaps, the terms and the general manner of the narration had their weight. He suffered much from a morbid acuteness of the senses; the most insipid food was alone endurable; he could wear only garments of certain texture; the odors of all flowers were oppressive; his eyes were tortured by even a faint light; and there were but peculiar sounds, and these from stringed instruments, which did not inspire him with horror.

To an anomalous species of terror I found him a bounden slave. "I shall perish," said he, "I *must* perish in this deplorable folly. Thus, thus, and not otherwise, shall I be lost. I dread the events of the future, not in themselves, but in their results. I shudder at the thought of any, even the most trivial, incident, which may operate upon this intolerable agitation of soul. I have, indeed, no abhorrence of danger, except in its absolute effect—in terror. In this unnerved—in this pitiable condition —I feel that the period will sooner or later arrive when I must abandon life and reason together, in some struggle with the grim phantasm, FEAR."

I learned, moreover, at intervals, and through broken and equivocal hints, another singular feature of his mental condition. He was enchained by certain superstitious impressions in regard to the dwelling which he tenanted, and whence, for many years, he had never ventured forth—in regard to an influence whose supposititious force was conveyed in terms too shadowy here to be re-stated—an influence which some peculiarities in the mere form and substance of his family mansion had, by dint of long sufferance, he said, obtained over his spirit— an effect which the *physique* of the gray wall and turrets, and of the dim tarn into which they all looked down, had, at length, brought about upon the *morale* of his existence.

He admitted, however, although with hesitation, that much of the peculiar gloom which thus afflicted him could be traced to a more natural and far more palpable origin—to the severe and long-continued illness—indeed to the evidently approaching dissolution—of a tenderly beloved sister—his sole companion for long years—his last and only relative on earth. "Her decease," he said, with a bitterness which I can never forget, "would leave him (him the hopeless and the frail) the last of the ancient race of the Ushers." While he spoke, the lady Madeline (for so was she called) passed slowly through a remote portion of the apartment, and, without having noticed my presence, disappeared. I regarded her with an utter astonishment not unmingled with dread—and yet I found it impossible to account for such feelings. A sensation of stupor oppressed me, as my eyes followed her retreating steps. When a door, at length, closed upon her, my glance sought instinctively and eagerly the countenance of the brother —but he had buried his face in his hands, and I could only perceive that a far more than ordinary wanness had overspread the emaciated fingers through which trickled many passionate tears.

The disease of the lady Madeline had long baffled the skill of her physicians. A settled apathy, a gradual wasting away of the person, and frequent although transient affections of a partially cataleptical character, were the unusual diagnosis. Hitherto she had steadily borne up against the pressure of her malady, and had not betaken herself finally to bed; but, on the closing in of the evening of my arrival at the house, she succumbed (as her brother told me at night with inexpressible agitation) to the prostrating power of the destroyer; and I learned that the glimpse I had obtained of her person would thus probably be the last I should obtain—that the lady, at least while living, would be seen by me no more.

For several days ensuing, her name was unmentioned by either Usher or myself: and during this period I was busied in earnest endeavors to alleviate the melancholy of my friend. We painted and read together; or I listened, as if in a dream, to the wild improvisations of his speaking guitar. And thus, as a closer and still closer intimacy admitted me more unreservedly into the recesses of his spirit, the more bitterly did I perceive the futility of all attempt at cheering a mind from which darkness, as if an inherent positive quality, poured forth upon all objects of the moral and physical universe, in one unceasing radiation of gloom.

I shall ever bear about me a memory of the many solemn hours I thus spent alone with the master of the House of Usher. Yet I should fail in any attempt to convey an idea of the exact character of the studies, or of the occupations, in which he involved me, or led me the way. An excited and highly distempered ideality threw a sulphureous lustre over all. His long improvised dirges will ring forever in my ears. Among other things, I hold painfully in mind a certain singular perversion and amplification of the wild air of the last waltz of Von Weber. From the paintings over which his elaborate fancy brooded, and which grew, touch by touch, into vaguenesses at which I shuddered the more thrillingly, because I shuddered knowing not why;— from these paintings (vivid as their images now are before me) I would in vain endeavor to educe more than a small portion which should lie within the compass of merely written words. By the utter simplicity, by the nakedness of his designs, he arrested and overawed attention. If ever mortal painted an idea, that mortal was Roderick Usher. For me at least—in the circumstances then surrounding me— there arose out of the pure abstractions which the hypochondriac contrived to throw upon his canvas, an intensity of intolerable awe, no shadow of which felt I ever yet in the contemplation of the certainly glowing yet too concrete reveries of Fuseli.

One of the phantasmagoric conceptions of my friend, partaking not so rigidly of the spirit of abstraction, may be shadowed forth, although feebly, in words. A small picture presented the interior of an immensely long and rectangular vault or tunnel, with low walls, smooth, white, and without interruption or device. Certain accessory points of the design served well to convey the idea that this excavation lay at an exceeding depth below the surface of the earth. No outlet was observed in any portion of its vast extent, and no torch or other artificial source of light was discernible; yet a flood of intense rays rolled throughout, and bathed the whole in a ghastly and inappropriate splendor.

I have just spoken of that morbid condition of the auditory nerve which rendered all music intolerable to the sufferer, with the exception of certain effects of stringed instruments. It was, perhaps, the narrow limits to which he thus confined himself upon the guitar, which gave birth, in great measure, to the fantastic character of his performances. But the fervid *facility* of his *impromptus* could not be so accounted for. They must have been, and were, in the notes, as well as in the words of his wild fantasias (for he not unfrequently accompanied himself with rhymed verbal improvisations), the result of that intense mental collectedness and concentration to which I have previously alluded as observable only in particular moments of the highest artificial excitement. The words of one of these rhapsodies I have easily remembered. I was, perhaps, the more forcibly impressed with it, as he gave it, because, in the under or mystic current of its meaning, I fancied that I perceived, and for the first time, a full consciousness on the part of Usher, of the tottering of his lofty reason upon her throne. The verses, which were entitled "The Haunted Palace," ran very nearly, if not accurately, thus:

I

In the greenest of our valleys,
    By good angels tenanted,
Once a fair and stately palace—
    Radiant palace—reared its head.
In the monarch Thought's dominion—
    It stood there!
Never seraph spread a pinion
    Over fabric half so fair.

II

Banners yellow, glorious, golden,
    On its roof did float and flow;
(This—all this—was in the olden
    Time long ago)
And every gentle air that dallied,
    In that sweet day,
Along the ramparts plumed and pallid,
    A winged odor went away.

III

Wanderers in that happy valley
    Through two luminous windows saw
Spirits moving musically
    To a lute's well-tunèd law,
Round about a throne, where sitting
    (Porphyrogene!)
In state his glory well befitting,
    The ruler of the realm was seen.

### IV

And all with pearl and ruby glowing
  Was the fair palace door,
Through which came flowing, flowing, flowing,
  And sparkling evermore,
A troop of Echoes whose sweet duty
  Was but to sing,
In voices of surpassing beauty,
  The wit and wisdom of their king.

### V

But evil things, in robes of sorrow,
  Assailed the monarch's high estate;
(Ah, let us mourn, for never morrow
  Shall dawn upon him, desolate!)
And, round about his home, the glory
  That blushed and bloomed
Is but a dim-remembered story
  Of the old time entombed.

### VI

And travellers now within that valley,
  Through the red-litten windows, see
Vast forms that move fantastically
  To a discordant melody;
While, like a rapid ghastly river,
  Through the pale door,
A hideous throng rush out forever,
  And laugh—but smile no more.

I well remember that suggestions arising from this ballad, led us into a train of thought wherein there became manifest an opinion of Usher's which I mention not so much on account of its novelty (for other men have thought thus), as on account of the pertinacity with which he maintained it. This opinion, in its general form, was that of the sentience of all vegetable things. But, in his disordered fancy, the idea had assumed a more daring character, and trespassed, under certain conditions, upon the kingdom of inorganization. I lack words to express the full extent, or the earnest *abandon* of his persuasion. The belief, however, was connected (as I have previously hinted) with the gray stones of the home of his forefathers. The conditions of the sentience had been here, he imagined, fulfilled in the method of collocation of these stones—in the order of their arrangement, as well as in that of the many *fungi* which overspread them, and of the decayed trees which stood around—above all, in the long undisturbed endurance of this arrangement, and in its reduplication in the still waters of the tarn. Its evidence—the evidence of the sentience—was to be seen, he said (and I here started as he spoke), in the gradual yet certain condensation of an atmosphere of their own about the waters and the walls. The result was discoverable, he added, in that silent yet importunate and terrible influence which for centuries had moulded the destinies of his family, and which made *him* what I now saw him— what he was. Such opinions need no comment, and I will make none.

Our books—the books which, for years, had formed no small portion of the mental existence of the invalid—were, as might be supposed, in strict keeping with this character of phantasm. We pored together over such works as the Ververt et Chartreuse of Gresset; the Belphegor of Machiavelli; the Heaven and Hell of Swedenborg; the Subterranean Voyage of Nicholas Klimm by Holberg; the Chiromancy of Robert Flud, of Jean D'Indaginé, and of De la Chambre; the Journey into the Blue Distance of Tieck; and the City of the Sun of Campanella. One favorite volume was a small octavo edition of the *Directorium Inquisitorium,* by the Dominican Eymeric de Gironne; and there were passages in Pomponius Mela, about the old African Satyrs and Œgipans, over which Usher would sit dreaming for hours. His chief delight, however, was found in the perusal of an exceedingly rare and curious book in quarto Gothic—the manual of a forgotten church—the *Vigilae Mortuorum secundum Chorum Ecclesiae Maguntinae.*

I could not help thinking of the wild ritual of this work, and of its probable influence upon the hypochondriac, when, one evening, having informed me abruptly that the lady Madeline was no more, he stated his intention of preserving her corpse for a fortnight (previously to its final interment), in one of the numerous vaults within the main walls of the building. The worldly reason, however, assigned for this singular proceeding, was one which I did not feel at liberty to dispute. The brother had been led to his resolution (so he told me) by consideration of the unusual character of the malady of the deceased, of certain obtrusive and eager inquiries on the part of her medical men, and of the remote and exposed situation of the burial-ground of the family. I will not deny that when I called to mind the sinister countenance of the person whom I met upon the staircase, on the day of my arrival at the house, I had no desire to oppose what I regarded as at best but a harmless, and by no means an unnatural, precaution.

At the request of Usher, I personally aided him in the arrangements for the temporary entombment. The body having been encoffined, we two alone bore it to its rest. The vault in which we placed it (and which had been so long unopened that our torches, half smothered in its oppressive atmosphere, gave us little opportunity for investigation) was small, damp, and entirely without means of admission for light; lying, at great depth, immediately beneath that portion of the building in which was my own sleeping apartment. It had been used, appar-ently, in remote feudal times, for the worst purposes of a donjon-keep, and, in later days, as a place of deposit for powder, or some other highly combustible substance, as a portion of its floor, and the whole interior of a long archway through which we reached it, were care-fully sheathed with copper. The door, of massive iron, had been, also, similarly protected. Its immense weight caused an unusually sharp grating sound, as it moved upon its hinges.

Having deposited our mournful burden upon tressels within this region of horror, we partially turned aside the yet unscrewed lid of the coffin, and looked upon the face of the tenant. A striking simili-tude between the brother and sister now first arrested my attention; and Usher, divining, perhaps, my thoughts, murmured out some few words from which I learned that the deceased and himself had been twins, and that sympathies of a scarcely intelligible nature had always existed between them. Our glances, however, rested not long upon the dead—for we could not regard her unawed. The disease which had thus entombed the lady in the maturity of youth, had left, as usual in all maladies of a strictly cataleptical character, the mockery of a faint blush upon the bosom and the face, and that suspiciously lingering smile upon the lip which is so terrible in death. We replaced and screwed down the lid, and, having secured the door of iron, made our way, with toil, into the scarcely less gloomy apartments of the upper portion of the house.

And now, some days of bitter grief having elapsed, an observable change came over the features of the mental disorder of my friend.

His ordinary manner had vanished. His ordinary occupations were neglected or forgotten. He roamed from chamber to chamber with hurried, unequal, and objectless step. The pallor of his countenance had assumed, if possible, a more ghastly hue—but the luminousness of his eye had utterly gone out. The once occasional huskiness of his tone was heard no more; and a tremulous quaver, as if of extreme terror, habitually characterized his utterance. There were times, indeed, when I thought his unceasingly agitated mind was laboring with some oppressive secret, to divulge which he struggled for the necessary courage. At times, again, I was obliged to resolve all into the mere inexplicable vagaries of madness, for I beheld him gazing upon vacancy for long hours, in an attitude of the profoundest attention, as if listening to some imaginary sound. It was no wonder that his condition terrified—that it infected me. I felt creeping upon me, by slow yet certain degrees, the wild influences of his own fantastic yet impressive superstitions.

It was, especially, upon retiring to bed late in the night of the seventh or eighth day after the placing of the lady Madeline within the donjon, that I experienced the full power of such feelings. Sleep came not near my couch—while the hours waned and waned away. I struggled to reason off the nervousness which had dominion over me. I endeavored to believe that much, if not all of what I felt, was due to the bewildering influence of the gloomy furniture of the room—of the dark and tattered draperies, which, tortured into motion by the breath of a rising tempest, swayed fitfully to and fro upon the walls, and rustled uneasily about the decorations of the bed. But my efforts were fruitless. An irrepressible tremor gradually pervaded my frame; and, at length, there sat upon my very heart an incubus of utterly causeless alarm. Shaking this off with a gasp and a struggle, I uplifted myself upon the pillows, and, peering earnestly within the intense darkness of the chamber, harkened—I know not why, except that an instinctive spirit prompted me—to certain low and indefinite sounds which came, through the pauses of the storm, at long intervals, I knew not whence. Overpowered by an intense sentiment of horror, unaccountable yet unendurable, I threw on my clothes with haste (for I felt that I should sleep no more during the night), and endeavored to arouse myself from the pitiable condition into which I had fallen, by pacing rapidly to and fro through the apartment.

I had taken but few turns in this manner, when a light step on an adjoining staircase arrested my attention. I presently recognized it as that of Usher. In an instant afterward he rapped, with a gentle touch, at my door, and entered, bearing a lamp. His countenance was, as usual, cadaverously wan—but, moreover, there was a species of mad hilarity in his eyes—an evidently restrained *hysteria* in his whole demeanor. His air appalled me—but anything was preferable to the solitude which I had so long endured, and I even welcomed his presence as a relief.

"And you have not seen it?" he said abruptly, after having stared about him for some moments in silence—"you have not then seen it?—but, stay! you shall." Thus speaking, and having carefully shaded his lamp, he hurried to one of the casements, and threw it freely open to the storm.

The impetuous fury of the entering gust nearly lifted us from our feet. It was, indeed, a tempestuous yet sternly beautiful night, and one wildly singular in its terror and its beauty. A whirlwind had apparently collected its force in our vicinity; for there were frequent and violent alterations in the direction of the wind; and the exceeding density of the clouds (which hung so low as to press upon the turrets of the house) did not prevent our perceiving the life-like velocity with which they flew careering from all points against each other, without passing away into the distance. I say that even their exceeding density did not prevent our perceiving this—yet we had no glimpse of the moon or stars—nor was there any flashing forth of the lightning. But the under surfaces of the huge masses of agitated vapor, as well as all terrestrial objects immediately around us, were glowing in the unnatural light of a faintly luminous and distinctly visible gaseous exhalation which hung about and enshrouded the mansion.

"You must not—you shall not behold this!" said I, shudderingly, to Usher, as I led him, with a gentle violence, from the window to a seat. "These appearances, which bewilder you, are merely electrical phenomena not uncommon—or it may be that they have their ghastly origin in the rank miasma of the tarn. Let us close this casement;—the air is chilling and dangerous to your frame. Here is one of your favorite romances. I will read, and you shall listen;—and so we will pass away this terrible night together."

The antique volume which I had taken up was the "Mad Trist" of Sir Launcelot Canning; but I had called it a favorite of Usher's more in sad jest than in earnest; for, in truth, there is little in its uncouth and unimaginative prolixity which could have had interest for the lofty and spiritual ideality of my friend. It was, however, the only book immediately at hand; and I indulged a vague hope that the excitement which now agitated the hypochondriac, might find relief (for the history of mental disorder is full of similar anomalies) even in the extremeness of the folly which I should read. Could I have judged, indeed, by the wild overstrained air of vivacity with which he harkened, or apparently harkened, to the words of the tale, I might well have congratulated myself upon the success of my design.

I had arrived at that well-known portion of the story where Ethelred, the hero of the Trist, having sought in vain for peaceable admission into the dwelling of the hermit, proceeds to make good an entrance by force. Here, it will be remembered the words of the narrative run thus:

"And Ethelred, who was by nature of a doughty heart, and who was now mighty withal, on account of the powerfulness of the wine which he had drunken, waited no longer to hold parley with the hermit, who, in sooth, was of an obstinate and maliceful turn, but, feeling the rain upon his shoulders, and fearing the rising of the tempest, uplifted his mace outright, and, with blows, made quickly room in the plankings of the door for his gauntleted hand; and now pulling therewith sturdily, he so cracked, and ripped, and tore all asunder, that the noise of the dry and hollow-sounding wood alarumed and reverberated throughout the forest."

At the termination of this sentence I started, and for a moment, paused; for it appeared to me (although I at once concluded that my excited fancy had deceived me)—it appeared to me that, from some very remote portion of the mansion, there came, indistinctly, to my ears, what might have been, in its exact similarity of character, the echo (but a stifled and dull one certainly) of the very cracking and ripping sound which Sir Launcelot had had so particularly described. It was, beyond doubt, the coincidence alone which had arrested my attention; for, amid the rattling of the sashes of the casements, and the ordinary commingled noises of the still increasing storm, the sound, in itself, had nothing, surely, which should have interested or disturbed me. I continued the story:

"But the good champion Ethelred, now entering within the door, was sore enraged and amazed to perceive no signal of the maliceful hermit; but, in the stead thereof, a dragon of a scaly and prodigious

demeanor, and of a fiery tongue, which sate in guard before a palace
of gold, with a floor of silver; and upon the wall there hung a shield
of shining brass with this legend enwritten—

> Who entereth herein, a conqueror hath bin;
> Who slayeth the dragon, the shield he shall win.

And Ethelred upliften his mace, and struck upon the head of the
dragon, which fell before him, and gave up his pesty breath, with a
shriek so horrid and harsh, and withal so piercing, that Ethelred had
fain to close his ears with his hands against the dreadful noise of it,
the like whereof was never before heard."

Here again I paused abruptly, and now with a feeling of wild
amazement—for there could be no doubt whatever that, in this instance, I did actually hear (although from what direction it proceeded
I found it impossible to say) a low and apparently distant, but harsh,
protracted, and most unusual screaming or grating sound—the exact
counterpart of what my fancy had already conjured up for the dragon's
unnatural shriek as described by the romancer.

Oppressed, as I certainly was, upon the occurrence of this second
and most extraordinary coincidence, by a thousand conflicting sensations, in which wonder and extreme terror were predominant, I still
retained sufficient presence of mind to avoid exciting, by any observation, the sensitive nervousness of my companion. I was by no means
certain that he had noticed the sounds in question; although, assuredly,
a strange alteration had, during the last few minutes, taken place in
his demeanor. From a position fronting my own, he had gradually
brought round his chair, so as to sit with his face to the door of the
chamber; and thus I could but partially perceive his features, although
I saw that his lips trembled as if he were murmuring inaudibly. His
head had dropped upon his breast—yet I knew that he was not asleep,
from the wide and rigid opening of the eye as I caught a glance of it
in profile. The motion of his body, too, was at variance with this idea
—for he rocked from side to side with a gentle yet constant and uniform sway. Having rapidly taken notice of all this, I resumed the
narrative of Sir Launcelot, which thus proceeded:

"And now, the champion, having escaped from the terrible fury
of the dragon, bethinking himself of the brazen shield, and of the
breaking up of the enchantment which was upon it, removed the
carcass from out of the way before him, and approached valorously

over the silver pavement of the castle to where the shield was upon the wall; which in sooth tarried not for his full coming, but fell down at his feet upon the silver floor, with a mighty great and terrible ringing sound."

No sooner had these syllables passed my lips, than—as if a shield of brass had indeed, at the moment, fallen heavily upon a floor of silver—I became aware of a distinct, hollow, metallic, and clangorous, yet apparently muffled reverberation. Completely unnerved, I leaped to me feet; but the measured rocking movement of Usher was undisturbed. I rushed to the chair in which he sat. His eyes were bent fixedly before him, and throughout his whole countenance there reigned a stony rigidity. But, as I placed my hand upon his shoulder, there came a strong shudder over his whole person; a sickly smile quivered about his lips; and I saw that he spoke in a low, hurried, and gibbering murmur, as if unconscious of my presence. Bending closely over him, I at length drank in the hideous import of his words.

"Not hear it?—yes, I hear it, and *have* heard it. Long—long—long—many minutes, many hours, many days, have I heard it—yet I dared not—oh, pity me, miserable wretch that I am!—I dared not—I *dared* not speak! *We have put her living in the tomb!* Said I not that my senses were acute? I *now* tell you that I heard her first feeble movements in the hollow coffin. I heard them—many, many days ago—yet I dared not—I *dared not speak!* And now—to-night—Ethelred—ha! ha!—the breaking of the hermit's door, and the death-cry of the dragon, and the clangor of the shield!—say, rather, the rending of her coffin, and the grating of the iron hinges of her prison, and her struggles within the coppered archway of the vault! Oh whither shall I fly? Will she not be here anon? Is she not hurrying to upbraid me for my haste? Have I not heard her footstep on the stair? Do I not distinquish that heavy and horrible beating of her heart? Madman!"—here he sprang furiously to his feet, and shrieked out his syllables, as if in the effort he were giving up his soul—"*Madman! I tell you that she now stands without the door;*"

As if in the superhuman energy of his utterance there had been found the potency of a spell—the huge antique panels to which the speaker pointed, threw slowly back, upon the instant, their ponderous and ebony jaws. It was the work of the rushing gust—but then without those doors there *did* stand the lofty and enshrouded figure of the lady Madeline of Usher. There was blood upon her white robes, and

the evidence of some bitter struggle upon every portion of her emaciated frame. For a moment she remained trembling and reeling to and
fro upon the threshold—then, with a low moaning cry, fell heavily
inward upon the person of her brother, and in her violent and now
final death-agonies, bore him to the floor a corpse, and a victim to the
terrors he had anticipated.

From that chamber, and from that mansion, I fled aghast. The
storm was still abroad in all its wrath as I found myself crossing the
old causeway. Suddenly there shot along the path a wild light, and
I turned to see whence a gleam so unusual could have issued; for the
vast house and its shadows were alone behind me. The radiance was
that of the full, setting, and blood-red moon, which now shone vividly
through that once barely-discernible fissure, of which I have before
spoken as extending from the roof of the building, in a zigzag direction, to the base. While I gazed, this fissure rapidly widened—there
came a fierce breath of the whirlwind—the entire orb of the satellite
burst at once upon my sight—my brain reeled as I saw the mighty
walls rushing asunder—there was a long tumultuous shouting sound
like the voice of a thousand waters—and the deep and dank tarn at
my feet closed sullenly and silently over the fragments of the *"House
of Usher."*

# A Hunger Artist

## FRANZ KAFKA

DURING these last decades the interest in professional fasting has markedly diminished. It used to pay very well to stage such great performances under one's own management, but today that is quite impossible. We live in a different world now. At one time the whole town took a lively interest in the hunger artist; from day to day of his fast the excitement mounted; everybody wanted to see him at least once a day; there were people who bought season tickets for the last few days and sat from morning till night in front of his small barred cage; even in the nighttime there were visiting hours, when the whole effect was heightened by torch flares; on fine days the cage was set out in the open air, and then it was the children's special treat to see the hunger artist; for their elders he was often just a joke that happened to be in fashion, but the children stood open-mouthed, holding each other's hands for greater security, marveling at him as he sat there pallid in black tights, with his ribs sticking out so prominently, not even on a seat but down among straw on the ground, sometimes giving a courteous nod, answering questions with a constrained smile, or perhaps stretching an arm through the bars so that one might feel how thin it was, and then again withdrawing deep into himself, paying no attention to anyone or anything, not even to the all-important striking of the clock that was the only piece of furniture in his cage, but merely staring into vacancy with half-shut eyes, now and then taking a sip from a tiny glass of water to moisten his lips.

Besides casual onlookers there were also relays of permanent watchers selected by the public, usually butchers, strangely enough, and it was their task to watch the hunger artist day and night, three of them at a time, in case he should have some secret recourse to nourishment.

This was nothing but a formality, instituted to reassure the masses, for the initiates knew well enough that during his fast the artist would never in any circumstances, not even under forcible compulsion, swallow the smallest morsel of food; the honor of his profession forbade it. Not every watcher, of course, was capable of understanding this, there were often groups of night watchers who were very lax in carrying out their duties and deliberately huddled together in a retired corner to play cards with great absorption, obviously intending to give the hunger artist the chance of a little refreshment, which they supposed he could draw from some private hoard. Nothing annoyed the artist more than such watchers; they made him miserable; they made his fast seem unendurable; sometimes he mastered his feebleness sufficiently to sing during their watch for as long as he could keep going, to show them how unjust their suspicions were. But that was of little use; they only wondered at his cleverness in being able to fill his mouth even while singing. Much more to his taste were the watchers who sat close up to the bars, who were not content with the dim night lighting of the hall but focused him in the full glare of the electric pocket torch given them by the impresario. The harsh light did not trouble him at all. In any case he could never sleep properly, and he could always drowse a little, whatever the light, at any hour, even when the hall was thronged with noisy onlookers. He was quite happy at the prospect of spending a sleepless night with such watchers; he was ready to exchange jokes with them, to tell them stories out of his nomadic life, anything at all to keep them awake and demonstrate to them again that he had no eatables in his cage and that he was fasting as not one of them could fast. But his happiest moment was when the morning came and an enormous breakfast was brought them, at his expense, on which they flung themselves with the keen appetite of healthy men after a weary night of wakefulness. Of course there were people who argued that this breakfast was an unfair attempt to bribe the watchers, but that was going rather too far, and when they were invited to take on a night's vigil without a breakfast, merely for the sake of the cause, they made themselves scarce, although they stuck stubbornly to their suspicions.

Such suspicions, anyhow, were a necessary accompaniment to the profession of fasting. No one could possibly watch the hunger artist continuously, day and night, and so no one could produce first-hand evidence that the fast had really been rigorous and continuous; only the artist himself could know that; he was therefore bound to be the sole completely satisfied spectator of his own fast. Yet for other reasons he was never satisfied; it was not perhaps mere fasting that had brought him to such skeleton thinness that many people had regretfully to keep away from his exhibitions, because the sight of him was too much for them, perhaps it was dissatisfaction with himself that had worn him down. For he alone knew, what no other initiate knew, how easy it was to fast. It was the easiest thing in the world. He made no secret of this, yet people did not believe him; at the best they set him down as modest, most of them, however, thought he was out for publicity or else was some kind of cheat who found it easy to fast because he had discovered a way of making it easy, and then had the impudence to admit the fact, more or less. He had to put up with all that, and in the course of time had got used to it, but his inner dissatisfaction always rankled, and never yet, after any term of fasting—this must be granted to his credit—had he left the cage of his own free will. The longest period of fasting was fixed by his impresario at forty days, beyond that term he was not allowed to go, not even in great cities, and there was good reason for it, too. Experience had proved that for about forty days the interest of the public could be stimulated by a steadily increasing pressure of advertisement, but after that the town began to lose interest, sympathetic support began notably to fall off; there were of course local variations as between one town and another or one country and another, but as a general rule forty days marked the limit. So on the fortieth day the flower-bedecked cage was opened, enthusiastic spectators filled the hall, a military band played, two doctors entered the cage to measure the results of the fast, which were announced through a megaphone, and finally two young ladies appeared, blissful at having been selected for the honor, to help the hunger artist down the few steps leading to a small table on which was spread a carefully chosen invalid repast. And at this very moment the artist always turned stubborn. True, he would entrust his bony arms to the outstretched helping hands of the ladies bending over him, but stand up he would not. Why stop fasting at this particular moment, after forty days of it? He had held out for a long time, an illimitably long time; why stop now, when he was in his best fasting form, or rather, not yet quite in his best fasting form? Why should he be cheated of the fame he would get for fasting longer, for being not only the record hunger artist of all time, which presumably he was already, but for beating his own record by a performance beyond human imagination, since he felt that there were no limits to his capacity for fasting? His public pretended to admire him so much, why should it have so little patience with him; if he could endure fasting longer, why shouldn't the public endure it? Besides, he was tired, he was comfortable sitting in the straw, and now he was supposed to lift himself to his full height and go down to a meal the very thought of which gave him a nausea that only the presence of the ladies kept him from betraying, and even that with an effort. And he looked up into the eyes of the ladies who were apparently so friendly and in reality so cruel, and shook his head, which felt too heavy on its strengthless neck. But then there happened yet again what always happened. The impresario came forward, without a word—for the band made speech impossible—lifted his arms in the air above the artist, as if inviting Heaven to look down upon its creature here in the straw, this suffering martyr, which indeed he was, although in quite another sense; grasped him round the emaciated waist, with exaggerated caution, so that the frail condition he was in might be appreciated; and committed him to the care of the blenching ladies, not without secretly giving him a shaking so that his legs and body tottered and swayed. The artist now submitted completely; his head lolled on his breast as if it had landed there by chance; his body was hollowed out; his legs in a spasm of self-preservation clung close to each other at the knees, yet scraped on the ground as if it were not really solid ground, as if they were only trying to find solid ground; and the whole weight of his body, a featherweight after all, relapsed onto one of the ladies, who, looking round for help and panting a little—this post of honor was not at all what she had expected it to be —first stretched her neck as far as she could to keep her face at least free from contact with the artist, then finding this impossible, and her more fortunate companion not coming to her aid but merely holding extended on her own trembling hand the little bunch of knucklebones that was the artist's, to the great delight of the spectators burst into tears and had to be replaced by an attendant who had long been stationed in readiness. Then came the food, a little of which the impresario managed to get between the artist's lips, while he sat in a kind of half-fainting trance, to the accompaniment of cheerful patter designed to distract the public's attention from the artist's condition; after that, a toast was drunk to the public, supposedly prompted by a whisper from the artist in the impresario's ear; the band confirmed it with a mighty flourish, the spectators melted away, and no one had any cause to be dissatisfied with the proceedings, no one except the hunger artist himself, he only, as always.

So he lived for many years, with small regular intervals of recuperation, in visible glory, honored by the world, yet in spite of that troubled in spirit, and all the more troubled because no one would take his trouble seriously. What comfort could he possibly need? What more could he possibly wish for? And if some good-natured person, feeling sorry for him, tried to console him by pointing out that his melancholy was probably caused by fasting, it could happen, especially when he had been fasting for some time, that he reacted with an outburst of fury and to the general alarm began to shake the bars of his cage like a wild animal. Yet the impresario had a way of punishing these outbreaks which he rather enjoyed putting into operation. He would apologize publicly for the artist's behavior, which was only to be excused, he admitted, because of the irritability caused by fasting; a condition hardly to be understood by well-fed people; then by natural transition he went on to mention the artist's equally incomprehensible boast that he could fast for much longer than he was doing; he praised the high ambition, the good will, the great self-denial undoubtedly implicit in such a statement; and then quite simply countered it by bringing out photographs, which were also on sale to the public, showing the artist on the fortieth day of a fast lying in bed almost dead from exhaustion. This perversion of the truth, familiar to the artist though it was, always unnerved him afresh and proved too much for him. What was a consequence of the premature ending of his fast was here presented as the cause of it! To fight against this lack of understanding, against a whole world of nonunderstanding, was impossible. Time and again in good faith he stood by the bars listening to the impresario, but as soon as the photographs appeared he always let go and sank with a groan back on to his straw, and the reassured public could once more come close and gaze at him.

A few years later when the witnesses of such scenes called them to mind, they often failed to understand themselves at all. For meanwhile the aforementioned change in public interest had set in; it seemed to happen almost overnight; there may have been profound causes for it, but who was going to bother about that; at any rate the pampered hunger artist suddenly found himself deserted one fine day by the amusement seekers, who went streaming past him to other more favored attraction. For the last time the impresario hurried him over half Europe to discover whether the old interest might still survive here and there; all in vain; everywhere, as if by secret agreement, a positive revulsion from professional fasting was in evidence. Of course it could not really have sprung up so suddenly as all that, and many premonitory symptoms which had not been sufficiently remarked or suppressed during the rush and glitter of success now came retrospectively to mind, but it was now too late to take any countermeasures. Fasting would surely come into fashion again at some future date, yet that was no comfort for those living in the present. What, then, was the hunger artist to do? He had been applauded by thousands in his time and could hardly come down to showing himself in a street booth at village fairs, and as for adopting another profession, he was not only too old for that but too fanatically devoted to fasting. So he took leave of the impresario, his partner in an unparalleled career, and hired himself to a large circus; in order to spare his own feelings he avoided reading the conditions of his contract.

A large circus with its enormous traffic in replacing and recruiting men, animals and apparatus can always find a use for people at any time, even for a hunger artist, provided of course that he does not ask too much, and in this particular case anyhow it was not only the artist who was taken on but his famous and long-known name as well; indeed considering the peculiar nature of his performance, which was not impaired by advancing age, it could not be objected that here was an artist past his prime, no longer at the height of his professional skill, seeking a refuge in some quiet corner of a circus; on the contrary, the hunger artist averred that he could fast as well as ever, which was entirely credible; he even alleged that if he were allowed to fast as he liked, and this was at once promised him without more ado, he could astound the world by establishing a record never yet achieved, a statement which certainly provoked a smile among the other professionals, since it left out of account the change in public opinion, which the hunger artist in his zeal conveniently forgot.

He had not, however, actually lost his sense of the real situation and took it as a matter of course that he and his cage should be stationed, not in the middle of the ring as a main attraction, but outside, near the animal cages, on a site that was after all easily accessible. Large and gaily painted placards made a frame for the cage and announced what was to be seen inside it. When the public came thronging out in the intervals to see the animals, they could hardly avoid passing the hunger artist's cage and stopping there for a moment, perhaps they might even have stayed longer had not those pressing behind them in the narrow gangway, who did not understand why they should be held up on their way towards the excitements of the menagerie, made it impossible for anyone to stand gazing quietly for any length of time. And that was the reason why the hunger artist, who had of course been looking forward to these visiting hours as the main achievement of his life, began instead to shrink from them. At first he could hardly wait for the intervals; it was exhilarating to watch the crowds come streaming his way, until only too soon—not even the most obstinate self-deception, clung to almost consciously, could hold out against the fact—the conviction was borne in upon him that these people, most of them, to judge from their actions, again and again, without exception, were all on their way to the menagerie. And the first sight of him from the distance remained the best. For when they reached his cage he was at once deafened by the storm of shouting and abuse that arose from the two contending factions, which renewed themselves continuously, of those who wanted to stop and stare at him—he soon began to dislike them more than the others—not out of real interest but only out of obstinate self-assertiveness, and those who wanted to go straight on to the animals. When the first great rush was past, the stragglers came along, and these, whom nothing could have prevented from stopping to look at him as long as they had breath, raced past with long strides, hardly even glancing at him, in their haste to get to the menagerie in time. And all too rarely did it happen that he had a stroke of luck, when some father of a family fetched up before him with his children, pointed a finger at the hunger artist and explained at length what the phenomenon meant, telling stories of earlier years when he himself had watched similar but much more thrilling performances, and the children, still rather uncomprehending, since neither inside nor outside school had they been sufficiently prepared for this lesson—what did they care about fasting?—yet showed by the brightness of their intent eyes that new and better times might be coming. Perhaps, said the hunger artist to himself many a time, things would be a little better if his cage were set not quite so near the menagerie. That made it too easy for people to make their choice, to say nothing of what he suffered from the stench of the menagerie, the animals' restlessness by night, the carrying past of raw lumps of flesh for the beasts of prey, the roaring at feeding times, which depressed him continually. But he did not dare to lodge a complaint with the management; after all, he had the animals to thank for the troops of people who passed his cage, among whom there might always be one here and there to take an interest in him, and who could tell where they might seclude him if he called attention to his existence and thereby to the fact that, strictly speaking, he was only an impediment on the way to the menagerie.

A small impediment, to be sure, one that grew steadily less. People grew familiar with the strange idea that they could be expected, in times like these, to take an interest in a hunger artist, and with this familiarity the verdict went out against him. He might fast as much as he could, and he did so; but nothing could save him now, people passed him by. Just try to explain to anyone the art of fasting! Anyone who has no feeling for it cannot be made to understand it. The fine placards grew dirty and illegible, they were torn down; the little notice board telling the number of fast days achieved, which at first was changed carefully every day, had long stayed at the same figure, for after the first few weeks even this small task seemed pointless to the staff; and so the artist simply fasted on and on, as he had once dreamed of doing, and it was no trouble to him, just as he had always foretold, but no one counted the days, no one, not even the artist himself, knew what records he was already breaking, and his heart grew heavy. And when once in a time some leisurely passer-by stopped, made merry over the old figure on the board and spoke of swindling, that was in its way the stupidest lie ever invented by indifference and inborn malice, since it was not the hunger artist who was cheating; he was working honestly, but the world was cheating him of his reward.

Many more days went by, however, and that too came to an end. An overseer's eye fell on the cage one day and he asked the attendants why this perfectly good cage should be left standing there unused with dirty straw inside it; nobody knew, until one man, helped out by the notice board, remembered about the hunger artist. They poked into the straw with sticks and found him in it. "Are you still fasting?" asked the overseer. "When on earth do you mean to stop?" "Forgive me, everybody," whispered the hunger artist; only the overseer, who had his ear to the bars, understood him. "Of course," said the overseer, and tapped his forehead with a finger to let the attendants know what state the man was in, "we forgive you." "I always wanted you to ad-mire my fasting," said the hunger artist. "We do admire it," said the overseer, "but why shouldn't we admire it?" "Because I have to fast, I can't help it," said the hunger artist, lifting his head a little and speaking, with his lips pursed, as if for a kiss, right into the over-seer's ear, so that no syllable might be lost, "because I couldn't find the food I liked. If I had found it, believe me, I should have made no fuss and stuffed myself like you or anyone else." These were his last words, but in his dimming eyes remained the firm though no longer proud persuasion that he was still continuing to fast.

"Well, clear this out now!" said the overseer, and they buried the hunger artist, straw and all. Into the cage they put a young panther. Even the most insensitive felt it refreshing to see this wild creature leaping around the cage that had so long been dreary. The panther was all right. The food he liked was brought him without hesitation by the attendants; he seemed not even to miss his freedom; his noble body, furnished almost to the bursting point with all that it needed, seemed to carry freedom around with it too; somewhere in his jaws it seemed to lurk; and the joy of life streamed with such ardent pas-sion from his throat that for the onlookers it was not easy to stand the shock of it. But they braced themselves, crowded round the cage, and did not want ever to move away.

# Norfolk Isle and the Chola Widow

[Sketch 8 of "The Encantadas" from
·*The Piazza Tales* (1856).]

## HERMAN MELVILLE

*At last they in a island did espy*
*A seemly woman sitting by the shore,*
*That with great sorrow and sad agony*
*Seemed some great misfortune to deplore,*
*And loud to them for succor called evermore.*

*Black his eyes as the midnight sky,*
*White his neck as the driven snow,*
*Red his cheek as the morning light;—*
*Cold he lies in the ground below.*
*My love is dead,*
*Gone to his death-bed,*
*All under the cactus tree.*

FAR TO the northeast of Charles's Isle, sequestered from the rest, lies Norfolk Isle; and, however insignificant to most voyagers, to me, through sympathy, that lone island has become a spot made sacred by the strongest trials of humanity.

It was my first visit to the Encantadas. Two days had been spent ashore in hunting tortoises. There was not time to capture many; so on the third afternoon we loosed our sails. We were just in the act of getting under way, the uprooted anchor yet suspended and invisibly swaying beneath the wave, as the good ship gradually turned her heel to leave the isle behind, when the seaman who heaved with me at the windlass paused suddenly, and directed my attention to something moving on the land, not along the beach, but somewhat back, fluttering from a height.

In view of the sequel of this little story, be it here narrated how it came to pass, that an object which partly from its being so small was quite lost to every other man on board, still caught the eye of my hand-spike companion. The rest of the crew, myself included, merely stood up to our spikes in heaving; whereas, unwontedly exhilarated at every turn of the ponderous windlass, my belted comrade leaped atop of it, with might and main giving a downward, thewey, perpendicular heave, his raised eye bent in cheery animation upon the slowly receding shore. Being high lifted above all others was the reason he perceived the object, otherwise unperceivable; and this elevation of his eye was owing to the elevation of his spirits; and this again—for truth must out—to a dram of Peruvian pisco, in guerdon for some kindness done, secretly administered to him that morning by our mulatto steward. Now, certainly, pisco does a deal of mischief in the world; yet seeing that, in the present case, it was the means, though indirect, of rescuing a human being from the most dreadful fate, must we not also needs admit that sometimes pisco does a deal of good?

Glancing across the water in the direction pointed out, I saw some white thing hanging from an inland rock, perhaps half a mile from the sea.

"It is a bird; a white-winged bird; perhaps a—no; it is—it is a handkerchief!"

"Aye, a handkerchief!" echoed my comrade, and with a louder shout apprised the captain.

Quickly now—like the running out and training of a great gun—the long cabin spy-glass was thrust through the mizzen rigging from the high platform of the poop; whereupon a human figure was plainly seen upon the inland rock, eagerly waving towards us what seemed to be the handkerchief.

Our captain was a prompt, good fellow. Dropping the glass, he lustily ran forward, ordering the anchor to be dropped again; hands to stand by a boat, and lower away.

In a half-hour's time the swift boat returned. It went with six and came with seven; and the seventh was a woman.

It is not artistic heartlessness, but I wish I could but draw in crayons; for this woman was a most touching sight; and crayons, tracing softly melancholy lines, would best depict the mournful image of the dark-damasked Chola widow.

Her story was soon told, and though given in her own strange language was as quickly understood, for our captain from long trading on the Chilian coast was well versed in the Spanish. A *cholo,* or half-breed Indian woman of Payta in Peru, three years gone by, with her young new-wedded husband Felipe, of pure Castilian blood, and her one only Indian brother, Truxill, Hunilla had taken passage on the main in a French whaler, commanded by a joyous man; which vessel, bound to the cruising grounds beyond the Enchanted Isles, proposed passing close by their vicinity. The object of the little party was to procure tortoise oil, a fluid which for its great purity and delicacy is held in high estimation wherever known; and it is well known all along this part of the Pacific coast. With a chest of clothes, tools, cooking utensils, a rude apparatus for trying out the oil, some casks of biscuit, and other things, not omitting two favourite dogs, of which faithful animal all the Cholos are very fond, Hunilla and her companions were safely landed at their chosen place; the Frenchman, according to the contract made ere sailing, engaged to take them off upon returning from a four months' cruise in the westward seas; which interval the three adventurers deemed quite sufficient for their purposes.

On the isle's lone beach they paid him in silver for their passage out, the stranger having declined to carry them at all except upon that condition; though willing to take every means to insure the due fulfilment of his promise. Felipe had striven hard to have this payment put off to the period of the ship's return. But in vain. Still, they thought they had, in another way, ample pledge of the good faith of the Frenchman. It was arranged that the expenses of the passage home should not be payable in silver, but in tortoises; one hundred tortoises ready captured to the returning captain's hand. These the Cholos meant to secure after their own work was done, against the probable time of the Frenchman's coming back; and no doubt in prospect already felt, that in those hundred tortoises—now somewhere ranging in the isle's interior—they possessed one hundred hostages. Enough: the vessel sailed; the gazing three on shore answered the loud glee of the singing crew; and ere evening, the French craft was hull down in the distant sea, its masts three faintest lines which quickly faded from Hunilla's eye.

The stranger had given a blithesome promise, and had anchored it with oaths; but oaths and anchors equally will drag; nought else abides on fickle earth but unkept promises of joy. Contrary winds from out unstable skies, or contrary moods of his more varying mind, or shipwreck and sudden death in solitary waves; whatever was the cause, the blithe stranger never was seen again.

Yet, however dire a calamity was here in store, misgivings of it ere due time never disturbed the Cholos' busy mind, now all intent upon the toilsome matter which had brought them hither. Nay, by swift doom coming like the thief at night, ere seven weeks went by, two of the little party were removed from all anxieties of land or sea. No more they sought to gaze with feverish fear, or still more feverish hope, beyond the present's horizon line; but into the furthest future their own silent spirits sailed. By persevering labour beneath that burning sun, Felipe and Truxill had brought down to their hut many scores of tortoises, and tried out the oil, when, elated with their good success, and to reward themselves for such hard work, they, too hastily, made a catamaran, or Indian raft, much used on the Spanish main, and merrily started a fishing trip just without a long reef with many jagged gaps, running parallel with the shore, about half a mile from it. By some bad tide or hap—or natural negligence of joyfulness (for though they could not be heard, yet by their gestures they seemed singing at the time), forced in deep water against that iron bar—the ill-made catamaran was overset, and came all to pieces; when, dashed by broad-chested swells between their broken logs and the sharp teeth of the reef, both adventurers perished before Hunilla's eyes.

Before Hunilla's eyes they sank. The real woe of this event passed before her sight as some sham tragedy on the stage. She was seated on a rude bower among the withered thickets, crowning a lofty cliff, a little back from the beach. The thickets were so disposed, that in looking upon the sea at large she peered out from among the branches as from the lattice of a high balcony. But, upon the day we speak of here, the better to watch the adventure of those two hearts she loved, Hunilla had withdrawn the branches to one side and held them so. They formed an oval frame through which the bluey boundless sea rolled like a painted one. And there, the invisible painter painted to her view the wave-tossed and disjointed raft, its once level logs slantingly upheaved, as raking masts, and the four struggling arms un-distinguishable among them; and then all subsided into smooth-flowing creamy waters, slowly drifting the splintered wreck; while first and last, no sound of any sort was heard. Death in a silent picture; a dream of the eye; such vanishing shapes as the mirage shows.

So instant was the scene, so trance-like its mild pictorial effect, so distant from her blasted tower and her common sense of things, that Hunilla gazed and gazed, nor raised a finger or a wail. But as good to sit thus dumb, in stupor staring on that dumb show, for all that otherwise might be done. With half a mile of sea between, could her two enchanted arms aid those four fated ones? The distance long, the time one sand. After the lightning is beheld, what fool shall ever stay the thunderbolt? Felipe's body was washed ashore, but Truxill's never came; only his gay, braided hat of golden straw—that same sunflower thing he waved to her, pushing from the strand—and now, to the last gallant, it still saluted her. But Felipe's body floated to the marge, with one arm encirclingly outstretched. Lock-jawed in grim death, the lover-husband softly clasped his bride—true to her even in death's dream. Ah, Heaven, when man thus keeps his faith, wilt thou be faithless who created the faithful one? But they cannot break faith who never plighted it.

It needs not to be said what nameless misery now wrapped the lonely widow. In telling her own story she passed this almost entirely over, simply recounting the event. Construe the comment of her features as you might; from her mere words little would you have weened that Hunilla was herself the heroine of her tale. But not thus did she defraud us of our tears. All hearts bled that grief could be so brave.

She but showed us her soul's lid, and the strange ciphers thereon engraved; all within, with pride's timidity, was withheld. Yet was there one exception. Holding out her small olive hand before our captain, she said in mild and slowest Spanish, "Señor, I buried him;" then paused, struggled as against the writhed coilings of a snake, and cringing suddenly, leaped up, repeating in impassioned pain, "I buried him, my life, my soul!"

Doubtless it was by half-unconscious, automatic motions of her hands, that this heavy-hearted one performed the final offices for Felipe, and planted a rude cross of withered sticks—no green ones might be had—at the head of that lonely grave, where rested now in lasting uncomplaint and quiet haven he whom untranquil seas had overthrown.

But some dull sense of another body that should be interred, of another cross that should hallow another grave—unmade as yet; some dull anxiety and pain touching her undiscovered brother now haunted the oppressed Hunilla. Her hands fresh from the burial earth, she slowly went back to the beach, with unshaped purposes wandered there, her spellbound eye bent upon the incessant waves. But they bore nothing to her but a dirge, which maddened her to think that murderers should mourn. As time went by, and these things came less dreamingly to her mind, the strong persuasions of her Romish faith, which sets peculiar store by consecrated urns, prompted her to resume in waking earnest that pious search which had but been begun as in somnambulism. Day after day, week after week, she trod the cindery beach, till at length a double motive edged every eager glance. With equal longing she now looked for the living and the dead; the brother and the captain; alike vanished, never to return. Little accurate note of time had Hunilla taken under such emotions as were hers, and little, outside herself, served for calendar or dial. As to poor Crusoe in the self-same sea, no saint's bell pealed forth the lapse of week or month; each day went by unchallenged; no chanticleer announced those sultry dawns, no lowing herds those poisonous nights. All wonted and steadily recurring sounds, human or humanized by sweet fellowship with man, but one stirred that torrid trance,—the cry of dogs; save which nought but the rolling sea invaded it, an all pervading monotone; and to the widow that was the least loved voice she could have heard.

No wonder that as her thoughts now wandered to the unreturning ship, and were beaten back again, the hope against hope so struggled in her soul, that at length she desperately said, "Not yet, not yet; my foolish heart runs on too fast." She forced patience for some further weeks. But to those whom earth's sure indraft draws, patience or impatience is still the same.

Hunilla now sought to settle precisely in her mind, to an hour, how long it was since the ship had sailed; and then, with the same precision, how long a space remained to pass. But this proved impossible. What present day or month it was she could not say. Time was her labyrinth, in which Hunilla was entirely lost.

And now follows—

Against my own purposes a pause descends upon me here. One knows not whether nature doth not impose some secrecy upon him who has been privy to certain things. At least, it is to be doubted whether it be good to blazon such. If some books are deemed most baneful and their sale forbid, how then with deadlier facts, not dreams of doting men? Those whom books will hurt will not be proof against events. Events, not books, should be forbid. But in all things man sows upon the wind, which bloweth just there whither it listeth; for ill or good man cannot know. Often ill comes from the good, as good from ill.

When Hunilla—

Dire sight it is to see some silken beast long dally with a golden lizard ere she devour. More terrible, to see how feline Fate will sometimes dally with a human soul, and by a nameless magic make it repulse one sane despair with another which is but mad. Unwittingly I imp this cat-like thing, sporting with the heart of him who reads; for if he feel not, he does read in vain.

—"The ship sails this day, to-day," at last said Hunilla to herself; "this gives me certain time to stand on; without certainty I go mad. In loose ignorance I have hoped and hoped; now in firm knowledge I will but wait. Now I live and no longer perish in bewilderings. Holy Virgin, aid me! Thou wilt waft back the ship. Oh, past length of weary weeks—all to be dragged over—to buy the certainty of to-day, I freely give ye, though I tear ye from me!"

As mariners tossed in tempest on some desolate ledge patch them a boat out of the remnants of their vessel's wreck, and launch it in the self-same waves—see here Hunilla, this lone shipwrecked soul, out of treachery invoking trust. Humanity, thou strong thing. I worship thee, not in the laurelled victor, but in this vanquished one.

Truly, Hunilla leaned upon a reed, a real one; no metaphor; a real Eastern reed. A piece of hollow cane, drifted from unknown isles, and found upon the beach, its once jagged ends rubbed smoothly even as by sandpaper; its golden glazing gone. Long ground between the sea and land, upper and nether stone, the unvarnished substance was filed bare, and wore another polish now, one with itself, the polish of its agony. Circular lines at intervals cut all round this surface, divided it into six panels of unequal length. In the first were scored the days, each tenth one marked by a longer and deeper notch; the second was

scored for the number of sea-fowl eggs for sustenance, picked out from
the rocky nests; the third, how many fish had been caught from the
shore; the fourth, how many small tortoises found inland; the fifth,
how many days of sun; the sixth, of clouds; which last, of the two,
was the greater one. Long night of busy numbering, misery's mathe-
matics, to weary her too-wakeful soul to sleep; yet sleep for that was
none.

The panel of the days was deeply worn, the long tenth notches half
effaced, as alphabets of the blind. Ten thousand times the longing
widow had traced her finger over the bamboo—dull flute, which
played on, gave no sound—as if counting birds flown by in air, would
hasten tortoises creeping through the woods.

After the one hundred and eightieth day no further mark was seen;
that last one was the faintest, as the first the deepest.

"There were more days," said our Captain; "many, many more;
why did you not go on and notch them too, Hunilla?"

"Señor, ask me not."

"And meantime, did no other vessel pass the isle?"

"Nay, Señor;—but—"

"You do not speak; but *what*, Hunilla?"

"Ask me not, Señor."

"You saw ships pass, far away; you waved to them; they passed on;
—was that it, Hunilla?"

"Señor, be it as you say."

Braced against her woe, Hunilla would not—durst not—trust the
weakness of her tongue. Then when our Captain asked whether any
whale-boats had—

But no, I will not file this thing complete for scoffing souls to quote,
and call it firm proof upon their side. The half shall here remain un-
told. Those two unnamed events which befell Hunilla on this isle, let
them abide between her and her God. In nature, as in law, it may be
libellous to speak some truths.

Still, how it was that, although our vessel had lain three days
anchored nigh the isle, its one human tenant should not have discovered us till just upon the point of sailing, never to revisit so lone
and far a spot; this needs explaining ere the sequel come.

The place where the French captain had landed the little party was
on the farther and opposite end of the isle. There too it was that they
had afterwards built their hut. Nor did the widow in her solitude

desert the spot where her loved ones had dwelt with her, and where the dearest of the twain now slept his last long sleep, and all her plaints awaked him not, and he of husbands the most faithful during life.

Now, high broken land rises between the opposite extremities of the isle. A ship anchored at one side is invisible from the other. Neither is the isle so small but a considerable company might wander for days through the wilderness of one side, and never be seen, or their halloos heard, by any stranger holding aloof on the other. Hence Hunilla, who naturally associated the possible coming of ships with her own part of the isle, might to the end have remained quite ignorant of the presence of our vessel, were it not for a mysterious presentiment, borne to her, so our mariners averred, by this isle's enchanted air. Nor did the widow's answer undo the thought.

"How did you come to cross the isle this morning then, Hunilla?" said our Captain.

"Señor, something came flitting by me. It touched my cheek, my heart, Señor."

"What do you say, Hunilla?"

"I have said, Señor; something came through the air."

It was a narrow chance. For when in crossing the isle Hunilla gained the high land in the centre, she must then for the first have perceived our masts, and also marked that their sails were being loosed, perhaps even heard the echoing chorus of the windlass song. The strange ship was about to sail, and she behind. With all haste she now descends the height on the hither side, but soon loses sight of the ship among the sunken jungles at the mountain's base. She struggles on through the withered branches, which seek at every step to bar her path, till she comes to the isolated rock, still some way from the water. This she climbs, to reassure herself. The ship is still in plainest sight. But now, worn out with over tension, Hunilla all but faints; she fears to step down from her giddy perch; she is feign to pause, there where she is, and as a last resort catches the turban from her head, unfurls and waves it over the jungles towards us.

During the telling of her story the mariners formed a voiceless circle round Hunilla and the Captain; and when at length the word was given to man the fastest boat, and pull round to the isle's thither side, to bring away Hunilla's chest and the tortoise-oil—such alacrity of both cheery and sad obedience seldom before was seen. Little ado was made. Already the anchor had been recommitted to the bottom and the ship swung calmly to it.

But Hunilla insisted upon accompanying the boat as indispensable pilot to her hidden hut. So, being refreshed with the best the steward could supply, she started with us. Nor did ever any wife of the most famous admiral in her husband's barge receive more silent reverence of respect, than poor Hunilla from this boat's crew.

Rounding many a vitreous cape and bluff, in two hours' time we shot inside the fatal reef; wound into a secret cove, looked up along a green many-gabled lava wall, and saw the island's solitary dwelling.

It hung upon an impending cliff, sheltered on two sides by tangled thickets, and half-screened from view in front by juttings of the rude stairway, which climbed the precipice from the sea. Built of canes, it was thatched with long, mildewed grass. It seemed an abandoned hayrick, whose haymakers were now no more. The roof inclined but one way; the eaves coming to within two feet of the ground. And here was a simple apparatus to collect the dews, or rather doubly-distilled and finest winnowed rains, which, in mercy or in mockery, the night skies sometimes drop upon these blighted Encantadas. All along beneath the eave, a spotted sheet, quite weather-stained, was spread, pinned to short, upright stakes, set in the shallow sand. A small clinker, thrown into the cloth, weighed its middle down, thereby straining all moisture into a calabash placed below. This vessel supplied each drop of water ever drunk upon the isle by the Cholos. Hunilla told us the calabash would sometimes, but not often, be half filled over-night. It held six quarts, perhaps. "But," said she, "we were used to thirst. At Sandy Payta, where I live, no shower from heaven ever fell; all the water there is brought on mules from the inland vales."

Tied among the thickets were some twenty moaning tortoises, supplying Hunilla's lonely larder; while hundreds of vast tableted black bucklers, like displaced, shattered tombstones of dark slate, were also scattered round. These were the skeleton backs of those great tortoises from which Felipe and Truxill had made their precious oil. Several large calabashes and two goodly kegs were filled with it. In a pot near by were the caked crusts of a quantity which had been permitted to evaporate. "They meant to have strained it off next day," said Hunilla, as she turned aside.

I forgot to mention the most singular sight of all, though the first that greeted us after landing; memory keeps not in all things to the order of occurrence.

Some ten small, soft-haired, ringleted dogs, of a beautiful breed, peculiar to Peru, set up a concert of glad welcomings when we gained the beach, which was responded to by Hunilla. Some of these dogs had, since her widowhood, been born upon the isle, the progeny of the two brought from Payta. Owing to the jagged steeps and pitfalls, tortuous thickets, sunken clefts and perilous intricacies of all sorts in the interior, Hunilla, admonished by the loss of one favourite among them, never allowed these delicate creatures to follow her in her occasional bird's-nests climbs and other wanderings; so that, through long habituation, they offered not to follow, when that morning she crossed the land; and her own soul was then too full of other things to heed their lingering behind. Yet, all along she had so clung to them, that, besides what moisture they lapped up at early daybreak from the small scoop-holes among the adjacent rocks, she had shared the dew of her calabash among them; never laying by any considerable store against those prolonged and utter droughts, which in some disastrous seasons warp these isles.

Having pointed out, at our desire, what few things she would like transported to the ship—her chest, the oil, not omitting the live tortoises which she intended for a grateful present to our Captain—we immediately set to work, carrying them to the boat down the long, sloping stair of deeply-shadowed rock. While my comrades were thus employed, I looked, and Hunilla had disappeared.

It was not curiosity alone, but, it seems to me, something different mingled with it, which prompted me to drop my tortoises and once more gaze slowly around. I remembered the husband buried by Hunilla's hands. A narrow pathway led into a dense part of the thickets. Following it through many mazes, I came out upon a small, round, open space, deeply chambered there.

The mound rose in the middle; a bare heap of finest sand, like that unverdured heap found at the bottom of an hourglass run out. At its head stood the cross of withered sticks; the dry, peeled bark still fraying from it; its transverse limb tied up with rope, and forlornly adroop in the silent air.

Hunilla was partly prostrate upon the grave; her dark head bowed, and lost in her long, loosened Indian hair; her hands extended to the crossfoot, with a little brass crucifix clasped between; a crucifix worn featureless, like an ancient graven knocker long plied in vain. She did not see me, and I made no noise but slid aside and left the spot.

A few moments, ere all was ready for our going, she reappeared among us. I looked into her eyes, but saw no tear. There was something which seemed strangely haughty in her air, and yet it was the air of woe. A Spanish and an Indian grief, which would not visibly lament. Pride's height in vain abased to proneness on the rock; nature's pride subduing nature's torture.

Like pages the small and silken dogs surrounded her, as she slowly descended towards the beach. She caught the two most eager creatures in her arms:—"Mia Teeta! Mia Tomoteeta!" and fondling them, inquired how many could we take on board.

The mate commanded the boat's crew; not a hard-hearted man, but his way of life had been such that in most things, even in the smallest, simple utility was his leading motive.

"We cannot take them all, Hunilla; our supplies are short; the winds are unreliable; we may be a good many days going to Tombez. So take those you have, Hunilla; but no more."

She was in the boat; the oarsmen too were seated; all save one, who stood ready to push off and then spring himself. With the sagacity of their race, the dogs now seemed aware that they were in the very instant of being deserted upon a barren strand. The gunwales of the boat were high; its prow—presented inland—was lifted; so, owing to the water, which they seemed instinctively to shun, the dogs could not well leap into the little craft. But their busy paws hard scraped the prow, as it had been some farmer's door shutting them out from shelter in a winter storm. A clamorous agony of alarm. They did not howl, or whine; they all but spoke.

"Push off! Give way!" cried the mate. The boat gave one heavy drag and lurch, and next moment shot swiftly from the beach, turned on her heel, and sped. The dogs ran howling along the water's marge; now pausing to gaze at the flying boat, then motioning as if to leap in chase, but mysteriously withheld themselves; and again ran howling along the beach. Had they been human beings hardly would they have more vividly inspired the sense of desolation. The oars were plied as confederate feathers of two wings. No one spoke. I looked back upon the beach, and then upon Hunilla, but her face was set in a stern dusky calm. The dogs crouching in her lap vainly licked her rigid hands. She never looked behind her; but sat motionless, till we turned a promontory of the coast and lost all sights and sounds astern. She seemed as one who, having experienced the sharpest of mortal pangs, was henceforth content to have all lesser heartstrings riven, one by one. To Hunilla, pain seemed so necessary, that pain in other beings— though by love and sympathy made her own—was unrepiningly to be borne. A heart of yearning in a frame of steel. A heart of earthly yearning, frozen by the frost which falleth from the sky.

The sequel is soon told. After a long passage, vexed by calms and baffling winds, we made the little port of Tombez in Peru, there to recruit the ship. Payta was not very distant. Our captain sold the tortoise oil to a Tombez merchant; and adding to the silver a contribution from all hands, gave it to our silent passenger, who knew not what the mariners had done.

The last seen of lone Hunilla she was passing into Payta town, riding upon a small gray ass; and before her on the ass's shoulders, she eyed the jointed workings of the beast's armorial cross.

# The Wall

## JEAN-PAUL SARTRE

THEY pushed us into a large white room and my eyes began to blink because the light hurt them. Then I saw a table and four fellows seated at the table, civilians, looking at some papers. The other prisoners were herded together at one end and we were obliged to cross the entire room to join them. There were several I knew, and others who must have been foreigners. The two in front of me were blond with round heads. They looked alike. I imagine they were French. The smaller one kept pulling at his trousers, out of nervousness.

This lasted about three hours. I was dog-tired and my head was empty. But the room was well-heated, which struck me as rather agreeable; we had not stopped shivering for twenty-four hours. The guards led the prisoners in one after the other in front of the table. Then the four fellows asked them their names and what they did. Most of the time that was all—or perhaps from time to time they would ask such questions as: "Did you help sabotage the munitions?" or, "Where were you on the morning of the ninth and what were you doing?" They didn't even listen to the replies, or at least they didn't seem to. They just remained silent for a moment and looked straight ahead, then they began to write. They asked Tom if it was true he had served in the International Brigade. Tom couldn't say he hadn't because of the papers they had found in his jacket. They didn't ask Juan anything, but after he told them his name, they wrote for a long while.

"It's my brother José who's the anarchist," Juan said. "You know perfectly well he's not here now. I don't belong to any party. I never did take part in politics." They didn't answer.

Then Juan said, "I didn't do anything. And I'm not going to pay for what the others did."

His lips were trembling. A guard told him to stop talking and led him away. It was my turn.

"Your name is Pablo Ibbieta?"

I said yes.

The fellow looked at his papers and said, "Where is Ramon Gris?"

"I don't know."

"You hid him in your house from the sixth to the nineteenth."

"I did not."

They continued to write for a moment and the guards led me away. In the hall, Tom and Juan were waiting between two guards. We started walking. Tom asked one of the guards, "Was that just the preliminary questioning, or was that the trial?" "That was the trial," the guard said. "So now what? What are they going to do with us?" The guard answered drily, "The verdict will be told you in your cell."

In reality, our cell was one of the cellars of the hospital. It was terribly cold there because it was very drafty. We had been shivering all night long and it had hardly been any better during the day. I had spent the preceding five days in a cellar in the archbishop's palace, a sort of dungeon that must have dated back to the Middle Ages. There were lots of prisoners and not much room, so they housed them just anywhere. But I was not homesick for my dungeon. I hadn't been cold there, but I had been alone, and that gets to be irritating. In the cellar I had company. Juan didn't say a word; he was afraid, and besides, he was too young to have anything to say. But Tom was a good talker and knew Spanish well.

In the cellar there were a bench and four straw mattresses. When they led us back we sat down and waited in silence. After a while Tom said, "Our goose is cooked."

"I think so too," I said. "But I don't believe they'll do anything to the kid."

Tom said, "They haven't got anything on him. He's the brother of a fellow who's fighting, and that's all."

I looked at Juan. He didn't seem to have heard.

Tom continued, "You know what they do in Saragossa? They lay the guys across the road and then they drive over them with trucks. It was a Moroccan deserter who told us that. They say it's just to save ammunition."

I said, "Well, it doesn't save gasoline."

I was irritated with Tom; he shouldn't have said that.

He went on, "There are officers walking up and down the roads with their hands in their pockets, smoking, and they see that it's done right. Do you think they'd put 'em out of their misery? Like hell they do. They just let 'em holler. Sometimes as long as an hour. The Moroccan said the first time he almost puked."

"I don't believe they do that here," I said, "unless they really are short of ammunition."

The daylight came in through four air vents and a round opening that had been cut in the ceiling, to the left, and which opened directly onto the sky. It was through this hole, which was ordinarily closed by means of a trapdoor, that they unloaded coal into the cellar. Directly under the hole, there was a big pile of coal dust; it had been intended for heating the hospital, but at the beginning of the war they had evacuated the patients and the coal had stayed there unused; it even got rained on from time to time, when they forgot to close the trapdoor.

Tom started to shiver. "God damn it," he said, "I'm shivering. There, it is starting again."

He rose and began to do gymnastic exercises. At each movement, his shirt opened and showed his white, hairy chest. He lay down on his back, lifted his legs in the air and began to do the scissors movement. I watched his big buttocks tremble. Tom was tough, but he had too much fat on him. I kept thinking that soon bullets and bayonet points would sink into that mass of tender flesh as though it were a pat of butter.

I wasn't exactly cold, but I couldn't feel my shoulders or my arms. From time to time, I had the impression that something was missing and I began to look around for my jacket. Then I would suddenly remember they hadn't given me a jacket. It was rather awkward. They had taken our clothes to give them to their own soldiers and had left us only our shirts and these cotton trousers the hospital patients wore in mid-summer. After a moment, Tom got up and sat down beside me, breathless.

"Did you get warmed up?"

"Damn it, no. But I'm all out of breath."

Around eight o'clock in the evening, a Major came in with two falangists.

"What are the names of those three over there?" he asked the guard.

"Steinbock, Ibbieta and Mirbal," said the guard.

The Major put on his glasses and examined his list.

"Steinbock—Steinbock. . . . Here it is. You are condemned to death. You'll be shot tomorrow morning."

He looked at his list again.

"The other two, also," he said.

"That's not possible," said Juan. "Not me."

The Major looked at him with surprise. "What's your name?"

"Juan Mirbal."

"Well, your name is here," said the Major, "and you're condemned to death."

"I didn't do anything," said Juan.

The Major shrugged his shoulders and turned toward Tom and me.

"You are both Basque?"

"No, nobody's Basque."

He appeared exasperated.

"I was told there were three Basques. I'm not going to waste my time running after them. I suppose you don't want a priest?"

We didn't even answer.

Then he said, "A Belgian doctor will be around in a little while. He has permission to stay with you all night."

He gave a military salute and left.

"What did I tell you?" Tom said. "We're in for something swell."

"Yes," I said. "It's a damned shame for the kid."

I said that to be fair, but I really didn't like the kid. His face was too refined and it was disfigured by fear and suffering, which had twisted all his features. Three days ago, he was just a kid with a kind of affected manner some people like. But now he looked like an aging fairy, and I thought to myself he would never be young again, even if they let him go. It wouldn't have been a bad thing to show him a little pity, but pity makes me sick, and besides, I couldn't stand him. He hadn't said anything more, but he had turned gray. His face and hands were gray. He sat down again and stared, round-eyed, at the ground. Tom was good-hearted and tried to take him by the arm, but the kid drew himself away violently and made an ugly face. "Leave him alone," I said quietly. "Can't you see he's going to start to bawl?" Tom obeyed regretfully. He would have liked to console the kid; that would have kept him occupied and he wouldn't have been tempted to think about himself. But it got on my nerves. I had never thought about death, for the reason that the question had never come up. But now it had come up, and there was nothing else to do but think about it.

Tom started talking. "Say, did you ever bump anybody off?" he asked me. I didn't answer. He started to explain to me that he had bumped off six fellows since August. He hadn't yet realized what we were in for, and I saw clearly he didn't *want* to realize it. I myself hadn't quite taken it in. I wondered if it hurt very much. I thought about the bullets; I imagined their fiery hail going through my body. All that was beside the real question; but I was calm, we had all night in which to realize it. After a while Tom stopped talking and I looked at him out of the corner of my eye. I saw that he, too, had turned gray and that he looked pretty miserable. I said to myself, "It's starting." It was almost dark, a dull light filtered through the air vents across the coal pile and made a big spot under the sky. Through the hole in the ceiling I could already see a star. The night was going to be clear and cold.

The door opened and two guards entered. They were followed by a blond man in a tan uniform. He greeted us.

"I'm the doctor," he said. "I've been authorized to give you any assistance you may require in these painful circumstances."

He had an agreeable, cultivated voice.

I said to him, "What are you going to do here?"

"Whatever you want me to do. I shall do everything in my power to lighten these few hours."

"Why did you come to us? There are lots of others: the hospital's full of them."

"I was sent here," he answered vaguely. "You'd probably like to smoke, wouldn't you?" he added suddenly. "I've got some cigarettes and even some cigars."

He passed around some English cigarettes and some *puros,* but we refused them. I looked him straight in the eye and he appeared uncomfortable.

"You didn't come here out of compassion," I said to him. "In fact, I know who you are. I saw you with some fascists in the barracks yard the day I was arrested."

I was about to continue, when all at once something happened to me which surprised me: the presence of this doctor had suddenly ceased to interest me. Usually, when I've got hold of a man I don't let go. But somehow the desire to speak had left me. I shrugged my shoulders and turned away. A little later, I looked up and saw he was watching me with an air of curiosity. The guards had sat down on one of the mattresses. Pedro, the tall thin one, was twiddling his thumbs, while the other one shook his head occasionally to keep from falling asleep.

"Do you want some light?" Pedro suddenly asked the doctor. The other fellow nodded, "Yes." I think he was not over-intelligent, but doubtless he was not malicious. As I looked at his big, cold, blue eyes, it seemed to me the worst thing about him was his lack of imagination. Pedro went out and came back with an oil lamp which he set on the corner of the bench. It gave a poor light, but it was better than nothing; the night before we had been left in the dark. For a long while I stared at the circle of light the lamp threw on the ceiling. I was fascinated. Then, suddenly, I came to, the light circle paled, and I felt as if I were being crushed under an enormous weight. It wasn't the thought of death, and it wasn't fear; it was something anonymous. My cheeks were burning hot and my head ached.

I roused myself and looked at my two companions. Tom had his head in his hands and only the fat, white nape of his neck was visible. Juan was by far the worst off; his mouth was wide open and his nostrils were trembling. The doctor came over to him and touched him on the shoulder, as though to comfort him; but his eyes remained cold. Then I saw the Belgian slide his hand furtively down Juan's arm to his wrist. Indifferent, Juan let himself be handled. Then, as though absent-mindedly, the Belgian laid three fingers over his wrist; at the same time, he drew away somewhat and managed to turn his back to me. But I leaned over backward and saw him take out his watch and look at it a moment before relinquishing the boy's wrist. After a moment, he let the inert hand fall and went and leaned against the wall. Then, as if he had suddenly remembered something very important that had to be noted down immediately, he took a notebook from his pocket and wrote a few lines in it. "The son-of-a-bitch," I thought angrily. "He better not come and feel my pulse; I'll give him a punch in his dirty jaw."

He didn't come near me, but I felt he was looking at me. I raised my head and looked back at him. In an impersonal voice, he said, "Don't you think it's frightfully cold here?"

He looked purple with cold.

"I'm not cold," I answered him.

He kept looking at me with a hard expression. Suddenly I understood, and I lifted my hands to my face. I was covered with sweat. Here, in this cellar, in mid-winter, right in a draft, I was sweating. I ran my fingers through my hair, which was stiff with sweat; at the same time, I realized my shirt was damp and sticking to my skin. I had been streaming with perspiration for an hour, at least, and had felt nothing. But this fact hadn't escaped that Belgian swine. He had seen the drops rolling down my face and had said to himself that it showed an almost pathological terror; and he himself had felt normal and proud of it because he was cold. I wanted to get up and go punch his face in, but I had hardly started to make a move before my shame and anger had disappeared. I dropped back onto the bench with indifference.

I was content to rub my neck with my handkerchief because now I felt the sweat dripping from my hair onto the nape of my neck and that was disagreeable. I soon gave up rubbing myself, however, for it didn't do any good; my handkerchief was already wringing wet and I was still sweating. My buttocks, too, were sweating, and my damp trousers stuck to the bench.

Suddenly, Juan said, "You're a doctor, aren't you?"

"Yes," said the Belgian.

"Do people suffer—very long?"

"Oh! When . . . ? No, no," said the Belgian, in a paternal voice, "it's quickly over."

His manner was as reassuring as if he had been answering a paying patient.

"But I . . . Somebody told me—they often have to fire two volleys."

"Sometimes," said the Belgian, raising his head, "it just happens that the first volley doesn't hit any of the vital organs."

"So then they have to reload their guns and aim all over again?" Juan thought for a moment, then added hoarsely, "But that takes time!"

He was terribly afraid of suffering. He couldn't think about anything else, but that went with his age. As for me, I hardly thought about it any more and it certainly was not fear of suffering that made me perspire.

I rose and walked toward the pile of coal dust. Tom gave a start and looked at me with a look of hate. I irritated him because my shoes squeaked. I wondered if my face was as putty-colored as his. Then I noticed that he, too, was sweating. The sky was magnificent; no light at all came into our dark corner and I had only to lift my head to see the Big Bear. But it didn't look the way it had looked before. Two days ago, from my cell in the archbishop's palace, I could see a big patch of sky and each time of day brought back a different memory. In the morning, when the sky was a deep blue, and light, I thought of beaches along the Atlantic; at noon, I could see the sun, and I remembered a bar in Seville where I used to drink manzanilla and eat anchovies and olives; in the afternoon, I was in the shade, and I thought of the deep shadow which covers half of the arena while the other half gleams in the sunlight: it really gave me a pang to see the whole earth reflected in the sky like that. Now, however, no matter how much I looked up in the air, the sky no longer recalled anything. I liked it better that way. I came back and sat down next to Tom. There was a long silence.

Then Tom began to talk in a low voice. He had to keep talking, otherwise he lost his way in his own thoughts. I believe he was talking to me, but he didn't look at me. No doubt he was afraid to look at me, because I was gray and sweating. We were both alike and worse than mirrors for each other. He looked at the Belgian, the only one who was alive.

"Say, do you understand? I don't."

Then I, too, began to talk in a low voice. I was watching the Belgian. "Understand what? What's the matter?"

"Something's going to happen to us that I don't understand."

There was a strange odor about Tom. It seemed to me that I was more sensitive to odors than ordinarily. With a sneer, I said, "You'll understand, later."

"That's not so sure," he said stubbornly. "I'm willing to be courageous, but at least I ought to know. . . . Listen, they're going to take us out into the courtyard. All right. The fellows will be standing in line in front of us. How many of them will there be?"

"Oh, I don't know. Five, or eight. Not more."

"That's enough. Let's say there'll be eight of them. Somebody will shout 'Shoulder arms!' and I'll see all eight rifles aimed at me. I'm sure I'm going to feel like going through the wall. I'll push against the wall as hard as I can with my back, and the wall won't give in.

The way it is in a nightmare. . . . I can imagine all that. Ah, if you only knew how well I can imagine it!"

"Skip it!" I said. "I can imagine it too."

"It must hurt like the devil. You know they aim at your eyes and mouth so as to disfigure you," he added maliciously. "I can feel the wounds already. For the last hour I've been having pains in my head and neck. Not real pains—it's worse still. They're the pains I'll feel tomorrow morning. And after that, then what?"

I understood perfectly well what he meant, but I didn't want to seem to understand. As for the pains, I, too, felt them all through my body, like a lot of little gashes. I couldn't get used to them, but I was like him, I didn't think they were very important.

"After that," I said roughly, "you'll be eating daisies."

He started talking to himself, not taking his eyes off the Belgian, who didn't seem to be listening to him. I knew what he had come for, and that what we were thinking didn't interest him. He had come to look at our bodies, our bodies which were dying alive.

"It's like in a nightmare," said Tom. "You want to think of something, you keep having the impression you've got it, that you're going to understand, and then it slips away from you, it eludes you and it's gone again. I say to myself, afterwards, there won't be anything. But I don't really understand what that means. There are moments when I almost do—and then it's gone again. I start to think of the pains, the bullets, the noise of the shooting. I am a materialist, I swear it; and I'm not going crazy, either. But there's something wrong. I see my own corpse. That's not hard, but it's *I* who see it, with *my* eyes. I'll have to get to the point where I think—where I think I won't see anything more. I won't hear anything more, and the world will go on for the others. We're not made to think that way, Pablo. Believe me, I've already stayed awake all night waiting for something. But this is not the same thing. This will grab us from behind, Pablo, and we won't be ready for it."

"Shut up," I said. "Do you want me to call a father confessor?"

He didn't answer. I had already noticed that he had a tendency to prophesy and call me "Pablo" in a kind of pale voice. I didn't like that very much, but it seems all the Irish are like that. I had a vague impression that he smelled of urine. Actually, I didn't like Tom very much, and I didn't see why, just because we were going to die together, I should like him any better. There are certain fellows with

whom it would be different—with Ramon Gris, for instance. But between Tom and Juan, I felt alone. In fact, I liked it better that way.
With Ramon I might have grown soft. But I felt terribly hard at that
moment, and I wanted to stay hard.

Tom kept on muttering, in a kind of absent-minded way. He was
certainly talking to keep from thinking. Naturally, I agreed with him,
and I could have said everything he was saying. It's not *natural* to die.
And since I was going to die, nothing seemed natural any more:
neither the coal pile, nor the bench, nor Pedro's dirty old face. Only
it was disagreeable for me to think the same things Tom thought.
And I knew perfectly well that all night long, within five minutes of
each other, we would keep on thinking things at the same time,
sweating or shivering at the same time. I looked at him sideways and,
for the first time, he seemed strange to me. He had death written on
his face. My pride was wounded. For twenty-four hours I had lived
side by side with Tom, I had listened to him, I had talked to him,
and I knew we had nothing in common. And now we were as alike
as twin brothers, simply because we were going to die together. Tom
took my hand without looking at me.

"Pablo, I wonder . . . I wonder if it's true that we just cease to
exist."

I drew my hand away.

"Look between your feet, you dirty dog."

There was a puddle between his feet and water was dripping from
his trousers.

"What's the matter?" he said, frightened.

"You're wetting your pants," I said to him.

"It's not true," he said furiously. "I can't be . . . I don't feel anything."

The Belgian had come closer to him. With an air of false concern,
he asked, "Aren't you feeling well?"

Tom didn't answer. The Belgian looked at the puddle without comment.

"I don't know what that is," Tom said savagely, "but I'm not afraid.
I swear to you, I'm not afraid."

The Belgian made no answer. Tom rose and went to the corner. He
came back, buttoning his fly, and sat down, without a word. The
Belgian was taking notes.

We were watching the doctor. Juan was watching him too. All three of us were watching him because he was alive. He had the gestures of a living person, the interests of a living person; he was shivering in this cellar the way living people shiver; he had an obedient, well-fed body. We, on the other hand, didn't feel our bodies any more—not the same way, in any case. I felt like touching my trousers, but I didn't dare to. I looked at the Belgian, well-planted on his two legs, master of his muscles—and able to plan for tomorrow. We were like three shadows deprived of blood; we were watching him and sucking his life like vampires.

Finally he came over to Juan. Was he going to lay his hand on the nape of Juan's neck for some professional reason, or had he obeyed a charitable impulse? If he had acted out of charity, it was the one and only time during the whole night. He fondled Juan's head and the nape of his neck. The kid let him do it, without taking his eyes off him. Then, suddenly, he took hold of the doctor's hand and looked at it in a funny way. He held the Belgian's hand between his own two hands and there was nothing pleasing about them, those two gray paws squeezing that fat red hand. I sensed what was going to happen and Tom must have sensed it, too. But all the Belgian saw was emotion, and he smiled paternally. After a moment, the kid lifted the big red paw to his mouth and started to bite it. The Belgian drew back quickly and stumbled toward the wall. For a second, he looked at us with horror. He must have suddenly understood that we were not men like himself. I began to laugh, and one of the guards started up. The other had fallen asleep with his eyes wide open, showing only the whites.

I felt tired and over-excited at the same time. I didn't want to think any more about what was going to happen at dawn—about death. It didn't make sense, and I never got beyond just words, or emptiness. But whenever I tried to think about something else I saw the barrels of rifles aimed at me. I must have lived through my execution twenty times in succession; one time I thought it was the real thing; I must have dozed off for a moment. They were dragging me toward the wall and I was resisting; I was imploring their pardon. I woke with a start and looked at the Belgian. I was afraid I had cried out in my sleep. But he was smoothing his mustache; he hadn't noticed anything. If I had wanted to, I believe I could have slept for a while. I had been awake for the last forty-eight hours, and I was worn out. But I didn't want to lose two hours of life. They would have had to come and wake me at dawn. I would have followed them, drunk with sleep, and I would have gone off without so much as "Gosh!" I didn't want it that way, I didn't want to die like an animal. I wanted to understand. Besides, I was afraid of having nightmares. I got up and began to walk up and down and, so as to think about something else, I began to think about my past life. Memories crowded in on me, helter-skelter. Some were good and some were bad—at least that was how I had thought of them *before*. There were faces and happenings. I saw the face of a little *novilero* who had gotten himself horned during the *Feria,* in Valencia. I saw the face of one of my uncles, of Ramon Gris. I remembered all kinds of things that had happened: how I had been on strike for three months in 1926, and had almost died of hunger. I recalled a night I had spent on a bench in Granada; I hadn't eaten for three days, I was nearly wild, I didn't want to give up the sponge. I had to smile. With what eagerness I had run after happiness, and women, and liberty! And to what end? I had wanted to liberate Spain, I admired Py Margall, I had belonged to the anarchist movement, I had spoken at public meetings. I took everything as seriously as if I had been immortal.

At that time I had the impression that I had my whole life before me, and I thought to myself, "It's all a god-damned lie." Now it wasn't worth anything because it was finished. I wondered how I had ever been able to go out and have a good time with girls. I wouldn't have lifted my little finger if I had ever imagined that I would die like this. I saw my life before me, finished, closed, like a bag, and yet what was inside was not finished. For a moment I tried to appraise it. I would have liked to say to myself, "It's been a good life." But it couldn't be appraised, it was only an outline. I had spent my time writing checks on eternity, and had understood nothing. Now, I didn't miss anything. There were a lot of things I might have missed: the taste of manzanilla, for instance, or the swims I used to take in summer in a little creek near Cadiz. But death had taken the charm out of everything.

Suddenly the Belgian had a wonderful idea.

"My friends," he said to us, "if you want me to—and providing the military authorities give their consent—I could undertake to deliver a word or some token from you to your loved ones. . . ."

Tom growled, "I haven't got anybody."

I didn't answer. Tom waited for a moment, then he looked at me with curiosity. "Aren't you going to send any message to Concha?"

"No."

I hated that sort of sentimental conspiracy. Of course, it was my fault, since I had mentioned Concha the night before, and I should have kept my mouth shut. I had been with her for a year. Even as late as last night, I would have cut my arm off with a hatchet just to see her again for five minutes. That was why I had mentioned her. I couldn't help it. Now I didn't care any more about seeing her. I hadn't anything more to say to her. I didn't even want to hold her in my arms. I loathed my body because it had turned gray and was sweating—and I wasn't even sure that I didn't loathe hers too. Concha would cry when she heard about my death; for months she would have no more interest in life. But still it was I who was going to die. I thought of her beautiful, loving eyes. When she looked at me something went from her to me. But I thought to myself that it was all over; if she looked at me *now* her gaze would not leave her eyes, it would not reach out to me. I was alone.

Tom too, was alone, but not the same way. He was seated astride his chair and had begun to look at the bench with a sort of smile, with surprise, even. He reached out his hand and touched the wood cautiously, as though he were afraid of breaking something, then he drew his hand back hurriedly, and shivered. I wouldn't have amused myself touching that bench, if I had been Tom, that was just some more Irish play-acting. But somehow it seemed to me too that the different objects had something funny about them. They seemed to have grown paler, less massive than before. I had only to look at the bench, the lamp or the pile of coal dust to feel I was going to die. Naturally, I couldn't think clearly about my death, but I saw it everywhere, even on the different objects, the way they had withdrawn and kept their distance, tactfully, like people talking at the bedside of a dying person. It was *his own death* Tom had just touched on the bench.

In the state I was in, if they had come and told me I could go home quietly, that my life would be saved, it would have left me cold. A few hours, or a few years of waiting are all the same, when you've lost the illusion of being eternal. Nothing mattered to me any more. In a way, I was calm. But it was a horrible kind of calm—because of my body. My body—I saw with its eyes and I heard with its ears, but it was no longer I. It sweat and trembled independently, and I didn't recognize it any longer. I was obliged to touch it and look at it to know what was happening to it, just as if it had been someone else's body. At times I still felt it, I felt a slipping, a sort of headlong plunging, as in a falling airplane, or else I heard my heart beating. But this didn't give me confidence. In fact, everything that came from my body had something damned dubious about it. Most of the time it was silent, it stayed put and I didn't feel anything other than a sort of heaviness, a loathsome presence against me. I had the impression of being bound to an enormous vermin.

The Belgian took out his watch and looked at it.

"It's half-past three," he said.

The son-of-a-bitch! He must have done it on purpose. Tom jumped up. We hadn't yet realized the time was passing. The night surrounded us like a formless, dark mass; I didn't even remember it had started.

Juan started to shout. Wringing his hands, he implored, "I don't want to die! I don't want to die!"

He ran the whole length of the cellar with his arms in the air, then he dropped down onto one of the mattresses, sobbing. Tom looked at him with dismal eyes and didn't even try to console him any more. The fact was, it was no use; the kid made more noise than we did, but he was less affected, really. He was like a sick person who defends himself against his malady with a high fever. When there's not even any fever left, it's much more serious.

He was crying. I could tell he felt sorry for himself; he was thinking about death. For one second, one single second, I too felt like crying, crying out of pity for myself. But just the contrary happened. I took one look at the kid, saw his thin, sobbing shoulders, and I felt I was inhuman. I couldn't feel pity either for these others or for myself. I said to myself, "I want to die decently."

Tom had gotten up and was standing just under the round opening looking out for the first signs of daylight. I was determined, I wanted to die decently, and I only thought about that. But underneath, ever since the doctor had told us the time, I felt time slipping, flowing by, one drop at a time.

It was still dark when I heard Tom's voice.

"Do you hear them?"

"Yes."

People were walking in the courtyard.

"What the hell are they doing? After all, they can't shoot in the dark."

After a moment, we didn't hear anything more. I said to Tom, "There's the daylight."

Pedro got up yawning, and came and blew out the lamp. He turned to the man beside him. "It's hellish cold."

The cellar had grown gray. We could hear shots at a distance.

"It's about to start," I said to Tom. "That must be in the back courtyard."

Tom asked the doctor to give him a cigarette. I didn't want any; I didn't want either cigarettes or alcohol. From that moment on, the shooting didn't stop.

"Can you take it in?" Tom said.

He started to add something, then he stopped and began to watch the door. The door opened and a lieutenant came in with four soldiers. Tom dropped his cigarette.

"Steinbock?"

Tom didn't answer. Pedro pointed him out.

"Juan Mirbal?"

"He's the one on the mattress."

"Stand up," said the Lieutenant.

Juan didn't move. Two soldiers took hold of him by the armpits and stood him up on his feet. But as soon as they let go of him he fell down.

The soldiers hesitated a moment.

"He's not the first one to get sick," said the Lieutenant. "You'll have to carry him, the two of you. We'll arrange things when we get there." He turned to Tom. "All right, come along."

Tom left between two soldiers. Two other soldiers followed, carrying the kid by his arms and legs. He was not unconscious; his eyes were wide open and tears were rolling down his cheeks. When I started to go out, the Lieutenant stopped me.

"Are you Ibbieta?"

"Yes."

"You wait here. They'll come and get you later on."

They left. The Belgian and the two jailers left too, and I was alone. I didn't understand what had happened to me, but I would have liked it better if they had ended it all right away. I heard the volleys at almost regular intervals; at each one, I shuddered. I felt like howling and tearing my hair. But instead, I gritted my teeth and pushed my hands deep into my pockets, because I wanted to stay decent.

An hour later, they came to fetch me and took me up to the first floor in a little room which smelt of cigar smoke and was so hot it seemed to me suffocating. Here there were two officers sitting in comfortable chairs, smoking, with papers spread out on their knees.

"Your name is Ibbieta?"

"Yes."

"Where is Ramon Gris?"

"I don't know."

The man who questioned me was small and stocky. He had hard eyes behind his glasses.

"Come nearer," he said to me.

I went nearer. He rose and took me by the arms, looking at me in a way calculated to make me go through the floor. At the same time he pinched my arms with all his might. He didn't mean to hurt me; it was quite a game; he wanted to dominate me. He also seemed to think it was necessary to blow his fetid breath right into my face. We stood like that for a moment, only I felt more like laughing than anything else. It takes a lot more than that to intimidate a man who's about to die: it didn't work. He pushed me away violently and sat down again.

"It's your life or his," he said. "You'll be allowed to go free if you tell us where he is."

After all, these two bedizened fellows with their riding crops and boots were just men who were going to die one day. A little later than I, perhaps, but not a great deal. And there they were, looking for names among their papers, running after other men in order to put them in prison or do away with them entirely. They had their opinions on the future of Spain and on other subjects. Their petty activities seemed to me to be offensive and ludicrous. I could no longer put myself in their place. I had the impression they were crazy.

The little fat fellow kept looking at me, tapping his boots with his riding crop. All his gestures were calculated to make him appear like a spirited, ferocious animal.

"Well? Do you understand?"

"I don't know where Gris is," I said. "I thought he was in Madrid."

The other officer lifted his pale hand indolently. This indolence was also calculated. I saw through all their little tricks, and I was dumb-founded that men should still exist who took pleasure in that kind of thing.

"You have fifteen minutes to think it over," he said slowly. "Take him to the linen-room, and bring him back here in fifteen minutes. If he continues to refuse, he'll be executed at once."

They knew what they were doing. I had spent the night waiting. After that, they had made me wait another hour in the cellar, while they shot Tom and Juan, and now they locked me in the linen-room. They must have arranged the whole thing the night before. They figured that sooner or later people's nerves wear out and they hoped to get me that way.

They made a big mistake. In the linen-room I sat down on a ladder because I felt very weak, and I began to think things over. Not their proposition, however. Naturally I knew where Gris was. He was hiding in his cousins' house, about two miles outside of the city. I knew, too, that I would not reveal his hiding place, unless they tortured me (but they didn't seem to be considering that). All that was definitely settled and didn't interest me in the least. Only I would have liked to understand the reasons for my own conduct. I would rather die than betray Gris. Why? I no longer liked Ramon Gris. My friendship for him had died shortly before dawn along with my love for Concha, along with my own desire to live. Of course I still admired him—he was hard. But it was not for that reason that I was willing to die in his place; his life was no more valuable than mine. No life was of any value. A man was going to be stood up against a wall and fired at till he dropped dead. It didn't make any difference whether it was I or Gris or somebody else. I knew perfectly well he was more useful to the Spanish cause than I was, but I didn't give a God damn about Spain or anarchy, either; nothing had any importance now. And yet, there I was. I could save my skin by betraying Gris and I refused to do it. It seemed more ludicrous to me than anything else; it was stubbornness.

I thought to myself, "Am I hard-headed!" And I was seized with a strange sort of cheerfulness.

They came to fetch me and took me back to the two officers. A rat darted out under our feet and that amused me. I turned to one of the falangists and said to him, "Did you see that rat?"

He made no reply. He was gloomy, and took himself very seriously.

As for me, I felt like laughing, but I restrained myself because I was afraid that if I started, I wouldn't be able to stop. The falangist wore mustaches. I kept after him, "You ought to cut off those mustaches, you fool."

I was amused by the fact that he let hair grow all over his face while he was still alive. He gave me a kind of half-hearted kick, and I shut up.

"Well," said the fat officer, "have you thought things over?"

I looked at them with curiosity, like insects of a very rare species.

"I know where he is," I said. "He's hiding in the cemetery. Either in one of the vaults, or in the gravediggers' shack."

I said that just to make fools of them. I wanted to see them get up and fasten their belts and bustle about giving orders.

They jumped to their feet.

"Fine. Moles, go ask Lieutenant Lopez for fifteen men. And as for you," the little fat fellow said to me, "if you've told the truth, I don't go back on my word. But you'll pay for this, if you're pulling our leg."

They left noisily and I waited in peace, still guarded by the falangists. From time to time I smiled at the thought of the face they were going to make. I felt dull and malicious. I could see them lifting up the gravestones, or opening the doors of the vaults one by one. I saw the whole situation as though I were another person: the prisoner determined to play the hero, the solemn falangists with their mustaches and the men in uniform running around among the graves. It was irresistibly funny.

After half an hour, the little fat fellow came back alone. I thought he had come to give the order to execute me. The others must have stayed in the cemetery.

The officer looked at me. He didn't look at all foolish.

"Take him out in the big courtyard with the others," he said. "When military operations are over, a regular tribunal will decide his case."

I thought I must have misunderstood.

"So they're not—they're not going to shoot me?" I asked.

"Not now, in any case. Afterwards, that doesn't concern me."

I still didn't understand.

"But why?" I said to him.

He shrugged his shoulders without replying, and the soldiers led me away. In the big courtyard there were a hundred or so prisoners, women, children and a few old men. I started to walk around the grass plot in the middle. I felt absolutely idiotic. At noon we were fed in the dining hall. Two or three fellows spoke to me. I must have known them, but I didn't answer. I didn't even know where I was.

Toward evening, about ten new prisoners were pushed into the courtyard. I recognized Garcia, the baker.

He said to me, "Lucky dog! I didn't expect to find you alive."

"They condemned me to death," I said, "and then they changed their minds. I don't know why."

"I was arrested at two o'clock," Garcia said.

"What for?"

Garcia took no part in politics.

"I don't know," he said. "They arrest everybody who doesn't think the way they do."

He lowered his voice.

"They got Gris."

I began to tremble.

"When?"

"This morning. He acted like a damned fool. He left his cousins' house Tuesday because of a disagreement. There were any number of fellows who would have hidden him, but he didn't want to be indebted to anybody any more. He said, 'I would have hidden at Ibbieta's, but since they've got him, I'll go hide in the cemetery.' "

"In the cemetery?"

"Yes. It was the god-damnedest thing. Naturally they passed by there this morning; that had to happen. They found him in the gravediggers' shack. They opened fire at him and they finished him off."

"In the cemetery!"

Everything went around in circles, and when I came to I was sitting on the ground. I laughed so hard the tears came to my eyes.

# Death in the Woods

## SHERWOOD ANDERSON

### I

SHE WAS an old woman and lived on a farm near the town in which I lived. All country and small-town people have seen such old women, but no one knows much about them. Such an old woman comes into town driving an old worn-out horse or she comes afoot carrying a basket. She may own a few hens and have eggs to sell. She brings them in a basket and takes them to a grocer. There she trades them in. She gets some salt pork and some beans. Then she gets a pound or two of sugar and some flour.

Afterwards she goes to the butcher's and asks for some dog-meat. She may spend ten or fifteen cents, but when she does she asks for something. Formerly the butchers gave liver to anyone who wanted to carry it away. In our family we were always having it. Once one of my brothers got a whole cow's liver at the slaughterhouse near the fair grounds in our town. We had it until we were sick of it. It never cost a cent. I have hated the thought of it ever since.

The old farm woman got some liver and a soup-bone. She never visited with anyone, and as soon as she got what she wanted she lit out for home. It made quite a load for such an old body. No one gave her a lift. People drive right down a road and never notice an old woman like that.

There was such an old woman who used to come into town past our house one summer and fall when I was a young boy and was sick with what was called inflammatory rheumatism. She went home later carrying a heavy pack on her back. Two or three large gaunt-looking dogs followed at her heels.

The old woman was nothing special. She was one of the nameless ones that hardly anyone knows, but she got into my thoughts. I have just suddenly now, after all these years, remembered her and what happened. It is a story. Her name was Grimes, and she lived with her husband and a son in a small unpainted house on the bank of a small creek four miles from town.

The husband and son were a tough lot. Although the son was but twenty-one, he had already served a term in jail. It was whispered about that the woman's husband stole horses and ran them off to some other county. Now and then, when a horse turned up missing, the man had also disappeared. No one ever caught him. Once, when I was loafing at Tom Whitehead's livery-barn, the man came there and sat on the bench in front. Two or three other men were there, but no one spoke to him. He sat for a few minutes and then got up and went away. When he was leaving he turned around and stared at the men. There was a look of defiance in his eyes. "Well, I have tried to be friendly. You don't want to talk to me. It has been so wherever I have gone in this town. If, some day, one of your fine horses turns up missing, well, then what?" He did not say anything actually. "I'd like to bust one of you on the jaw," was about what his eyes said. I remember how the look in his eyes made me shiver.

The old man belonged to a family that had had money once. His name was Jake Grimes. It all comes back clearly now. His father, John Grimes, had owned a sawmill when the country was new, and had made money. Then he got to drinking and running after women. When he died there wasn't much left.

Jake blew in the rest. Pretty soon there wasn't any more lumber to cut and his land was nearly all gone.

He got his wife off a German farmer, for whom he went to work one June day in the wheat harvest. She was a young thing then and scared to death. You see, the farmer was up to something with the girl—she was, I think, a bound girl and his wife had her suspicions. She took it out on the girl when the man wasn't around. Then, when the wife had to go off to town for supplies, the farmer got after her. She told young Jake that nothing really ever happened, but he didn't know whether to believe it or not.

He got her pretty easy himself, the first time he was out with her. He wouldn't have married her if the German farmer hadn't tried to tell him where to get off. He got her to go riding with him in his buggy one night when he was threshing on the place, and then he came for her the next Sunday night.

She managed to get out of the house without her employer's seeing, but when she was getting into the buggy he showed up. It was almost dark, and he just popped up suddenly at the horse's head. He grabbed the horse by the bridle and Jake got out his buggy-whip.

They had it out all right! The German was a tough one. Maybe he didn't care whether his wife knew or not. Jake hit him over the face and shoulders with the buggy-whip, but the horse got to acting up and he had to get out.

Then the two men went for it. The girl didn't see it. The horse started to run away and went nearly a mile down the road before the girl got him stopped. Then she managed to tie him to a tree beside the road. (I wonder how I know all this. It must have stuck in my mind from small-town tales when I was a boy.) Jake found her there after he got through with the German. She was huddled up in the buggy seat, crying, scared to death. She told Jake a lot of stuff, how the German had tried to get her, how he chased her once into the barn, how another time, when they happened to be alone in the house together, he tore her dress open clear down the front. The German, she said, might have got her that time if he hadn't heard his old woman drive in at the gate. She had been off to town for supplies. Well, she would be putting the horse in the barn. The German managed to sneak off to the fields without his wife seeing. He told the girl he would kill her if she told. What could she do? She told a lie about ripping her dress in the barn when she was feeding the stock. I remember now that she was a bound girl and did not know where her father and mother were. Maybe she did not have any father. You know what I mean.

Such bound children were often enough cruelly treated. They were children who had no parents, slaves really. There were very few orphan homes then. They were legally bound into some home. It was a matter of pure luck how it came out.

## II

She married Jake and had a son and daughter, but the daughter died.

Then she settled down to feed stock. That was her job. At the

German's place she had cooked the food for the German and his wife. The wife was a strong woman with big hips and worked most of the time in the fields with her husband. She fed them and fed the cows in the barn, fed the pigs, the horses and the chickens. Every moment of every day, as a young girl, was spent feeding something.

Then she married Jake Grimes and he had to be fed. She was a slight thing, and when she had been married for three or four years, and after the two children were born, her slender shoulders became stooped.

Jake always had a lot of big dogs around the house, that stood near the unused sawmill near the creek. He was always trading horses when he wasn't stealing something and had a lot of poor bony ones about. Also he kept three or four pigs and a cow. They were all pastured in the few acres left of the Grimes place and Jake did little enough work.

He went into debt for a threshing outfit and ran it for several years, but it did not pay. People did not trust him. They were afraid he would steal the grain at night. He had to go a long way off to get work and it cost too much to get there. In the winter he hunted and cut a little firewood, to be sold in some nearby town. When the son grew up he was just like the father. They got drunk together. If there wasn't anything to eat in the house when they came home the old man gave his old woman a cut over the head. She had a few chickens of her own and had to kill one of them in a hurry. When they were all killed she wouldn't have any eggs to sell when she went to town, and then what would she do?

She had to scheme all her life about getting things fed, getting the pigs fed so they would grow fat and could be butchered in the fall. When they were butchered her husband took most of the meat off to town and sold it. If he did not do it first the boy did. They fought sometimes and when they fought the old woman stood aside trembling.

She had got the habit of silence anyway—that was fixed. Sometimes, when she began to look old—she wasn't forty yet—and when the husband and son were both off, trading horses or drinking or hunting or stealing, she went around the house and the barnyard muttering to herself.

How was she going to get everything fed?—that was her problem. The dogs had to be fed. There wasn't enough hay in the barn for the horses and the cow. If she didn't feed the chickens how could they lay eggs? Without eggs to sell how could she get things in town, things she had to have to keep the life of the farm going? Thank heaven, she did not have to feed her husband—in a certain way. That hadn't lasted long after their marriage and after the babies came. Where he went on his long trips she did not know. Sometimes he was gone from home for weeks, and after the boy grew up they went off together.

They left everything at home for her to manage and she had no money. She knew no one. No one ever talked to her in town. When it was winter she had to gather sticks of wood for her fire, had to try to keep the stock fed with very little grain.

The stock in the barn cried to her hungrily, the dogs followed her about. In the winter the hens laid few enough eggs. They huddled in the corners of the barn and she kept watching them. If a hen lays an egg in the barn in winter and you do not find it, it freezes and breaks.

One day in winter the old woman went off to town with a few eggs and the dogs followed her. She did not get started until nearly three o'clock and the snow was heavy. She hadn't been feeling very well for several days and so she went muttering along, scantily clad, her shoulders stooped. She had an old grain bag in which she carried her eggs, tucked away down in the bottom. There weren't many of them, but in winter the price of eggs is up. She would get a little meat in exchange for the eggs, some salt pork, a little sugar, and some coffee perhaps. It might be the butcher would give her a piece of liver.

When she had got to town and was trading in her eggs the dogs lay by the door outside. She did pretty well, got the things she needed, more than she had hoped. Then she went to the butcher and he gave her some liver and some dog-meat.

It was the first time anyone had spoken to her in a friendly way for a long time. The butcher was alone in his shop when she came in and was annoyed by the thought of such a sick-looking woman out on such a day. It was bitter cold and the snow, that had let up during the afternoon, was falling again. The butcher said something about her husband and her son, swore at them, and the old woman stared at him, a look of mild surprise in her eyes as he talked. He said that if either the husband or the son were going to get any of the liver or the heavy bones with scraps of meat hanging to them that he had put into the grain bag, he'd see him starve first.

Starve, eh? Well, things had to be fed. Men had to be fed, and the horses that weren't any good but maybe could be traded off, and the poor thin cow that hadn't given any milk for three months.

Horses, cows, pigs, dogs, men.

## III

The old woman had to get back before darkness came if she could. The dogs followed at her heels, sniffing at the heavy grain bag she had fastened on her back. When she got to the edge of town she stopped by a fence and tied the bag on her back with a piece of rope she had carried in her dress-pocket for just that purpose. That was an easier way to carry it. Her arms ached. It was hard when she had to crawl over fences and once she fell over and landed in the snow. The dogs went frisking about. She had to struggle to get to her feet again, but she made it. The point of climbing over the fences was that there was a short cut over a hill and through a woods. She might have gone around by the road, but it was a mile farther that way. She was afraid she couldn't make it. And then, besides, the stock had to be fed. There was a little hay left and a little corn. Perhaps her husband and son would bring some home when they came. They had driven off in the only buggy the Grimes family had, a rickety thing, a rickety horse hitched to the buggy, two other rickety horses led by halters. They might come home drunk. It would be well to have something in the house when they came back.

The son had an affair on with a woman at the county seat, fifteen miles away. She was a rough enough woman, a tough one. Once, in the summer, the son had brought her to the house. Both she and the son had been drinking. Jake Grimes was away and the son and his woman ordered the old woman about like a servant. She didn't mind much; she was used to it. Whatever happened she never said anything. That was her way of getting along. She had managed that way when she was a young girl at the German's and ever since she had married Jake. That time her son brought his woman to the house they stayed all night, sleeping together just as though they were married. It hadn't shocked the old woman, not much. She had got past being shocked early in life.

With the pack on her back she went painfully along across an open field, wading in the deep snow, and got into the woods.

There was a path, but it was hard to follow. Just beyond the top of the hill, where the woods was thickest, there was a small clearing. Had someone once thought of building a house there? The clearing was as large as a building lot in town, large enough for a house and a garden. The path ran along the side of the clearing, and when she got there the old woman sat down to rest at the foot of a tree.

It was a foolish thing to do. When she got herself placed, the pack against the tree's trunk, it was nice, but what about getting up again? She worried about that for a moment and then quietly closed her eyes.

She must have slept for a time. When you are about so cold you can't get any colder. The afternoon grew a little warmer and the snow came thicker than ever. Then after a time the weather cleared. The moon even came out.

There were four Grimes dogs that had followed Mrs. Grimes into town, all tall gaunt fellows. Such men as Jake Grimes and his son always keep such dogs. They kick and abuse them, but they stay. The Grimes dogs, in order to keep from starving, had to do a lot of foraging for themselves, and they had been at it while the old woman slept with her back to the tree at the side of the clearing. They had been chasing rabbits in the woods and in adjoining fields and in their ranging had picked up three other farm dogs.

After a time all the dogs came back to the clearing. They were excited about something. Such nights, cold and clear and with a moon, do things to dogs. It may be that some old instinct, come down from the time when they were wolves and ranged the woods in packs on winter nights, comes back into them.

The dogs in the clearing, before the old woman, had caught two or three rabbits and their immediate hunger had been satisfied. They began to play, running in circles in the clearing. Round and round they ran, each dog's nose at the tail of the next dog. In the clearing, under the snow-laden trees and under the wintry moon they made a strange picture, running thus silently, in a circle their running had beaten in the soft snow. The dogs made no sound. They ran around and around in the circle.

It may have been that the old woman saw them doing that before she died. She may have awakened once or twice and looked at the strange sight with dim old eyes.

She wouldn't be very cold now, just drowsy. Life hangs on a long time. Perhaps the old woman was out of her head. She may have dreamed of her girlhood, at the German's and before that, when she was a child and before her mother lit out and left her.

Her dreams couldn't have been very pleasant. Not many pleasant things had happened to her. Now and then one of the Grimes dogs left the running circle and came to stand before her. The dog thrust his face close to her face. His red tongue was hanging out.

The running of the dogs may have been a kind of death ceremony. It may have been that the primitive instinct of the wolf, having been aroused in the dogs by the night and the running, made them somehow afraid.

"Now we are no longer wolves. We are dogs, the servants of men. Keep alive, man! When man dies we become wolves again."

When one of the dogs came to where the old woman sat with her back against the tree and thrust his nose close to her face he seemed satisfied and went back to run with the pack. All the Grimes dogs did it at some time during the evening, before she died. I knew all about it afterward, when I grew to be a man, because once in a woods in Illinois, on another winter night, I saw a pack of dogs act just like that. The dogs were waiting for me to die as they had waited for the old woman that night when I was a child, but when it happened to me I was a young man and had no intention whatever of dying.

The old woman died softly and quietly. When she was dead and when one of the Grimes dogs had come to her and had found her dead all the dogs stopped running.

They gathered about her.

Well, she was dead now. She had fed the Grimes dogs when she was alive, what about now?

There was the pack on her back, the grain bag containing the piece of salt pork, the liver the butcher had given her, the dog-meat, the soup bones. The butcher in town, having been suddenly overcome with a feeling of pity, had loaded her grain bag heavily. It had been a big haul for the old woman.

It was a big haul for the dogs now.

## IV

One of the Grimes dogs sprang suddenly out from among the others and began worrying the pack on the old woman's back. Had the dogs really been wolves that one would have been the leader of the pack. What he did, all the others did.

All of them sank their teeth into the grain bag the old woman had fastened with ropes to her back.

They dragged the old woman's body out into the open clearing. The wornout dress was quickly torn from her shoulders. When she was found, a day or two later, the dress had been torn from her body clear to the hips, but the dogs had not touched her body. They had got the meat out of the grain bag, that was all. Her body was frozen stiff when it was found, and the shoulders were so narrow and the body so slight that in death it looked like the body of some charming young girl.

Such things happened in towns of the Middle West, on farms near town, when I was a boy. A hunter out after rabbits found the old woman's body and did not touch it. Something, the beaten round path in the little snow-covered clearing, the silence of the place, the place where the dogs had worried the body trying to pull the grain bag away to tear it open—something startled the man and he hurried off to town.

I was in Main Street with one of my brothers who was town newsboy and who was taking the afternoon papers to the stores. It was almost night.

The hunter came into a grocery and told his story. Then he went to a hardware shop and into a drugstore. Men began to gather on the sidewalks. Then they started out along the road to the place in the woods.

My brother should have gone on about his business of distributing papers but he didn't. Everyone was going to the woods. The undertaker went and the town marshal. Several men got on a dray and rode out to where the path left the road and went into the woods, but the horses weren't very sharply shod and slid about on the slippery roads. They made no better time than those of us who walked.

The town marshal was a large man whose leg had been injured in the Civil War. He carried a heavy cane and limped rapidly along the road. My brother and I followed at his heels, and as we went other men and boys joined the crowd.

It had grown dark by the time we got to where the old woman had left the road but the moon had come out. The marshal was thinking there might have been a murder. He kept asking the hunter questions.

The hunter went along with his gun across his shoulders, a dog following at his heels. It isn't often a rabbit hunter has a chance to be so conspicuous. He was taking full advantage of it, leading the procession with the town marshal. "I didn't see any wounds. She was a beautiful young girl. Her face was buried in the snow. No, I didn't know her." As a matter of fact, the hunter had not looked closely at the body. He had been frightened. She might have been murdered and someone might spring out from behind a tree and murder him. In a woods, in the late afternoon, when the trees are all bare and there is white snow on the ground, when all is silent, something creepy steals over the mind and body. If something strange or uncanny has happened in the neighborhood all you think about is getting away from there as fast as you can.

The crowd of men and boys had got to where the old woman had crossed the field and went, following the marshal and the hunter, up the slight incline and into the woods.

My brother and I were silent. He had his bundle of papers in a bag slung across his shoulder. When he got back to town he would have to go on distributing his papers before he went home to supper. If I went along, as he had no doubt already determined I should, we would both be late. Either mother or our older sister would have to warm our supper.

Well, we would have something to tell. A boy did not get such a chance very often. It was lucky we just happened to go into the grocery when the hunter came in. The hunter was a country fellow. Neither of us had ever seen him before.

Now the crowd of men and boys had got to the clearing. Darkness comes quickly on such winter nights, but the full moon made everything clear. My brother and I stood near the tree, beneath which the old woman had died.

She did not look old, lying there in that light, frozen and still. One of the men turned her over in the snow and I saw everything. My body trembled with some strange mystical feeling and so did my brother's. It might have been the cold.

Neither of us had ever seen a woman's body before. It may have been the snow, clinging to the frozen flesh, that made it look so white and lovely, so like marble. No woman had come with the party from town; but one of the men, he was the town blacksmith, took off his overcoat and spread it over her. Then he gathered her into his arms and started off to town, all the others following silently. At that time no one knew who she was.

## V

I had seen everything, had seen the oval in the snow, like a miniature race track, where the dogs had run, had seen how the men were mystified, had seen the white bare young-looking shoulders, had heard the whispered comments of the men.

The men were simply mystified. They took the body to the undertaker's, and when the blacksmith, the hunter, the marshal and several others had got inside they closed the door. If father had been there perhaps he could have got in, but we boys couldn't.

I went with my brother to distribute the rest of his papers and when we got home it was my brother who told the story.

I kept silent and went to bed early. It may have been I was not satisfied with the way he told it.

Later, in the town, I must have heard other fragments of the old woman's story. She was recognized the next day and there was an investigation.

The husband and son were found somewhere and brought to town and there was an attempt to connect them with the woman's death, but it did not work. They had perfect enough alibis.

However, the town was against them. They had to get out. Where they went I never heard.

I remember only the picture there in the forest, the men standing about, the naked girlish-looking figure, face down in the snow, the tracks made by the running dogs and the clear cold winter sky above. White fragments of clouds were drifting across the sky. They went racing across the little open space among the trees.

The scene in the forest had become for me, without my knowing it, the foundation for the real story I am now trying to tell. The fragments, you see, had to be picked up slowly, long afterwards.

Things happened. When I was a young man I worked on the farm of a German. The hired-girl was afraid of her employer. The farmer's wife hated her.

I saw things at that place. Once later, I had a half-uncanny, mystical adventure with dogs in an Illinois forest on a clear, moonlit winter night. When I was a schoolboy, and on a summer day, I went with a boy friend out along a creek some miles from town and came to the house where the old woman had lived. No one had lived in the house since her death. The doors were broken from the hinges; the window lights were all broken. As the boy and I stood in the road outside, two dogs, just roving farm dogs no doubt, came running around the corner of the house. The dogs were tall, gaunt fellows and came down to the fence and glared through at us, standing in the road.

The whole thing, the story of the old woman's death, was to me as I grew older like music heard from far off. The notes had to be picked up slowly one at a time. Something had to be understood.

The woman who died was one destined to feed animal life. Anyway, that is all she ever did. She was feeding animal life before she was born, as a child, as a young woman working on the farm of the German, after she married, when she grew old and when she died. She fed animal life in cows, in chickens, in pigs, in horses, in dogs, in men. Her daughter had died in childhood and with her one son she had no articulate relations. On the night when she died she was hurrying homeward, bearing on her body food for animal life.

She died in the clearing in the woods and even after her death continued feeding animal life.

You see it is likely that, when my brother told the story, that night when we got home and my mother and sister sat listening, I did not think he got the point. He was too young and so was I. A thing so complete has its own beauty.

I shall not try to emphasize the point. I am only explaining why I was dissatisfied then and have been ever since. I speak of that only that you may understand why I have been impelled to try to tell the simple story over again.

# The Pupil

## HENRY JAMES

### I

THE POOR young man hesitated and procrastinated: it cost him such an effort to broach the subject of terms, to speak of money to a person who spoke only of feelings and, as it were, of the aristocracy. Yet he was unwilling to take leave, treating his engagement as settled, without some more conventional glance in that direction than he could find an opening for in the manner of the large affable lady who sat there drawing a pair of soiled *gants de Suède* through a fat jewelled hand and, at once pressing and gliding, repeated over and over everything but the thing he would have liked to hear. He would have liked to hear the figure of his salary; but just as he was nervously about to sound that note the little boy came back—the little boy Mrs. Moreen had sent out of the room to fetch her fan. He came back without the fan, only with the casual observation that he couldn't find it. As he dropped this cynical confession he looked straight and hard at the candidate for the honour of taking his education in hand. This personage reflected somewhat grimly that the first thing he should have to teach his little charge would be to appear to address himself to his mother when he spoke to her—especially not to make her such an improper answer as that.

When Mrs. Moreen bethought herself of this pretext for getting rid of their companion Pemberton supposed it was precisely to approach the delicate subject of his remuneration. But it had been only to say some things about her son that it was better a boy of eleven shouldn't catch. They were extravagantly to his advantage save when she lowered her voice to sigh, tapping her left side familiarly, "And all over-

clouded by *this,* you know; all at the mercy of a weakness—!"
Pemberton gathered that the weakness was in the region of the heart.
He had known the poor child was not robust: this was the basis on
which he had been invited to treat, through an English lady, an Oxford acquaintance, then at Nice, who happened to know both his
needs and those of the amiable American family looking out for something really superior in the way of a resident tutor.

The young man's impression of his prospective pupil, who had come
into the room as if to see for himself the moment Pemberton was
admitted, was not quite the soft solicitation the visitor had taken for
granted. Morgan Moreen was somehow sickly without being "delicate,"
and that he looked intelligent—it is true Pemberton would have enjoyed his being stupid—only added to the suggestion that, as with his
big mouth and big ears he really couldn't be called pretty, he might
too utterly fail to please. Pemberton was modest, was even timid; and
the chance that his small scholar would prove cleverer than himself
had quite figured, to his anxiety, among the dangers of an untried
experiment. He reflected, however, that these were risks one had to
run when one accepted a position, as it was called, in a private family;
when as yet one's university honours had, pecuniarily speaking, remained barren. At any rate when Mrs. Moreen got up as to intimate
that, since it was understood he would enter upon his duties within
the week she would let him off now, he succeeded, in spite of the
presence of the child, in squeezing out a phrase about the rate of payment. It was not the fault of the conscious smile which seemed a
reference to the lady's expensive identity, it was not the fault of this
demonstration, which had, in a sort, both vagueness and point, if the
allusion didn't sound rather vulgar. This was exactly because she became still more gracious to reply: "Oh I can assure you that all that
will be quite regular."

Pemberton only wondered, while he took up his hat, what "all that"
was to amount to—people had such different ideas. Mrs. Moreen's
words, however, seemed to commit the family to a pledge definite
enough to elicit from the child a strange little comment in the shape
of the mocking foreign ejaculation "Oh la-la!"

Pemberton, in some confusion, glanced at him as he walked slowly
to the window with his back turned, his hands in his pockets and the
air in his elderly shoulders of a boy who didn't play. The young man
wondered if he should be able to teach him to play, though his mother

had said it would never do that this was why school was impossible. Mrs. Moreen exhibited no discomfiture; she only continued blandly: "Mr. Moreen will be delighted to meet your wishes. As I told you, he has been called to London for a week. As soon as he comes back you shall have it out with him."

This was so frank and friendly that the young man could only reply, laughing as his hostess laughed: "Oh I don't imagine we shall have much of a battle."

"They'll give you anything you like," the boy remarked unexpectedly, returning from the window. "We don't mind what anything costs—we live awfully well."

"My darling, you're too quaint!" his mother exclaimed, putting out to caress him a practised but ineffectual hand. He slipped out of it, but looked with intelligent innocent eyes at Pemberton, who had already had time to notice that from one moment to the other his small satiric face seemed to change its time of life. At this moment it was infantine, yet it appeared also to be under the influence of curious intuitions and knowledges. Pemberton rather disliked precocity and was disappointed to find gleams of it in a disciple not yet in his teens. Nevertheless he divined on the spot that Morgan wouldn't prove a bore. He would prove on the contrary a source of agitation. This idea held the young man, in spite of a certain repulsion.

"You pompous little person! We're not extravagant!" Mrs. Moreen gaily protested, making another unsuccessful attempt to draw the boy to her side. "You must know what to expect," she went on to Pemberton.

"The less you expect the better!" her companion interposed. "But we *are* people of fashion."

"Only so far as *you* make us so!" Mrs. Moreen tenderly mocked. "Well then, on Friday—don't tell me you're superstitious—and mind you don't fail us. Then you'll see us all. I'm so sorry the girls are out. I guess you'll like the girls. And, you know, I've another son, quite different from this one."

"He tries to imitate me," Morgan said to their friend.

"He tries? Why he's twenty years old!" cried Mrs. Moreen.

"You're very witty," Pemberton remarked to the child—a proposition his mother echoed with enthusiasm, declaring Morgan's sallies to be the delight of the house.

The boy paid no heed to this; he only enquired abruptly of the visitor, who was surprised afterwards that he hadn't struck him as offensively forward: "Do you *want* very much to come?"

"Can you doubt it after such a description of what I shall hear?" Pemberton replied. Yet he didn't want to come at all; he was coming because he had to go somewhere, thanks to the collapse of his fortune at the end of a year abroad spent on the system of putting his scant patrimony into a single full wave of experience. He had had his full wave but couldn't pay the score at his inn. Moreover he had caught in the boy's eyes the glimpse of a far-off appeal.

"Well, I'll do the best I can for you," said Morgan; with which he turned away again. He passed out of one of the long windows; Pemberton saw him go and lean on the parapet of the terrace. He remained there while the young man took leave of his mother, who, on Pemberton's looking as if he expected a farewell from him interposed with: "Leave him, leave him; he's so strange!" Pemberton supposed her to fear something he might say. "He's a genius—you'll love him," she added. "He's much the most interesting person in the family." And before he could invent some civility to oppose to this she wound up with: "But we're all good, you know!"

"He's a genius—you'll love him!" were words that recurred to our aspirant before the Friday, suggesting among many things that geniuses were not invariably loveable. However, it was all the better if there was an element that would make tutorship absorbing: he had perhaps taken too much for granted it would only disgust him. As he left the villa after his interview he looked up at the balcony and saw the child leaning over it. "We shall have great larks!" he called up.

Morgan hung fire a moment and then gaily returned: "By the time you come back I shall have thought of something witty!"

This made Pemberton say to himself "After all he's rather nice."

## II

On the Friday he saw them all, as Mrs. Moreen had promised, for her husband had come back and the girls and the other son were at home. Mr. Moreen had a white moustache, a confiding manner and, in his buttonhole, the ribbon of a foreign order—bestowed, as Pemberton eventually learned, for services. For what services he never clearly ascertained: this was a point—one of a larger number—that Mr. Moreen's manner never confided. What it emphatically did confide was that he was even more a man of the world than you might first make out. Ulick, the firstborn, was in visible training for the same profession—under the disadvantage as yet, however, of a buttonhole but feebly floral and a moustache with no pretensions to type. The girls had hair and figures and manners and small fat feet, but had never been out alone. As for Mrs. Moreen, Pemberton saw on a nearer view that her elegance was intermittent and her parts didn't always match. Her husband, as she had promised, met with enthusiasm Pemberton's ideas in regard to a salary. The young man had endeavoured to keep these stammerings modest, and Mr. Moreen made it no secret that *he* found them wanting in "style." He further mentioned that he aspired to be intimate with his children, to be their best friend, and that he was always looking out for them. That was what he went off for, to London and other places—to look out; and this vigilance was the theory of life, as well as the real occupation, of the whole family. They all looked out, for they were very frank on the subject of its being necessary. They desired it to be understood that they were earnest people, and also that their fortune, though quite adequate for earnest people, required the most careful administration. Mr. Moreen, as the parent bird, sought sustenance for the nest. Ulick invoked support mainly at the club, where Pemberton guessed that it was usually served on green cloth. The girls used to do up their hair and their frocks themselves, and our young man felt appealed to to be glad, in regard to Morgan's education, that, though it must naturally be of the best, it didn't cost too much. After a little he *was* glad, forgetting at times his own needs in the interest inspired by the child's character and culture and the pleasure of making easy terms for him.

During the first weeks of their acquaintance Morgan had been as puzzling as a page in an unknown language—altogether different from the obvious little Anglo-Saxons who had misrepresented childhood to Pemberton. Indeed the whole mystic volume in which the boy had been amateurishly bound demanded some practice in translation. Today, after a considerable interval, there is something phantasmagoric, like a prismatic reflexion or a serial novel, in Pemberton's memory of the queerness of the Moreens. If it were not for a few tangible tokens—a lock of Morgan's hair cut by his own hand, and the half-dozen letters received from him when they were disjoined— the whole episode and the figures peopling it would seem too inconsequent for anything but dreamland. Their supreme quaintness was their success—as it appeared to him for a while at the time; since he had never seen a family so brilliantly equipped for failure. Wasn't it success to have drawn him in that first morning at déjeuner, the Friday he came—it was enough to *make* one superstitious—so that he utterly committed himself, and this not by calculation or on a signal, but from a happy instinct which made them, like a band of gipsies, work so neatly together? They amused him as much as if they had really been a band of gipsies. He was still young and had not seen much of the world—his English years had been properly arid; therefore the reversed conventions of the Moreens—for they had *their* desperate properties—struck him as topsy-turvy. He had encountered nothing like them at Oxford; still less had any such note been struck to his younger American ear during the four years at Yale in which he had richly supposed himself to be reacting against a Puritan strain. The reaction of the Moreens, at any rate, went ever so much further. He had thought himself very sharp that first day in hitting them all off in his mind with the "cosmopolite" label. Later it seemed feeble and colourless—confessedly helplessly provisional.

He yet when he first applied it felt a glow of joy—for an instructor he was still empirical—rise from the apprehension that living with them would really be to see life. Their sociable strangeness was an imitation of that—their chatter of tongues, their gaiety and good humour, their infinite dawdling (they were always getting themselves up, but it took for ever, and Pemberton had once found Mr. Moreen shaving in the drawingroom), their French, their Italian and cropping up in the foreign fluencies, their cold tough slices of American. They lived on macaroni and coffee—they had these articles prepared in perfection—but they knew recipes for a hundred other dishes. They overflowed with music and song, were always humming and catching each other up, and had a sort of professional acquaintance with Continental cities. They talked of "good places" as if they had been pickpockets or strolling players. They had at Nice a villa, a carriage, a piano and a banjo, and they went to official parties. They were a perfect calendar of the "days" of their friends, which Pemberton knew them, when they were indisposed, to get out of bed to go to, and which made the week larger than life when Mrs. Moreen talked of them with Paula and Amy. Their initiations gave their new inmate at first an almost dazzling sense of culture. Mrs. Moreen had translated something at some former period—an author whom it made

Pemberton feel *borné* never to have heard of. They could imitate
Venetian and sing Neapolitan, and when they wanted to say something very particular communicated with each other in an ingenious
dialect of their own, an elastic spoken cipher which Pemberton at first
took for some patois of one of their countries, but which he "caught
on to" as he would not have grasped provincial development of Spanish or German.

"It's the family language—Ultramoreen," Morgan explained to him
drolly enough; but the boy rarely condescended to use it himself,
though he dealt in colloquial Latin as if he had been a little prelate.

Among the "days" with which Mrs. Moreen's memory was taxed
she managed to squeeze in one of her own, which her friends sometimes forgot. But the house drew a frequented air from the number
of fine people who were freely named there and from several mysterious men with foreign titles and English clothes whom Morgan
called the Princes and who, on sofas with the girls, talked French
very loud—though sometimes with some oddity of accent—as if to
show they were saying nothing improper. Pemberton wondered how
the Princes could ever propose in that tone and so publicly: he took
for granted cynically that this was what was desired of them. Then
he recognized that even for the chance of such an advantage Mrs.
Moreen would never allow Paula and Amy to receive alone. These
young ladies were not at all timid, but it was just the safeguards that
made them so candidly free. It was a houseful of Bohemians who
wanted tremendously to be Philistines.

In one respect, however, certainly, they achieved no rigour—they
were wonderfully amiable and ecstatic about Morgan. It was a genuine
tenderness, an artless admiration, equally strong in each. They even
praised his beauty, which was small, and were as afraid of him as if
they felt him of finer clay. They spoke of him as a little angel and a
prodigy—they touched on his want of health with long vague faces.
Pemberton feared at first an extravagance that might make him hate
the boy, but before this happened he had become extravagant himself.
Later, when he had grown rather to hate the others, it was a bribe to
patience for him that they were at any rate nice about Morgan, going
on tiptoe if they fancied he was showing symptoms, and even giving
up somebody's "day" to procure him a pleasure. Mixed with this too
was the oddest wish to make him independent, as if they had felt
themselves not good enough for him. They passed him over to the

new members of their circle very much as if wishing to force some
charity of adoption on so free an agent and get rid of their own charge.
They were delighted when they saw Morgan take so to his kind play-
fellow, and could think of no higher praise for the young man. It
was strange how they contrived to reconcile the appearance, and indeed the essential fact, of adoring the child with their eagerness to
wash their hands of him. Did they want to get rid of him before he
should find them out? Pemberton was finding them out month by
month. The boy's fond family, however this might be, turned their
backs with exaggerated delicacy, as if to avoid the reproach of inter-
fering. Seeing in time how little he had in common with them—it
was by *them* he first observed it; they proclaimed it with complete
humility—his companion was moved to speculate on the mysteries of
transmission, the far jumps of heredity. Where his detachment from
most of the things they represented had come from was more than
an observer could say—it certainly had burrowed under two or three
generations.

As for Pemberton's own estimate of his pupil, it was a good while
before he got the point of view, so little had he been prepared for it
by the smug young barbarians to whom the tradition of tutorship, as
hitherto revealed to him, had been adjusted. Morgan was scrappy and
surprising, deficient in many properties supposed common to the *genus*
and abounding in others that were the portion only of the supernaturally clever. One day his friend made a great stride: it cleared
up the question to perceive that Morgan *was* supernaturally clever and
that, though the formula was temporarily meagre, this would be the
only assumption on which one could successfully deal with him. He
had the general quality of a child for whom life had not been simpli-
fied by school, a kind of homebred sensibility which might have been
bad for himself but was charming for others, and a whole range of
refinement and perception—little musical vibrations as taking as
picked-up airs—begotten by wandering about Europe at the tail of
his migratory tribe. This might not have been an education to recom-
mend in advance, but its results with so special a subject were as ap-
preciable as the marks on a piece of fine porcelain. There was at the
same time in him a small strain of stoicism, doubtless the fruit of
having had to begin early to bear pain, which counted for pluck and
made it of less consequence that he might have been thought at school
rather a polyglot little beast. Pemberton indeed quickly found himself

rejoicing that school was out of the question: in any million of boys
it was probably good for all but one, and Morgan was that millionth.
It would have made him comparative and superior—it might have
made him really require kicking. Pemberton would try to be school
himself—a bigger seminary than five hundred grazing donkeys, so
that, winning no prizes, the boy would remain unconscious and ir-
responsible and amusing—amusing, because, though life was already
intense in his childish nature, freshness still made there a strong
draught for jokes. It turned out that even in the still air of Morgan's
various disabilities jokes flourished greatly. He was a pale lean acute
undeveloped little cosmopolite, who liked intellectual gymnastics and
who also, as regards the behaviour of mankind, had noticed more
things than you might suppose, but who nevertheless had his proper
playroom of superstitions, where he smashed a dozen toys a day.

### III

At Nice once, toward evening, as the pair rested in the open air
after a walk, and looked over the sea at the pink western lights, he
said suddenly to his comrade: "Do you like it, you know—being with
us all in this intimate way?"

"My dear fellow, why should I stay if I didn't?"

"How do I know you'll stay? I'm almost sure you won't, very long."

"I hope you don't mean to dismiss me," said Pemberton.

Morgan debated, looking at the sunset. "I think if I did right I
ought to."

"Well, I know I'm supposed to instruct you in virtue; but in that
case don't do right."

"You're very young—fortunately," Morgan went on, turning to him
again.

"Oh yes, compared with you!"

"Therefore it won't matter so much if you do lose a lot of time."

"That's the way to look at it," said Pemberton accommodatingly.

They were silent a minute; after which the boy asked: "Do you like
my father and my mother very much?"

"Dear me, yes. Charming people."

Morgan received this with another silence; then unexpectedly, familiarly, but at the same time affectionately, he remarked: "You're a
jolly old humbug!"

For a particular reason the words made our young man change colour. The boy noticed in an instant that he had turned red, whereupon he turned red himself and pupil and master exchanged a longish glance in which there was a consciousness of many more things than are usually touched upon, even tacitly, in such a relation. It produced for Pemberton an embarrassment; it raised in a shadowy form a question—this was the first glimpse of it—destined to play a singular and, as he imagined, owing to the altogether peculiar conditions, an unprecedented part in his intercourse with his little companion. Later, when he found himself talking with the youngster in a way in which few youngsters could ever have been talked with, he thought of that clumsy moment on the bench at Nice as the dawn of an understanding that had broadened. What had added to the clumsiness then was that he thought it his duty to declare to Morgan that he might abuse him, Pemberton, as much as he liked, but must never abuse his parents. To this Morgan had the easy retort that he hadn't dreamed of abusing them; which appeared to be true: it put Pemberton in the wrong.

"Then why am I a humbug for saying *I* think them charming?" the young man asked, conscious of a certain rashness.

"Well—they're not your parents."

"They love you better than anything in the world—never forget that," said Pemberton.

"Is that why you like them so much?"

"They're very kind to me," Pemberton replied evasively.

"You *are* a humbug!" laughed Morgan, passing an arm into his tutor's. He leaned against him looking off at the sea again and swinging his long thin legs.

"Don't kick my shins," said Pemberton while he reflected "Hang it, I can't complain of them to the child!"

"There's another reason too," Morgan went on, keeping his legs still.

"Another reason for what?"

"Besides their not being your parents."

"I don't understand you," said Pemberton.

"Well, you will before long. All right!"

He did understand fully before long, but he made a fight even with himself before he confessed it. He thought it the oddest thing to have a struggle with the child about. He wondered he didn't hate the hope of the Moreens for bringing the struggle on. But by the time it began any such sentiment for that scion was closed to him. Morgan was a special case, and to know him was to accept him on his own odd terms. Pemberton had spent his aversion to special cases before arriving at knowledge. When at last he did arrive his quandary was great. Against every interest he had attached himself. They would have to meet things together. Before they went home that evening at Nice the boy had said, clinging to his arm:

"Well, at any rate you'll hang on to the last."

"To the last?"

"Till you're fairly beaten."

"*You* ought to be fairly beaten!" cried the young man, drawing him closer.

## IV

A year after he had come to live with them Mr. and Mrs. Moreen suddenly gave up the villa at Nice. Pemberton had got used to suddenness, having seen it practised on a considerable scale during two jerky little tours—one in Switzerland the first summer, and the other late in the winter, when they all ran down to Florence and then, at the end of ten days, liking it much less than they had intended, straggled back in mysterious depression. They had returned to Nice "for ever," as they said; but this didn't prevent their squeezing, one rainy muggy May night, into a second-class railway-carriage—you could never tell by which class they would travel—where Pemberton helped them to stow away a wonderful collection of bundles and bags. The explanation of this manoeuvre was that they had determined to spend the summer "in some bracing place"; but in Paris they dropped into a small furnished apartment—a fourth floor in a third-rate avenue, where there was a smell on the staircase and the *portier* was hateful—and passed the next four months in blank indigence.

The better part of this baffled sojourn was for the preceptor and his pupil, who, visiting the Invalides and Notre Dame, the Conciergerie and all the museums, took a hundred remunerative rambles. They learned to know their Paris, which was useful, for they came back another year for a longer stay, the general character of which in Pemberton's memory to-day mixed pitiably and confusedly with that of the first. He sees Morgan's shabby knickerbockers—the everlasting pair that didn't match his blouse and that as he grew longer could only grow faded. He remembers the particular holes in his three or four pairs of coloured stockings.

Morgan was dear to his mother, but he never was better dressed than was absolutely necessary—partly, no doubt, by his own fault, for he was as indifferent to his appearance as a German philosopher. "My dear fellow, you *are* coming to pieces," Pemberton would say to him in sceptical remonstrance; to which the child would reply, looking at him serenely up and down: "My dear fellow, so are you! I don't want to cast you in the shade." Pemberton could have no rejoinder for this —the assertion so closely represented the fact. If however the deficiencies of his own wardrobe were a chapter by themselves he didn't like his little charge to look too poor. Later he used to say "Well, if we're poor, why, after all, shouldn't we look it?" and he consoled himself with thinking there was something rather elderly and gentlemanly in Morgan's disrepair—it differed from the untidiness of the urchin who plays and spoils his things. He could trace perfectly the degrees by which, in proportion as her little son confined himself to his tutor for society, Mrs. Moreen shrewdly forbore to renew his garments. She did nothing that didn't show, neglected him because he escaped notice, and then, as he illustrated this clever policy, discouraged at home his public appearances. Her position was logical enough—those members of her family who did show had to be showy.

During this period and several others Pemberton was quite aware of how he and his comrade might strike people; wandering languidly through the Jardin des Plantes as if they had nowhere to go, sitting on the winter days in the galleries of the Louvre, so splendidly ironical to the homeless, as if for the advantage of the *calorifère*. They joked about it sometimes: it was the sort of joke that was perfectly within the boy's compass. They figured themselves as part of the vast vague hand-to-mouth multitude of the enormous city and pretended they were proud of their position in it—it showed them "such a lot of life" and made them conscious of a democratic brotherhood. If Pemberton couldn't feel a sympathy in destitution with his small companion—for after all Morgan's fond parents would never have let him really suffer —the boy would at least feel it with him, so it came to the same thing. He used sometimes to wonder what people would think they were— to fancy they were looked askance at, as if it might be a suspected case of kidnapping. Morgan wouldn't be taken for a young patrician with a preceptor—he wasn't smart enough; though he might pass for his companion's sickly little brother. Now and then he had a five-franc piece, and except once, when they bought a couple of lovely neckties, one of which he made Pemberton accept, they laid it out scientifically in old books. This was sure to be a great day, always spent on the quays, in a rummage of the dusty boxes that garnish the parapets. Such occasions helped them to live, for their books ran low very soon after the beginning of their acquaintance. Pemberton had a good many in England, but he was obliged to write to a friend and ask him kindly to get some fellow to give him something for them.

If they had to relinquish that summer the advantage of the bracing climate the young man couldn't but suspect this failure of the cup when at their very lips to have been the effect of a rude jostle of his own. This had represented his first blow-out, as he called it, with his patrons; his first successful attempt—though there was little other success about it—to bring them to a consideration of his impossible position. As the ostensible eve of a costly journey the moment had struck him as favourable to an earnest protest, the presentation of an ultimatum. Ridiculous as it sounded, he had never yet been able to compass an uninterrupted private interview with the elder pair or with either of them singly. They were always flanked by their elder children, and poor Pemberton usually had his own little charge at his side. He was conscious of its being a house in which the surface of one's delicacy got rather smudged; nevertheless he had preserved the bloom of his scruple against announcing to Mr. and Mrs. Moreen with publicity that he shouldn't be able to go on longer without a little money. He was still simple enough to suppose Ulick and Paula and Amy might not know that since his arrival he had only had a hundred and forty francs; and he was magnanimous enough to wish not to compromise their parents in their eyes. Mr. Moreen now listened to him, as he listened to every one and to everything, like a man of the world, and seemed to appeal to him—though not of course too grossly—to try and be a little more of one himself. Pemberton recognised in fact the importance of the character—from the advantage it gave Mr. Moreen. He was not even confused or embarrassed, whereas the young man in his service was more so than there was any reason for. Neither was he surprised—at least any more than a gentleman had to be who freely confessed himself a little shocked—though not perhaps strictly at Pemberton.

"We must go into this, mustn't we, dear?" he said to his wife. He assured his young friend that the matter should have his very best attention; and he melted into space as elusively as if, at the door, he were taking an inevitable but deprecatory precedence. When, the next moment, Pemberton found himself alone with Mrs. Moreen it was to hear her say "I see, I see"—stroking the roundness of her chin and looking as if she were only hesitating between a dozen easy remedies. If they didn't make their push Mr. Moreen could at least disappear for several days. During his absence his wife took up the subject again spontaneously, but her contribution to it was merely that she had thought all the while they were getting on so beautifully. Pemberton's reply to this revelation was that unless they immediately put down something on account he would leave them on the spot and for ever. He knew she would wonder how he would get away, and for a moment expected her to enquire. She didn't, for which he was almost grateful to her, so little was he in a position to tell.

"You won't, you *know* you won't—you're too interested," she said. "You *are* interested, you know you are, you dear kind man!" She laughed with almost condemnatory archness, as if it were a reproach —though she wouldn't insist; and flirted a soiled pocket-handkerchief at him.

Pemberton's mind was fully made up to take his step the following week. This would give him time to get an answer to a letter he had dispatched to England. If he did in the event nothing of the sort—that is if he stayed another year and then went away only for three months —it was not merely because before the answer to his letter came (most unsatisfactory when it did arrive) Mr. Moreen generously counted out to him, and again with the sacrifice to "form" of a marked man of the world, three hundred francs in elegant ringing gold. He was irritated to find that Mrs. Moreen was right, that he couldn't at the pinch bear to leave the child. This stood out clearer for the very reason that, the night of his desperate appeal to his patrons, he had seen fully for the first time where he was. Wasn't it another proof of the success with which those patrons practised their arts that they had managed to avert for so long the illuminating flash? It descended on our friend with a breadth of effect which perhaps would have struck a spectator as comical, after he had returned to his little servile room, which looked into a close court where a bare dirty opposite wall took, with the sound of shrill clatter, the reflexion of lighted back windows. He had simply given himself away to a band of adventurers. The idea, the word itself, wore a romantic horror for him—he had always lived on such safe lines. Later it assumed a more interesting, almost a soothing, sense: it pointed a moral, and Pemberton could enjoy a moral. The Moreens were adventurers not merely because they didn't pay their debts, because they lived on society, but because their whole view of life, dim and confused and instinctive, like that of clever colour-blind animals, was speculative and rapacious and mean. Oh they were "respectable," and that only made them more *immondes!* The young man's analysis, while he brooded, put it at last very simply —they were adventurers because they were toadies and snobs. That was the completest account of them—it was the law of their being. Even when this truth became vivid to their ingenious inmate he remained unconscious of how much his mind had been prepared for it by the extraordinary little boy who had now become such a complication in his life. Much less could he then calculate on the information he was still to owe the extraordinary little boy.

## V

But it was during the ensuing time that the real problem came up— the problem of how far it was excusable to discuss the turpitude of parents with a child of twelve, of thirteen, of fourteen. Absolutely inexcusable and quite impossible it of course at first appeared; and indeed the question didn't press for some time after Pemberton had received his three hundred francs. They produced a temporary lull, a relief from the sharpest pressure. The young man frugally amended his wardrobe and even had a few francs in his pocket. He thought the Moreens looked at him as if he were almost too smart, as if they ought to take care not to spoil him. If Mr. Moreen hadn't been such a man of the world he would perhaps have spoken of the freedom of such neckties on the part of a subordinate. But Mr. Moreen was always enough a man of the world to let things pass—he had certainly shown that. It was singular how Pemberton guessed that Morgan, though saying nothing about it, knew something had happened. But three hundred francs, especially when one owed money, couldn't last for ever; and when the treasure was gone—the boy knew when it had failed—Morgan did break ground. The party had returned to Nice at the beginning of the winter, but not to the charming villa. They went to an hotel, where they stayed three months, and then moved to another establishment, explaining that they had left the first because, after waiting and waiting, they couldn't get the rooms they wanted. These apartments, the rooms they wanted, were generally very splendid; but fortunately they never *could* get them—fortunately, I mean, for Pemberton, who reflected always that if they had got them there would have been a still scanter educational fund. What Morgan said at last was said suddenly, irrelevantly, when the moment came, in the middle of a lesson, and consisted of the apparently unfeeling words: "You ought to *filer,* you know—you really ought."

Pemberton stared. He had learnt enough Franch slang from Morgan to know that to *filer* meant to cut sticks. "Ah my dear fellow, don't turn me off!"

Morgan pulled a Greek lexicon toward him—he used a Greek-German—to look out a word, instead of asking it of Pemberton. "You can't go on like this, you know."

"Like what, my boy?"

"You know they don't pay you up," said Morgan, blushing and turning his leaves.

"Don't pay me?" Pemberton stared again and feigned amazement. "What on earth put that into your head?"

"It has been there a long time," the boy replied rummaging his book.

Pemberton was silent, then he went on: "I say, what are you hunting for? They pay me beautifully."

"I'm hunting for the Greek for awful whopper," Morgan dropped.

"Find that rather for gross impertinence and disabuse your mind. What do I want of money?"

"Oh that's another question!"

Pemberton wavered—he was drawn in different ways. The severely correct thing would have been to tell the boy that such a matter was none of his business and bid him go on with his lines. But they were really too intimate for that; it was not the way he was in the habit of treating him; there had been no reason it should be. On the other hand Morgan had quite lighted on the truth—he really shouldn't be able to keep it up much longer; therefore why not let him know one's real motive for forsaking him? At the same time it wasn't decent to abuse to one's pupil the family of one's pupil; it was better to misrepresent than to do that. So in reply to his comrade's last exclamation he just declared, to dismiss the subject, that he had received several payments.

"I say—I say!" the boy ejaculated, laughing.

"That's all right," Pemberton insisted. "Give me your written rendering."

Morgan pushed a copybook across the table, and he began to read

the page, but with something running in his head that made it no
sense. Looking up after a minute or two he found the child's eyes
fixed on him and felt in them something strange. Then Morgan said:
"I'm not afraid of the stern reality."

"I haven't yet seen the thing you *are* afraid of—I'll do you that
justice!"

This came out with a jump—it was perfectly true—and evidently
gave Morgan pleasure. "I've thought of it a long time," he presently
resumed.

"Well, don't think of it any more."

The boy appeared to comply, and they had a comfortable and even
an amusing hour. They had a theory that they were very thorough,
and yet they seemed always to be in the amusing part of lessons, the
intervals between the dull dark tunnels, where there were waysides
and jolly views. Yet the morning was brought to a violent end by
Morgan's suddenly leaning his arms on the table, burying his head
in them and bursting into tears: at which Pemberton was the more
startled that, as it then came over him, it was the first time he had
ever seen the boy cry and that the impression was consequently quite
awful.

The next day, after much thought, he took a decision and, believing
it to be just, immediately acted on it. He cornered Mr. and Mrs.
Moreen again and let them know that if on the spot they didn't pay
him all they owed him he wouldn't only leave their house but would
tell Morgan exactly what had brought him to it.

"Oh you *haven't* told him?" cried Mrs. Moreen with a pacifying
hand on her well-dressed bosom.

"Without warning you? For what do you take me?" the young man
returned.

Mr. and Mrs. Moreen looked at each other; he could see that they
appreciated, as tending to their security, his superstition of delicacy,
and yet that there was a certain alarm in their relief. "My dear fellow,"
Mr. Moreen demanded, "what use *can* you have, leading the quiet life
we all do, for such a lot of money?"—a question to which Pemberton
made no answer, occupied as he was in noting that what passed in the
mind of his patrons was something like: "Oh then, if we've felt that
the child, dear little angel, has judged us and how he regards us, and
we haven't been betrayed, he must have guessed—and in short it's
*general!*" an inference that rather stirred up Mr. and Mrs. Moreen, as

Pemberton had desired it should. At the same time, if he had supposed his threat would do something towards bringing them round,
he was disappointed to find them taking for granted—how vulgar
their perception *had* been!—that he had already given them away.
There was a mystic uneasiness in their parental breasts, and that had
been the inferior sense of it. None the less, however, his threat did
touch them; for if they had escaped it was only to meet a new danger.
Mr. Moreen appealed to him on every precedent, as a man of the
world; but his wife had recourse, for the first time since his domesti-
cation with them, to a fine *hauteur,* reminding him that a devoted
mother, with her child, had arts that protected her against gross mis-
representation.

"I should misrepresent you grossly if I accused you of common
honesty!" our friend replied; but as he closed the door behind him
sharply, thinking he had not done himself much good, while Mr.
Moreen lighted another cigarette, he heard his hostess shout after him
more touchingly:

"Oh you do, you *do,* put the knife to one's throat!"

The next morning, very early, she came to his room. He recognised
her knock, but had no hope she brought him money; as to which he
was wrong, for she had fifty francs in her hand. She squeezed forward
in her dressing-gown, and he received her in his own, between his
bath-tub and his bed. He had been tolerably schooled by this time to
the "foreign ways" of his hosts. Mrs. Moreen was ardent, and when
she was ardent she didn't care what she did; so she now sat down on
his bed, his clothes being on the chairs, and, in her preoccupation, forgot, as she glanced round, to be ashamed of giving him such a horrid
room. What Mrs. Moreen's ardour now bore upon was the design of
persuading him that in the first place she was very good-natured to
bring him fifty francs, and that in the second, if he would only see
it, he was really too absurd to expect to be *paid.* Wasn't he paid
enough without perpetual money—wasn't he paid by the comfortable
luxurious home he enjoyed with them all, without a care, an anxiety,
a solitary want? Wasn't he sure of his position, and wasn't that everything to a young man like him, quite unknown, with singularly little
to show, the ground of whose exorbitant pretensions it had never been
easy to discover? Wasn't he paid above all by the sweet relation he
had established with Morgan—quite ideal as from master to pupil—
and by the simple privilege of knowing and living with so amazingly

gifted a child; than whom really (and she meant literally what she said) there was no better company in Europe? Mrs. Moreen herself took to appealing to him as a man of the world; she said "Voyons, mon cher," and "My dear man, look here now"; and urged him to be reasonable, putting it before him that it was truly a chance for him. She spoke as if, according as he *should* be reasonable, he would prove himself worthy to be her son's tutor and of the extraordinary confidence they had placed in him.

After all, Pemberton reflected, it was only a difference of theory and the theory didn't matter much. They had hitherto gone on that of remunerated, as now they would go on that of gratuitous, service; but why should they have so many words about it? Mrs. Moreen at all events continued to be convincing; sitting there with her fifty francs she talked and reiterated as women reiterate, and bored and irritated him, while he leaned against the wall with his hands in the pockets of his wrapper, drawing it together round his legs and looking over the head of his visitor at the grey negations of his window. She wound up with saying: "You see I bring you a definite proposal."

"A definite proposal?"

"To make our relations regular, as it were—to put them on a comfortable footing."

"I see—it's a system," said Pemberton. "A kind of organised blackmail."

Mrs. Moreen bounded up, which was exactly what he wanted. "What do you mean by that?"

"You practise on one's fears—one's fears about the child if one should go away."

"And pray what would happen to him in that event?" she demanded with majesty.

"Why he'd be alone with *you*."

"And pray with whom *should* a child be but with those whom he loves most?"

"If you think that, why don't you dismiss me?"

"Do you pretend he loves you more than he loves *us*?" cried Mrs. Moreen.

"I think he ought to. I make sacrifices for him. Though I've heard of those *you* make I don't see them."

Mrs. Moreen stared a moment; then with emotion she grasped her inmate's hand. "*Will* you make it—the sacrifice?"

He burst out laughing. "I'll see. I'll do what I can. I'll stay a little longer. Your calculation's just—I *do* hate intensely to give him up; I'm fond of him and he thoroughly interests me, in spite of the inconvenience I suffer. You know my situation perfectly. I haven't a penny in the world and, occupied as you see me with Morgan, am unable to earn money."

Mrs. Moreen tapped her undressed arm with her folded bank-note. "Can't you write articles: Can't you translate as *I* do?"

"I don't know about translating; it's wretchedly paid."

"I'm glad to earn what I can," said Mrs. Moreen with prodigious virtue.

"You ought to tell me who you do it for." Pemberton paused a moment, and she said nothing; so he added: "I've tried to turn off some little sketches, but the magazines won't have them—they're declined with thanks."

"You see then you're not such a phoenix," his visitor pointedly smiled—"to pretend to abilities you're sacrificing for our sake."

"I haven't time to do things properly," he ruefully went on. Then as it came over him that he was almost abjectly good-natured to give these explanations he added: "If I stay on longer it must be on one condition—that Morgan shall know distinctly on what footing I am."

Mrs. Moreen demurred. "Surely you don't want to show off to a child?"

"To show *you* off, do you mean?"

Again she cast about, but this time it was to produce a still finer flower. "And *you* talk of blackmail!"

"You can easily prevent it," said Pemberton.

"And *you* talk of practising on fears!" she bravely pushed on.

"Yes, there's no doubt I'm a great scoundrel."

His patroness met his eyes—it was clear she was in straits. Then she thrust out her money at him. "Mr. Moreen desired me to give you this on account."

"I'm much obliged to Mr. Moreen, but we *have* no account."

"You won't take it?"

"That leaves me more free," said Pemberton.

"To poison my darling's mind?" groaned Mrs. Moreen.

"Oh your darling's mind—!" the young man laughed.

She fixed him a moment, and he thought she was going to break out tormentedly, pleadingly: "For God's sake, tell me what *is* in it!"

But she checked this impulse—another was stronger. She pocketed the money—the crudity of the alternative was comical—and swept out of the room with the desperate concession: "You may tell him any horror you like!"

## VI

A couple of days after this, during which he had failed to profit by so free a permission, he had been for a quarter of an hour walking with his charge in silence when the boy became sociable again with the remark: "I'll tell you how I know it; I know it through Zénobie."

"Zénobie? Who in the world is *she?*"

"A nurse I used to have—ever so many years ago. A charming woman. I liked her awfully, and she liked me."

"There's no accounting for tastes. What is it you know through her?"

"Why what their idea is. She went away because they didn't fork out. She did like me awfully, and she stayed two years. She told me all about it—that at last she could never get her wages. As soon as they saw how much she liked me they stopped giving her anything. They thought she'd stay for nothing—just *because,* don't you know?" And Morgan had a queer little conscious lucid look. "She did stay ever so long—as long as she could. She was only a poor girl. She used to send money to her mother. At last she couldn't afford it any longer, and went away in a fearful rage one night—I mean of course in a rage against *them.* She cried over me tremendously, she hugged me nearly to death. She told me all about it," the boy repeated. "She told me it was their idea. So I guessed, ever so long ago, that they have had the same idea with you."

"Zénobie was very sharp," said Pemberton. "And she made you so."

"Oh that wasn't Zénobie; that was nature. And experience!" Morgan laughed.

"Well, Zénobie was a part of your experience."

"Certainly I was a part of hers, poor dear!" the boy wisely sighed. "And I'm part of yours."

"A very important part. But I don't see how you know I've been treated like Zénobie."

"Do you take me for the biggest dunce you've known?" Morgan

asked. "Haven't I been conscious of what we've been through to-gether?"

"What we've been through?"

"Our privations—our dark days."

"Oh our days have been bright enough."

Morgan went on in silence for a moment. Then he said: "My dear chap, you're a hero!"

"Well, you're another!" Pemberton retorted.

"No I'm not, but I ain't a baby. I won't stand it any longer. You must get some occupation that pays. I'm ashamed, I'm ashamed!" quavered the boy with a ring of passion, like some high silver note from a small cathedral chorister, that deeply touched his friend.

"We ought to go off and live somewhere together," the young man said.

"I'll go like a shot if you'll take me."

"I'd get some work that would keep us both afloat," Pemberton continued.

"So would I. Why shouldn't *I* work? I ain't such a beastly little muff as *that* comes to."

"The difficulty is that your parents wouldn't hear of it. They'd never part with you; they worship the ground you tread on. Don't you see the proof of it?" Pemberton developed. "They don't dislike me; they wish me no harm; they're very amiable people; but they're perfectly ready to expose me to any awkwardness in life for your sake."

The silence in which Morgan received his fond sophistry struck Pemberton somehow as expressive. After a moment the child repeated: "You *are* a hero!" Then he added: "They leave me with you alto-gether. You've all the responsibility. They put me off on you from morning till night. Why then should they object to my taking up with you completely? I'd help you."

"They're not particularly keen about my being helped, and they delight in thinking of you as *theirs*. They're tremendously proud of you."

"I'm not proud of *them*. But you know that," Morgan returned.

"Except for the little matter we speak of they're charming people," said Pemberton, not taking up the point made for his intelligence, but wondering greatly at the boy's own, and especially at this fresh re-minder of something he had been conscious of from the first—the strangest thing in his friend's large little composition, a temper, a sensibility, even a private ideal, which made him as privately disown the stuff his people were made of. Morgan had in secret a small loftiness which made him acute about betrayed meanness; as well as a critical sense for the manners immediately surrounding him that was quite without precedent in a juvenile nature, especially when one noted that it had not made this nature "old-fashioned," as the word is of children—quaint or wizened or offensive. It was as if he had been a little gentleman and had paid the penalty by discovering that he was the only such person in his family. This comparison didn't make him vain, but it could make him melancholy and a trifle austere. While Pemberton guessed at these dim young things, shadows of shadows, he was partly drawn on and partly checked, as for a scruple, by the charm of attempting to sound the little cool shallows that were so quickly growing deeper. When he tried to figure to himself the morning twilight of childhood, so as to deal with it safely, he saw it was never fixed, never arrested, that ignorance at the instant he touched it, was already flushing faintly into knowledge, that there was nothing that at a given moment you could say an intelligent child didn't know. It seemed to him that he himself knew too much to imagine Morgan's simplicity and too little to disembroil his tangle.

The boy paid no heed to his last remark; he only went on: "I'd have spoken to them about their idea, as I call it, long ago, if I hadn't been sure what they'd say."

"And what would they say?"

"Just what they said about what poor Zénobie told me—that it was a horrid dreadful story, that they had paid her every penny they owed her."

"Well, perhaps they had," said Pemberton.

"Perhaps they've paid you!"

"Let us pretend they have, and *n'en parlons plus.*"

"They accused her of lying and cheating"—Morgan stuck to historic truth. "That's why I don't want to speak to them."

"Lest they should accuse me too?" To this Morgan made no answer, and his companion, looking down at him—the boy turned away his eyes, which had filled—saw that he couldn't have trusted himself to utter. "You're right. Don't worry them," Pemberton pursued. "Except for that, they *are* charming people."

"Except for *their* lying and *their* cheating?"

"I say—I say!" cried Pemberton, imitating a little tone of the lad's which was itself an imitation.

"We must be frank, at the last; we *must* come to an understanding," said Morgan with the importance of the small boy who lets himself think he is arranging great affairs—almost playing at shipwreck or at Indians. "I know all about everything."

"I dare say your father has his reasons," Pemberton replied, but too vaguely, as he was aware.

"For lying and cheating?"

"For saving and managing and turning his means to the best account. He has plenty to do with his money. You're an expensive family."

"Yes, I'm very expensive," Morgan concurred in a manner that made his preceptor burst out laughing.

"He's saving for *you*," said Pemberton. "They think of you in everything they do."

"He might, while he's about it, save a little—" The boy paused, and his friend waited to hear what. Then Morgan brought out oddly: "A little reputation."

"Oh there's plenty of that. That's all right!"

"Enough of it for the people they know, no doubt. The people they know are awful."

"Do you mean the princes? We mustn't abuse the princes."

"Why not? They haven't married Paula—they haven't married Amy. They only clean out Ulick."

"You *do* know everything!" Pemberton declared.

"No I don't after all. I don't know what they live on, or how they live, or *why* they live! What have they got and how did they get it? Are they rich, are they poor, or have they a *modeste aisance?* Why are they always chiveying me about—living one year like ambassadors and the next like paupers? Who are they, anyway, and what are they? I've thought of all that—I've thought of a lot of things. They're so beastly worldly. That's what I hate most—oh I've *seen* it! All they care about is to make an appearance and to pass for something or other. What the dickens do they want to pass for? What *do* they, Mr. Pemberton?"

"You pause for a reply," said Pemberton, treating the question as a joke, yet wondering too and greatly struck with his mate's intense if imperfect vision. "I haven't the least idea."

"And what good does it do? Haven't I seen the way people treat them—the 'nice' people, the ones they want to know? They'll take anything from them—they'll lie down and be trampled on. The nice ones hate that—they just sicken them. You're the only really nice person we know."

"Are you sure? They don't lie down for me!"

"Well, you shan't lie down for them. You've got to go—that's what you've got to do," said Morgan.

"And what will become of you?"

"Oh I'm growing up. I shall get off before long. I'll see you later."

"You had better let me finish you," Pemberton urged, lending himself to the child's strange superiority.

Morgan stopped in their walk, looking up at him. He had to look up much less than a couple of years before—he had grown, in his loose leanness, so long and high. "Finish me?" he echoed.

"There are such a lot of jolly things we can do together yet. I want to turn you out—I want you to do me credit."

Morgan continued to look at him. "To give you credit—do you mean?"

"My dear fellow, you're too clever to live."

"That's just what I'm afraid you think. No, no; it isn't fair—I can't endure it. We'll separate next week. The sooner it's over the sooner to sleep."

"If I hear of anything—any other chance—I promise to go," Pemberton said.

Morgan consented to consider this. "But you'll be honest," he demanded; "you won't pretend you haven't heard?"

"I'm much more likely to pretend I have."

"But what can you hear of, this way, stuck in a hole with us? You ought to be on the spot, to go to England—you ought to go to America."

"One would think you were *my* tutor!" said Pemberton.

Morgan walked on and after a little had begun again: "Well, now that you know I know and that we look at the facts and keep nothing back—it's much more comfortable, isn't it?"

"My dear boy, it's so amusing, so interesting, that it will surely be quite impossible for me to forego such hours as these."

This made Morgan stop once more. "You *do* keep something back. Oh you're not straight—*I* am!"

"How am I not straight?"

"Oh you've got your idea!"

"My idea?"

"Why that I probably shan't make—make older—bones, and that you can stick it out till I'm removed."

"You *are* too clever to live!" Pemberton repeated.

"I call it a mean idea," Morgan pursued. "But I shall punish you by the way I hang on."

"Look out or I'll poison you!" Pemberton laughed.

"I'm stronger and better every year. Haven't you noticed that there hasn't been a doctor near me since you came?"

"*I'm* your doctor," said the young man, taking his arm and drawing him tenderly on again.

Morgan proceeded and after a few steps gave a sigh of mingled weariness and relief. "Ah now that we look at the facts it's all right!"

## VII

They looked at the facts a good deal after this; and one of the first consequences of their doing so was that Pemberton stuck it out, in his friend's parlance, for the purpose. Morgan made the facts so vivid and so droll, and at the same time so bald and so ugly, that there was fascination in talking them over with him, just as there would have been heartlessness in leaving him alone with them. Now that the pair had such perceptions in common it was useless for them to pretend they didn't judge such people; but the very judgement and the exchange of perceptions created another tie. Morgan had never been so interesting as now that he himself was made plainer by the side light of these confidences. What came out in it most was the small fine passion of his pride. He had plenty of that, Pemberton felt—so much that one might perhaps wisely wish for it some early bruises. He would have liked his people to have a spirit and had waked up to the sense of their perpetually eating humble-pie. His mother would consume any amount, and his father would consume even more than his mother. He had a theory that Ulick had wriggled out of an "affair" at Nice: there had once been a flurry at home, a regular panic, after which they all went to bed and took medicine, not to be accounted for on any other supposition. Morgan had a romantic imagination, fed by poetry and history, and he would have liked those who "bore his

name"—as he used to say to Pemberton with the humour that made
his queer delicacies manly—to carry themselves with an air. But their
one idea was to get in with people who didn't want them and to take
snubs as if they were honourable scars. Why people didn't want them
more he didn't know—that was people's own affair; after all they
weren't superficially repulsive, they were a hundred times cleverer
than most of the dreary grandees, the "poor swells" they rushed about
Europe to catch up with. "After all they *are* amusing—they are!" he
used to pronounce with the wisdom of the ages. To which Pemberton
always replied: "Amusing—the great Moreen troupe? Why they're
altogether delightful; and if it weren't for the hitch that you and I
(feeble performers!) make in the *ensemble* they'd carry everything
before them."

What the boy couldn't get over was the fact that this particular
blight seemed, in a tradition of self-respect, so undeserved and so
arbitrary. No doubt people had a right to take the line they liked; but
why should *his* people have liked the line of pushing and toadying
and lying and cheating? What had their forefathers—all decent folk,
so far as he knew—done to them, or what had *he* done to them? Who
had poisoned their blood with the fifth-rate social ideal, the fixed idea
of making smart acquaintances and getting into the *monde chic,* especially when it was foredoomed to failure and exposure? They
showed so what they were after; that was what made the people they
wanted not want *them.* And never a wince for dignity, never a throb
of shame at looking each other in the face, never any independence
or resentment or disgust. If his father or his brother would only knock
some one down once or twice a year! Clever as they were they never
guessed the impression they made. They were good-natured, yes—as
good-natured as Jews at the doors of clothing-shops! But was that the
model one wanted one's family to follow? Morgan had dim memories
of an old grandfather, the maternal, in New York, whom he had been
taken across the ocean at the age of five to see: a gentleman with a
high neck-cloth and a good deal of pronunciation, who wore a dress-
coat in the morning, which made one wonder what he wore in the
evening, and had, or was supposed to have, "property" and something
to do with the Bible Society. It couldn't have been but that *he* was a
good type. Pemberton himself remembered Mrs. Clancy, a widowed
sister of Mr. Moreen's, who was as irritating as a moral tale and had
paid a fortnight's visit to the family at Nice shortly after he came to

live with them. She was "pure and refined," as Amy said over the
banjo, and had the air of not knowing what they meant when they
talked, and of keeping something rather important back. Pemberton
judged that what she kept back was an approval of many of their
ways; therefore it was to be supposed that she too was of a good type,
and that Mr. and Mrs. Moreen and Ulick and Paula and Amy might
easily have been of a better one if they would.

But that they wouldn't was more and more perceptible from day to
day. They continued to "chivey," as Morgan called it, and in due time
became aware of a variety of reasons for proceeding to Venice. They
mentioned a great many of them—they were always strikingly frank
and had the brightest friendly chatter, at the late foreign breakfast in
especial, before the ladies had made up their faces, when they leaned
their arms on the table, had something to follow the *demi-tasse,* and,
in the heat of familiar discussion as to what they "really ought" to do,
fell inevitably into the languages in which they could *tutoyer.* Even
Pemberton liked them then; he could endure even Ulick when he
heard him give his little flat voice for the "sweet sea-city." That was
what made him have a sneaking kindness for them—that they were
so out of the workaday world and kept him so out of it. The summer
had waned when, with cries of ecstasy, they all passed out on the
balcony that overhung the Grand Canal. The sunsets then were splendid and the Dorringtons had arrived. The Dorringtons were the only
reason they hadn't talked of at breakfast; but the reasons they didn't
talk of at breakfast always came out in the end. The Dorringtons on
the other hand came out very little; or else when they did they stayed—
as was natural—for hours, during which periods Mrs. Moreen and the
girls sometimes called at their hotel (to see if they had returned) as
many as three times running. The gondola was for the ladies, as in
Venice too there were "days," which Mrs. Moreen knew in their order
an hour after she arrived. She immediately took one herself, to which
the Dorringtons never came, though on a certain occasion when
Pemberton and his pupil were together at Saint Mark's—where, taking the best walks they had ever had and haunting a hundred churches,
they spent a great deal of time—they saw the old lord turn up with
Mr. Moreen and Ulick, who showed him the dim basilica as if it belonged to them. Pemberton noted how much less, among its curiosities,
Lord Dorrington carried himself as a man of the world; wondering
too whether, for such services, his companions took a fee from him.

The autumn at any rate waned, the Dorringtons departed, and Lord Verschoyle, the eldest son, had proposed neither for Amy nor for Paula.

One sad November day, while the wind roared round the old palace and the rain lashed the lagoon, Pemberton, for exercise and even somewhat for warmth—the Moreens were horribly frugal about fires; it was a cause of suffering to their inmate—walked up and down the big bare *sala* with his pupil. The scagliola floor was cold, the high battered casements shook in the storm, and the stately decay of the place was unrelieved by a particle of furniture. Pemberton's spirits were low, and it came over him that the fortune of the Moreens was now even lower. A blast of desolation, a portent of disgrace and disaster, seemed to draw through the comfortless hall. Mr. Moreen and Ulick were in the Piazza, looking out for something, strolling drearily, in mackintoshes, under the arcades; but still, in spite of mackintoshes, unmistakable men of the world. Paula and Amy were in bed—it might have been thought they were staying there to keep warm. Pemberton looked askance at the boy at his side, to see to what extent he was conscious of these dark omens. But Morgan, luckily for him, was now mainly conscious of growing taller and stronger and indeed of being in his fifteenth year. This fact was intensely interesting to him and the basis of a private theory—which, however, he had imparted to his tutor—that in a little while he should stand on his own feet. He considered that the situation would change—that in short he should be "finished," grown up, producible in the world of affairs and ready to prove himself of sterling ability. Sharply as he was capable at times of analysing, as he called it, his life, there were happy hours when he remained, as he also called it—and as the name, really, of their right ideal—"jolly" superficial; the proof of which was his fundamental assumption that he should presently go to Oxford, to Pemberton's college, and aided and abetted by Pemberton, do the most wonderful things. It depressed the young man to see how little in such a project he took account of ways and means: in other connexions he mostly kept to the measure. Pemberton tried to imagine the Moreens at Oxford and fortunately failed; yet unless they were to adopt it as a residence there would be no *modus vivendi* for Morgan. How could he live without an allowance, and where was the allowance to come from? He, Pemberton, might live on Morgan; but how could Morgan live on *him*? What was to become of him anyhow? Somehow the fact that he was a big boy now, with better prospects of health, made the question of his future more difficult. So long as he was markedly frail the great consideration he inspired seemed enough of an answer to it. But at the bottom of Pemberton's heart was the recognition of his probably being strong enough to live and not yet strong enough to struggle or to thrive. Morgan himself at any rate was in the first flush of the rosiest consciousness of adolescence, so that the beating of the tempest seemed to him after all but the voice of life and the challenge of fate. He had on his shabby little overcoat, with the collar up, but was enjoying his walk.

It was interrupted at last by the appearance of his mother at the end of the *sala*. She beckoned him to come to her, and while Pemberton saw him, complaisant, pass down the long vista and over the damp false marble, he wondered what was in the air. Mrs. Moreen said a word to the boy and made him go into the room she had quitted. Then, having closed the door after him, she directed her steps swiftly to Pemberton. There *was* something in the air, but his wildest flight of fancy wouldn't have suggested what it proved to be. She signified that she had made a pretext to get Morgan out of the way, and then she enquired—without hesitation—if the young man could favour her with the loan of three louis. While, before bursting into a laugh, he stared at her with surprise, she declared that she was awfully pressed for the money; she was desperate for it—it would save her life.

"Dear lady, *c'est trop fort!*" Pemberton laughed in the manner and with the borrowed grace of idiom that marked the best colloquial, the best anecdotic, moments of his friends themselves. "Where in the world do you suppose I should get three louis, *du train dont vous allez?*"

"I thought you worked—wrote things. Don't they pay you?"

"Not a penny."

"Are you such a fool as to work for nothing?"

"You ought surely to know that."

Mrs. Moreen stared, then she coloured a little. Pemberton saw she had quite forgotten the terms—if "terms" they could be called—that he had ended by accepting from herself; they had burdened her memory as little as her conscience. "Oh yes, I see what you mean— you've been very nice about that; but why drag it in so often?" She had been perfectly urbane with him ever since the rough scene of explanation in his room the morning he made her accept *his* "terms"—

the necessity of his making his case known to Morgan. She had felt no resentment after seeing there was no danger Morgan would take the matter up with her. Indeed, attributing this immunity to the good taste of his influence with the boy, she had once said to Pemberton "My dear fellow, it's an immense comfort you're a gentleman." She repeated this in substance now. "Of course you're a gentleman—that's a bother the less!" Pemberton reminded her that he had not "dragged in" anything that wasn't already in as much as his foot was in his shoe; and she also repeated her prayer that, somewhere and somehow, he would find her sixty francs. He took the liberty of hinting that if he could find them it wouldn't be to lend them to *her*—as to which he consciously did himself injustice, knowing that if he had them he would certainly put them at her disposal. He accused himself, at bottom and not unveraciously, of a fantastic, a demoralised sympathy with her. If misery made strange bed-fellows it also made strange sympathies. It was moreover a part of the abasement of living with such people that one had to make vulgar retorts, quite out of one's own tradition of good manners. "Morgan, Morgan, to what pass have I come for you?" he groaned while Mrs. Moreen floated voluminously down the *sala* again to liberate the boy, wailing as she went that everything was too odious.

Before their young friend was liberated there came a thump at the door communicating with the staircase, followed by the apparition of a dripping youth who poked in his head. Pemberton recognised him as the bearer of a telegram and recognised the telegram as addressed to himself. Morgan came back as, after glancing at the signature—that of a relative in London—he was reading the words: "Found jolly job for you, engagement to coach opulent youth on own terms. Come at once." The answer happily was paid and the messenger waited. Morgan, who had drawn near, waited too and looked hard at Pemberton; and Pemberton, after a moment, having met his look, handed him the telegram. It was really by wise looks—they knew each other so well now—that, while the telegraph-boy, in his waterproof cape, made a great puddle on the floor, the thing was settled between them. Pemberton wrote the answer with a pencil against the frescoed wall, and the messenger departed. When he had gone the young man explained himself.

"I'll make a tremendous charge; I'll earn a lot of money in a short time, and we'll live on it."

"Well, I hope the opulent youth will be a dismal dunce—he probably will," Morgan parenthesised—"and keep you a long time a-hammering of it in."

"Of course the longer he keeps me the more we shall have for our old age."

"But suppose *they* don't pay you!" Morgan awfully suggested.

"Oh there are not two such—!" But Pemberton pulled up; he had been on the point of using too invidious a term. Instead of this he said "Two such fatalities."

Morgan flushed—the tears came to his eyes. *"Dites toujours* two such rascally crews!" Then in a different tone he added: "Happy opulent youth!"

"Not if he's a dismal dunce."

"Oh they're happier then. But you can't have everything, can you?" the boy smiled.

Pemberton held him fast, hands on his shoulders—he had never loved him so. "What will become of *you*, what will you do?" He thought of Mrs. Moreen, desperate for sixty francs.

"I shall become an *homme fait*." And then as if he recognised all the bearings of Pemberton's allusion: "I shall get on with them better when you're not here."

"Ah don't say that—it sounds as if I set you against them!"

"You do—the sight of you. It's all right; you know what I mean. I shall be beautiful. I'll take their affairs in hand; I'll marry my sisters."

"You'll marry yourself!" joked Pemberton; as high, rather tense pleasantry would evidently be the right, or the safest, tone for their separation.

It was, however, not purely in this strain that Morgan suddenly asked: "But I say—how will you get to your jolly job? You'll have to telegraph to the opulent youth for money to come on."

Pemberton bethought himself. "They won't like that, will they?"

"Oh look out for them!"

Then Pemberton brought out his remedy. "I'll go to the American Consul; I'll borrow some money of him—just for the few days, on the strength of the telegram."

Morgan was hilarious. "Show him the telegram—then collar the money and stay!"

Pemberton entered into the joke sufficiently to reply that for Morgan he was really capable of that; but the boy, growing more serious, and

to prove he hadn't meant what he said, not only hurried him off to
the Consulate—since he was to start that evening, as he had wired to
his friend—but made sure of their affair by going with him. They
splashed through the tortuous perforations and over the humpbacked
bridges, and they passed through the Piazza, where they saw Mr.
Moreen and Ulick go into a jeweller's shop. The Consul proved ac-
commodating—Pemberton said it wasn't the letter, but Morgan's grand
air—and on their way back they went into Saint Mark's for a hushed
ten minutes. Later they took up and kept up the fun of it to the very
end; and it seemed to Pemberton a part of that fun that Mrs. Moreen,
who was very angry when he had announced her his intention, should
charge him grotesquely and vulgarly and in reference to the loan she
had vainly endeavoured to effect, with bolting lest they should "get
something out" of him. On the other hand he had to do Mr. Moreen
and Ulick the justice to recognise that when on coming in *they* heard
the cruel news they took it like perfect men of the world.

## VIII

When he got at work with the opulent youth, who was to be taken
in hand for Balliol, he found himself unable to say if this aspirant had
really such poor parts or if the appearance were only begotten of his
own long association with an intensely living little mind. From
Morgan he heard half a dozen times: the boy wrote charming young
letters, a patchwork of tongues, with indulgent postscripts in the family
Volapuk and, in little squares and rounds and crannies of the text,
the drollest illustrations—letters that he was divided between the impulse to show his present charge as a vain, a wasted incentive, and the
sense of something in them that publicity would profane. The opulent
youth went up in due course and failed to pass; but it seemed to add
to the presumption that brilliancy was not expected of him all at once
that his parents, condoning the lapse, which they good-naturedly
treated as little as possible as if it were Pemberton's, should have
sounded the rally again, begged the young coach to renew the siege.

The young coach was now in a position to lend Mrs. Moreen three
louis, and he sent her a post-office order even for a larger amount. In
return for his favour he received a frantic scribbled line from her:
"Implore you to come back instantly—Morgan dreadfully ill." They
were on the rebound, once more in Paris—often as Pemberton had

seen them depressed he had never seen them crushed—and communication was therefore rapid. He wrote to the boy to ascertain the state of his health, but awaited the answer in vain. He accordingly, after three days, took an abrupt leave of the opulent youth and, crossing the Channel, alighted at the small hotel, in the quarter of the Champs Elysées, of which Mrs. Moreen had given him the address. A deep if dumb dissatisfaction with this lady and her companions bore him company: they couldn't be vulgarly honest, but they could live at hotels, in velvety *entresols,* amid a smell of burnt pastilles, surrounded by the most expensive city in Europe. When he had left them in Venice it was with an irrepressible suspicion that something was going to happen; but the only thing that could have taken place was again their masterly retreat. "How is he? where is he?" he asked of Mrs. Moreen; but before she could speak these questions were answered by the pressure round his neck of a pair of arms, in shrunken sleeves, which still were perfectly capable of an effusive young foreign squeeze.

"Dreadfully ill—I don't see it!" the young man cried. And then to Morgan: "Why on earth didn't you relieve me? Why didn't you answer my letter?"

Mrs. Moreen declared that when she wrote he was very bad, and Pemberton learned at the same time from the boy that he had answered every letter he had received. This led to the clear inference that Pemberton's note had been kept from him so that the game to be practised should not be interfered with. Mrs. Moreen was prepared to see the fact exposed, as Pemberton saw the moment he faced her that she was prepared for a good many other things. She was prepared above all to maintain that she had acted from a sense of duty, that she was enchanted she had got him over, whatever they might say, and that it was useless of him to pretend he didn't know in all his bones that his place at such a time was with Morgan. He had taken the boy away from them and now had no right to abandon him. He had created for himself the gravest responsibilities and must at least abide by what he had done.

"Taken him away from you?" Pemberton exclaimed indignantly.

"Do it—do it for pity's sake; that's just what I want. I can't stand *this*—and such scenes. They're awful frauds—poor dears!" These words broke from Morgan, who had intermitted his embrace, in a key which made Pemberton turn quickly to him and see that he had suddenly seated himself, was breathing in great pain and was very pale.

"*Now* do you say he's not in a state, my precious pet?" shouted his mother, dropping on her knees before him with clasped hands, but touching him no more than if he had been a gilded idol. "It will pass —it's only for an instant; but don't say such dreadful things!"

"I'm all right—all right," Morgan panted to Pemberton, whom he sat looking up at with a strange smile, his hands resting on either side of the sofa.

"Now do you pretend I've been dishonest, that I've deceived?" Mrs. Moreen flashed at Pemberton as she got up.

"It isn't *he* says it, it's I!" the boy returned, apparently easier but sinking back against the wall; while his restored friend, who had sat down beside him, took his hand and bent over him.

"Darling child, one does what one can; there are so many things to consider," urged Mrs. Moreen. "It's his *place*—his only place. You see *you* think it is now."

"Take me away—take me away," Morgan went on, smiling to Pemberton with his white face.

"Where shall I take you, and how—oh *how,* my boy?" the young man stammered, thinking of the rude way in which his friends in London held that, for his convenience, with no assurance of prompt return, he had thrown them over; of the just resentment with which they would already have called in a successor, and of the scant help to finding fresh employment that resided for him in the grossness of his having failed to pass his pupil.

"Oh we'll settle that. You used to talk about it," said Morgan. "If we can only go all the rest's a detail."

"Talk about it as much as you like, but don't think you can attempt it. Mr. Moreen would never consent—it would be so *very* hand-to-mouth," Pemberton's hostess beautifully explained to him. Then to Morgan she made it clearer: "It would destroy our peace, it would break our hearts. Now that he's back it will be all the same again. You'll have your life, your work and your freedom, and we'll all be happy as we used to be. You'll bloom and grow perfectly well, and we won't have any more silly experiments, will we? They're too absurd. It's Mr. Pemberton's place—every one in his place. You in yours, your papa in his, me in mine—*n'est-ce pas, chéri?* We'll all forget how foolish we've been and have lovely times."

She continued to talk and to surge vaguely about the little draped stuffy salon while Pemberton sat with the boy, whose colour gradually came back; and she mixed up her reasons, hinting that there were going to be changes, that the other children might scatter (who knew? —Paula had her ideas) and that then it might be fancied how much the poor old parent-birds would want the little nestling. Morgan looked at Pemberton, who wouldn't let him move; and Pemberton knew exactly how he felt at hearing himself called a little nestling. He admitted that he had had one or two bad days, but he protested afresh against the wrong of his mother's having made them the ground of an appeal to poor Pemberton. Poor Pemberton could laugh now, apart from the comicality of Mrs. Moreen's mustering so much philosophy for her defense—she seemed to shake it out of her agitated petticoats, which knocked over the light gilt chairs—so little did their young companion, *marked,* unmistakably marked at the best, strike him as qualified to repudiate any advantage.

He himself was in for it at any rate. He should have Morgan on his hands again indefinitely; though indeed he saw the lad had a private theory to produce which would be intended to smooth this down. He was obliged to him for it in advance; but the suggested amendment didn't keep his heart rather from sinking, any more than it prevented him from accepting the prospect on the spot, with some confidence moreover that he should do even better if he could have a little supper. Mrs. Moreen threw out more hints about the changes that were to be looked for, but she was such a mixture of smiles and shudders—she confessed she was very nervous—that he couldn't tell if she were in high feather or only in hysterics. If the family was really at last going to pieces why shouldn't she recognise the necessity of pitching Morgan into some sort of lifeboat? This presumption was fostered by the fact that they were established in luxurious quarters in the capital of pleasure; that was exactly where they naturally *would* be established in view of going to pieces. Moreover didn't she mention that Mr. Moreen and the others were enjoying themselves at the opera with Mr. Granger, and wasn't *that* also precisely where one would look for them on the eve of a smash? Pemberton gathered that Mr. Granger was a rich vacant American—a big bill with a flourishy heading and no items; so that one of Paula's "ideas" was probably that this time she hadn't missed fire—by which straight shot indeed she would have shattered the general cohesion. And if the cohesion was to crumble what would become of poor Pemberton? He felt quite enough bound up with them to figure to his alarm as a dislodged block in the edifice.

It was Morgan who eventually asked if no supper had been ordered for him; sitting with him below, later, at the dim delayed meal, in the presence of a great deal of corded green plush, a plate of ornamental biscuit and an aloofness marked on the part of the waiter. Mr. Moreen had explained that they had been obliged to secure a room for the visitor out of the house; and Morgan's consolation—he offered it while Pemberton reflected on the nastiness of luke-warm sauces—proved to be, largely, that this circumstance would facilitate their escape. He talked of their escape—recurring to it often afterwards—as if they were making up a "boy's book" together. But he likewise expressed his sense that there was something in the air, that the Moreens couldn't keep it up much longer. In point of fact, as Pemberton was to see, they kept it up for five or six months. All the while, however, Morgan's contention was designed to cheer him. Mr. Moreen and Ulick, whom he had met the day after his return, accepted that return like perfect men of the world. If Paula and Amy treated it even with less formality an allowance was to be made for them, inasmuch as Mr. Granger hadn't come to the opera after all. He had only placed his box at their service, with a bouquet for each of the party; there was even one apiece, embittering the thought of his profusion, for Mr. Moreen and Ulick. "They're all like that," was Morgan's comment; "at the very last, just when we think we've landed them they're back in the deep sea!"

Morgan's comments in these days were more and more free; they even included a large recognition of the extraordinary tenderness with which he had been treated while Pemberton was away. Oh yes, they couldn't do enough to be nice to him, to show him they had him on their mind and make up for his loss. That was just what made the whole thing so sad and caused him to rejoice after all in Pemberton's return—he had to keep thinking of their affection less, had less sense of obligation. Pemberton laughed out at this last reason, and Morgan blushed and said "Well, dash it, you know what I mean." Pemberton knew perfectly what he meant; but there were a good many things that—dash it too!—it didn't make any clearer. This episode of his second sojourn in Paris stretched itself out wearily, with their resumed readings and wanderings and maunderings, their potterings on the quays, their hauntings of the museums, their occasional lingerings in the Palais Royal when the first sharp weather came on and there was a comfort in warm emanations, before Chevet's wonderful succulent window. Morgan wanted to hear all about the opulent youth—he took an immense interest in him. Some of the details of his opulence— Pemberton could spare him none of them—evidently fed the boy's appreciation of all his friend had given up to come back to him; but in addition to the greater reciprocity established by that heroism he had always his little brooding theory, in which there was a frivolous gaiety too, that their long probation was drawing to a close. Morgan's conviction that the Moreens couldn't go on much longer kept pace with their unexpended impetus with which, from month to month, they did go on. Three weeks after Pemberton had rejoined them they went on to another hotel, a dingier one than the first; but Morgan rejoiced that his tutor had at least still not sacrificed the advantage of a room outside. He clung to the romantic utility of this when the day, or rather the night, should arrive for their escape.

For the first time, in this complicated connexion, our friend felt his collar gall him. It was, as he had said to Mrs. Moreen in Venice, *trop fort*—everything was *trop fort*. He could neither really throw off his blighting burden nor find in it the benefit of a pacified conscience or of a rewarded affection. He had spent all the money accruing to him in England, and he saw his youth going and that he was getting nothing back for it. It was all very well of Morgan to count it for reparation that he should now settle on him permanently—there was an irritating flaw in such a view. He saw what the boy had in his mind; the conception that as his friend had had the generosity to come back he must show his gratitude by giving him his life. But the poor friend didn't desire the gift—what could he do with Morgan's dreadful little life? Of course at the same time that Pemberton was irritated he remembered the reason, which was very honourable to Morgan and which dwelt simply in his making one so forget that he was no more than a patched urchin. If one dealt with him on a different basis one's misadventures were one's own fault. So Pemberton waited in a queer confusion of yearning and alarm for the catastrophe which was held to hang over the house of Moreen, of which he certainly at moments felt the symptoms brush his cheek and as to which he wondered much in what form it would find its liveliest effect.

Perhaps it would take the form of sudden dispersal—a frightened *sauve qui peut,* a scuttling into selfish corners. Certainly they were

less elastic than of yore; they were evidently looking for something
they didn't find. The Dorringtons hadn't re-appeared, the princes had
scattered; wasn't that the beginning of the end? Mrs. Moreen had lost
her reckoning of the famous "days"; her social calendar was blurred
—it had turned its face to the wall. Pemberton suspected that the great,
the cruel discomfiture had been the unspeakable behaviour of Mr.
Granger, who seemed not to know what he wanted, or, what was
much worse, what *they* wanted. He kept sending flowers, as if to
bestrew the path of his retreat, which was never the path of a return.
Flowers were all very well, but—Pemberton could complete the proposition. It was now positively conspicuous that in the long run the
Moreens were a social failure; so that the young man was almost
grateful the run had not been short. Mr. Moreen indeed was still
occasionally able to get away on business and, what was more surprising, was likewise able to get back. Ulick had no club, but you couldn't
have discovered it from his appearance, which was as much as ever
that of a person looking at life from the window of such an institution;
therefore Pemberton was doubly surprised at an answer he once heard
him make his mother in the desperate tone of a man familiar with
the worst privations. Her question Pemberton had not quite caught;
it appeared to be an appeal for a suggestion as to whom they might
get to take Amy. "Let the Devil take her!" Ulick snapped; so that
Pemberton could see that they had not only lost their amiability but
had ceased to believe in themselves. He could also see that if Mrs.
Moreen was trying to get people to take her children she might be
regarded as closing the hatches for the storm. But Morgan would be
the last she would part with.

One winter afternoon—it was a Sunday—he and the boy walked
far together in the Bois de Boulogne. The evening was so splendid,
the cold lemon-coloured sunset so clear, the stream of carriages and
pedestrians so amusing and the fascination of Paris so great, that they
stayed out later than usual and became aware that they should have
to hurry home to arrive in time for dinner. They hurried accordingly,
arm-in-arm, good-humoured and hungry, agreeing that there was
nothing like Paris after all and that after everything too that had come
and gone they were not yet sated with innocent pleasures. When they
reached the hotel they found that, though scandalously late, they were
in time for all the dinner they were likely to sit down to. Confusion
reigned in the apartments of the Moreens—very shabby ones this time,

but the best in the house—and before the interrupted service of the table, with objects displaced almost as if there had been a scuffle and a great wine-stain from an overturned bottle, Pemberton couldn't blink the fact that there had been a scene of the last proprietary firmness. The storm had come—they were all seeking refuge. The hatches were down, Paula and Amy were invisible—they had never tried the most casual art upon Pemberton, but he felt they had enough of an eye to him not to wish to meet him as young ladies whose frocks had been confiscated—and Ulick appeared to have jumped overboard. The host and his staff, in a word, had ceased to "go on" at the pace of their guests, and the air of embarrassed detention, thanks to a pile of gaping trunks in the passage, was strangely commingled with the air of indignant withdrawal.

When Morgan took all this in—and he took it in very quickly—he coloured to the roots of his hair. He had walked from his infancy among difficulties and dangers, but he had never seen a public exposure. Pemberton noticed in a second glance at him that the tears had rushed into his eyes and that they were tears of a new and untasted bitterness. He wondered an instant, for the boy's sake, whether he might successfully pretend not to understand. Not successfully, he felt, as Mr. and Mrs. Moreen, dinnerless by their extinguished hearth, rose before him in their little dishonoured salon, casting about with glassy eyes for the nearest port in such a storm. They were not prostrate but were horribly white, and Mrs. Moreen had evidently been crying. Pemberton quickly learned however that her grief was not for the loss of her dinner, much as she usually enjoyed it, but the fruit of a blow that struck even deeper, as she made all haste to explain. He would see for himself, so far as that went, how the great change had come, the dreadful bolt had fallen, and how they would now all have to turn themselves about. Therefore cruel as it was to them to part with their darling she must look to him to carry a little further the influence he had so fortunately acquired with the boy—to induce his young charge to follow him into some modest retreat. They depended on him—that was the fact—to take their delightful child temporarily under his protection: it would leave Mr. Moreen and herself so much more free to give the proper attention (too little, alas! had been given) to the readjustment of their affairs.

"We trust you—we feel we *can*," said Mrs. Moreen, slowly rubbing her plump white hands and looking with compunction hard at Morgan, whose chin, not to take liberties, her husband stroked with a tentative paternal forefinger.

"Oh yes—we feel that we *can*. We trust Mr. Pemberton fully, Morgan," Mr. Moreen pursued.

Pemberton wondered again if he might pretend not to understand; but everything good gave way to the intensity of Morgan's understanding. "Do you mean he may take me to live with him for ever and ever?" cried the boy. "May take me away, away, anywhere he likes?"

"For ever and ever? *Comme vous-y-allez!*" Mr. Moreen laughed indulgently. "For as long as Mr. Pemberton may be so good."

"We've struggled, we've suffered," his wife went on; "but you've made him so your own that we've already been through the worst of the sacrifice."

Morgan had turned away from his father—he stood looking at Pemberton with a light in his face. His sense of shame for their common humiliated state had dropped; the case had another side—the thing was to clutch at *that*. He had a moment of boyish joy, scarcely mitigated by the reflexion that with this unexpected consecration of his hope—too sudden and too violent; the turn taken was away from a *good* boy's book—the "escape" was left on their hands. The boyish joy was there an instant, and Pemberton was almost scared at the rush of gratitude and affection that broke through his first abasement. When he stammered "My dear fellow, what do you say to *that?*" how could one not say something enthusiastic? But there was more need for courage at something else that immediately followed and that made the lad sit down quickly on the nearest chair. He had turned quite livid and had raised his hand to his left side. They were all three looking at him, but Mrs. Moreen suddenly bounded forward. "Ah his darling little heart!" she broke out; and this time, on her knees before him and without respect for the idol, she caught him ardently in her arms. "You walked him too far, you hurried him too fast!" she hurled over her shoulder at Pemberton. Her son made no protest, and the next instant, still holding him, she sprang up with her face convulsed and with the terrified cry "Help, help! he's going, he's gone!" Pemberton saw with equal horror, by Morgan's own stricken face, that he was beyond their wildest recall. He pulled him half out of his mother's hands, and for a moment, while they held him together, they looked all their dismay into each other's eyes. "He couldn't stand it with his weak organ," said Pemberton—"the shock, the whole scene, the violent emotion."

"But I thought he *wanted* to go to you!" wailed Mrs. Moreen.

"I *told* you he didn't, my dear," her husband made answer. Mr. Moreen was trembling all over and was in his way as deeply affected as his wife. But after the very first he took his bereavement as a man of the world.

# The Death of Iván Ilých

## LEO TOLSTOY

## I

Dᴜʀɪɴɢ an interval in the Melvínski trial in the large building of
the Law Courts the members and public prosecutor met in Iván
Egórobich Shébek's private room, where the conversation turned on
the celebrated Krasóvski case. Fëdor Vasílievich warmly maintained
that it was not subject to their jurisdiction, Iván Egórovich maintained
the contrary, while Peter Ivánovich, not having entered into the discussion at the start, took no part in it but looked through the *Gazette*
which had just been handed in.

"Gentleman," he said "Iván Ilých has died!"

"You don't say so!"

"Here, read it yourself," replied Peter Ivánovich, handing Fëdor
Vasílievich the paper still damp from the press. Surrounded by a black
border were the words: "Praskóvya Fëdorovna Goloviná, with profound sorrow, informs relatives and friends of the demise of her beloved husband Iván Ilých Golovín, Member of the Court of Justice,
which occurred on February the 4th of this year 1882. The funeral
will take place on Friday at one o'clock in the afternoon."

Iván Ilých had been a colleague of the gentlemen present and was
liked by them all. He had been ill for some weeks with an illness said
to be incurable. His post had been kept open for him, but there had
been conjectures that in case of his death Alexéev might receive his
appointment, and that either Vínnikov or Shtábel would succeed
Alexéev. So on receiving the news of Iván Ilých's death the first
thought of each of the gentlemen in that private room was of the

changes and promotions it might occasion among themselves or their acquaintances.

"I shall be sure to get Shtábel's place or Vínnikov's," thought Fëdor Vasílievich. "I was promised that long ago, and the promotion means an extra eight hundred rubles a year for me besides the allowance."

"Now I must apply for my brother-in law's transfer from Kalúga," thought Peter Ivánovich. "My wife will be very glad, and then she won't be able to say that I never do anything for her relations."

"I thought he would never leave his bed again," said Peter Ivánovich aloud. "It's very sad."

"But what really was the matter with him?"

"The doctors couldn't say—at least they could, but each of them said something different. When last I saw him I thought he was getting better."

"And I haven't been to see him since the holidays. I always meant to go."

"Had he any property?"

"I think his wife had a little—but something quite trifling."

"We shall have to go to see her, but they live so terribly far away."

"Far away from you, you mean. Everything's far away from your place."

"You see, he never can forgive my living on the other side of the river," said Peter Ivánovich, smiling at Shébek. Then, still talking of the distances between different parts of the city, they returned to the Court.

Besides considerations as to the possible transfers and promotions likely to result from Iván Ilých's death, the mere fact of the death of a near acquaintance aroused, as usual, in all who heard of it the complacent feeling that, "it is he who is dead and not I."

Each one thought or felt, "Well, he's dead but I'm alive!" But the more intimate of Iván Ilých's acquaintances, his so-called friends, could not help thinking also that they would now have to fulfill the very tiresome demands of propriety by attending the funeral service and paying a visit of condolence to the widow.

Fëdor Vasílievich and Peter Ivánovich had been his nearest acquaintances. Peter Ivánovich had studied law with Iván Ilých and had considered himself to be under obligations to him.

Having told his wife at dinner-time of Iván Ilých's death, and of his conjecture that it might be possible to get her brother transferred to their circuit, Peter Ivánovich sacrificed his usual nap, put on his evening clothes, and drove to Iván Ilých's house.

At the entrance stood a carriage and two cabs. Leaning against the wall in the hall downstairs near the cloak-stand was a coffin-lid covered with cloth of gold, ornamented with gold cord and tassels, that had been polished up with metal powder. Two ladies in black were taking off their fur cloaks. Peter Ivánovich recognized one of them as Iván Ilých's sister, but the other was a stranger to him. His colleague Schwartz was just coming downstairs, but on seeing Peter Ivánovich enter he stopped and winked at him, as if to say: "Iván Ilých has made a mess of things—not like you and me."

Schwartz's face with his Piccadilly whiskers, and his slim figure in evening dress, had as usual an air of elegant solemnity which contrasted with the playfulness of his character and had a special piquancy here, or so it seemed to Peter Ivánovich.

Peter Ivánovich allowed the ladies to precede him and slowly followed them upstairs. Schwartz did not come down but remained where he was, and Peter Ivánovich understood that he wanted to arrange where they should play bridge that evening. The ladies went upstairs to the widow's room, and Schwartz with seriously compressed lips but a playful look in his eyes, indicated by a twist of his eyebrows the room to the right where the body lay.

Peter Ivánovich, like everyone else on such occasions, entered feeling uncertain what he would have to do. All he knew was that at such times it is always safe to cross oneself. But he was not quite sure whether one should make obeisances while doing so. He therefore adopted a middle course. On entering the room he began crossing himself and made a slight movement resembling a bow. At the same time, as far as the motion of his head and arm allowed, he surveyed the room. Two young men—apparently nephews, one of whom was a high-school pupil—were leaving the room, crossing themselves as they did so. An old woman was standing motionless, and a lady with strangely arched eyebrows was saying something to her in a whisper. A vigorous, resolute Church Reader, in a frock-coat, was reading something in a loud voice with an expression that precluded any contradiction. The butler's assistant, Gerásim, stepping lightly in front of Peter Ivánovich, was strewing something on the floor. Noticing this, Peter

Ivánovich, was immediately aware of a faint odour of a decomposing body.

The last time he had called on Iván Ilých, Peter Ivánovich had seen Gerásim in the study. Iván Ilých had been particularly fond of him and he was performing the duty of a sick-nurse.

Peter Ivánovich continued to make the sign of the cross slightly inclining his head in an intermediate direction between the coffin, the Reader, and the icons on the table in a corner of the room. Afterwards, when it seemed to him that this movement of his arm in crossing himself had gone on too long, he stopped and began to look at the corpse.

The dead man lay, as dead men alway lie, in a specially heavy way, his rigid limbs sunk in the soft cushions of the coffin, with the head forever bowed on the pillow. His yellow waxen brow with bald patches over his sunken temples was thrust up in the way peculiar to the dead, the protruding nose seeming to press on the upper lip. He was much changed and had grown even thinner since Peter Ivánovich had last seen him, but, as is always the case with the dead, his face was handsomer and above all more dignified than when he was alive. The expression on the face said that what was necessary had been accomplished, and accomplished rightly. Besides this there was in that expression a reproach and a warning to the living. This warning seemed to Peter Ivánovich out of place, or at least not applicable to him. He felt a certain discomfort and so he hurriedly crossed himself once more and turned and went out of the door—too hurriedly and too regardless of propriety, as he himself was aware.

Schwartz was waiting for him in the adjoining room with legs spread wide apart and both hands toying with his top-hat behind his back. The mere sight of that playful, well-groomed, and elegant figure refreshed Peter Ivánovich. He felt that Schwartz was above all these happenings and would not surrender to any depressing influences. His very look said that this incident of a church service for Iván Ilých could not be a sufficient reason for infringing the order of the session —in other words, that it would certainly not prevent his unwrapping a new pack of cards and shuffling them that evening while a footman placed four fresh candles on the table: in fact, there was no reason for supposing that this incident would hinder their spending the evening agreeably. Indeed he said this in a whisper as Peter Ivánovich passed him, proposing that they should meet for a game at Fëdor Vasílievich's. But apparently Peter Ivánovich was not destined to play bridge that evening. Praskóvya Fëdorovna (a short, fat woman who despite all efforts to the contrary had continued to broaden steadily from her shoulders downwards and who had the same extraordinarily arched eyebrows as the lady who had been standing by the coffin), dressed all in black, her head covered with lace, came out of her own room with some other ladies, conducted them to the room where the dead body lay, and said: "The service will begin immediately. Please go in."

Schwartz, making an indefinite bow, stood still, evidently neither accepting nor declining this invitation. Praskóvya Fëdorovna recognizing Peter Ivánovich, sighed, went close up to him, took his hand, and said: "I know you were a true friend to Iván Ilých . . ." and looked at him awaiting some suitable response. And Peter Ivánovich knew that, just as it had been the right thing to cross himself in that room, so what he had to do here was to press her hand, sigh, and say, "Believe me . . ." So he did all this and as he did it felt that the desired result had been achieved: that both he and she were touched.

"Come with me. I want to speak to you before it begins," said the widow. "Give me your arm."

Peter Ivánovich gave her his arm and they went to the inner rooms, passing Schwartz who winked at Peter Ivánovich compassionately. "That does for our bridge! Don't object if we find another player. Perhaps you can cut in when you do escape," said his playful look.

Peter Ivánovich sighed still more deeply and despondently, and Praskóvya Fëdorovna pressed his arm gratefully. When they reached the drawing-room, upholstered in pink cretonne and lighted by a dim lamp, they sat down at the table—she on a sofa and Peter Ivánovich on a low pouffe, the springs of which yielded spasmodically under his weight. Praskóvya Fëdorovna had been on the point of warning him to take another seat, but felt that such a warning was out of keeping with her present condition and so changed her mind. As he sat down on the pouffe Peter Ivánovich recalled how Iván Ilých had arranged this room and had consulted him regarding this pink cretonne with green leaves. The whole room was full of furniture and knick-knacks, and on her way to the sofa the lace of the widow's black shawl caught on the carved edge of the table. Peter Ivánovich rose to detach it, and the springs of the pouffe, relieved of his weight, rose also and gave him a push. The widow began detaching her shawl herself, and Peter Ivánovich again sat down, suppressing the rebellious springs of the pouffe under him. But the widow had not quite freed herself and Peter Ivánovich got up again, and again the pouffe rebelled and even creaked. When this was all over she took out a clean cambric handkerchief and began to weep. The episode with the shawl and the struggle with the pouffe had cooled Peter Ivánovich's emotions and he sat there with a sullen look on his face. This awkward situation was interrupted by Sokolóv, Iván Ilých's butler, who came to report that the plot in the cemetery that Praskóvya Fëdorovna had chosen would cost two hundred rubles. She stopped weeping and, looking at Peter Ivánovich with the air of a victim, remarked in French that it was very hard for her. Peter Ivánovich made a silent gesture signifying his full conviction that it must indeed be so.

"Please smoke," she said in a magnanimous yet crushed voice, and turned to discuss with Sokolóv the price of the plot for the grave.

Peter Ivánovich while lighting his cigarette heard her inquiring very circumstantially into the price of different plots in the cemetery and finally decide which she would take. When that was done she gave instructions about engaging the choir. Sokolóv then left the room.

"I look after everything myself," she told Peter Ivánovich, shifting the albums that lay on the table; and noticing that the table was endangered by his cigarette-ash, she immediately passed him an ashtray, saying as she did so: "I consider it an affectation to say that my grief prevents my attending to practical affairs. On the contrary, if anything can—I won't say console me, but—distract me, it is seeing to everything concerning him." She again took out her handkerchief as if preparing to cry, but suddenly, as if mastering her feeling, she shook herself and began to speak calmly. "But there is something I want to talk to you about."

Peter Ivánovich bowed, keeping control of the springs of the pouffe, which immediately began quivering under him.

"He suffered terribly the last few days."

"Did he?" said Peter Ivánovich.

"Oh, terribly! He screamed unceasingly, not for minutes but for hours. For the last three days he screamed incessantly. It was unendurable. I cannot understand how I bore it; you could hear him three rooms off. Oh, what I have suffered!"

"Is it possible that he was conscious all that time?" asked Peter Ivánovich.

"Yes," she whispered. "To the last moment. He took leave of us a quarter of an hour before he died, and asked us to take Volódya away."

The thought of the sufferings of this man he had known so intimately, first as a merry little boy, then as a school-mate, and later as a grown-up colleague, suddenly struck Peter Ivánovich with horror, despite an unpleasant consciousness of his own and this woman's dissimulation. He again saw that brow, and that nose pressing down on the lip, and felt afraid for himself.

"Three days of frightful suffering and then death! Why, that might suddenly, at any time, happen to me," he thought, and for a moment felt terrified. But—he did not himself know how—the customary reflection at once occurred to him that this had happened to Iván Ilých and not to him, and that it should not and could not happen to him, and that to think that it could would be yielding to depression which he ought not to do, as Schwartz's expression plainly showed. After which reflection Peter Ivánovich felt reassured, and began to ask with interest about the details of Iván Ilých's death, as though death was an accident natural to Iván Ilých but certainly not to himself.

After many details of the really dreadful physical sufferings Iván Ilých had endured (which details he learnt only from the effect those sufferings had produced on Praskóvya Fëdorovna's nerves) the widow apparently found it necessary to get to business.

"Oh, Peter Ivánovich, how hard it is! How terribly, terribly hard!" and she again began to weep.

Peter Ivánovich sighed and waited for her to finish blowing her nose. When she had done so he said, "Believe me . . ." and she again began talking and brought out what was evidently her chief concern with him—namely, to question him as to how she could obtain a grant of money from the government on the occasion of her husband's death. She made it appear that she was asking Peter Ivánovich's advice about her pension, but he soon saw that she already knew about that to the minutest detail, more even than he did himself. She knew how much could be got out of the government in consequence of her husband's death, but wanted to find out whether she could not possibly extract something more. Peter Ivánovich tried to think of some means of doing so, but after reflecting for a while and, out of propriety, condemning the government for its niggardliness, he said he thought that nothing more could be got. Then she sighed and evidently began to devise means of getting rid of her visitor. Noticing this, he put out his cigarette, rose, pressed her hand, and went out into the anteroom.

In the dining-room where the clock stood that Iván Ilých had liked so much and had bought at an antique shop, Peter Ivánovich met a priest and a few acquaintances who had come to attend the service, and he recognized Iván Ilých's daughter, a handsome young woman. She was in black and her slim figure appeared slimmer than ever. She had a gloomy, determined, almost angry expression, and bowed to Peter Ivánovich as though he were in some way to blame. Behind her, with the same offended look, stood a wealthy young man, an examining magistrate, whom Peter Ivánovich also knew and who was her fiancé, as he had heard. He bowed mournfully to them and was about to pass into the death-chamber, when from under the stairs appeared the figure of Iván Ilých's schoolboy son, who was extremely like his father. He seemed a little Iván Ilých, such as Peter Ivánovich remembered when they studied law together. His tear-stained eyes had in them the look that is seen in the eyes of boys of thirteen or fourteen who are not pure-minded. When he saw Peter Ivánovich he scowled morosely and shame-facedly. Peter Ivánovich nodded to him and entered the death-chamber. The service began: candles, groans, incense, tears, and sobs. Peter Ivánovich stood looking gloomily down at his feet. He did not look once at the dead man, did not yield to any depressing influence, and was one of the first to leave the room. There was no one in the anteroom, but Gerásim darted out of the dead man's room, rummaged with his strong hands among the fur coats to find Peter Ivánovich's and helped him on with it.

"Well, friend Gerásim," said Peter Ivánovich, so as to say something. "It's a sad affair, isn't it?"

"It's God's will. We shall all come to it some day," said Gerásim, displaying his teeth—the even, white teeth of a healthy peasant—and, like a man in the thick of urgent work, he briskly opened the front door, called the coachman, helped Peter Ivánovich into the sledge, and sprang back to the porch as if in readiness for what he had to do next.

Peter Ivánovich found the fresh air particularly pleasant after the smell of incense, the dead body, and carbolic acid.

"Where to, sir?" asked the coachman.

"It's not too late even now. . . . I'll call round on Fëdor Vasílievich."

He accordingly drove there and found them just finishing the first rubber, so that it was quite convenient for him to cut in.

## II

Iván Ilých's life had been most simple and most ordinary and therefore most terrible.

He had been a member of the Court of Justice, and died at the age of forty-five. His father had been an official who after serving in various ministries and departments in Petersburg had made the sort of career which brings men to positions from which by reason of their long service they cannot be dismissed, though they are obviously unfit to hold any responsible position, and for whom therefore posts are specially created, which though fictitious carry salaries of from six to ten thousand rubles that are not fictitious, and in receipt of which they live on to a great age.

Such was the Privy Councillor and superfluous member of various superfluous institutions, Ilýa Epímovich Golovín.

He had three sons, of whom Iván Ilých was the second. The eldest son was following in his father's footsteps only in another department, and was already approaching that stage in the service at which a similar sinecure would be reached. The third son was a failure. He had ruined his prospects in a number of positions and was now serving in the railway department. His father and brothers, and still more their wives, not merely disliked meeting him, but avoided remembering his existence unless compelled to do so. His sister had married Baron Greff, a Petersburg official of her father's type. Iván Ilých was *le phénix de la famille* as people said. He was neither as cold and formal as his elder brother nor as wild as the younger, but was a happy mean between them—an intelligent, polished, lively and agreeable man. He had studied with his younger brother at the School of Law, but the latter had failed to complete the course and was expelled when he was in the fifth class. Iván Ilých finished the course well. Even when he was at the School of Law he was just what he remained for the rest of his life: a capable, cheerful, good-natured, and sociable man, though strict in the fulfilment of what he considered to be his duty: and he considered his duty to be what was so considered by those in authority. Neither as a boy nor as a man was he a toady, but from early youth was by nature attracted to people of high station as a fly is drawn to the light, assimilating their ways and views of life and establishing friendly relations with them. All the enthusiasms of childhood and youth passed without leaving much trace on him; he succumbed to sensuality, to vanity, and latterly among the highest classes to liberalism, but always within limits which his instinct unfailingly indicated to him as correct.

At school he had done things which had formerly seemed to him very horrid and made him feel disgusted with himself when he did them; but when later on he saw that such actions were done by people of good position and that they did not regard them as wrong, he was able not exactly to regard them as right, but to forget about them entirely or not be at all troubled at remembering them.

Having graduated from the School of Law and qualified for the tenth rank of the civil service, and having received money from his father for his equipment, Iván Ilých ordered himself clothes at Scharmer's, the fashionable tailor, hung a medallion inscribed *respice finen* on his watch-chain, took leave of his professor and the prince who was patron of the school, had a farewell dinner with his comrades at Donon's first-class restaurant, and with his new and fashionable portmanteau, linen, clothes, shaving and other toilet appliances, and a travelling rug, all purchased at the best shops, he set off for one of the provinces where, through his father's influence, he had been attached to the Governor as an official for special service.

In the province Iván Ilých soon arranged as easy and agreeable a position for himself as he had had at the School of Law. He performed his official tasks, made his career, and at the same time amused himself pleasantly and decorously. Occasionally he paid official visits to country districts, where he behaved with dignity both to his superiors and inferiors, and performed the duties entrusted to him, which related chiefly to the sectarians, with an exactness and incorruptible honesty of which he could not but feel proud.

In official matters, despite his youth and taste for frivolous gaiety, he was exceedingly reserved, punctilious, and even severe; but in society he was often amusing and witty, and always good-natured, correct in his manner, and *bon enfant,* as the governor and his wife— with whom he was like one of the family—used to say of him.

In the provinces he had an affair with a lady who made advances to the elegant young lawyer, and there was also a milliner; and there were carousals with aides-de-camp who visited the district, and after-supper visits to a certain outlying street of doubtful reputation; and there was too some obsequiousness to his chief and even to his chief's wife, but all this was done with such a tone of good breeding that no hard names could be applied to it. It all came under the heading of the French saying: *"Il faut que jeunesse se passe."* It was all done with clean hands, in clean linen, with French phrases, and above all among people of the best society and consequently with the approval of people of rank.

So Iván Ilých served for five years and then came a change in his official life. The new and reformed judicial institutions were introduced, and new men were needed. Iván Ilých became such a new man. He was offered the post of Examining Magistrate, and he accepted it though the post was in another province and obliged him to give up the connexions he had formed and to make new ones. His friends met to give him a send-off; they had a group-photograph taken and presented him with a silver cigarette-case, and he set off to his new post.

As examining magistrate Iván Ilých was just as *comme il faut* and decorous a man, inspiring general respect and capable of separating his official duties from his private life, as he had been when acting as an official on special service. His duties now as examining magistrate were far more interesting and attractive than before. In his former position it had been pleasant to wear an undress uniform made by Scharmer, and to pass through the crowd of petitioners and officials who were timorously awaiting an audience with the governor, and who envied him as with free and easy gait he went straight into his chief's private room to have a cup of tea and a cigarette with him. But not many people had then been directly dependent on him—only police officials and the sectarians when he went on special missions—and he liked to treat them politely, almost as comrades, as if he were letting them feel that he who had the power to crush them was treating them in this simple, friendly way. There were then but few such people. But now, as an examining magistrate, Iván Ilých felt that everyone without exception, even the most important and self-satisfied, was in his power, and that he need only write a few words on a sheet of paper with a certain heading, and this or that important, self-satisfied person would be brought before him in the role of an accused person or a witness, and if he did not choose to allow him to sit down, would have to stand before him and answer his questions. Iván Ilých never abused his power; he tried on the contrary to soften its expression, but the consciousness of it and of the possibility of softening its effect, supplied the chief interest and attraction of his office. In his work itself, especially in his examinations, he very soon acquired a method of eliminating all considerations irrelevant to the legal aspect of the case, and reducing even the most complicated case to a form in which it would be presented on paper only in its externals, completely excluding his personal opinion of the matter, while above all observing every prescribed formality. The work was new and Iván Ilých was one of the first men to apply the new Code of 1864.[1]

On taking up the post of examining magistrate in a new town, he made new acquaintances and connexions, placed himself on a new footing, and assumed a somewhat different tone. He took up an attitude of rather dignified aloofness towards the provincial authorities, but picked out the best circle of legal gentlemen and wealthy gentry living in the town and assumed a tone of slight dissatisfaction with the government, of moderate liberalism, and of enlightened citizenship. At the same time, without at all altering the elegance of his toilet, he ceased shaving his chin and allowed his beard to grow as it pleased.

Iván Ilých settled down very pleasantly in this new town. The society there, which inclined towards opposition to the Governor, was friendly, his salary was larger, and he began to play *vint* [a form of bridge], which he found added not a little to the pleasure of life, for he had a capacity for cards, played good-humouredly, and calculated rapidly and astutely, so that he usually won.

After living there for two years he met his future wife, Praskóvya Fëdorovna Míkhel, who was the most attractive, clever, and brilliant girl of the set in which he moved, and among other amusements and relaxation from his labours as examining magistrate, Iván Ilých established light and playful relations with her.

While he had been an official on special service he had been accustomed to dance, but now as an examining magistrate it was exceptional for him to do so. If he danced now, he did it as if to show that though he served under the reformed order of things, and had reached the fifth official rank, yet when it came to dancing he could do it better than most people. So at the end of an evening he sometimes danced with Praskóvya Fëdorovna, and it was chiefly during these dances that he captivated her. She fell in love with him. Iván Ilých had at first no definite intention of marrying, but when the girl

---

[1] The emancipation of the serfs in 1861 was followed by a thorough all-round reform of judicial proceedings.—Aylmer Maud [translator].

fell in love with him he said to himself: "Really, why shouldn't I marry?"

Praskóvya Fëdorovna came of a good family, was not bad looking, and had some little property. Iván Ilých might have aspired to a more brilliant match, but even this was good. He had his salary, and she, he hoped, would have an equal income. She was well connected, and was a sweet, pretty, and thoroughly correct young woman. To say that Iván Ilých married because he fell in love with Praskóvya Fëdorovna and found that she sympathized with his views of life would be as incorrect as to say that he married because his social circle approved of the match. He was swayed by both these considerations: the marriage gave him personal satisfaction, and at the same time it was considered the right thing by the most highly placed of his associates.

So Iván Ilých got married.

The preparations for marriage and the beginning of married life, with its conjugal caresses, the new furniture, new crockery, and new linen, were very pleasant until his wife became pregnant—so that Iván Ilých had begun to think that marriage would not impair the easy, agreeable, gay and always decorous character of his life, approved of by society and regarded by himself as natural, but would even improve it. But from the first months of his wife's pregnancy, something new, unpleasant, depressing, and unseemly, and from which there was no way of escape, unexpectedly showed itself.

His wife, without any reason—*de gaieté de coeur* as Iván Ilých expressed it to himself—began to disturb the pleasure and propriety of their life. She began to be jealous without any cause, expected him to devote his whole attention to her, found fault with everything, and made coarse and ill-mannered scenes.

At first Iván Ilých hoped to escape from the unpleasantness of this state of affairs by the same easy and decorous relation to life that had served him heretofore: he tried to ignore his wife's disagreeable moods, continued to live in his usual easy and pleasant way, invited friends to his house for a game of cards, and also tried going out to his club of spending his evenings with friends. But one day his wife began upbraiding him so vigorously, using such coarse words, and continued to abuse him every time he did not fulfil her demands, so resolutely and with such evident determination not to give way till he submitted —that is, till he stayed at home and was bored just as she was—that he became alarmed. He now realized that matrimony—at any rate with Praskóvya Fëdorovna—was not always conducive to the pleasures and amenities of life but on the contrary often infringed both comfort and propriety, and that he must therefore entrench himself against such infringement. And Iván Ilých began to seek for means of doing so. His official duties were the one thing that imposed upon Praskóvya Fëdorovna, and by means of his official work and the duties attached to it he began struggling with his wife to secure his own independence.

With the birth of their child, the attempts to feed it and the various failures in doing so, and with the real and imaginary illnesses of mother and child, in which Iván Ilých's sympathy was demanded but about which he understood nothing, the need of securing for himself an existence outside his family life became still more imperative.

As his wife grew more irritable and exacting and Iván Ilých trans-ferred the centre of gravity of his life more and more to his official work, so did he grow to like his work better and became more am-bitious than before.

Very soon, within a year of his wedding, Iván Ilých had realized that marriage, though it may add some comforts to life, is in fact a very intricate and difficult affair towards which in order to perform one's duty, that is, to lead a decorous life approved of by society, one must adopt a definite attitude just as towards one's official duties.

And Iván Ilých evolved such an attitude towards married life. He only required of it those conveniences—dinner at home, housewife, and bed—which it could give him, and above all that propriety of ex-ternal forms required by public opinion. For the rest he looked for light-hearted pleasure and propriety, and was very thankful when he found them, but if he met with antagonism and querulousness he at once retired into his separate fenced-off world of official duties, where he found satisfaction.

Iván Ilých was esteemed a good official, and after three years was made Assistant Public Prosecutor. His new duties, their importance, the possibility of indicting and imprisoning anyone he chose, the publicity his speeches received, and the success he had in all these things, made his work still more attractive.

More children came. His wife became more and more querulous and ill-tempered, but the attitude Iván Ilých had adopted towards his home life rendered him almost impervious to her grumbling.

After seven years' service in that town he was transferred to another province as Public Prosecutor. They moved, but were short of money and his wife did not like the place they moved to. Though the salary was higher the cost of living was greater, besides which two of their children died and family life became still more unpleasant for him.

Praskóvya Fëdorovna blamed her husband for every inconvenience they encountered in their new home. Most of the conversations between husband and wife, especially as to the children's education, led to topics which recalled former disputes, and those disputes were apt to flare up at any moment. There remained only those rare periods of amorousness which still came to them at times but did not last long. These were islets at which they anchored for a while and then again set out upon that ocean of veiled hostility which showed itself in their aloofness from one another. This aloofness might have grieved Iván Ilých had he considered that it ought not to exist, but he now regarded the position as normal, and even made it the goal at which he aimed in family life. His aim was to free himself more and more from those unpleasantnesses and to give them a semblance of harmlessness and propriety. He attained this by spending less and less time with his family, and when obliged to be at home he tried to safeguard his position by the presence of outsiders. The chief thing however was that he had his official duties. The whole interest of his life now centred in the official world and that interest absorbed him. The consciousness of his power, being able to ruin anybody he wished to ruin, the importance, even the external dignity of his entry into court, or meetings with his subordinates, his success with superiors and inferiors, and above all his masterly handling of cases, of which he was conscious—all this gave him pleasure and filled his life, together with chats with his colleagues, dinners, and bridge. So that on the whole Iván Ilých's life continued to flow as he considered it should do—pleasantly and properly.

So things continued for another seven years. His eldest daughter was already sixteen, another child had died, and only one son was left, a schoolboy and a subject of dissension. Iván Ilých wanted to put him in the School of Law, but to spite him Praskóvya Fëdorovna entered him at the High School. The daughter had been educated at home and had turned out well: the boy did not learn badly either.

### III

So Iván Ilých lived for seventeen years after his marriage. He was already a Public Prosecutor of long standing, and had declined several proposed transfers while awaiting a more desirable post, when an unanticipated occurrence quite upset the peaceful course of his life. He was expecting to be offered the post of presiding judge in a University town, but Happe somehow came to the front and obtained the appointment instead. Iván Ilých became irritable, reproached Happe, and quarrelled both with him and with his immediate superiors—who became colder to him and again passed him over when other appointments were made.

This was in 1880, the hardest year of Iván Ilých's life. It was then that it became evident on the one hand that his salary was insufficient for them to live on, and on the other that he had been forgotten, and not only this, but that what was for him the greatest and most cruel injustice appeared to others a quite ordinary occurrence. Even his father did not consider it his duty to help him. Iván Ilých felt himself abandoned by everyone, and that they regarded his position with a salary of 3,500 rubles [about $2,000] as quite normal and even fortunate. He alone knew that with the consciousness of the injustices done him, with his wife's incessant nagging, and with the debts he had contracted by living beyond his means, his position was far from normal.

In order to save money that summer he obtained leave of absence and went with his wife to live in the country at her brother's place.

In the country, without his work, he experienced *ennui* for the first time in his life, and not only *ennui* but intolerable depression, and he decided that it was impossible to go on living like that, and that it was necessary to take energetic measures.

Having passed a sleepless night pacing up and down the veranda, he decided to go to Petersburg and bestir himself, in order to punish those who had failed to appreciate him and to get transferred to another ministry.

Next day, despite many protests from his wife and her brother, he started for Petersburg with the sole object of obtaining a post with a salary of five thousand rubles a year. He was no longer bent on any particular department, or tendency, or kind of activity. All he now wanted was an appointment to another post with a salary of five thousand rubles, either in the administration, in the banks, with the railways, in one of the Empress Márya's Institutions, or even in the customs—but it had to carry with it a salary of five thousand rubles and be in a ministry other than that in which they had failed to appreciate him.

And this quest of Iván Ilých's was crowned with remarkable and unexpected success. At Kursk an acquaintance of his, F. I. Ilyín, got into the first-class carriage, sat down beside Iván Ilých, and told him of a telegram just received by the Governor of Kursk announcing that a change was about to take place in the ministry: Peter Ivánovich was to be superseded by Iván Semënovich.

The proposed change, apart from its significance for Russia, had a special significance for Iván Ilých, because by bringing forward a new man, Peter Petróvich, and consequently his friend Zachár Ivánovich, it was highly favourable for Iván Ilých, since Zachár Ivánovich was a friend and colleague of his.

In Moscow this news was confirmed, and on reaching Petersburg Iván Ilých found Zachár Ivánovich and received a definite promise of an appointment in his former Department of Justice.

A week later he telegraphed to his wife: "Zachár in Miller's place. I shall receive appointment on presentation of report."

Thanks to this change of personnel, Iván Ilých had unexpectedly obtained an appointment in his former ministry which placed him two stages above his former colleagues besides giving him five thousand rubles salary and three thousand five hundred rubles for expenses connected with his removal. All his ill humour towards his former enemies and the whole department vanished, and Iván Ilých was completely happy.

He returned to the country more cheerful and contented than he had been for a long time. Praskóvya Fëdorovna also cheered up and a truce was arranged between them. Iván Ilých told of how he had been fêted by everybody in Petersburg, how all those who had been his enemies were put to shame and now fawned on him, how envious they were of his appointment, and how much everybody in Petersburg had liked him.

Praskóvya Fëdorovna listened to all this and appeared to believe it. She did not contradict anything, but only made plans for their life in the town to which they were going. Iván Ilých saw with delight that these plans were his plans, that he and his wife agreed, and that, after a stumble, his life was regaining its due and natural character of pleasant lightheartedness and decorum.

Iván Ilých had come back for a short time only, for he had to take up his new duties on the 10th of September. Moreover, he needed time to settle into the new place, to move all his belongings from the province, and to buy and order many additional things: in a word, to make such arrangements as he had resolved on, which were almost exactly what Praskóvya Fëdorovna too had decided on.

Now that everything had happened so fortunately, and that he and his wife were at one in their aims and moreover saw so little of one another, they got on together better than they had done since the first years of marriage. Iván Ilých had thought of taking his family away with him at once, but the insistence of his wife's brother and her sister-in-law, who had suddenly become particularly amiable and friendly to him and his family, induced him to depart alone.

So he departed, and the cheerful state of mind induced by his success and by the harmony between his wife and himself, the one intensifying the other, did not leave him. He found a delightful house, just the thing both he and his wife had dreamt of. Spacious, lofty reception rooms in the old style, a convenient and dignified study, rooms for his wife and daughter, a study for his son—it might have been specially built for them. Iván Ilých himself superintended the arrangements, chose the wall-papers, supplemented the furniture (preferably with antiques which he considered particularly *comme il faut*), and supervised the upholstering. Everything progressed and progressed and approached the ideal he had set himself: even when things were only half completed they exceeded his expectations. He saw what a refined and elegant character, free from vulgarity, it would all have when it was ready. On falling asleep he pictured to himself how the reception-room would look. Looking at the yet unfinished drawing-room he could see the fireplace, the screen, the what-not, the little chairs dotted here and there, the dishes and plates on the walls, and the bronzes, as they would be when everything was in place. He was pleased by the thought of how his wife and daughter, who shared his taste in this matter, would be impressed by it. They were certainly not expecting as much. He had been particularly successful in finding, and buying cheaply, antiques which gave a particularly aristocratic character to the whole place. But in his letters he intentionally understated everything in order to be able to surprise them. All this so absorbed him that his new duties—though he liked his official work —interested him less than he had expected. Sometimes he even had moments of absent-mindedness during the Court Sessions, and would consider whether he should have straight or curved cornices for his curtains. He was so interested in it all that he often did things himself, rearranging the furniture, or rehanging the curtains. Once when mounting a step-ladder to show the upholsterer, who did not understand, how he wanted the hangings draped, he made a false step and slipped, but being a strong and agile man he clung on and only knocked his side against the knob of the window frame. The bruised place was painful but the pain soon passed, and he felt particularly bright and well just then. He wrote: "I feel fifteen years younger." He thought he would have everything ready by September, but it dragged on till mid-October. But the result was charming not only in his eyes but to everyone who saw it.

In reality it was just what is usually seen in the houses of people of moderate means who want to appear rich, and therefore succeed only in resembling others like themselves: there were damasks, dark wood, plants, rugs, and dull and polished bronzes—all the things people of a certain class have in order to resemble other people of that class. His house was so like the others that it would never have been noticed, but to him it all seemed to be quite exceptional. He was very happy when he met his family at the station and brought them to the newly furnished house all lit up, where a footman in a white tie opened the door into the hall decorated with plants, and when they went on into the drawing-room and the study uttering exclamations of delight. He conducted them everywhere, drank in their praises eagerly, and beamed with pleasure. At tea that evening, when Praskóvya Fëdorovna among other things asked him about his fall, he laughed, and showed them how he had gone flying and had frightened the upholsterer.

"It's a good thing I'm a bit of an athlete. Another man might have been killed, but I merely knocked myself, just here; it hurts when it's touched, but it's passing off already—it's only a bruise."

So they began living in their new home—in which, as always happens, when they got thoroughly settled in they found they were just one room short—and with the increased income, which as always was just a little (some five hundred rubles) too little, but it was all very nice.

Things went particularly well at first, before everything was finally arranged and while something had still to be done: this thing bought, that thing ordered, another thing moved, and something else adjusted. Though there were some disputes between husband and wife, they were both so well satisfied and had so much to do that it all passed off without any serious quarrels. When nothing was left to arrange it became rather dull and something seemed to be lacking, but they were then making acquaintances, forming habits, and life was growing fuller.

Iván Ilých spent his mornings at the law court and came home to dinner, and at first he was generally in a good humour, though he occasionally became irritable just on account of his house. (Every spot on the tablecloth or the upholstery, and every broken window-blind string, irritated him. He had devoted so much trouble to arranging it all that every disturbance of it distressed him.) But on the whole his life ran its course as he believed life should do: easily, pleasantly, and decorously.

He got up at nine, drank his coffee, read the paper, and then put on his undress uniform and went to the law courts. There the harness in which he worked had already been stretched to fit him and he donned it without a hitch: petitioners, inquiries at the chancery, the chancery itself, and the sittings public and administrative. In all this the thing was to exclude everything fresh and vital, which always disturbs the regular course of official business, and to admit only official relations with people, and then only on official grounds. A man would come, for instance, wanting some information. Iván Ilých, as one in whose sphere the matter did not lie, would have nothing to do with him: but if the man had some business with him in his official capacity, something that could be expressed on officially stamped paper, he would do everything, positively everything he could within the limits of such relations, and in doing so would maintain the semblance of friendly human relations, that is, would observe the courtesies of life. As soon as the official relations ended, so did everything else. Iván Ilých possessed this capacity to separate his real life from the official side of affairs and not mix the two, in the highest degree, and by long practice and natural aptitude had brought it to such a pitch that sometimes, in the manner of a virtuoso, he would even allow himself to let the human and official relations mingle. He let himself do this just because he felt that he could at any time he chose resume the strictly official attitude again and drop the human relation. And he did it all easily, pleasantly, correctly, and even artistically. In the intervals between the sessions he smoked, drank tea, chatted a little about politics, a little about general topics, a little about cards, but most of all about official appointments. Tired, but with the feelings of a virtuoso—one of the first violins who has played his part in an orchestra with precision—he would return home to find that his wife and daughter had been out paying calls, or had a visitor, and that his son had been to school, had done his homework with his tutor, and was duly learning what is taught at High Schools. Everything was as it should be. After dinner, if they had no visitors, Iván Ilých sometimes read a book that was being much discussed at the time, and in the evening settled down to work, that is, read official papers, compared the depositions of witnesses, and noted paragraphs of the Code applying to them. This was neither dull nor amusing. It was dull when he might have been playing bridge, but if no bridge was available it was at any rate better than doing nothing or sitting with his wife. Iván Ilých's chief pleasure was giving little dinners to which he invited men and women of good social position, and just as his drawing-room resembled all other drawing-rooms so did his enjoyable little parties resemble all other such parties.

Once they even gave a dance. Iván Ilých enjoyed it and everything went off well, except that it led to a violent quarrel with his wife about the cakes and sweets. Praskóvya Fëdorovna had made her own plans, but Iván Ilých insisted on getting everything from an expensive confectioner and ordered too many cakes, and the quarrel occurred because some of those cakes were left over and the confectioner's bill came to forty-five rubles. It was a great and disagreeable quarrel. Praskóvya Fëdorovna called him "a fool and an imbecile," and he clutched at his head and made angry allusions to divorce.

But the dance itself had been enjoyable. The best people were there, and Iván Ilých had danced with Princess Trúfonova, a sister of the distinguished founder of the Society "Bear by Burden."

The pleasures connected with his work were pleasure of ambition; his social pleasures were those of vanity; but Iván Ilých's greatest pleasure was playing bridge. He acknowledged that whatever disagreeable incident happened in his life, the pleasure that beamed like a ray of light above everything else was to sit down to bridge with good players, not noisy partners, and of course to four-handed bridge (with five players it was annoying to have to stand out, though one pretended not to mind), to play a clever and serious game (when the cards allowed it) and then to have supper and drink a glass of wine.

After a game of bridge, especially if he had won a little (to win a large sum was unpleasant), Iván Ilých went to bed in specially good humour.

So they lived. They formed a circle of acquaintances among the best people and were visited by people of importance and by young folk. In their views as to their acquaintances, husband, wife and daughter were entirely agreed, and tacitly and unanimously kept at arm's length and shook off the various shabby friends and relations who, with much show of affection, gushed into the drawing-room with its Japanese plates on the walls. Soon these shabby friends ceased to obtrude themselves and only the best people remained in the Golovíns' set.

Young men made up to Lisa, and Petríshchev, an examining magistrate and Dmítri Ivánovich Petríshchev's son and sole heir, began to be so attentive to her that Iván Ilých had already spoken to Praskóvya Fëdorovna about it, and considered whether they should not arrange a party for them, or get up some private theatricals.

So they lived, and all went well, without change, and life flowed pleasantly.

## IV

They were all in good health. It could not be called ill health if Iván Ilých sometimes said that he had a queer taste in his mouth and felt some discomfort in his left side.

But this discomfort increased and, though not exactly painful, grew into a sense of pressure in his side accompanied by ill humour. And his irritability became worse and worse and began to mar the agreeable, easy, and correct life that had established itself in the Golovín family. Quarrels between husband and wife became more and more frequent, and soon the ease and amenity disappeared and even the decorum was rarely maintained. Scenes again became frequent, and very few of those islets remained on which husband and wife could meet without an explosion. Praskóvya Fëdorovna now had good reason to say that her husband's temper was trying. With characteristic exaggeration she said he had always had a dreadful temper, and that it had needed all her good nature to put up with it for twenty years. It was true that now the quarrels were started by him. His bursts of temper always came just before dinner, often just as he began to eat his soup. Sometimes he noticed that a plate or dish was chipped, or the food was not right, or his son put his elbow on the table, or his daughter's hair was not done as he liked it, and for all this he blamed Praskóvya Fëdorovna. At first she retorted and said disagreeable things to him, but once or twice he fell into such a rage at the beginning of dinner that she realized it was due to some physical derangement brought on by taking food, and so she restrained herself and did not answer, but only hurried to get the dinner over. She regarded this self-restraint as highly praiseworthy. Having come to the conclusion that her husband had a dreadful temper and made her life miserable, she began to feel sorry for herself, and the more she pitied herself the more she hated her husband. She began to wish he would die; yet she did not want him to die because then his salary would cease. And this irritated her against him still more. She considered herself dreadfully unhappy just because not even his death could save her, and though she concealed her exasperation, that hidden exasperation of hers increased his irritation also.

After one scene in which Iván Ilých had been particularly unfair and after which he had said in explanation that he certainly was irritable but that it was due to his not being well, she said that if he was ill it should be attended to, and insisted on his going to see a celebrated doctor.

He went. Everything took place as he had expected and as it always does. There was the usual waiting and the important air assumed by the doctor, with which he was so familiar (resembling that which he himself assumed in court), and the sounding and listening, and the questions which called for answers that were foregone conclusions and were evidently unnecessary, and the look of importance which implied that "if only you put yourself in our hands we will arrange everything —we know indubitably how it has to be done, always in the same way for everybody alike." It was all just as it was in the law courts. The doctor put on just the same air towards him as he himself put on towards an accused person.

The doctor said that so-and-so indicated that there was so-and-so inside the patient, but if the investigation of so-and-so did not confirm this, then he must assume that and that. If he assumed that and that, then . . . and so on. To Iván Ilých only one question was important: was his case serious or not? But the doctor ignored that inappropriate question. From his point of view it was not the one under consideration, the real question was to decide between a floating kidney, chronic catarrh, or appendicitis. It was not a question of Iván Ilých's life or death, but one between a floating kidney and appendicitis. And that question the doctor solved brilliantly, as it seemed to Iván Ilých, in favour of the appendix, with the reservation that should an examination of the urine give fresh indications the matter would be reconsidered. All this was just what Iván Ilých had himself brilliantly accomplished a thousand times in dealing with men on trial. The doctor summed up just as brilliantly, looking over his spectacles triumphantly and even gaily at the accused. From the doctor's summing up Iván Ilých concluded that things were bad, but that for the doctor, and perhaps for everybody else, it was a matter of indifference, though for him it was bad. And this conclusion struck him painfully, arousing in him a great feeling of pity for himself and of bitterness towards the doctor's indifference to a matter of such importance.

He said nothing of this, but rose, placed the doctor's fee on the table, and remarked with a sigh: "We sick people probably often put inappropriate questions. But tell me, in general, is this complaint dangerous, or not? . . ."

The doctor looked at him sternly over his spectacles with one eye, as if to say: "Prisoner, if you will not keep to the questions put to you, I shall be obliged to have you removed from the court."

"I have already told you what I consider necessary and proper. The analysis may show something more." And the doctor bowed.

Iván Ilých went out slowly, seated himself disconsolately in his sledge, and drove home. All the way home he was going over what the doctor had said, trying to translate those complicated, obscure, scientific phrases into plain language and find in them an answer to the question: "Is my condition bad? Is it very bad? Or is there as yet nothing much wrong?" And it seemed to him that the meaning of what the doctor had said was that it was very bad. Everything in the streets seemed depressing. The cabmen, the houses, the passers-by, and the shops, were dismal. His ache, this dull gnawing ache that never ceased for a moment, seemed to have acquired a new and more serious significance from the doctor's dubious remarks. Iván Ilých now watched it with a new and oppressive feeling.

He reached home and began to tell his wife about it. She listened, but in the middle of his account his daughter came in with her hat on, ready to go out with her mother. She sat down reluctantly to listen to this tedious story, but could not stand it long, and her mother too did not hear him to the end.

"Well, I am very glad," she said. "Mind now to take your medicine regularly. Give me the prescription and I'll send Gerásim to the chemist's." And she went to get ready to go out.

While she was in the room Iván Ilých had hardly taken time to breathe, but he sighed deeply when she left it.

"Well," he thought, "perhaps it isn't so bad after all."

He began taking his medicine and following the doctor's directions, which had been altered after the examination of the urine. But then it happened that there was a contradiction between the indications drawn from the examination of the urine and the symptoms that showed themselves. It turned out that what was happening differed from what the doctor had told him, and that he had either forgotten, or blundered, or hidden something from him. He could not, however, be blamed for that, and Iván Ilých still obeyed his orders implicitly and at first derived some comfort from doing so.

From the time of his visit to the doctor, Iván Ilých's chief occupation was the exact fulfilment of the doctor's instructions regarding hygiene and the taking of medicine, and the observation of his pain and his excretions. His chief interests came to be people's ailments and people's health. When sickness, deaths, or recoveries, were mentioned in his presence, especially when the illness resembled his own, he listened with agitation which he tried to hide, asked questions, and applied what he heard to his own case.

The pain did not grow less, but Iván Ilých made efforts to force himself to think that he was better. And he could do this so long as nothing agitated him. But as soon as he had any unpleasantness with his wife, any lack of success in his official work, or held bad cards at bridge, he was at once acutely sensible of his disease. He had formerly borne such mischances, hoping soon to adjust what was wrong, to master it and attain success, or make a grand slam. But now every mischance upset him and plunged him into despair. He would say to himself: "There now, just as I was beginning to get better and the medicine had begun to take effect, comes this accursed misfortune, or unpleasantness. . . ." And he was furious with the mishap, or with the people who were causing the unpleasantness and killing him, for he felt that his fury was killing him but could not restrain it. One would have thought that it should have been clear to him that this exasperation with circumstances and people aggravated his illness, and that he ought therefore to ignore unpleasant occurrences. But he drew the very opposite conclusion: he said that he needed peace, and he watched for everything that might disturb it and became irritable at the slightest infringement of it. His condition was rendered worse by the fact that he read medical books and consulted doctors. The progress of his disease was so gradual that he could deceive himself when comparing one day with another—the difference was so slight. But when he consulted the doctors it seemed to him that he was getting worse, and even very rapidly. Yet despite this he was continually consulting them.

That month he went to see another celebrity, who told him almost the same as the first had done but put his questions rather differently, and the interview with this celebrity only increased Iván Ilých's doubts and fears. A friend of a friend of his, a very good doctor, diagnosed his illness again quite differently from the others, and though he predicted recovery, his questions and suppositions bewildered Iván Ilých still more and increased his doubts. A homoeopathist diagnosed the disease in yet another way, and prescribed medicine which Iván Ilých took secretly for a week. But after a week, not feeling any improvement and having lost confidence both in the former doctor's treatment and in this one's, he became still more despondent. One day a lady acquaintance mentioned a cure effected by a wonder-working icon. Iván Ilých caught himself listening attentively and beginning to believe that it had occurred. This incident alarmed him. "Has my mind really weakened to such an extent?" he asked himself. "Nonsense! It's all rubbish. I mustn't give way to nervous fears but having chosen a doctor must keep strictly to his treatment. That is what I will do. Now it's all settled. I won't think about it, but will follow the treatment seriously till summer, and then we shall see. From now there must be no more of this wavering!" This was easy to say but impossible to carry out. The pain in his side oppressed him and seemed to grow worse and more incessant, while the taste in his mouth grew stranger and stranger. It seemed to him that his breath had a disgusting smell, and he was conscious of a loss of appetite and strength. There was no deceiving himself: something terrible, new, and more important than anything before in his life, was taking place within him of which he alone was aware. Those about him did not understand or would not understand it, but thought everything in the world was going on as usual. That tormented Iván Ilých more than anything. He saw that his household, especially his wife and daughter who were in a perfect whirl of visiting, did not understand anything of it and were annoyed that he was so depressed and so exacting, as if he were to blame for it. Though they tried to disguise it he saw that he was an obstacle in their path, and that his wife had adopted a definite line in regard to his illness and kept to it regardless of anything he said or did. Her attitude was this: "You know," she would say to her friends, "Iván Ilých can't do as other people do, and keep to the treatment prescribed for him. One day he'll take his drops and keep strictly to his diet and go to bed in good time, but the next day unless I watch him he'll suddenly forget his medicine, eat sturgeon—which is forbidden—and sit up playing cards till one o'clock in the morning."

"Oh, come, when was that?" Iván Ilých would ask in vexation. "Only once at Peter Ivánovich's."

"And yesterday with Shébek."

"Well, even if I hadn't stayed up, this pain would have kept me awake."

"Be that as it may you'll never get well like that, but will always make us wretched."

Praskóvya Fëdorovna's attitude to Iván Ilých's illness, as she expressed it both to others and to him, was that it was his own fault and was another of the annoyances he caused her. Iván Ilých felt that this opinion escaped her involuntarily—but that did not make it easier for him.

As the law courts too, Iván Ilých noticed, or thought he noticed, a strange attitude towards himself. It sometimes seemed to him that people were watching him inquisitively as a man whose place might soon be vacant. Then again, his friends would suddenly begin to chaff him in a friendly way about his low spirits, as if the awful, horrible, and unheard-of thing that was going on within him, incessantly gnawing at him and irresistibly drawing him away, was a very agreeable subject for jests. Schwartz in particular irritated him by his jocularity, vivacity, and *savoir-faire*, which reminded him of what he himself had been ten years ago.

Friends came to make up a set and they sat down to cards. They dealt, bending the new cards to soften them, and he sorted the diamonds in his hand and found he had seven. His partner said "No trumps" and supported him with two diamonds. What more could be wished for? It ought to be jolly and lively. They would make a grand slam. But suddenly Iván Ilých was conscious of that gnawing pain, that taste in his mouth, and it seemed ridiculous that in such circumstances he should be pleased to make a grand slam.

He looked at his partner Mikháil Mikháylovich, who rapped the table with his strong hand and instead of snatching up the tricks pushed the cards courteously and indulgently towards Iván Ilých that he might have the pleasure of gathering them up without the trouble of stretching out his hand for them. "Does he think I am too weak to stretch out my arm?" thought Iván Ilých, and forgetting what he was doing he over-trumped his partner, missing the grand slam by three tricks. And what was most awful of all was that he saw how upset Mikháil Mikháylovich was about it but did not himself care. And it was dreadful to realize why he did not care.

They all saw that he was suffering, and said: "We can stop if you are tired. Take a rest." Lie down? No, he was not at all tired, and he finished the rubber. All were gloomy and silent. Iván Ilých felt that he had diffused this gloom over them and could not dispel it. They had supper and went away, and Iván Ilých was left alone with the consciousness that his life was poisoned and was poisoning the lives of others, and that this poison did not weaken but penetrated more and more deeply into his whole being.

With this consciousness, and with physical pain besides the terror, he must go to bed, often to lie awake the greater part of the night. Next morning he had to get up again, dress, go to the law courts, speak, and write; or if he did not go out, spend at home those twenty four hours a day each of which was a torture. And he had to live thus all alone on the brink of an abyss, with no one who understood or pitied him.

## V

So one month passed and then another. Just before the New Year his brother-in law came to town and stayed at their house. Iván Ilých was at the law courts and Praskóvya Fëdorovna had gone shopping. When Iván Ilých came home and entered his study he found his brother-in-law there—a healthy, florid man—unpacking his portmanteau himself. He raised his head on hearing Iván Ilých's footsteps and looked up at him for a moment without a word. That stare told Iván Ilých everything. His brother-in-law opened his mouth to utter an exclamation of surprise but checked himself, and that action confirmed it all.

"I have changed, eh?"

"Yes, there is a change."

And after that, try as he would to get his brother-in-law to return to the subject of his looks, the latter would say nothing about it. Praskóvya Fëdorovna came home and her brother went out to her. Iván Ilých locked the door and began to examine himself in the glass, first full face, then in profile. He took up a portrait of himself taken with his wife, and compared it with what he saw in the glass. The change in him was immense. Then he bared his arms to the elbow, looked at them, drew the sleeves down again, sat down on an ottoman, and grew blacker than night.

"No, no, this won't do!" he said to himself, and jumped up, went to the table, took up some law papers and began to read them, but could not continue. He unlocked the door and went into the reception-room. The door leading to the drawing-room was shut. He approached it on tiptoe and listened.

"No, you are exaggerating!" Praskóvya Fëdorovna was saying.

"Exaggerating! Don't you see it? Why, he's a dead man! Look at his eyes—there's no light in them. But what is it that is wrong with him?"

"No one knows. Nikoláevich [that was another doctor] said something, but I don't know what. And Leshchetítsky [this was the celebrated specialist] said quite the contrary. . . ."

Iván Ilých walked away, went to his own room, lay down, and began musing: "The kidney, a floating kidney." He recalled all the doctors had told him of how it detached itself and swayed about. And by an effort of imagination he tried to catch that kidney and arrest it and support it. So little was needed for this, it seemed to him. "No, I'll go to see Peter Ivánovich again." [That was the friend whose friend was a doctor.] He rang, ordered the carriage, and got ready to go.

"Where are you going, Jean?" asked his wife, with a specially sad and exceptionally kind look.

This exceptionally kind look irritated him. He looked morosely at her.

"I must go to see Peter Ivánovich."

He went to see Peter Ivánovich, and together they went to see his friend, the doctor. He was in, and Iván Ilých had a long talk with him.

Reviewing the anatomical and physiological details of what in the doctor's opinion was going on inside him, he understood it all.

There was something, a small thing, in the vermiform appendix. It might all come right. Only stimulate the energy of one organ and check the activity of another, then absorption would take place and everything would come right. He got home rather late for dinner, ate his dinner, and conversed cheerfully, but could not for a long time bring himself to go back to work in his room. At last, however, he went to his study and did what was necessary, but the consciousness that he had put something aside—an important, intimate matter which he would revert to when his work was done—never left him. When he had finished his work he remembered that this intimate matter was the thought of his vermiform appendix. But he did not give himself up to it, and went to the drawing-room for tea. There were callers there, including the examining magistrate who was a desirable match for his daughter, and they were conversing, playing the piano and singing. Iván Ilých, as Praskóvya Fëdorovna remarked, spent that evening more cheerfully than usual, but he never for a moment forgot that he had postponed the important matter of the appendix. At eleven o'clock he said good-night and went to his bedroom. Since his illness he had slept alone in a small room next to his study. He undressed and took up a novel by Zola, but instead of reading it he fell into thought, and in his imagination that desired improvement in the vermiform appendix occurred. There was the absorption and evacuation and the re-establishment of normal activity. "Yes, that's it" he said to himself. "One need only assist nature, that's all." He remembered his medicine, rose, took it, and lay down on his back watching for the beneficent action of the medicine and for it to lessen the pain. "I need only take it regularly and avoid all injurious influences. I am already feeling better, much better." He began touching his side: it was not painful to the touch. "There, I really don't feel it. It's much better already." He put out the light and turned on his side . . . "The appendix is getting better, absorption is occurring." Suddenly he felt the old, familiar, dull, gnawing pain, stubborn and serious. There was the same familiar loathsome taste in his mouth. His heart sank and he felt dazed. "My God! My God!" he muttered. "Again, again! And it will never cease." And suddenly the matter presented itself in a quite different aspect. "Vermiform appendix! Kidney!" he said to himself.

"It's not a question of appendix or kidney, but of life . . . and death. Yes, life was there and now it is going, going and I cannot stop it. Yes. Why deceive myself? Isn't it obvious to everyone but me that I'm dying, and that it's only a question of weeks, days . . . it may happen this moment. There was light and now there is darkness. I was here and now I'm going there! Where?" A chill came over him, his breathing ceased, and he felt only the throbbing of his heart.

"When I am not, what will there be? There will be nothing. Then where shall I be when I am no more? Can this be dying? No, I don't want to!" He jumped up and tried to light the candle, felt for it with trembling hands, dropped candle and candlestick on the floor, and fell back on his pillow.

"What's the use? It makes no difference," he said to himself, staring with wide-open eyes into the darkness. "Death. Yes, death. And none of them know or wish to know it, and they have no pity for me. Now they are playing." (He heard through the door the distant sound of a song and its accompaniment.) "It's all the same to them, but they will die too! Fools! I first, and they later, but it will be the same for them. And now they are merry . . . the beasts!"

Anger choked him and he was agonizingly, unbearably miserable. "It is impossible that all men have been doomed to suffer this awful horror!" He raised himself.

"Something must be wrong. I must calm myself—must think it all over from the beginning." And he again began thinking. "Yes, the beginning of my illness: I knocked my side, but I was still quite well that day and the next. It hurt a little, then rather more. I saw the doctors, then followed despondency and anguish, more doctors, and I drew nearer to the abyss. My strength grew less and I kept coming nearer and nearer, and now I have wasted away and there is no light in my eyes. I think of the appendix—but this is death! I think of mending the appendix, and all the while here is death! Can it really be death?" Again terror seized him and he gasped for breath. He leant down and began feeling for the matches, pressing with his elbow on the stand beside the bed. It was in his way and hurt him, he grew furious with it, pressed on it still harder, and upset it. Breathless and in despair he fell on his back, expecting death to come immediately.

Meanwhile the visitors were leaving. Praskóvya Fëdorovna was seeing them off. She heard something fall and came in.

"What has happened?"

"Nothing. I knocked it over accidentally."

She went out and returned with a candle. He lay there panting heavily, like a man who has run a thousand yards, and stared upwards at her with a fixed look.

"What is it, Jean?"

"No . . . o . . . thing. I upset it." ("Why speak of it? She won't understand," he thought.)

And in truth she did not understand. She picked up the stand, lit his candle, and hurried away to see another visitor off. When she came back he still lay on his back, looking upwards.

"What is it? Do you feel worse?"

"Yes."

She shook her head and sat down.

"Do you know, Jean, I think we must ask Leshchetítsky to come and see you here."

This meant calling in the famous specialist, regardless of expense. He smiled malignantly and said "No." She remained a little longer and then went up to him and kissed his forehead.

While she was kissing him he hated her from the bottom of his soul and with difficulty refrained from pushing her away.

"Good-night. Please God you'll sleep."

"Yes."

## VI

Iván Ilých saw that he was dying, and he was in continual despair.

In the depth of his heart he knew he was dying, but not only was he not accustomed to the thought, he simply did not and could not grasp it.

The syllogism he had learnt from Kiezewetter's Logic: "Caius is a man, men are mortal, therefore Caius is mortal," had always seemed to him correct as applied to Caius, but certainly not as applied to himself. That Caius—man in the abstract—was mortal, was perfectly correct, but he was not Caius, not an abstract man, but a creature quite, quite separate from all others. He had been little Ványa, with a mamma and a papa, with Mitya and Volódya, with the toys, a coachman and a nurse, afterwards with Kátenka and with all the joys, griefs, and delights of childhood, boyhood, and youth. What did Caius know of the smell of that striped leather ball Ványa had been so fond of?

Had Caius kissed his mother's hand like that, and did the silk of her dress rustle so for Caius? Had he rioted like that at school when the pastry was bad? Had Caius been in love like that? Could Caius preside at a session as he did? "Caius really was mortal, and it was right for him to die; but for me, little Ványa, Iván Ilých, with all my thoughts and emotions, it's altogether a different matter. It cannot be that I ought to die. That would be too terrible."

Such was his feeling.

"If I had to die like Caius I should have known it was so. An inner voice would have told me so, but there was nothing of the sort in me and I and all my friends felt that our case was quite different from that of Caius. And now here it is!" he said to himself. "It can't be. It's impossible! But here it is. How is this? How is one to understand it?"

He could not understand it, and tried to drive this false, incorrect, morbid thought away and to replace it by other proper and healthy thoughts. But that thought, and not the thought only but the reality itself, seemed to come and confront him.

And to replace that thought he called up a succession of others, hoping to find in them some support. He tried to get back into the former current of thoughts that had once screened the thought of death from him. But strange to say, all that had formerly shut off, hidden, and destroyed, his consciousness of death, no longer had that effect. Iván Ilých now spent most of his time in attempting to re-establish that old current. He would say to himself: "I will take up my duties again—after all I used to live by them." And banishing all doubts he would go to the law courts, enter into conversation with his colleagues, and sit carelessly as was his wont, scanning the crowd with a thoughtful look and leaning both his emaciated arms on the arms of his oak chair; bending over as usual to a colleague and drawing his papers nearer he would interchange whispers with him, and then suddenly raising his eyes and sitting erect would pronounce certain words and open the proceedings. But suddenly in the midst of those proceedings the pain in his side, regardless of the stage the proceedings had reached, would begin its own gnawing work. Iván Ilých would turn his attention to it and try to drive the thought of it away, but without success. *It* would come and stand before him and look at him, and he would be petrified and the light would die out of his eyes, and he would again begin asking himself whether *It* alone

was true. And his colleagues and subordinates would see with surprise
and distress that he, the brilliant and subtle judge, was becoming confused and making mistakes. He would shake himself, try to pull himself together, manage somehow to bring the sitting to a close, and
return home with the sorrowful consciousness that his judicial labours
could not as formerly hide from him what he wanted them to hide,
and could not deliver him from *It*. And what was worst of all was
that It drew his attention to itself not in order to make him take some
action but only that he should look at *It,* look it straight in the face:
look at it and without doing anything, suffer inexpressibly.

And to save himself from this condition Iván Ilých looked for con-
solations—new screens—and new screens were found and for a while
seemed to save him, but then they immediately fell to pieces or rather
became transparent, as if *It* penerated them and nothing could veil *It*.

In these latter days he would go into the drawing-room he had arranged—that drawing-room where he had fallen and for the sake of
which (how bitterly ridiculous it seemed) he had sacrificed his life—
for he knew that his illness originated with that knock. He would
enter and see that something had scratched the polished table. He
would look for the cause of this and find that it was the bronze ornamentation of an album, that had got bent. He would take up the
expensive album which he had lovingly arranged, and feel vexed with
his daughter and her friends for their untidiness—for the album was
torn here and there and some of the photographs turned upside down.
He would put it carefully in order and bend the ornamentation back
into position. Then it would occur to him to place all those things in
another corner of the room, near the plants. He would call the footman, but his daughter or wife would come to help him. They would
not agree, and his wife would contradict him, and he would dispute
and grow angry. But that was all right, for then he did not think about
*It. It* was invisible.

But then, when he was moving something himself, his wife would
say: "Let the servants do it. You will hurt yourself again." And suddenly *It* would flash through the screen and he would see it. *It* was
just a flash, and he hoped it would disappear, but he would involuntarily pay attention to his side. "It sits there as before, gnawing just
the same!" And he could no longer forget *It,* but could distinctly see
it looking at him from behind the flowers. "What is it all for?"

"It really is so I lost my life over that curtain as I might have done when storming a fort. It that possible? How terrible and how stupid. It can't be true! It can't, but it is."

He would go to his study, lie down, and again be alone with *It:* face to face with *It.* And nothing could be done with *It* except to look at it and shudder.

## VII

How it happened it is impossible to say because it came about step by step, unnoticed, but in the third month of Iván Ilych's illness, his wife, his daughter, his son, his acquaintances, the doctors, the servants, and above all he himself, were aware that the whole interest he had for other people was whether he would soon vacate his place, and at last release the living from the discomfort caused by his presence and be himself released from his sufferings.

He slept less and less. He was given opium and hypodermic injections of morphine, but this did not relieve him. The dull depression he experienced in a somnolent condition at first gave him a little relief, but only as something new, afterwards it became as distressing as the pain itself or even more so.

Special foods were prepared for him by the doctors' orders, but all those foods became increasingly distasteful and disgusting to him.

For his excretions also special arrangements had to be made, and this was a torment to him every time—a torment from the uncleanliness, the unseemliness, and the smell, and from knowing that another person had to take part in it.

But just through this most unpleasant matter Iván Ilých obtained comfort. Gerásim, the butler's young assistant, always came in to carry the things out. Gerásim was a clean, fresh peasant lad, grown stout on town food and always cheerful and bright. At first the sight of him, in his clean Russian peasant costume, engaged on that disgusting task embarrassed Iván Ilých.

Once when he got up from the commode too weak to draw up his trousers, he dropped into a soft armchair and looked with horror at his bare, enfeebled thighs with the muscles so sharply marked on them.

Gerásim with a firm light tread, his heavy boots emitting a pleasant smell of tar and fresh winter air, came in wearing a clean Hessian apron, the sleeves of his print shirt tucked up over his strong bare young arms; and refraining from looking at his sick master out of consideration for his feelings, and restraining the joy of life that beamed from his face, went up to the commode.

"Gerásim!" said Iván Ilých in a weak voice.

Gerásim started, evidently afraid he might have committed some blunder, and with a rapid movement turned his fresh, kind, simple young face which just showed the first downy signs of a beard.

"Yes, sir?"

"That must be very unpleasant for you. You must forgive me. I am helpless."

"Oh, why, sir," and Gerásim's eyes beamed and he showed his glistening white teeth, "what's a little trouble? It's a case of illness with you, sir."

And his deft strong hands did their accustomed task, and he went out of the room stepping lightly. Five minutes later he as lightly returned.

Iván Ilých was still sitting in the same position in the armchair.

"Gerásim," he said when the latter had replaced the freshly-washed utensil. "Please come here and help me." Gerásim went up to him. "Lift me up. It is hard for me to get up. and I have seen Dmítri away."

Gerásim went up to him, grasped his master with his strong arms deftly but gently, in the same way that he stepped—lifted him, supported him with one hand, and with the other drew up his trousers and would have set him down again, but Iván Ilých asked to be led to the sofa. Gerásim, without an effort and without apparent pressure, led him, almost lifting him, to the sofa and placed him on it.

"Thank you. How easily and well you do it all!"

Gerásim smiled again and turned to leave the room. But Iván Ilých felt his presence such a comfort that he did not want to let him go.

"One thing more, please move up that chair. No, the other one—under my feet. It is easier for me when my feet are raised."

Gerásim brought the chair, set it down gently in place, and raised Iván Ilých's legs on to it. It seemed to Iván Ilých that he felt better while Gerásim was holding up his legs.

"It's better when my legs are higher," he said. "Place that cushion under them."

Gerásim did so. He again lifted the legs and placed them, and again Iván Ilých felt better while Gerásim held his legs. When he set them down Iván Ilých fancied he felt worse.

"Gerásim," he said. "Are you busy now?"

"Not at all, sir," said Gerásim, who had learnt from the townsfolk how to speak to gentlefolk.

"What have you still to do?"

"What have I to do? I've done everything except chopping the logs for to-morrow."

"Then hold my legs up a bit higher, can you?"

"Of course I can. Why not?" And Gerásim raised his master's legs higher and Iván Ilých thought that in that position he did not feel any pain at all.

"And how about the logs?"

"Don't trouble about that, sir. There's plenty of time."

Iván Ilých told Gerásim to sit down and hold his legs, and began to talk to him. And strange to say it seemed to him that he felt better while Gerásim held his legs up.

After that Iván Ilých would sometimes call Gerásim and get him to hold his legs on his shoulders, and he liked talking to him. Gerásim did it all easily, willingly, simply, and with a good nature that touched Iván Ilých. Health, strength, and vitality in other people were offensive to him, but Gerásim's strength and vitality did not mortify but soothed him.

What tormented Iván Ilych most was the deception, the lie, which for some reason they all accepted, that he was not dying but was simply ill, and that he only need keep quiet and undergo a treatment and then something very good would result. He however knew that do what they would nothing would come of it, only still more agonizing suffering and death. This deception tortured him—their not wishing to admit what they all knew and what he knew, but wanting to lie to him concerning his terrible condition, and wishing and forcing him to participate in that lie. Those lies—lies enacted over him on the eve of his death and destined to degrade this awful, solemn act to the level of their visitings, their curtains, their sturgeon for dinner—were a terrible agony for Iván Ilých. And strangely enough, many times when they were going through their antics over him he had been within a hairbreadth of calling out to them: "Stop lying! You know and I know that I am dying. Then at least stop lying about it!" But he had never had the spirit to do it. The awful, terrible act of his dying was, he could see, reduced by those about him to the level of a casual, unpleasant, and almost indecorous incident (as if someone entered a drawing-room diffusing an unpleasant odour) and this was done by that very decorum which he had served all his life long. He saw that no one felt for him, because no one even wished to grasp his position. Only Gerásim recognized it and pitied him. And so Iván Ilých felt at ease only with him. He felt comforted when Gerásim supported his legs (sometimes all night long) and refused to go to bed saying: "Don't you worry, Iván Ilých. I'll get sleep enough later on," or when he suddenly became familiar and exclaimed: "If you weren't sick it would be another matter, but as it is, why should I grudge a little trouble?" Gerásim alone did not lie; everything showed that he alone understood the facts of the case and did not consider it necessary to disguise them, but simply felt sorry for his emaciated and enfeebled master. Once when Iván Ilých was sending him away he even said straight out: "We shall all of us die, so why should I grudge a little trouble?"—expressing the fact that he did not think his work burdensome, because he was doing it for a dying man and hoped someone would do the same for him when his time came.

Apart from this lying, or because of it, what most tormented Iván Ilých was that no one pitied him as he wished to be pitied. At certain moments after prolonged suffering he wished most of all (though he would have been ashamed to confess it) for someone to pity him as a sick child is pitied. He longed to be petted and comforted. He knew he was an important functionary, that he had a beard turning grey, and that therefore what he longed for was impossible, but still he longed for it. And in Gerásim's attitude towards him there was something akin to what he wished for, and so that attitude comforted him. Iván Ilých wanted to weep, wanted to be petted and cried over, and then his colleague Shébek would come, and instead of weeping and being petted, Iván Ilých would assume a serious, severe, and profound air, and by force of habit would express his opinion on a decision of the Court of Cassation and would stubbornly insist on that view. This falsity around him and within him did more than anything else to poison his last days.

## VIII

It was morning. He knew it was morning because Gerásim had gone, and Peter the footman had come and put out the candles, drawn back one of the curtains, and begun quietly to tidy up. Whether it was morning or evening, Friday or Sunday, made no difference, it was all just the same: the gnawing, unmitigated, agonizing pain, never ceasing for an instant, the consciousness of life inexorably waning but not yet extinguished, that approach of that ever dreaded and hateful Death which was the only reality, and always the same falsity. What were days, weeks, hours, in such a case?

"Will you have some tea, sir?"

"He wants things to be regular, and wishes the gentlefolk to drink tea in the morning," thought Iván Ilých, and only said "No."

"Wouldn't you like to move onto the sofa, sir?"

"He wants to tidy up the room, and I'm in the way. I am uncleanliness and disorder," he thought, and said only:

"No, leave me alone."

The man went on bustling about. Iván Ilých stretched out his hand. Peter came up, ready to help.

"What is it, sir?"

"My watch."

Peter took the watch which was close at hand and gave it to his master.

"Half-past eight. Are they up?"

"No sir, except Vladímir Ivánich" (the son) "who has gone to school. Praskóvya Fëdorovna ordered me to wake her if you asked for her. Shall I do so?"

"No, there's no need to." "Perhaps I'd better have some tea," he thought, and added aloud: "Yes, bring me some tea."

Peter went to the door but Iván Ilých dreaded being left alone. "How can I keep him here? Oh yes, my medicine." "Peter, give me my medicine." "Why not? Perhaps it may still do me some good." He took a spoonful and swallowed it. "No, it won't help. It's all tomfoolery, all deception," he decided as soon as he became aware of the familiar, sickly, hopeless taste. "No, I can't believe in it any longer. But the pain, why this pain? If it would only cease just for a moment!" And he moaned. Peter turned towards him. "It's all right. Go and fetch me some tea."

Peter went out. Left alone Iván Ilých groaned not so much with pain, terrible though that was, as from mental anguish. Always and for ever the same, always these endless days and nights. If only it would come quicker! If only *what* would come quicker? Death, darkness? . . . No, no! Anything rather than death!

When Peter returned with the tea on a tray, Iván Ilých stared at him for a time in perplexity, not realizing who and what he was. Peter was disconcerted by that look and his embarrassment brought Iván Ilých to himself.

"Oh, tea! All right, put it down. Only help me to wash and put on a clean shirt."

And Iván Ilých began to wash. With pauses for rest, he washed his hands and then his face, cleaned his teeth, brushed his hair, and looked in the glass. He was terrified by what he saw, especially by the limp way in which his hair clung to his pallid forehead.

While his shirt was being changed he knew that he would be still more frightened at the sight of his body, so he avoided looking at it. Finally he was ready. He drew on a dressing-gown, wrapped himself in a plaid, and sat down in the armchair to take his tea. For a moment he felt refreshed, but as soon as he began to drink the tea he was again aware of the same taste, and the pain also returned. He finished it with an effort, and then lay down stretching out his legs, and dismissed Peter.

Always the same. Now a spark of hope flashes up, then a sea of despair rages, and always pain; always pain, always despair, and always the same. When alone he had a dreadful and distressing desire to call someone, but he knew beforehand that with others present it would be still worse. "Another dose of morphine—to lose consciousness. I will tell him, the doctor, that he must think of something else. It's impossible, impossible, to go on like this."

An hour and another pass like that. But now there is a ring at the door bell. Perhaps it's the doctor? It is. He comes in fresh, hearty, plump, and cheerful, with that look on his face that seems to say: "There now, you're in a panic about something, but we'll arrange it all for you directly!" The doctor knows this expression is out of place here, but he has put it on once for all and can't take it off—like a man who has put on a frock-coat in the morning to pay a round of calls.

The doctor rubs his hands vigorously and reassuringly.

"Brr! How cold it is! There's such a sharp frost; just let me warm myself!" he says, as if it were only a matter of waiting till he was warm, and then he would put everything right.

"Well now, how are you?"

Iván Ilých feels that the doctor would like to say: "Well, how are our affairs?" but that even he feels that this would not do, and says instead: "What sort of a night have you had?"

Iván Ilých looks at him as much as to say: "Are you really never ashamed of lying?" But the doctor does not wish to understand this question, and Iván Ilých says: "Just as terrible as ever. The pain never leaves me and never subsides. If only something. . . ."

"Yes, you sick people are always like that. . . . There, now I think I am warm enough. Even Praskóvya Fëdorovna, who is so particular, could find no fault with my temperature. Well, now I can say good-morning," and the doctor presses his patient's hand.

Then, dropping his former playfulness, he begins with a most serious face to examine the patient, feeling his pulse and taking his temperature, and then begins the sounding and auscultation.

Iván Ilých knows quite well and definitely that all this is nonsense and pure deception, but when the doctor, getting down on his knee, leans over him, putting his ear first higher then lower, and performs various gymnastic movements over him with a significant expression on his face, Iván Ilých submits to it all as he used to submit to the speeches of the lawyers, though he knew very well that they were all lying and why they were lying.

The doctor, kneeling on the sofa, is still sounding him when Pras-kóvya Fëdorovna's silk dress rustles at the door and she is heard scolding Peter for not having let her know of the doctor's arrival.

She comes in, kisses her husband, and at once proceeds to prove that she has been up a long time already, and only owing to a misunder-standing failed to be there when the doctor arrived.

Iván Ilých looks at her, scans her all over, sets against her the white-ness and plumpness and cleanness of her hands and neck, the gloss of her hair, and the sparkle of her vivacious eyes. He hates her with his whole soul. And the thrill of hatred he feels for her makes him suffer from her touch.

Her attitude towards him and his disease is still the same. Just as the doctor had adopted a certain relation to his patient which he could not abandon, so had she formed one towards him—that he was not doing something he ought to do and was himself to blame, and that she reproached him lovingly for this—and she could not now change that attitude.

"You see he doesn't listen to me and doesn't take his medicine at the proper time. And above all he lies in a position that is no doubt bad for him—with his legs up."

She described how he made Gerásim hold his legs up.

The doctor smiled with a contemptuous affability that said;

"What's to be done? These sick people do have foolish fancies of that kind, but we must forgive them."

When the examination was over the doctor looked at his watch, and then Praskóvya Fëdorovna announced to Iván Ilých that it was of course as he pleased, but she had sent to-day for a celebrated specialist who would examine him and have a consultation with Michael Danílovich (their regular doctor).

"Please don't raise any objections. I am doing this for my own sake," she said ironically, letting it be felt that she was doing it all for his sake and only said this to leave him no right to refuse. He remained silent, knitting his brows. He felt that he was so surrounded and involved in a mesh of falsity that it was hard to unravel anything.

Everything she did for him was entirely for her own sake, and she told him she was doing for herself what she actually was doing for herself, as if that was so incredible that he must understand the opposite.

At half-past eleven the celebrated specialist arrived. Again the sounding began and the significant conversations in his presence and in another room, about the kidneys and the appendix, and the questions and answers, with such an air of importance that again, instead of the real question of life and death which now alone confronted him, the question arose of the kidney and appendix which were not behaving as they ought to and would now be attacked by Michael Danílovich and the specialist and forced to amend their ways.

The celebrated specialist took leave of him with a serious though not hopeless look, and in reply to the timid question Iván Ilých, with eyes glistening with fear and hope, put to him as to whether there was a chance of recovery, said that he could not vouch for it but there was a possibility. The look of hope with which Iván Ilých watched the doctor out was so pathetic that Praskóvya Fëdorovna, seeing it, even wept as she left the room to hand the doctor his fee.

The gleam of hope kindled by the doctor's encouragement did not last long. The same room, the same pictures, curtains, wall-paper, medicine bottles, were all there, and the same aching suffering body, and Iván Ilých began to moan. They gave him a subcutaneous injection and he sank into oblivion.

It was twilight when he came to. They brought him his dinner and he swallowed some beef tea with difficulty, and then everything was the same again and night was coming on.

After dinner, at seven o'clock, Praskóvya Fëdorovna came into the room in evening dress, her full bosom pushed up by her corset, and with traces of powder on her face. She had reminded him in the morning that they were going to the theatre. Sarah Bernhardt was visiting the town and they had a box, which he had insisted on their taking. Now he had forgotten about it and her toilet offended him, but he concealed his vexation when he remembered that he had himself insisted on their securing a box and going because it would be an instructive and aesthetic pleasure for the children.

Praskóvya Fëdorovna came in, self-satisfied but yet with a rather guilty air. She sat down and asked how he was but, as he saw, only for the sake of asking and not in order to learn about it, knowing that there was nothing to learn—and then went on to what she really wanted to say: that she would not on any account have gone but that the box had been taken and Helen and their daughter were going, as well as Petríshchev (the examining magistrate, their daughter's fiancé) and that it was out of the question to let them go alone; but that she would have much preferred to sit with him for a while; and he must be sure to follow the doctor's orders while she was away.

"Oh, and Fëdor Petróvich" (the fiancé) "would like to come in. May he? And Lisa?"

"All right."

Their daughter came in in full evening dress, her fresh young flesh exposed (making a show of that very flesh which in his own case caused so much suffering), strong, healthy, evidently in love, and impatient with illness, suffering, and death, because they interfered with her happiness.

Fëdor Petróvich came in too, in evening dress, his hair curled *à la Capoul,* a tight still collar round his long sinewy neck, an enormous white shirt-front and narrow black trousers tightly stretched over his strong thighs. He had one white glove tightly drawn on, and was holding his opera hat in his hand.

Following him the schoolboy crept in unnoticed, in a new uniform, poor little fellow, and wearing gloves. Terribly dark shadows showed under his eyes, the meaning of which Iván Ilých knew well.

His son had always seemed pathetic to him, and now it was dreadful to see the boy's frightened look of pity. It seemed to Iván Ilých that Vásya was the only one besides Gerásim who understood and pitied him.

They all sat down and again asked how he was. A silence followed. Lisa asked her mother about the opera-glasses, and there was an altercation between mother and daughter as to who had taken them and where they had been put. This occasioned some unpleasantness.

Fëdor Petróvich inquired of Iván Ilých whether he had ever seen Sarah Bernhardt. Iván Ilých did not at first catch the question, but then replied: "No, have you seen her before?"

"Yes, in *Adrienne Lecouvreur*."

Praskóvya Fëdorovna mentioned some roles in which Sarah Bernhardt was particularly good. Her daughter disagreed. Conversation sprang up at to the elegance and realism of her acting—the sort of conversation that is always repeated and is always the same.

In the midst of the conversation Fëdor Petróvich glanced at Iván Ilých and became silent. The others also looked at him and grew silent. Iván Ilých was staring with glittering eyes straight before him, evidently indignant with them. This had to be rectified, but it was impossible to do so. The silence had to be broken, but for a time no one dared to break it and they all became afraid that the conventional deception would suddenly become obvious and the truth become plain to all. Lisa was the first to pluck up courage and break that silence, but by trying to hide what everybody was feeling, she betrayed it.

"Well, if we are going it's time to start," she said, looking at her watch, a present from her father, and with a faint and significant smile at Fëdor Petróvich relating to something known only to them. She got up with a rustle of her dress.

They all rose, said good-night, and went away.

When they had gone it seemed to Iván Ilých that he felt better; the falsity had gone with them. But the pain remained—that same pain and that same fear that made everything monotonously alike, nothing harder and nothing easier. Everything was worse.

Again minute followed minute and hour followed hour. Everything remained the same and there was no cessation. And the inevitable end of it all became more and more terrible.

"Yes, send Gerásim here," he replied to a question Peter asked.

## IX

His wife returned late at night. She came in on tiptoe, but he heard her, opened his eyes, and made haste to close them again. She wished to send Gerásim away and to sit with him herself, but he opened his eyes and said: "No, go away."

"Are you in great pain?"

"Always the same."

"Take some opium."

He agreed and took some. She went away.

Till about three in the morning he was in a state of stupefied misery. It seemed to him that he and his pain were being thrust into a narrow, deep black sack, but though they were pushed further and further in they could not be pushed to the bottom. And this, terrible enough in itself, was accompanied by suffering. He was frightened yet wanted to fall through the sack, he struggled but yet co-operated. And suddenly he broke through, fell, and regained consciousness. Gerásim was sitting at the foot of the bed dozing quietly and patiently, while he himself lay with his emaciated stockinged legs resting on Gerásim's shoulders; the same shaded candle was there and the same unceasing pain.

"Go away, Gerásim," he whispered.

"It's all right, sir. I'll stay a while."

"No. Go away."

He removed his legs from Gerásim's shoulders, turned sideways onto his arm, and felt sorry for himself. He only waited till Gerásim had gone into the next room and then restrained himself no longer but wept like a child. He wept on account of his helplessness, his terrible loneliness, the cruelty of man, the cruelty of God, and the absence of God.

"Why hast Thou done all this? Why hast Thou brought me here? Why, why dost Thou torment me so terribly?"

He did not expect an answer and yet wept because there was no answer and could be none. The pain again grew more acute, but he did not stir and did not call. He said to himself: "Go on! Strike me! But what is it for? What have I done to Thee? What is it for?"

Then he grew quiet and not only ceased weeping but even held his breath and became all attention. It was as though he were listening not to an audible voice but to the voice of his soul, to the current of thoughts arising within him.

"What is it you want?" was the first clear conception capable of expression in words, that he heard.

"What do you want? What do you want?" he repeated to himself. "What do I want? To live and not to suffer," he answered.

And again he listened with such concentrated attention that even his pain did not distract him.

"To live? How?" asked his inner voice.

"Why, to live as I used to—well and pleasantly."

"As you lived before, well and pleasantly?" the voice repeated.

And in imagination he began to recall the best moments of his pleasant life. But strange to say none of these best moments of his pleasant life now seemed at all what they had then seemed—none of them except the first recollections of childhood. There, in childhood, there had been something really pleasant with which it would be possible to live if it could return. But the child who had experienced that happiness existed no longer, it was like a reminiscence of somebody else.

As soon as the period began which had produced the present Iván Ilých, all that had then seemed joys now melted before his sight and turned into something trivial and often nasty.

And the further he departed from childhood and the nearer he came to the present the more worthless and doubtful were the joys. This began with the School of Law. A little that was really good was still found there—there was light-heartedness, friendship, and hope. But in the upper classes there had already been fewer of such good moments. Then during the first years of his official career, when he was in the service of the Governor, some pleasant moments again occurred: they were the memories of love for a woman. Then all became confused and there was still less of what was good; later on again there was still less that was good, and the further he went the less there was. His marriage, a mere accident, then the disenchantment that followed it, his wife's bad breath and the sensuality and hypocrisy: then that deadly official life and those preoccupations about money, a year of it, and two, and ten, and twenty, and always the same thing. And the longer it lasted the more deadly it became. "It is as if I had been going downhill while I imagined I was going up. And that is really what it was. I was going up in public opinion, but to the same extent life was ebbing away from me. And now it is all done and there is only death."

"Then what does it mean? Why? It can't be that life is so senseless and horrible. But if it really has been so horrible and senseless, why must I die in agony? There is something wrong!"

"Maybe I did not live as I ought to have done," it suddenly occurred to him. "But how could that be, when I did everything properly?" he replied, and immediately dismissed from his mind this, the sole solution of all the riddles of life and death, as something quite impossible.

"Then what do you want now? To live: Live how? Live as you lived in the law courts when the usher proclaimed "The judge is coming!" "The judge is coming, the judge!" he repeated to himself. "Here he is, the judge. But I am not guilty!" he exclaimed angrily. "What is it for?" And he ceased crying, but turning his face to the wall continued to ponder on the same question: Why, and for what purpose, is there all this horror? But however much he pondered he found no answer. And whenever the thought occurred to him, as it often did, that it all resulted from his not having lived as he ought to have done, he at once recalled the correctness of his whole life and dismissed so strange an idea.

## X

Another fortnight passed. Iván Ilých now no longer left his sofa. He would not lie in bed but lay on the sofa, facing the wall nearly all the time. He suffered ever the same unceasing agonies and in his loneliness pondered always on the same insoluble question: "What is this? Can it be that it is Death?" And the inner voice answered: "Yes, it is Death."

"Why these sufferings?" And the voice answered, "For no reason—they just are so." Beyond and besides this there was nothing.

From the very beginning of his illness, ever since he had first been to see the doctor, Iván Ilých's life had been divided between two contrary and alternating moods: now it was despair and the expectation of this uncomprehended and terrible death, and now hope and an intently interested observation of the functioning of his organs. Now before his eyes there was only a kidney or an intestine that temporarily evaded its duty, and now only that incomprehensible and dreadful death from which it was impossible to escape.

These two states of mind had alternated from the very beginning of his illness, but the further it progressed the more doubtful and fantastic became the conception of the kidney, and the more real the sense of impending death.

He had but to call to mind what he had been three months before and what he was now, to call to mind with what regularity he had been going downhill, for every possibility of hope to be shattered.

Latterly during that loneliness in which he found himself as he lay facing the back of the sofa, a loneliness in the midst of a populous town and surrounded by numerous acquaintances and relations but that yet could not have been more complete anywhere—either at the bottom of the sea or under the earth—during that terrible loneliness Iván Ilých had lived only in memories of the past. Pictures of his past rose before him one after another. They always began with what was nearest in time and then went back to what was most remote—to his childhood—and rested there. If he thought of the stewed prunes that had been offered him that day, his mind went back to the raw shrivelled French plums of his childhood, their peculiar flavour and the flow of saliva when he sucked their stones, and along with the memory of that taste came a whole series of memories of those days: his nurse, his brother, and their toys. "No, I mustn't think of that. . . . It is too painful," Iván Ilých said to himself, and brought himself back to the present—to the button on the back of the sofa and the creases in its morocco. "Morocco is expensive, but it does not wear well: there had been a quarrel about it. It was a different kind of quarrel and a different kind of morocco that time when we tore father's portfolio and were punished, and mamma brought us some tarts. . . ." And again his thoughts dwelt on his childhood, and again it was painful and he tried to banish them and fix his mind on something else.

Then again together with that chain of memories another series passed through his mind—of how his illness had progressed and grown worse. There also the further back he looked the more life there had been. There had been more of what was good in life and more of life itself. The two merged together. "Just as the pain went on getting worse and worse so my life grew worse and worse," he thought. "There is one bright spot there at the back, at the beginning of life, and afterwards all becomes blacker and blacker and proceeds more and more rapidly—in inverse ratio to the square of the distance from

death," thought Iván Ilých. And the example of a stone falling downwards with increasing velocity entered his mind. Life, a series of increasing sufferings, flies further and further towards its end—the most
terrible suffering. "I am flying. . . ." He shuddered, shifted himself,
and tried to resist, but was already aware that resistance was impossible, and again with eyes weary of gazing but unable to cease seeing
what was before them, he stared at the back of the sofa and waited—
awaiting that dreadful fall and shock and destruction.

"Resistance is impossible!" he said to himself. "If I could only understand what it is all for! But that too is impossible. An explanation
would be possible if it could be said that I have not lived as I ought
to. But it is impossible to say that," and he remembered all the legality,
correctitude, and propriety of his life. "That at any rate can certainly
not be admitted," he thought, and his lips smiled ironically as if someone could see that smile and be taken in by it. "There is no explanation! Agony, death. . . . What for?"

## XI

Another two weeks went by in this way and during that fortnight
an event occurred that Iván Ilých and his wife had desired. Petríschev
formally proposed. It happened in the evening. The next day Praskóvya Fëdorovna came into her husband's room considering how best
to inform him of it, but that very night there had been a fresh change
for the worse in his condition. She found him still lying on the sofa
but in a different position. He lay on his back, groaning and staring
fixedly straight in front of him.

She began to remind him of his medicines, but he turned his eyes
towards her with such a look that she did not finish what she was
saying; so great an animosity, to her in particular, did that look express.

"For Christ's sake, let me die in peace!" he said.

She would have gone away, but just then their daughter came in
and went up to say good morning. He looked at her as he had done
at his wife, and in reply to her inquiry about his health said dryly
that he would soon free them all of himself. They were both silent
and after sitting with him for a while went away.

"Is it our fault?" Lisa said to her mother. "It's as if we were to blame! I am sorry for papa, but why should we be tortured?"

The doctor came at his usual time. Iván Ilých answered "Yes" and "No," never taking his angry eyes from him, and at last said: "You know you can do nothing for me, so leave me alone."

"We can ease your sufferings."

"You can't even do that. Let me be."

The doctor went into the drawing-room and told Praskóvya Fëdorovna that the case was very serious and that the only resource left was opium to allay her husband's sufferings, which must be terrible.

It was true, as the doctor said, that Iván Ilých's physical sufferings were terrible, but worse than the physical sufferings were his mental sufferings which were his chief torture.

His mental sufferings were due to the fact that that night, as he looked at Gerásim's sleepy, good-natured face with its prominent cheek-bones, the question suddenly occurred to him: "What if my whole life has really been wrong?"

It occurred to him that what had appeared perfectly impossible before, namely that he had not spent his life as he should have done, might after all be true. It occurred to him that his scarcely perceptible attempts to struggle against what was considered good by the most highly placed people, those scarcely noticeable impulses which he had immediately suppressed, might have been the real thing, and all the rest false. And his professional duties and the whole arrangement of his life and of his family, and all his social and official interests, might all have been false. He tried to defend all those things to himself and suddenly felt the weakness of what he was defending. There was nothing to defend.

"But if that is so," he said to himself, "and I am leaving this life with the consciousness that I have lost all that was given me and it is impossible to rectify it—what then?"

He lay on his back and began to pass his life in review in quite a new way. In the morning when he saw first his footman, then his wife, then his daughter, and then the doctor, their every word and movement confirmed to him the awful truth that had been revealed to him during the night. In them he saw himself—all that for which he had lived—and saw clearly that it was not real at all, but a terrible and huge deception which had hidden both life and death. This consciousness intensified his physical suffering tenfold. He groaned and tossed about, and pulled at his clothing which choked and stifled him. And he hated them on that account.

He was given a large dose of opium and became unconscious, but at noon his sufferings began again. He drove everybody away and tossed from side to side.

His wife came to him and said:

"Jean, my dear, do this for me. It can't do any harm and often helps. Healthy people often do it."

He opened his eyes wide.

"What? Take communion? Why? It's unnecessary! However. . . ." She began to cry.

"Yes, do, my dear. I'll send for our priest. He is such a nice man."

"All right. Very well," he muttered.

When the priest came and heard his confession, Iván Ilých was softened and seemed to feel a relief from his doubts and consequently from his sufferings, and for a moment there came a ray of hope. He again began to think of the vermiform appendix and the possibility of correcting it. He received the sacrament with tears in his eyes.

When they laid him down again afterwards he felt a moment's ease, and the hope that he might live awoke in him again. He began to think of the operation that had been suggested to him. "To live! I want to live!" he said to himself.

His wife came in to congratulate him after his communion, and when uttering the usual conventional words she added:

"You feel better, don't you?"

Without looking at her he said "Yes."

Her dress, her figure, the expression of her face, the tone of her voice, all revealed the same thing. "This is wrong, it is not as it should be. All you have lived for and still live for is falsehood and deception, hiding life and death from you." And as soon as he admitted that thought, his hatred and his agonizing physical suffering again sprang up, and with that suffering a consciousness of the unavoidable, approaching end. And to this was added a new sensation of grinding shooting pain and a feeling of suffocation.

The expression of his face when he uttered that "yes" was dreadful. Having uttered it, he looked her straight in the eyes, turned on his face with a rapidity extraordinary in his weak state and shouted:

"Go away! Go away and leave me alone!"

## XII

From that moment the screaming began that continued for three days, and was so terrible that one could not hear it through two closed doors without horror. At the moment he answered his wife he realized that he was lost, that there was no return, that the end had come, the very end, and his doubts were still unsolved and remained doubts.

"Oh! Oh! Oh!" he cried in various intonations. He had begun by screaming "I won't!" and continued screaming on the letter "o."

For three whole days, during which time did not exist for him, he struggled in that black sack into which he was being thrust by an invisible, resistless force. He struggled as a man condemned to death struggles in the hands of the executioner, knowing that he cannot save himself. And every moment he felt that despite all his efforts he was drawing nearer and nearer to what terrified him. He felt that his agony was due to his being thrust into that black hole and still more to his not being able to get right into it. He was hindered from getting into it by his conviction that his life had been a good one. That very justification of his life held him fast and prevented his moving forward, and it caused him most torment of all.

Suddenly some force struck him in the chest and side, making it still harder to breathe, and he fell through the hole and there at the bottom was a light. What had happened to him was like the sensation one sometimes experiences in a railway carriage when one thinks one is going backwards while one is really going forwards and suddenly becomes aware of the real direction.

"Yes, it was all not the right thing," he said to himself, "but that's no matter. It can be done. But what *is* the right thing?" he asked himself, and suddenly grew quiet.

This occurred at the end of the third day, two hours before his death. Just then his schoolboy son had crept softly in and gone up to the bedside. The dying man was still screaming desperately and waving his arms. His hand fell on the boy's head, and the boy caught it, pressed it to his lips, and began to cry.

At that very moment Iván Ilých fell through and caught sight of the light, and it was revealed to him that though his life had not been what it should have been, this could still be rectified. He asked himself, "What *is* the right thing?" and grew still, listening. Then he felt that someone was kissing his hand. He opened his eyes, looked at his

son, and felt sorry for him. His wife came up to him and he glanced
at her. She was gazing at him open-mouthed, with undried tears on
her nose and cheek and a despairing look on her face. He felt sorry
for her too.

"Yes, I am making them wretched," he thought. "They are sorry,
but it will be better for them when I die." He wished to say this but
had not the strength to utter it. "Besides, why speak? I must act," he
thought. With a look at his wife he indicated his son and said: "Take
him away . . . sorry for him . . . sorry for you too. . . ." He tried to
add, "forgive me," but said "forego" and waved his hand, knowing
that He whose understanding mattered would understand.

And suddenly it grew clear to him that what had been oppressing
him and would not leave him was all dropping away at once from
two sides, from ten sides, and from all sides. He was sorry for them,
he must act so as not to hurt them: release them and free himself from
these sufferings. "How good and how simple!" he thought. "And the
pain?" he asked himself. "What has become of it? Where are you,
pain?"

He turned his attention to it.

"Yes, here it is. Well, what of it? Let the pain be."

"And death . . . where is it?"

He sought his former accustomed fear of death and did not find it.
"Where is it? What death?" There was no fear because there was no
death.

In place of death there was light.

"So that's what it is!" he suddenly exclaimed aloud. "What joy!"

To him all this happened in a single instant, and the meaning of
that instant did not change. For those present his agony continued for
another two hours. Something rattled in his throat, his emaciated body
twitched, then the gasping and rattle became less and less frequent.

"It is finished!" said someone near him.

He heard these words and repeated them in his soul.

"Death is finished," he said to himself. "It is no more!"

He drew in a breath, stopped in the midst of a sigh, stretched out,
and died.

# Drama

Henrik Ibsen · Anton Chekhov

# Ghosts

## HENRIK IBSEN

### CHARACTERS

MRS. ALVING, *a widow*
OSWALD ALVING, *her son, an artist*
MANDERS, *the Pastor of the parish*
ENGSTRAND, *a carpenter*
REGINA ENGSTRAND, *his daughter, in Mrs. Alving's service*

*The action takes place at* MRS. ALVING's *house on one of the larger fjords of western Norway.*

## ACT I

Scene.—*A large room looking upon a garden. A door in the left-hand wall, and two in the right. In the middle of the room, a round table with chairs set about it, and books, magazines and newspapers upon it. In the foreground on the left, a window, by which is a small sofa with a work-table in front of it. At the back the room opens into a conservatory rather smaller than the room. From the right-hand side of this a door leads to the garden. Through the large panes of glass that form the outer wall of the conservatory, a gloomy fjord landscape can be discerned, half obscured by steady rain.*

ENGSTRAND *is standing close up to the garden door. His left leg is slightly deformed, and he wears a boot with a clump of wood under the sole.* REGINA, *with an empty garden-syringe in her hand, is trying to prevent his coming in.*

REGINA [*below her breath*]. What is it you want? Stay where you are. The rain is dripping off you.

ENGSTRAND. God's good rain, my girl.

REGINA. The Devil's own rain, that's what it is!

ENGSTRAND. Lord, how you talk, Regina. [*Takes a few limping steps forward.*] What I wanted to tell you was this—

REGINA. Don't clump about like that, stupid! The young master is lying asleep upstairs.

ENGSTRAND. Asleep still? In the middle of the day?

REGINA. Well, it's no business of yours.

ENGSTRAND. Yes, we are poor weak mortals, my girl—

REGINA. We are indeed.

ENGSTRAND. —and the temptations of the world are manifold, you know—but, for all that, here I was at my work at half-past five this morning.

REGINA. Yes, yes, but make yourself scarce now. I am not going to stand here as if I had a *rendez-vous* with you.

ENGSTRAND. As if you had a what?

REGINA. I am not going to have any one find you here; so now you know, and you can go.

ENGSTRAND [*coming a few steps nearer*]. Not a bit of it! Not before we have had a little chat. This afternoon I shall have finished my job down at the school house, and I shall be off home to town by to-night's boat.

REGINA [*mutters*]. Pleasant journey to you!

ENGSTRAND. Thanks, my girl. To-morrow is the opening of the Orphanage, and I expect there will be a fine kick-up here and plenty of good strong drink, don't you know. And no one shall say of Jacob Engstrand that he can't hold off when temptation comes in his way.

REGINA. Oho!

ENGSTRAND. Yes, because there will be a lot of fine folk here to-morrow. Parson Manders is expected from town, too.

REGINA. What is more, he's coming to-day.

ENGSTRAND. There you are! And I'm going to be precious careful he doesn't have anything to say against me, do you see?

REGINA. Oh, that's your game, is it?

ENGSTRAND. What do you mean?

REGINA [*with a significant look at him*]. What is it you want to humbug Mr. Manders out of, this time?

ENGSTRAND. Sh! Sh! Are you crazy? Do you suppose *I* would want to humbug Mr. Manders? No, no—Mr. Manders has always been too kind a friend for me to do that. But what I wanted to talk to you about, was my going back home to-night.

REGINA. The sooner you go, the better I shall be pleased.

ENGSTRAND. Yes, only I want to take you with me, Regina.

REGINA [*open-mouthed*]. You want to take me—? What did you say?

ENGSTRAND. I want to take you home with me, I said.

REGINA [*contemptuously*]. You will never get me home with you.

ENGSTRAND. Ah, we shall see about that.

REGINA. Yes, you can be quite certain we *shall* see about that. I, who have been brought up by a lady like Mrs. Alving?—I, who have been treated almost as if I were her own child?—do you suppose I am going home with *you?*—to such a house as yours? Not likely!

ENGSTRAND. What the devil do you mean? Are you setting yourself up against your father, you hussy?

REGINA [*mutters, without looking at him*]. You have often told me I was none of yours.

ENGSTRAND. Bah!—why do you want to pay any attention to that?

REGINA. Haven't you many and many a time abused me and called me a—? For shame!

ENGSTRAND. I'll swear I never used such an ugly word.

REGINA. Oh, it doesn't matter what word you used.

ENGSTRAND. Besides, that was only when I was a bit fuddled—hm! Temptations are manifold in this world, Regina.

REGINA. Ugh!

ENGSTRAND. And it was when your mother was in a nasty temper. I had to find some way of getting my knife into her, my girl. She was always so precious genteel. [*Mimicking her.*] "Let go, Jacob! Let me be! Please to remember that I was three years with the Alvings at Rosenvold, and they were people who went to Court!" [*Laughs.*] Bless my soul, she never could forget that Captain Alving got a Court appointment while she was in service here.

REGINA. Poor mother—you worried her into her grave pretty soon.

ENGSTRAND [*shrugging his shoulders*]. Of course, of course; I have got to take the blame for everything.

REGINA [*beneath her breath, as she turns away*]. Ugh—that leg, too!

ENGSTRAND. What are you saying, my girl?

REGINA. *Pied de mouton.*

ENGSTRAND. Is that English?

REGINA. Yes.

ENGSTRAND. You have had a good education out here, and no mistake; and it may stand you in good stead now, Regina.

REGINA [*after a short silence*]. And what was it you wanted me to come to town for?

ENGSTRAND. Need you ask why a father wants his only child? Ain't I a poor lonely widower?

REGINA. Oh, don't come to me with that tale. Why do you want me to go?

ENGSTRAND. Well, I must tell you I am thinking of taking up a new line now.

REGINA [*whistles*]. You have tried that so often—but it has always proved a fool's errand.

ENGSTRAND. Ah, but this time you will just see, Regina! Strike me dead if—

REGINA [*stamping her feet*]. Stop swearing!

ENGSTRAND. Sh! Sh!—you're quite right, my girl, quite right! What I wanted to say was only this, that I have put by a tidy penny out of what I have made by working at this new Orphanage up here.

REGINA. Have you? All the better for you.

ENGSTRAND. What is there for a man to spend his money on, out here in the country?

REGINA. Well, what then?

ENGSTRAND. Well, you see, I thought of putting the money into something that would pay. I thought of some kind of an eating-house for seafaring folk—

REGINA. Heavens!

ENGSTRAND. Oh, a high-class eating-house, of course,—not a pigsty for common sailors. Damn it, no; it would be a place ships' captains and first mates would come to; really good sort of people, you know.

REGINA. And what should I—?

ENGSTRAND. You would help there. But only to make a show, you know. You wouldn't find it hard work, I can promise you, my girl. You should do exactly as you liked.

REGINA. Oh, yes, quite so!

ENGSTRAND. But we must have some women in the house; that is as clear as daylight. Because in the evening we must make the place a little attractive—some singing and dancing, and that sort of thing. Remember they are sea-folk—wayfarers on the waters of life! [*Com-*

*ing nearer to her.*] Now don't be a fool and stand in your own way, Regina. What good are you going to do here? Will this education, that your mistress has paid for, be of any use? You are to look after the children in the new Home, I hear. Is that the sort of work for you? Are you so frightfully anxious to go and wear out your health and strength for the sake of these dirty brats?

REGINA. No, if things were to go as I want them to, then—. Well, it may happen!

ENGSTRAND. What may happen?

REGINA. Never you mind. Is it much that you have put by, up here?

ENGSTRAND. Taking it all round, I should say about forty or fifty pounds.

REGINA. That's not so bad.

ENGSTRAND. It's enough to make a start with, my girl.

REGINA. Don't you mean to give me any of the money?

ENGSTRAND. No, I'm hanged if I do.

REGINA. Don't you mean to send me as much as a dress-length of stuff, just for once?

ENGSTRAND. Come and live in the town with me and you shall have plenty of dresses.

REGINA. Pooh!—I can get that much for myself, if I have a mind to.

ENGSTRAND. But it's far better to have a father's guiding hand, Regina. Just now I can get a nice house in Little Harbour Street. They don't want much money down for it—and we could make it like a sort of seamen's home, don't you know.

REGINA. But I have no intention of living with you! I have nothing whatever to do with you. So now, be off!

ENGSTRAND. You wouldn't be living with me long, my girl. No such luck—not if you knew how to play your cards. Such a fine wench as you have grown this last year or two—

REGINA. Well—?

ENGSTRAND. It wouldn't be very long before some first mate came along—or perhaps a captain.

REGINA. I don't mean to marry a man of that sort. Sailors have no *savoir-vivre*.

ENGSTRAND. What haven't they got?

REGINA. I know what sailors are, I tell you. They aren't the sort of people to marry.

ENGSTRAND. Well, don't bother about marrying them. You can make it pay just as well. [*More confidentially.*] That fellow—the English-man—the one with the yacht—he gave seventy pounds, he did; and she wasn't a bit prettier than you.

REGINA [*advancing towards him*]. Get out!

ENGSTRAND [*stepping back*]. Here! here!—you're not going to hit me, I suppose?

REGINA. Yes! If you talk like that of mother, I will hit you. Get out, I tell you! [*Pushes him up to the garden door.*] And don't bang the doors. Young Mr. Alving—

ENGSTRAND. Is asleep—I know. It's funny how anxious you are about young Mr. Alving. [*In a lower tone.*] Oho! is it possible that it is *he* that—?

REGINA. Get out, and be quick about it! Your wits are wandering, my good man. No, don't go that way; Mr. Manders is just coming along. Be off down the kitchen stairs.

ENGSTRAND [*moving towards the right*]. Yes, yes—all right. But have a bit of a chat with him that's coming along. He's the chap to tell you what a child owes to its father. For I am your father, anyway, you know. I can prove it by the Register.

[*He goes out through the farther door which* REGINA *has opened. She shuts it after him, looks hastily at herself in the mirror, fans herself with her handkerchief and sets her collar straight; then busies herself with the flowers.* MANDERS *enters the conservatory through the garden door. He wears an overcoat, carries an umbrella and has a small travelling-bag slung over his shoulder on a strap.*]

MANDERS. Good morning, Miss Engstrand.

REGINA [*turning round with a look of pleased surprise*]. Oh, Mr. Manders, good morning. The boat is in, then?

MANDERS. Just in. [*Comes into the room.*] It is most tiresome, this rain every day.

REGINA [*following him in*]. It's a splendid rain for the farmers, Mr. Manders.

MANDERS. Yes, you are quite right. We town-folk think so little about that. [*Begins to take off his overcoat.*]

REGINA. Oh, let me help you. That's it. Why, how wet it is! I will hang it up in the hall. Give me your umbrella, too; I will leave it open, so that it will dry.

[*She goes out with the things by the farther door on the right.*

MANDERS *lays his bag and his hat down on a chair.* REGINA *re-enters.*]

MANDERS. Ah, it's very pleasant to get indoors. Well, is everything going on well here?

REGINA. Yes, thanks.

MANDERS. Properly busy, though, I expect, getting ready for to-morrow?

REGINA. Oh, yes, there is plenty to do.

MANDERS. And Mrs. Alving is at home, I hope?

REGINA. Yes, she is. She has just gone upstairs to take the young master his chocolate.

MANDERS. Tell me—I heard down at the pier that Oswald had come back.

REGINA. Yes, he came the day before yesterday. We didn't expect him till to-day.

MANDERS. Strong and well, I hope?

REGINA. Yes, thank you, well enough. But dreadfully tired after his journey. He came straight from Paris without a stop—I mean, he came all the way without breaking his journey. I fancy he is having a sleep now, so we must talk a little bit more quietly, if you don't mind.

MANDERS. All right, we will be very quiet.

REGINA [*while she moves an armchair up to the table*]. Please sit down, Mr. Manders, and make yourself at home. [*He sits down; she puts a footstool under his feet.*] There! Is that comfortable?

MANDERS. Thank you, thank you. That is most comfortable. [*Looks at her.*] I'll tell you what, Miss Engstrand, I certainly think you have grown since I saw you last.

REGINA. Do you think so? Mrs. Alving says, too, that I have developed.

MANDERS. Developed? Well, perhaps a little—just suitably.

[*A short pause.*]

REGINA. Shall I tell Mrs. Alving you are here?

MANDERS. Thanks, there is no hurry, my dear child.—Now tell me, Regina my dear, how has your father been getting on here?

REGINA. Thank you, Mr. Manders, he is getting on pretty well.

MANDERS. He came to see me, the last time he was in town.

REGINA. Did he? He is always so glad when he can have a chat with you.

MANDERS. And I suppose you have seen him pretty regularly every day?

REGINA. I? Oh, yes, I do—whenever I have time, that is to say.

MANDERS. Your father has not a very strong character, Miss Engstrand. He sadly needs a guiding hand.

REGINA. Yes, I can quite believe that.

MANDERS. He needs someone with him that he can cling to, someone whose judgment he can rely on. He acknowledged that freely himself, the last time he came to see me.

REGINA. Yes, he has said something of the same sort to me. But I don't know whether Mrs. Alving could do without me—most of all just now, when we have the new Orphanage to see about. And I should be dreadfully unwilling to leave Mrs. Alving, too; she has always been so good to me.

MANDERS. But a daughter's duty, my good child—. Naturally we should have to get your mistress' consent first.

REGINA. Still I don't know whether it would be quite the thing, at my age, to keep house for a single man.

MANDERS. What!! My dear Miss Engstrand, it is your own father we are speaking of!

REGINA. Yes, I dare say, but still—. Now, if it were in a good house and with a real gentleman—

MANDERS. But, my dear Regina—

REGINA. —one whom I could feel an affection for, and really feel in the position of a daughter to—

MANDERS. Come, come—my dear good child—

REGINA. I should like very much to live in town. Out here it is terribly lonely; and you know yourself, Mr. Manders, what it is to be alone in the world. And, though I say it, I really am both capable and willing. Don't you know any place that would be suitable for me, Mr. Manders?

MANDERS. I? No, indeed I don't.

REGINA. But, dear Mr. Manders—at any rate don't forget me, in case—

MANDERS [getting up]. No, I won't forget you, Miss Engstrand.

REGINA. Because, if I—

MANDERS. Perhaps you will be so kind as to let Mrs. Alving know I am here?

REGINA. I will fetch her at once, Mr. Manders.

[*Goes out to the left.* MANDERS *walks up and down the room once or twice, stands for a moment at the farther end of the room with his hands behind his back and looks out into the garden. Then he comes back to the table, takes up a book and looks at the title page, gives a start and looks at some of the others.*]

MANDERS. Hm!—Really!

[MRS. ALVING *comes in by the door on the left. She is followed by* REGINA, *who goes out again at once through the nearer door on the right.*]

MRS. ALVING [*holding out her hand*]. I am very glad to see you, Mr. Manders.

MANDERS. How do you do, Mrs. Alving. Here I am, as I promised.

MRS. ALVING. Always punctual!

MANDERS. Indeed, I was hard put to it to get away. What with vestry meetings and committees—

MRS. ALVING. It was all the kinder of you to come in such good time; we can settle our business before dinner. But where is your luggage?

MANDERS [*quickly*]. My things are down at the village shop. I am going to sleep there to-night.

MRS. ALVING [*repressing a smile*]. Can't I really persuade you to stay the night here this time?

MANDERS. No, no; many thanks all the same; I will put up there, as usual. It is so handy for getting on board the boat again.

MRS. ALVING. Of course you shall do as you please. But it seems to me quite another thing, now we are two old people—

MANDERS. Ha! ha! You will have your joke! And it's natural you should be in high spirits to-day—first of all there is the great event to-morrow, and also you have got Oswald home.

MRS. ALVING. Yes, am I not a lucky woman! It is more than two years since he was home last, and he has promised to stay the whole winter with me.

MANDERS. Has he, really? That is very nice and filial of him; because there must be many more attractions in his life in Rome or in Paris, I should think.

MRS. ALVING. Yes, but he has his mother here, you see. Bless the dear boy, he has got a corner in his heart for his mother still.

MANDERS. Oh, it would be very sad if absence and preoccupation with such a thing as Art were to dull the natural affections.

MRS. ALVING. It would, indeed. But there is no fear of that with him,

I am glad to say. I am quite curious to see if you recognise him again. He will be down directly; he is just lying down for a little on the sofa upstairs. But do sit down, my dear friend.

MANDERS. Thank you. You are sure I am not disturbing you?

MRS. ALVING. Of course not.

[*She sits down at the table.*]

MANDERS. Good. Then I will show you—. [*He goes to the chair where his bag is lying and takes a packet of papers from it; then sits down at the opposite side of the table and looks for a clear space to put the papers down.*] Now first of all, here is—[*breaks off*]. Tell me, Mrs. Alving, what are these books doing here?

MRS. ALVING. These books? I am reading them.

MANDERS. Do you read this sort of thing?

MRS. ALVING. Certainly I do.

MANDERS. Do you feel any the better or the happier for reading books of this kind?

MRS. ALVING. I think it makes me, as it were, more self-reliant.

MANDERS. That is remarkable. But why?

MRS. ALVING. Well, they give me an explanation or a confirmation of lots of different ideas that have come into my own mind. But what surprises me, Mr. Manders, is that, properly speaking, there is nothing at all new in these books. There is nothing more in them than what most people think and believe. The only thing is, that most people either take no account of it or won't admit it to themselves.

MANDERS. But, good heavens, do you seriously think that most people—?

MRS. ALVING. Yes, indeed, I do.

MANDERS. But not here in the country at any rate? Not here amongst people like ourselves?

MRS. ALVING. Yes, amongst people like ourselves too.

MANDERS. Well, really, I must say—!

MRS. ALVING. But what is the particular objection that you have to these books?

MANDERS. What objection? You surely don't suppose that I take any particular interest in such productions?

MRS. ALVING. In fact, you don't know anything about what you are denouncing?

MANDERS. I have read quite enough about these books to disapprove of them.

Mrs. Alving.   Yes, but your own opinion—

Manders.   My dear Mrs. Alving, there are many occasions in life when one has to rely on the opinion of others. That is the way in this world, and it is quite right that it should be so. What would become of society, otherwise?

Mrs. Alving.   Well, you may be right.

Manders.   Apart from that, naturally I don't deny that literature of this kind may have a considerable attraction. And I cannot blame you, either, for wishing to make yourself acquainted with the intellectual tendencies which I am told are at work in the wider world in which you have allowed your son to wander for so long. But—

Mrs. Alving.   But—?

Manders [*lowering his voice*].   But one doesn't talk about it, Mrs. Alving. One certainly is not called upon to account to every one for what one reads or thinks in the privacy of one's own room.

Mrs. Alving.   Certainly not. I quite agree with you.

Manders.   Just think of the consideration you owe to this Orphanage, which you decided to build at a time when your thoughts on such subjects were very different from what they are now—as far as I am able to judge.

Mrs. Alving.   Yes, I freely admit that. But it was about the Orphanage—

Manders.   It was about the Orphanage we were going to talk; quite so. Well—walk warily, dear Mrs. Alving! And now let us turn to the business in hand. [*Opens an envelope and takes out some papers.*] You see these?

Mrs. Alving.   The deeds?

Manders.   Yes, the whole lot—and everything in order. I can tell you it has been no easy matter to get them in time. I had positively to put pressure on the authorities; they are almost painfully conscientious when it is a question of settling property. But here they are at last. [*Turns over the papers.*] Here is the deed of conveyance of that part of the Rosenvold estate known as the Solvik property, together with the building newly erected thereon—the school, the masters' houses and the chapel. And here is the legal sanction for the statutes of the institution. Here, you see—[*reads*] "Statutes for the Captain Alving Orphanage."

Mrs. Alving [*after a long look at the papers*].   That seems all in order.

Manders.   I thought "Captain" was the better title to use, rather than your husband's Court title of "Chamberlain." "Captain" seems less ostentatious.

MRS. ALVING. Yes, yes; just as you think best.

MANDERS. And here is the certificate for the investment of the capital in the bank, the interest being earmarked for the current expenses of the Orphanage.

MRS. ALVING. Many thanks; but I think it will be most convenient if you will kindly take charge of them.

MANDERS. With pleasure. I think it will be best to leave the money in the bank for the present. The interest is not very high, it is true; four per cent at six months' call. Later on, if we can find some good mortgage—of course it must be a first mortgage and on unexceptionable security—we can consider the matter further.

MRS. ALVING. Yes, yes, my dear Mr. Manders, you know best about all that.

MANDERS. I will keep my eye on it, anyway. But there is one thing in connection with it that I have often meant to ask you about.

MRS. ALVING. What is that?

MANDERS. Shall we insure the buildings, or not?

MRS. ALVING. Of course we must insure them.

MANDERS. Ah, but wait a moment, dear lady. Let us look into the matter a little more closely.

MRS. ALVING. Everything of mine is insured—the house and its contents, my livestock—everything.

MANDERS. Naturally. They are your own property. I do exactly the same, of course. But this, you see, is quite a different case. The Orphanage is, so to speak, dedicated to higher uses.

MRS. ALVING. Certainly, but—

MANDERS. As far as I am personally concerned, I can conscientiously say that I don't see the smallest objection to our insuring ourselves against all risks.

MRS. ALVING. That is exactly what I think.

MANDERS. But what about the opinion of the people hereabouts?

MRS. ALVING. Their opinion—?

MANDERS. Is there any considerable body of opinion here—opinion of some account, I mean—that might take exception to it?

MRS. ALVING. What, exactly, do you mean by opinion of some account?

MANDERS. Well, I was thinking particularly of persons of such independent and influential position that one could hardly refuse to attach weight to their opinion.

MRS. ALVING. There are a certain number of such people here, who might perhaps take exception to it if we—

MANDERS. That's just it, you see. In town there are lots of them. All my fellow-clergymen's congregations, for instance! It would be so extremely easy for them to interpret it as meaning that neither you nor I had a proper reliance on Divine protection.

MRS. ALVING. But as far as you are concerned, my dear friend, you have at all events the consciousness that—

MANDERS. Yes, I know, I know; my own mind is quite easy about it, it is true. But we should not be able to prevent a wrong and injurious interpretation of our action. And that sort of thing, moreover, might very easily end in exercising a hampering influence on the work of the Orphanage.

MRS. ALVING. Oh, well, if that is likely to be the effect of it—

MANDERS. Nor can I entirely overlook the difficult—indeed, I may say, painful—position I might possibly be placed in. In the best circles in town the matter of this Orphanage is attracting a great deal of attention. Indeed the Orphanage is to some extent built for the benefit of the town too, and it is to be hoped that it may result in the lowering of our poor-rate by a considerable amount. But as I have been your adviser in the matter and have taken charge of the business side of it, I should be afraid that it would be I that spiteful persons would attack first of all—

MRS. ALVING. Yet, you ought not to expose yourself to that.

MANDERS. Not to mention the attacks that would undoubtedly be made upon me in certain newspapers and reviews—

MRS. ALVING. Say no more about it, dear Mr. Manders; that quite decides it.

MANDERS. Then you don't wish it to be insured?

MRS. ALVING. No, we will give up the idea.

MANDERS [leaning back in his chair]. But suppose, now, that some accident happened?—one can never tell—would you be prepared to make good the damage?

MRS. ALVING. No; I tell you quite plainly I would not do so under any circumstances.

MANDERS. Still, you know, Mrs. Alving—after all, it is a serious responsibility that we are taking upon ourselves.

MRS. ALVING.   But do you think we can do otherwise?

MANDERS.   No, that's just it. We really can't do otherwise. We ought not to expose ourselves to a mistaken judgment; and we have no right to do anything that will scandalise the community.

MRS. ALVING.   You ought not to, as a clergyman, at any rate.

MANDERS.   And, what is more, I certainly think that we may count upon our enterprise being attended by good fortune—indeed, that it will be under a special protection.

MRS. ALVING.   Let us hope so, Mr. Manders.

MANDERS.   Then we will leave it alone?

MRS. ALVING.   Certainly.

MANDERS.   Very good. As you wish. [*Makes a note.*] No insurance, then.

MRS. ALVING.   It's a funny thing that you should just have happened to speak about that to-day—

MANDERS.   I have often meant to ask you about it—

MRS. ALVING.   —because yesterday we very nearly had a fire up there.

MANDERS.   Do you mean it!

MRS. ALVING.   Oh, as a matter of fact it was nothing of any consequence. Some shavings in the carpenter's shop caught fire.

MANDERS.   Where Engstrand works?

MRS. ALVING.   Yes. They say he is often so careless with matches.

MANDERS.   He has so many things on his mind, poor fellow—so many anxieties. Heaven be thanked, I am told he is really making an effort to live a blameless life.

MRS. ALVING.   Really? Who told you so?

MANDERS.   He assured me himself that it is so. He's a good workman, too.

MRS. ALVING.   Oh, yes, when he is sober.

MANDERS.   Ah, that sad weakness of his! But the pain in his poor leg often drives him to it, he tells me. The last time he was in town, I was really quite touched by him. He came to my house and thanked me so gratefully for getting him work here, where he could have the chance of being with Regina.

MRS. ALVING.   He doesn't see very much of her.

MANDERS.   But he assured me that he saw her every day.

MRS. ALVING.   Oh well, perhaps he does.

MANDERS.   He feels so strongly that he needs some one who can keep a hold on him when temptations assail him. That is the most winning thing about Jacob Engstrand; he comes to one like a helpless child and accuses himself and confesses his frailty. The last time he came and had a talk with me—. Suppose now, Mrs. Alving, that it were really a necessity of his existence to have Regina at home with him again—

MRS. ALVING [*standing up suddenly*]. Regina!

MANDERS. —you ought not to set yourself against him.

MRS. ALVING. Indeed, I set myself very definitely against that. And, besides, you know Regina is to have a post in the Orphanage.

MANDERS. But consider, after all he is her father—

MRS. ALVING. I know best what sort of a father he has been to her. No, she shall never go to him with my consent.

MANDERS [*getting up*]. My dear lady, don't judge so hastily. It is very sad how you misjudge poor Engstrand. One would really think you were afraid—

MRS. ALVING [*more calmly*]. That is not the question. I have taken Regina into my charge, and in my charge she remains. [*Listens.*] Hush, dear Mr. Manders, don't say any more about it. [*Her face brightens with pleasure.*] Listen! Oswald is coming downstairs. We will only think about him now.

[OSWALD ALVING, *in a light overcoat, hat in hand and smoking a big meerschaum pipe, comes in by the door on the left.*]

OSWALD [*standing in the doorway*]. Oh, I beg your pardon, I thought you were in the office. [*Comes in.*] Good morning, Mr. Manders.

MANDERS [*staring at him*]. Well! It's most extraordinary—

MRS. ALVING. Yes, what do you think of him, Mr. Manders?

MANDERS. I—I—no, can it possibly be—?

OSWALD. Yes, it really is the prodigal son, Mr. Manders.

MANDERS. Oh, my dear young friend—

OSWALD. Well, the son come home, then.

MRS. ALVING. Oswald is thinking of the time when you were so opposed to the idea of his being a painter.

MANDERS. We are only fallible, and many steps seem to us hazardous at first, that afterwards—[*grasps his hand*]. Welcome, welcome! Really, my dear Oswald—may I still call you Oswald?

OSWALD. What else would you think of calling me?

MANDERS. Thank you. What I mean, my dear Oswald, is that you

must not imagine that I have any unqualified disapproval of the
artist's life. I admit that there are many who, even in that career,
can keep the inner man free from harm.

OSWALD. Let us hope so.

MRS. ALVING [*beaming with pleasure*]. I know one who has kept
both the inner and the outer man free from harm. Just take a look
at him, Mr. Manders.

OSWALD [*walks across the room*]. Yes, yes, mother dear, of course.

MANDERS. Undoubtedly—no one can deny it. And I hear you have
begun to make a name for yourself. I have often seen mention of
you in the papers—and extremely favourable mention, too. Although,
I must admit, latterly I have not seen your name so often.

OSWALD [*going towards the conservatory*]. I haven't done so much
painting just lately.

MRS. ALVING. An artist must take a rest sometimes, like other people.

MANDERS. Of course, of course. At those times the artist is preparing
and strengthening himself for a greater effort.

OSWALD. Yes. Mother, will dinner soon be ready?

MRS. ALVING. In half an hour. He has a fine appetite, thank goodness.

MANDERS. And a liking for tobacco too.

OSWALD. I found father's pipe in the room upstairs, and—

MANDERS. Ah, that is what it was!

MRS. ALVING. What?

MANDERS. When Oswald came in at that door with the pipe in his
mouth, I thought for the moment it was his father in the flesh.

OSWALD. Really?

MRS. ALVING. How can you say so! Oswald takes after me.

MANDERS. Yes, but there is an expression about the corners of his
mouth—something about the lips—that reminds me so exactly of
Mr. Alving—especially when he smokes.

MRS. ALVING. I don't think so at all. To my mind, Oswald has much
more of a clergyman's mouth.

MANDERS. Well, yes—a good many of my colleagues in the church
have a similar expression.

MRS. ALVING. But put your pipe down, my dear boy. I don't allow
any smoking in here.

OSWALD [*puts down his pipe*]. All right, I only wanted to try it, because I smoked it once when I was a child.

MRS. ALVING. You?

OSWALD. Yes; it was when I was quite a little chap. And I can remember going upstairs to father's room one evening when he was in very good spirits.

MRS. ALVING. Oh, you can't remember anything about those days.

OSWALD. Yes, I remember plainly that he took me on his knee and let me smoke his pipe. "Smoke, my boy," he said, "have a good smoke, boy!" And I smoked as hard as I could, until I felt I was turning quite pale and the perspiration was standing in great drops on my forehead. Then he laughed—such a hearty laugh—

MANDERS. It was an extremely odd thing to do.

MRS. ALVING. Dear Mr. Manders, Oswald only dreamt it.

OSWALD. No indeed, mother, it was no dream. Because—don't you remember—you came into the room and carried me off to the nursery, where I was sick, and I saw that you were crying. Did father often play such tricks?

MANDERS. In his young days he was full of fun—

OSWALD. And, for all that, he did so much with his life—so much that was good and useful, I mean—short as his life was.

MANDERS. Yes, my dear Oswald Alving, you have inherited the name of a man who undoubtedly was both energetic and worthy. Let us hope it will be a spur to your energies—

OSWALD. It ought to be, certainly.

MANDERS. In any case it was nice of you to come home for the day that is to honour his memory.

OSWALD. I could do no less for my father.

MRS. ALVING. And to let me keep him so long here—that's the nicest part of what he has done.

MANDERS. Yes, I hear you are going to spend the winter at home.

OSWALD. I am here for an indefinite time, Mr. Manders. —Oh, it's good to be at home again!

MRS. ALVING [*beaming*]. Yes, isn't it!

MANDERS [*looking sympathetically at him*]. You went out into the world very young, my dear Oswald.

OSWALD. I did. Sometimes I wonder if I wasn't too young.

MRS. ALVING. Not a bit of it. It is the best thing for an active boy, and especially for an only child. It's a pity when they are kept at home with their parents and get spoilt.

MANDERS. That is a very debatable question, Mrs. Alving. A child's own home is, and always must be, his proper place.

OSWALD.   There I agree entirely with Mr. Manders.

MANDERS.   Take the case of your own son. Oh yes, we can talk about it before him. What has the result been in his case? He is six or seven and twenty, and has never yet had the opportunity of learning what a well-regulated home means.

OSWALD.   Excuse me, Mr. Manders, you are quite wrong there.

MANDERS.   Indeed? I imagined that your life abroad had practically been spent entirely in artistic circles.

OSWALD.   So it has.

MANDERS.   And chiefly amongst the younger artists.

OSWALD.   Certainly.

MANDERS.   But I imagined that those gentry, as a rule, had not the means necessary for family life and the support of a home.

OSWALD.   There are a considerable number of them who have not the means to marry, Mr. Manders.

MANDERS.   That is exactly my point.

OSWALD.   But they can have a home of their own, all the same; a good many of them have. And they are very well-regulated and very comfortable homes, too.

[MRS. ALVING, *who has listened to him attentively, nods assent, but says nothing.*]

MANDERS.   Oh, but I am not talking of bachelor establishments. By a home I mean family life—the life a man lives with his wife and children.

OSWALD.   Exactly, or with his children and his children's mother.

MANDERS [*starts and clasps his hands*].   Good heavens!

OSWALD.   What is the matter?

MANDERS.   Lives with—with—his children's mother!

OSWALD.   Well, would you rather he should repudiate his children's mother?

MANDERS.   Then what you are speaking of are those unprincipled conditions known as irregular unions!

OSWALD.   I have never noticed anything particularly unprincipled about these people's lives.

MANDERS.   But do you mean to say that it is possible for a man of any sort of bringing up, and a young woman, to reconcile themselves to such a way of living—and to make no secret of it, either?

OSWALD.   What else are they to do? A poor artist, and a poor girl—it costs a good deal to get married. What else are they to do?

MANDERS. What are they to do? Well, Mr. Alving, I will tell you what they ought to do. They ought to keep away from each other from the very beginning—that is what they ought to do!

OSWALD. That advice wouldn't have much effect upon hot-blooded young folk who are in love.

MRS. ALVING. No, indeed it wouldn't.

MANDERS [*persistently*]. And to think that the authorities tolerate such things! That they are allowed to go on, openly! [*Turns to* MRS. ALVING.] Had I so little reason, then, to be sadly concerned about your son? In circles where open immorality is rampant—where, one may say, it is honoured—

OSWALD. Let me tell you this, Mr. Manders. I have been a constant Sunday guest at one or two of these "irregular" households—

MANDERS. On Sunday, too!

OSWALD. Yes, that is the day of leisure. But never have I heard one objectionable word there, still less have I ever seen anything that could be called immoral. No; but do you know when and where I *have* met with immorality in artists' circles?

MANDERS. No, thank heaven, I don't!

OSWALD. Well, then, I shall have the pleasure of telling you. I have met with it when some one or other of your model husbands and fathers have come out there to have a bit of a look round on their own account, and have done the artists the honour of looking them up in their humble quarters. Then we had a chance of learning something, I can tell you. These gentlemen were able to instruct us about places and things that we had never so much as dreamt of.

MANDERS. What? Do you want me to believe that honourable men when they get away from home will—

OSWALD. Have you never, when these same honourable men come home again, heard them deliver themselves on the subject of the prevalence of immorality abroad?

MANDERS. Yes, of course, but—

MRS. ALVING. I have heard them, too.

OSWALD. Well, you take their word for it, unhesitatingly. Some of them are experts in the matter. [*Putting his hands to his head.*] To think that the glorious freedom of the beautiful life over there should be so besmirched!

MRS. ALVING. You mustn't get too heated, Oswald; you gain nothing by that.

OSWALD. No, you are quite right, mother. Besides, it isn't good for me. It's because I am so infernally tired, you know. I will go out and take a turn before dinner. I beg your pardon, Mr. Manders. It is impossible for you to realise the feeling; but it takes me that way.

[*Goes out by the farther door on the right.*]

MRS. ALVING. My poor boy!

MANDERS. You may well say so. This is what it has brought him to! [MRS. ALVING *looks steadily at him, but does not speak.*] He called himself the prodigal son. It's only too true, alas—only too true! [MRS. ALVING *looks steadily at him.*] And what do you say to all this?

MRS. ALVING. I say that Oswald was right in every single word he said.

MANDERS. Right? Right? To hold such principles as that?

MRS. ALVING. In my loneliness here I have come to just the same opinions as he, Mr. Manders. But I have never presumed to venture upon such topics in conversation. Now there is no need; my boy shall speak for me.

MANDERS. You deserve the deepest pity, Mrs. Alving. It is my duty to say an earnest word to you. It is no longer your business man and adviser, no longer your old friend and your dead husband's old friend, that stands before you now. It is your priest that stands before you, just as he did once at the most critical moment of your life.

MRS. ALVING. And what is it that my priest has to say to me?

MANDERS. First of all I must stir your memory. The moment is well chosen. To-morrow is the tenth anniversary of your husband's death; to-morrow the memorial to the departed will be unveiled; to-morrow I shall speak to the whole assembly that will be met together. But to-day I want to speak to you alone.

MRS. ALVING. Very well, Mr. Manders, speak!

MANDERS. Have you forgotten that after barely a year of married life you were standing at the very edge of a precipice?—that you forsook your house and home?—that you ran away from your husband—yes, Mrs. Alving, ran away, ran away—and refused to return to him in spite of his requests and entreaties?

MRS. ALVING. Have you forgotten how unspeakably unhappy I was during that first year?

MANDERS. To crave for happiness in this world is simply to be possessed by a spirit of revolt. What right have we to happiness? No! we must do our duty, Mrs. Alving. And your duty was to cleave to the man you had chosen and to whom you were bound by a sacred bond.

MRS. ALVING. You know quite well what sort of a life my husband was living at that time—what excesses he was guilty of.

MANDERS. I know only too well what rumour used to say of him; and I should be the last person to approve of his conduct as a young man, supposing that rumour spoke the truth. But it is not a wife's part to be her husband's judge. You should have considered it your bounden duty humbly to have borne the cross that a higher will had laid upon you. But, instead of that, you rebelliously cast off your cross, you deserted the man whose stumbling footsteps you should have supported, you did what was bound to imperil your good name and reputation, and came very near to imperilling the reputation of others into the bargain.

MRS. ALVING. Of others? Of one other, you mean.

MANDERS. It was the height of imprudence, your seeking refuge with me.

MRS. ALVING. With our priest? With our intimate friend?

MANDERS. All the more on that account. You should thank God that I possessed the necessary strength of mind—that I was able to turn you from your outrageous intention, and that it was vouchsafed to me to succeed in leading you back into the path of duty and back to your lawful husband.

MRS. ALVING. Yes, Mr. Manders, that certainly was your doing.

MANDERS. I was but the humble instrument of a higher power. And is it not true that my having been able to bring you again under the yoke of duty and obedience sowed the seeds of a rich blessing on all the rest of your life? Did things not turn out as I foretold to you? Did not your husband turn from straying in the wrong path as a man should? Did he not, after all, live a life of love and good report with you all his days? Did he not become a benefactor to the neighbourhood? Did he not so raise you up to his level, so that by degrees you became his fellow-worker in all his undertakings—and a noble fellow-worker, too, I know, Mrs. Alving; that praise I will give you.—But now I come to the second serious false step in your life.

MRS. ALVING. What do you mean?

MANDERS. Just as once you forsook your duty as a wife, so, since then, you have forsaken your duty as a mother.

MRS. ALVING. Oh—!

MANDERS. You have been overmastered all your life by a disastrous spirit of wilfulness. All your impulses have led you towards what is undisciplined and lawless. You have never been willing to submit to any restraint. Anything in life that has seemed irksome to you, you have thrown aside recklessly and unscrupulously, as if it were a burden that you were free to rid yourself of if you would. It did not please you to be a wife any longer, and so you left your husband. Your duties as a mother were irksome to you, so you sent your child away among strangers.

MRS. ALVING. Yes, that is true; I did that.

MANDERS. And that is why you have become a stranger to him.

MRS. ALVING. No, no, I am not that!

MANDERS. You are; you must be. And what sort of a son is it that you have got back? Think over it seriously, Mrs. Alving. You erred grievously in your husband's case—you acknowledge as much, by erecting this memorial to him. Now you are bound to acknowledge how much you have erred in your son's case; possibly there may still be time to reclaim him from the paths of wickedness. Turn over a new leaf, and set yourself to reform what there may still be that is capable of reformation in him. Because [*with uplifted forefinger*] in very truth, Mrs. Alving, you are a guilty mother!—That is what I have thought it my duty to say to you.

[*A short silence.*]

MRS. ALVING [*speaking slowly and with self-control*]. You have had your say, Mr. Manders, and to-morrow you will be making a public speech in memory of my husband. I shall not speak to-morrow. But now I wish to speak to you for a little, just as you have been speaking to me.

MANDERS. By all means; no doubt you wish to bring forward some excuses for your behaviour—

MRS. ALVING. No. I only want to tell you something.

MANDERS. Well?

MRS. ALVING. In all that you said just now about me and my husband, and about our life together after you had, as you put it, led me back into the path of duty—there was nothing that you knew at first hand. From that moment you never again set foot in our house— you, who had been our daily companion before that.

MANDERS. Remember that you and your husband moved out of town immediately afterwards.

MRS. ALVING. Yes, and you never once came out here to see us in my husband's lifetime. It was only the business in connection with the Orphanage that obliged you to come and see me.

MANDERS [*in a low and uncertain voice*]. Helen—if that is a reproach, I can only beg you to consider—

MRS. ALVING. —the respect you owed to your calling?—yes. All the more as I was a wife who had tried to run away from her husband. One can never be too careful to have nothing to do with such reckless women.

MANDERS. My dear—Mrs. Alving, you are exaggerating dreadfully—

MRS. ALVING. Yes, yes,—very well. What I mean is this, that when you condemn by conduct as a wife you have nothing more to go upon than ordinary public opinion.

MANDERS. I admit it. What then?

MRS. ALVING. Well—now, Mr. Manders, now I am going to tell you the truth. I had sworn to myself that you should know it one day— you, and you only!

MANDERS. And what may the truth be?

MRS. ALVING. The truth is this, that my husband died just as great a profligate as he had been all his life.

MANDERS [*feeling for a chair*]. What are you saying?

MRS. ALVING. After nineteen years of married life, just as profligate— in his desires at all events—as he was before you married us.

MANDERS. And can you talk of his youthful indiscretions—his irregularities—his excesses, if you like—as a profligate life!

MRS. ALVING. That was what the doctor who attended him called it.

MANDERS. I don't understand what you mean.

MRS. ALVING. It is not necessary you should.

MANDERS. It makes my brain reel. To think that your marriage—all the years of wedded life you spent with your husband—were nothing but a hidden abyss of misery.

MRS. ALVING. That and nothing else. Now you know.

MANDERS. This—this bewilders me. I can't understand it! I can't grasp it! How in the world was it possible—? How could such a state of things remain concealed?

MRS. ALVING. That was just what I had to fight for incessantly, day after day. When Oswald was born, I thought I saw a slight improvement. But it didn't last long. And after that I had to fight doubly hard—fight a desperate fight so that no one should know what sort of a man my child's father was. You know quite well what an attractive manner he had; it seemed as if people could believe nothing but good of him. He was one of those men whose mode of life seems to have no effect upon their reputations. But at last, Mr. Manders—you must hear this too—at last something happened more abominable than everything else.

MANDERS. More abominable than what you have told me!

MRS. ALVING. I had borne with it all, though I knew only too well what he indulged in in secret, when he was out of the house. But when it came to the point of the scandal coming within our four walls—

MANDERS. Can you mean it! Here?

MRS. ALVING. Yes, here, in our own home. It was in there [*pointing to the nearer door on the right*] in the dining-room that I got the first hint of it. I had something to do in there and the door was standing ajar. I heard our maid come up from the garden with water for the flowers in the conservatory.

MANDERS. Well—?

MRS. ALVING. Shortly afterwards I heard my husband come in too. I heard him say something to her in a low voice. And then I heard —[*with a short laugh*]—oh, it rings in my ears still, with its mixture of what was heartbreaking and what was so ridiculous—I heard my own servant whisper: "Let me go, Mr. Alving! Let me be!"

MANDERS. What unseemly levity on his part! But surely nothing more than levity, Mrs. Alving, believe me.

MRS. ALVING. I soon knew what to believe. My husband had his will of the girl—and that intimacy had consequences, Mr. Manders.

MANDERS [*as if turned to stone*]. And all that in this house! In this house!

MRS. ALVING. I have suffered a good deal in this house. To keep him at home in the evening—and at night—I have had to play the part of boon companion in his secret drinking-bouts in his room up there. I have had to sit there alone with him, have had to hobnob and drink with him, have had to listen to his ribald senseless talk, have had to fight with brute force to get him to bed—

MANDERS [*trembling*]. And you were able to endure all this!

MRS. ALVING. I had my little boy, and endured it for his sake. But when the crowning insult came—when my own servant—then I made up my mind that there should be an end of it. I took the upper hand in the house, absolutely—both with him and all the others. I had a weapon to use against him, you see; he didn't dare to speak. It was then that Oswald was sent away. He was about seven then, and was beginning to notice things and ask questions as children will. I could endure all that, my friend. It seemed to me that the child would be poisoned if he breathed the air of this polluted house. That was why I sent him away. And now you understand, too, why he never set foot here as long as his father was alive. No one knows what it meant to me.

MANDERS. You have indeed had a pitiable experience.

MRS. ALVING. I could never have gone through with it, if I had not had my work. Indeed, I can boast that I have worked. All the increase in the value of the property, all the improvements, all the useful arrangements that my husband got the honour and glory of —do you suppose that he troubled himself about any of them? He, who used to lie the whole day on the sofa reading old Official Lists! No, you may as well know that too. It was I that kept him up to the mark when he had his lucid intervals; it was I that had to bear the whole burden of it when he began his excesses again or took to whining about his miserable condition.

MANDERS. And this is the man you are building a memorial to!

MRS. ALVING. There you see the power of an uneasy conscience.

MANDERS. An uneasy conscience? What do you mean?

MRS. ALVING. I had always before me the fear that it was impossible that the truth should not come out and be believed. That is why the Orphanage is to exist, to silence all rumours and clear away all doubt.

MANDERS. You certainly have not fallen short of the mark in that, Mrs. Alving.

MRS. ALVING. I had another very good reason. I did not wish Oswald, my own son, to inherit a penny that belonged to his father.

MANDERS. Then it is with Mr. Alving's property—

MRS. ALVING. Yes. The sums of money that, year after year, I have given towards this Orphanage, make up the amount of property—I have reckoned it carefully—which in the old days made Lieutenant Alving a catch.

MANDERS. I understand.

MRS. ALVING. That was my purchase money. I don't wish it to pass into Oswald's hands. My son shall have everything from me, I am determined.

[OSWALD *comes in by the farther door on the right. He has left his hat and coat outside.*]

MRS. ALVING. Back again, my own dear boy?

OSWALD. Yes, what can one do outside in this everlasting rain? I hear dinner is nearly ready. That's good!

[REGINA *comes in from the dining-room, carrying a parcel.*]

REGINA. This parcel has come for you, ma'am.

[*Gives it to her.*]

MRS. ALVING [*glancing at* MANDERS]. The ode to be sung to-morrow, I expect.

MANDERS. Hm—!

REGINA. And dinner is ready.

MRS. ALVING. Good. We will come in a moment. I will just—[*begins to open the parcel*].

REGINA [*to* OSWALD]. Will you drink white or red wine, sir?

OSWALD. Both, Miss Engstrand.

REGINA. *Bien*—very good, Mr. Alving.

[*Goes into the dining-room.*]

OSWALD. I may as well help you to uncork it—.

[*Follows her into the dining-room, leaving the door ajar after him.*]

MRS. ALVING. Yes, I thought so. Here is the ode, Mr. Manders.

MANDERS [*clasping his hands*]. How shall I ever have the courage to-morrow to speak the address that—

MRS. ALVING. Oh, you will get through it.

MANDERS [*in a low voice, fearing to be heard in the dining-room*]. Yes, we must raise no suspicions.

MRS. ALVING [*quietly but firmly*]. No; and then this long dreadful comedy will be at an end. After to-morrow, I shall feel as if my dead husband had never lived in this house. There will be no one else here then but my boy and his mother.

[*From the dining-room is heard the noise of a chair falling; then*

Regina's *voice is heard in a loud whisper:* Oswald! Are you mad?
Let me go!]

Mrs. Alving [*starting in horror*]. Oh—!

[*She stares wildly at the half-open door.* Oswald *is heard coughing and humming, then the sound of a bottle being uncorked.*]

Manders [*in an agitated manner*]. What's the matter? What is it,
Mrs. Alving?

Mrs. Alving [*hoarsely*]. Ghosts. The couple in the conservatory—
over again.

Manders. What are you saying! Regina—? Is she—?

Mrs. Alving. Yes. Come. Not a word—!

[*Grips* Manders *by the arm and walks unsteadily with him into the dining-room.*]


## ACT II

*The same scene. The landscape is still obscured by mist.* Manders *and*
Mrs. Alving *come in from the dining-room.*

Mrs. Alving [*calls into the dining-room from the doorway*]. Aren't
you coming in here, Oswald?

Oswald. No, thanks; I think I will go out for a bit.

Mrs. Alving. Yes, do; the weather is clearing a little. [*She shuts the
dining-room door, then goes to the hall door and calls.*] Regina!

Regina [*from without*]. Yes, ma'am?

Mrs. Alving. Go down into the laundry and help with the garlands.

Regina. Yes, ma'am.

[Mrs. Alving *satisfies herself that she has gone, then shuts the
door.*]

Manders. I suppose he can't hear us?

Mrs. Alving. Not when the door is shut. Besides, he is going out.

Manders. I am still quite bewildered. I don't know how I managed
to swallow a mouthful of your excellent dinner.

Mrs. Alving [*walking up and down, and trying to control her agitation*]. Nor I. But what are we to do?

Manders. Yes, what are we to do? Upon my word I don't know; I
am so completely unaccustomed to things of this kind.

Mrs. Alving. I am convinced that nothing serious has happened yet.

Manders. Heaven forbid! But it is most unseemly behaviour, for all
that.

MRS. ALVING. It is nothing more than a foolish jest of Oswald's, you may be sure.

MANDERS. Well, of course, as I said, I am quite inexperienced in such matters; but it certainly seems to me—

MRS. ALVING. Out of the house she shall go—and at once. That part of it is as clear as daylight—

MANDERS. Yes, that is quite clear.

MRS. ALVING. But where is she to go? We should not be justified in—

MANDERS. Where to? Home to her father, of course.

MRS. ALVING. To whom, did you say?

MANDERS. To her—. No, of course Engstrand isn't—. But, great heavens, Mrs. Alving, how is such a thing possible? You surely may have been mistaken, in spite of everything.

MRS. ALVING. There was no chance of mistake, more's the pity. Joanna was obliged to confess it to me—and my husband couldn't deny it. So there was nothing else to do but to hush it up.

MANDERS. No, that was the only thing to do.

MRS. ALVING. The girl was sent away at once, and was given a tolerably liberal sum to hold her tongue. She looked after the rest herself when she got to town. She renewed an old acquaintance with the carpenter Engstrand; gave him a hint, I suppose, of how much money she had got, and told him some fairy tale about a foreigner who had been here in his yacht in the summer. So she and Engstrand were married in a great hurry. Why, you married them yourself!

MANDERS. I can't understand it—. I remember clearly Engstrand's coming to arrange about the marriage. He was full of contrition, and accused himself bitterly for the light conduct he and his fiancée had been guilty of.

MRS. ALVING. Of course he had to take the blame on himself.

MANDERS. But the deceitfulness of it! And with me, too! I positively would not have believed it of Jacob Engstrand. I shall most certainly give him a serious talking to.—And the immorality of such a marriage! Simply for the sake of the money—! What sum was it that the girl had?

MRS. ALVING. It was seventy pounds.

MANDERS. Just think of it—for a paltry seventy pounds to let yourself be bound in marriage to a fallen woman!

Mrs. Alving. What about myself, then?—I let myself be bound in marriage to a fallen man.

Manders. Heaven forgive you! what are you saying? A fallen man?

Mrs. Alving. Do you suppose my husband was any purer, when I went with him to the altar, than Joanna was when Engstrand agreed to marry her?

Manders. The two cases are as different as day from night—

Mrs. Alving. Not so very different, after all. It is true there was a great difference in the price paid, between a paltry seventy pounds and a whole fortune.

Manders. How can you compare such totally different things! I presume you consulted your own heart—and your relations.

Mrs. Alving [*looking away from him*]. I thought you understood where what you call my heart had strayed to at that time.

Manders [*in a constrained voice*]. If I had understood anything of the kind, I would not have been a daily guest in your husband's house.

Mrs. Alving. Well, at any rate this much is certain, that I didn't consult myself in the matter at all.

Manders. Still you consulted those nearest to you, as was only right— your mother, your two aunts.

Mrs. Alving. Yes, that is true. The three of them settled the whole matter for me. It seems incredible to me now, how clearly they made out that it would be sheer folly to reject such an offer. If my mother could only see what all that fine prospect has led to!

Manders. No one can be responsible for the result of it. Anyway, there is this to be said, that the match was made in complete conformity with law and order.

Mrs. Alving [*going to the window*]. Oh, law and order! I often think it is that that is at the bottom of all the misery in the world.

Manders. Mrs. Alving, it is very wicked of you to say that.

Mrs. Alving. That may be so; but I don't attach importance to those obligations and considerations any longer. I cannot! I must struggle for my freedom.

Manders. What do you mean?

Mrs. Alving [*tapping on the window panes*]. I ought never to have concealed what sort of a life my husband led. But I had not the courage to do otherwise then—for my own sake, either. I was too much of a coward.

MANDERS. A coward?

MRS. ALVING. If others had known anything of what happened, they would have said: "Poor man, it is natural enough that he should go astray, when he has a wife that has run away from him."

MANDERS. They would have had a certain amount of justification for saying so.

MRS. ALVING [*looking fixedly at him*]. If I had been the woman I ought, I would have taken Oswald into my confidence and said to him: "Listen, my son, your father was a dissolute man"—

MANDERS. Miserable woman—

MRS. ALVING. —and I would have told him all I have told you, from beginning to end.

MANDERS. I am almost shocked at you, Mrs. Alving.

MRS. ALVING. I know. I know quite well! I am shocked at myself when I think of it. [*Comes away from the window.*] I am coward enough for that.

MANDERS. Can you call it cowardice that you simply did your duty! Have you forgotten that a child should love and honour his father and mother?

MRS. ALVING. Don't let us talk in such general terms. Suppose we say: "Ought Oswald to love and honour Mr. Alving?"

MANDERS. You are a mother—isn't there a voice in your heart that forbids you to shatter your son's ideals?

MRS. ALVING. And what about the truth?

MANDERS. What about his ideals?

MRS. ALVING. Oh—ideals, ideals! If only I were not such a coward as I am!

MANDERS. Do not spurn ideals, Mrs. Alving—they have a way of avenging themselves cruelly. Take Oswald's own case, now. He hasn't many ideals, more's the pity. But this much I have seen, that his father is something of an ideal to him.

MRS. ALVING. You are right there.

MANDERS. And his conception of his father is what you inspired and encouraged by your letters.

MRS. ALVING. Yes, I was swayed by duty and consideration for others; that was why I lied to my son, year in and year out. Oh, what a coward—what a coward I have been!

MANDERS. You have built up a happy illusion in your son's mind,

Mrs. Alving—and that is a thing you certainly ought not to under-value.

MRS. ALVING. Ah, who knows if that is such a desirable thing after all!—But anyway I don't intend to put up with any goings on with Regina. I am not going to let him get the poor girl into trouble.

MANDERS. Good heavens, no—that would be a frightful thing!

MRS. ALVING. If only I knew whether he meant it seriously, and whether it would mean happiness for him—

MANDERS. In what way? I don't understand.

MRS. ALVING. But that is impossible; Regina is not equal to it, un-fortunately.

MANDERS. I don't understand. What do you mean?

MRS. ALVING. If I were not such a miserable coward, I would say to him: "Marry her, or make any arrangement you like with her—only let there be no deceit in the matter."

MANDERS. Heaven forgive you! Are you actually suggesting anything so abominable, so unheard of, as a marriage between them!

MRS. ALVING. Unheard of, do you call it? Tell me honestly, Mr. Manders, don't you suppose there are plenty of married couples out here in the country that are just as nearly related as they are?

MANDERS. I am sure I don't understand you.

MRS. ALVING. Indeed you do.

MANDERS. I suppose you are thinking of cases where possibly—. It is only too true, unfortunately, that family life is not always as stain-less as it should be. But as for the sort of thing you hint at—well, it's impossible to tell, at all events with any certainty. Here, on the other hand—for you, a mother, to be willing to allow your—

MRS. ALVING. But I am not willing to allow it. I would not allow it for anything in the world; that is just what I was saying.

MANDERS. No, because you are a coward, as you put it. But, supposing you were not a coward—! Great heavens—such a revolting union!

MRS. ALVING. Well, for the matter of that, we are all descended from a union of that description, so we are told. And who was it that was responsible for this state of things, Mr. Manders?

MANDERS. I can't discuss such questions with you, Mrs. Alving; you are by no means in the right frame of mind for that. But for you to dare to say that it is cowardly of you—!

MRS. ALVING. I will tell you what I mean by that. I am frightened and timid, because I am obsessed by the presence of ghosts that I never can get rid of.

MANDERS. The presence of what?

MRS. ALVING. Ghosts. When I heard Regina and Oswald in there, it was just like seeing ghosts before my eyes. I am half inclined to think we are all ghosts, Mr. Manders. It is not only what we have inherited from our fathers and mothers that exists again in us, but all sorts of old dead ideas and all kinds of old dead beliefs and things of that kind. They are not actually alive in us; but there they are dormant, all the same, and we can never be rid of them. Whenever I take up a newspaper and read it, I fancy I see ghosts creeping between the lines. There must be ghosts all over the world. They must be as countless as the grains of the sands, it seems to me. And we are so miserably afraid of the light, all of us.

MANDERS. Ah!—there we have the outcome of your reading. Fine fruit it has borne—this abominable, subversive, free-thinking literature!

MRS. ALVING. You are wrong there, my friend. You are the one who made me begin to think; and I owe you my best thanks for it.

MANDERS. I!

MRS. ALVING. Yes, by forcing me to submit to what you called my duty and my obligations; by praising as right and just what my whole soul revolted against, as it would against something abominable. That was what led me to examine your teachings critically. I only wanted to unravel one point in them; but as soon as I had got that unravelled, the whole fabric came to pieces. And then I realised that it was only machine-made.

MANDERS [*softly, and with emotion*]. Is that all I accomplished by the hardest struggle of my life?

MRS. ALVING. Call it rather the most ignominious defeat of your life.

MANDERS. It was the greatest victory of my life, Helen; victory over myself.

MRS. ALVING. It was a wrong done to both of us.

MANDERS. A wrong?—wrong for me to entreat you as a wife to go back to your lawful husband, when you came to me half distracted and crying: "Here I am, take me!" Was that a wrong?

MRS. ALVING. I think it was.

MANDERS. We two do not understand one another.

MRS. ALVING. Not now, at all events.

MANDERS. Never—even in my most secret thoughts—have I for a moment regarded you as anything but the wife of another.

MRS. ALVING. Do you believe what you say?

MANDERS. Helen—!

MRS. ALVING. One so easily forgets one's own feelings.

MANDERS. Not I. I am the same as I always was.

MRS. ALVING. Yes, yes—don't let us talk any more about the old days. You are buried up to your eyes now in committees and all sorts of business; and I am here, fighting with ghosts both without and within me.

MANDERS. I can at all events help you to get the better of those without you. After all that I have been horrified to hear from you to-day, I cannot conscientiously allow a young defenceless girl to remain in your house.

MRS. ALVING. Don't you think it would be best if we could get her settled?—by some suitable marriage, I mean.

MANDERS. Undoubtedly. I think, in any case, it would have been desirable for her. Regina is at an age now that—well, I don't know much about these things, but—

MRS. ALVING. Regina developed very early.

MANDERS. Yes, didn't she. I fancy I remember thinking she was remarkably well developed, bodily, at the time I prepared her for Confirmation. But, for the time being she must in any case go home. Under her father's care—no, but of course Engstrand is not—. To think that he, of all men, could so conceal the truth from me!

[*A knock is heard at the hall door.*]

MRS. ALVING. Who can that be? Come in!

[ENGSTRAND, *dressed in his Sunday clothes, appears in the doorway.*]

ENGSTRAND. I humbly beg pardon, but—

MANDERS. Aha! Hm!—

MRS. ALVING. Oh, it's you, Engstrand!

ENGSTRAND. There were none of the maids about, so I took the great liberty of knocking.

MRS. ALVING. That's all right. Come in. Do you want to speak to me?

ENGSTRAND [*coming in*]. No, thank you very much, ma'am. It was Mr. Manders I wanted to speak to for a moment.

MANDERS [*walking up and down*]. Hm!—do you. You want to speak to me, do you?

ENGSTRAND. Yes, sir, I wanted so very much to—

MANDERS [*stopping in front of him*]. Well, may I ask what it is you want?

ENGSTRAND. It's this way, Mr. Manders. We are being paid off now. And many thanks to you, Mrs. Alving. And now the work is quite finished, I thought it would be so nice and suitable if all of us, who have worked so honestly together all this time, were to finish up with a few prayers this evening.

MANDERS. Prayers? Up at the Orphanage?

ENGSTRAND. Yes, sir, but if it isn't agreeable to you, then—

MANDERS. Oh, certainly—but—hm!—

ENGSTRAND. I have made a practice of saying a few prayers there myself each evening—

MRS. ALVING. Have you?

ENGSTRAND. Yes, ma'am, now and then—just as a little edification, so to speak. But I am only a poor common man, and haven't rightly the gift, alas—and so I thought that as Mr. Manders happened to be here, perhaps—

MANDERS. Look here, Engstrand. First of all I must ask you a question. Are you in a proper frame of mind for such a thing? Is your conscience free and untroubled?

ENGSTRAND. Heaven have mercy on me a sinner! My conscience isn't worth our speaking about, Mr. Manders.

MANDERS. But it is just what we must speak about. What do you say to my question?

ENGSTRAND. My conscience? Well—it's uneasy sometimes, of course.

MANDERS. Ah, you admit that at all events. Now will you tell me, without any concealment—what is your relationship to Regina?

MRS. ALVING [*hastily*]. Mr. Manders!

MANDERS [*calming her*]. Leave it to me!

ENGSTRAND. With Regina? Good Lord, how you frightened me! [*Looks at* MRS. ALVING.] There is nothing wrong with Regina, is there?

MANDERS. Let us hope not. What I want to know is, what is your relationship to her? You pass as her father, don't you?

ENGSTRAND [*unsteadily*]. Well—hm!—you know, sir, what happened between me and my poor Joanna.

MANDERS. No more distortion of the truth! Your late wife made a full confession to Mrs. Alving, before she left her service.

ENGSTRAND. What!—do you mean to say—? Did she do that after all?

MANDERS. You see it has all come out, Engstrand.

ENGSTRAND. Do you mean to say that she, who gave me her promise and solemn oath—

MANDERS. Did she take an oath?

ENGSTRAND. Well, no—she only gave me her word, but as seriously as a woman could.

MANDERS. And all these years you have been hiding the truth from me—from me, who have had such complete and absolute faith in you.

ENGSTRAND. I am sorry to say I have, sir.

MANDERS. Did I deserve that from you, Engstrand? Haven't I been always ready to help you in word and deed as far as lay in my power? Answer me! Is it not so?

ENGSTRAND. Indeed there's many a time I should have been very badly off without you, sir.

MANDERS. And this is the way you repay me—by causing me to make false entries in the church registers, and afterwards keeping back from me for years the information which you owed it both to me and to your sense of the truth to divulge. Your conduct has been absolutely inexcusable, Engstrand, and from to-day everything is at an end between us.

ENGSTRAND [*with a sigh*]. Yes, I can see that's what it means.

MANDERS. Yes, because how can you possibly justify what you did?

ENGSTRAND. Was the poor girl to go and increase her load of shame by talking about it? Just suppose, sir, for a moment that your reverence was in the same predicament as my poor Joanna—

MANDERS. I!

ENGSTRAND. Good Lord, sir, I don't mean the same predicament. I mean, suppose there were something your reverence were ashamed of in the eyes of the world, so to speak. We men oughtn't to judge a poor woman too hardly, Mr. Manders.

MANDERS. But I am not doing so at all. It is you I am blaming.

ENGSTRAND. Will your reverence grant me leave to ask you a small question?

MANDERS. Ask away.

ENGSTRAND. Shouldn't you say it was right for a man to raise up the fallen?

MANDERS. Of course it is.

ENGSTRAND. And isn't a man bound to keep his word of honour?

MANDERS. Certainly he is; but—

ENGSTRAND. At the time when Joanna had her misfortune with this Englishman—or maybe he was an American or a Russian, as they call 'em—well, sir, then she came to town. Poor thing, she had refused me once or twice before; she only had eyes for good-looking men in those days, and I had this crooked leg then. Your reverence will remember how I had ventured up into a dancing-saloon where seafaring men were revelling in drunkenness and intoxication, as they say. And when I tried to exhort them to turn from their evil ways—

MRS. ALVING [*coughs from the window*]. Ahem!

MANDERS. I know, Engstrand, I know—the rough brutes threw you downstairs. You have told me about that incident before. The affliction to your leg is a credit to you.

ENGSTRAND. I don't want to claim credit for it, your reverence. But what I wanted to tell you was that she came then and confided in me with tears and gnashing of teeth. I can tell you, sir, it went to my heart to hear her.

MANDERS. Did it, indeed, Engstrand? Well, what then?

ENGSTRAND. Well, then I said to her: "The American is roaming about on the high seas, he is. And you, Joanna," I said, "you have committed a sin and are a fallen woman. But here stands Jacob Engstrand," I said, "on two strong legs"—of course that was only speaking in a kind of metaphor, as it were, your reverence.

MANDERS. I quite understand. Go on.

ENGSTRAND. Well, sir, that was how I rescued her and made her my lawful wife, so that no one should know how recklessly she had carried on with the stranger.

MANDERS. That was all very kindly done. The only thing I cannot justify was your bringing yourself to accept the money—

ENGSTRAND. Money? I? Not a farthing.

MANDERS [*to* MRS. ALVING, *in a questioning tone*]. But—

ENGSTRAND. Ah, yes!—wait a bit; I remember now. Joanna did have a trifle of money, you are quite right. But I didn't want to know anything about that. "Fie," I said, "on the mammon of unrighteousness, it's the price of your sin; as for this tainted gold"—or notes, or whatever it was—"we will throw it back in the American's face,"

I said. But he had gone away and disappeared on the stormy seas, your reverence.

MANDERS. Was that how it was, my good fellow?

ENGSTRAND. It was, sir. So then Joanna and I decided that the money should go towards the child's bringing-up, and that's what became of it; and I can give a faithful account of every single penny of it.

MANDERS. This alters the complexion of the affair very considerably.

ENGSTRAND. That's how it was, your reverence. And I make bold to say that I have been a good father to Regina—as far as was in my power—for I am a poor erring mortal, alas!

MANDERS. There, there, my dear Engstrand—

ENGSTRAND. Yes, I do make bold to say that I brought up the child, and made my poor Joanna a loving and careful husband, as the Bible says we ought. But it never occurred to me to go to your reverence and claim credit for it or boast about it because I had done one good deed in this world. No; when Jacob Engstrand does a thing like that, he holds his tongue about it. Unfortunately it doesn't often happen, I know that only too well. And whenever I do come to see your reverence, I never seem to have anything but trouble and wickedness to talk about. Because, as I said just now—and I say it again—conscience can be very hard on us sometimes.

MANDERS. Give me your hand, Jacob Engstrand.

ENGSTRAND. Oh, sir, I don't like—

MANDERS. No nonsense. [*Grasps his hand.*] That's it!

ENGSTRAND. And may I make bold humbly to beg your reverence's pardon—

MANDERS. You? On the contrary it is for me to beg your pardon—

ENGSTRAND. Oh no, sir.

MANDERS. Yes, certainly it is, and I do it with my whole heart. Forgive me for having so much misjudged you. And I assure you that if I can do anything for you to prove my sincere regret and my goodwill towards you—

ENGSTRAND. Do you mean it, sir?

MANDERS. It would give me the greatest pleasure.

ENGSTRAND. As a matter of fact, sir, you could do it now. I am thinking of using the honest money I have put away out of my wages up here, in establishing a sort of Sailors' Home in the town.

MRS. ALVING. You?

ENGSTRAND.  Yes, to be a sort of Refuge, as it were. There are such manifold temptations lying in wait for sailor men when they are roaming about on shore. But my idea is that in this house of mine they should have a sort of parental care looking after them.

MANDERS.  What do you say to that, Mrs. Alving!

ENGSTRAND.  I haven't much to begin such a work with, I know; but Heaven might prosper it, and if I found any helping hand stretched out to me, then—

MANDERS.  Quite so; we will talk over the matter further. Your project attracts me enormously. But in the meantime go back to the Orphanage and put everything tidy and light the lights, so that the occasion may seem a little solemn. And then we will spend a little edifying time together, my dear Engstrand, for now I am sure you are in a suitable frame of mind.

ENGSTRAND.  I believe I am, sir, truly. Good-bye, then, Mrs. Alving, and thank you for all your kindness; and take good care of Regina for me. [*Wipes a tear from his eye.*] Poor Joanna's child—it is an extraordinary thing, but she seems to have grown into my life and to hold me by the heartstrings. That's how I feel about it, truly.

[*Bows and goes out.*]

MANDERS.  Now then, what do you think of him, Mrs. Alving! That was quite another explanation that he gave us.

MRS. ALVING.  It was, indeed.

MANDERS.  There, you see how exceedingly careful we ought to be in condemning our fellow-men. But at the same time it gives one genuine pleasure to find that one was mistaken. Don't you think so?

MRS. ALVING.  What I think is that you are, and always will remain, a big baby, Mr. Manders.

MANDERS.  I?

MRS. ALVING [*laying her hands on his shoulders*].  And I think that I should like very much to give you a good hug.

MANDERS [*drawing back hastily*].  No, no, good gracious! What an idea!

MRS. ALVING [*with a smile*].  Oh, you needn't be afraid of me.

MANDERS [*standing by the table*].  You choose such an extravagant way of expressing yourself sometimes. Now I must get these papers together and put them in my bag. [*Does so.*] That's it. And now good-bye, for the present. Keep your eyes open when Oswald comes back. I will come back and see you again presently.

[*He takes his hat and goes out by the hall door.* MRS. ALVING *sighs, glances out of the window, puts one or two things tidy in the room and turns to go into the dining-room. She stops in the doorway with a stifled cry.*]

MRS. ALVING. Oswald, are you still sitting at table!

OSWALD [*from the dining-room*]. I am only finishing my cigar.

MRS. ALVING. I thought you had gone out for a little turn.

OSWALD [*from within the room*]. In weather like this? [*A glass is heard clinking.* MRS. ALVING *leaves the door open and sits down with her knitting on the couch by the window.*] Wasn't that Mr. Manders that went out just now?

MRS. ALVING. Yes, he has gone over to the Orphanage.

OSWALD. Oh.

[*The clink of a bottle on a glass is heard again.*]

MRS. ALVING. [*with an uneasy expression*]. Oswald, dear, you should be careful with that liqueur. It is strong.

OSWALD. It's a good protective against the damp.

MRS. ALVING. Wouldn't you rather come in here?

OSWALD. You know you don't like smoking in there.

MRS. ALVING. You may smoke a cigar in here, certainly.

OSWALD. All right; I will come in then. Just one drop more. There! [*Comes in, smoking a cigar, and shuts the door after him. A short silence.*] Where has the parson gone?

MRS. ALVING. I told you he had gone over to the Orphanage.

OSWALD. Oh, so you did.

MRS. ALVING. You shouldn't sit so long at table, Oswald.

OSWALD [*holding his cigar behind his back*]. But it's so nice and cosy, mother dear. [*Caresses her with one hand.*] Think what it means to me—to have come home; to sit at my mother's own table, in my mother's own room and to enjoy the charming meals she gives me.

MRS. ALVING. My dear, dear boy!

OSWALD [*a little impatiently, as he walks up and down smoking*]. And what else is there for me to do here? I have no occupation—

MRS. ALVING. No occupation?

OSWALD. Not in this ghastly weather, when there isn't a blink of sunshine all day long. [*Walks up and down the floor.*] Not to be able to work, it's—!

MRS. ALVING. I don't believe you were wise to come home.

OSWALD. Yes, mother; I had to.

MRS. ALVING.  Because I would ten times rather give up the happiness of having you with me, sooner than that you should—

OSWALD [*standing still by the table*].  Tell me, mother—is it really such a great happiness for you to have me at home?

MRS. ALVING.  Can you ask?

OSWALD [*crumpling up a newspaper*].  I should have thought it would have been pretty much the same to you whether I were here or away.

MRS. ALVING.  Have you the heart to say that to your mother, Oswald?

OSWALD.  But you have been quite happy living without me so far.

MRS. ALVING.  Yes, I have lived without you—that is true.

[*A silence. The dusk falls by degrees.* OSWALD *walks restlessly up and down. He has laid aside his cigar.*]

OSWALD [*stopping beside* MRS. ALVING].  Mother, may I sit on the couch beside you?

MRS. ALVING.  Of course, my dear boy.

OSWALD [*sitting down*].  Now I must tell you something, mother.

MRS. ALVING [*anxiously*].  What?

OSWALD [*staring in front of him*].  I can't bear it any longer.

MRS. ALVING.  Bear what? What do you mean?

OSWALD [*as before*].  I couldn't bring myself to write to you about it; and since I have been at home—

MRS. ALVING [*catching him by the arm*].  Oswald, what is it?

OSWALD.  Both yesterday and to-day I have tried to push my thoughts away from me—to free myself from them. But I can't.

MRS. ALVING [*getting up*].  You must speak plainly, Oswald!

OSWALD [*drawing her down to her seat again*].  Sit still, and I will try and tell you. I have made a great deal of the fatigue I felt after my journey—

MRS. ALVING.  Well, what of that?

OSWALD.  But that isn't what is the matter. It is no ordinary fatigue—

MRS. ALVING [*trying to get up*].  You are not ill, Oswald!

OSWALD [*pulling her down again*].  Sit still, mother. Do take it quietly. I am not exactly ill—not ill in the usual sense. [*Takes his head in his hands.*] Mother, it's my mind that has broken down—gone to pieces—I shall never be able to work any more!

[*Buries his face in his hands and throws himself at her knees in an outburst of sobs.*]

MRS. ALVING [*pale and trembling*].  Oswald! Look at me! No, no, it isn't true!

Oswald [*looking up with a distracted expression*]. Never to be able to work any more! Never—never! A living death! Mother, can you imagine anything so horrible!

Mrs. Alving. My poor unhappy boy? How has this terrible thing happened?

Oswald [*sitting up again*]. That is just what I cannot possibly understand. I have never lived recklessly, in any sense. You must believe that of me, mother! I have never done that.

Mrs. Alving. I haven't a doubt of it, Oswald.

Oswald. And yet this comes upon me all the same!—this terrible disaster!

Mrs. Alving. Oh, but it will all come right again, my dear precious boy. It is nothing but overwork. Believe me, that is so.

Oswald [*dully*]. I thought so too, at first; but it isn't so.

Mrs. Alving. Tell me all about it.

Oswald. Yes, I will.

Mrs. Alving. When did you first feel anything?

Oswald. It was just after I had been home last time and had got back to Paris. I began to feel the most violent pains in my head—mostly at the back, I think. It was as if a tight band of iron was pressing on me from my neck upwards.

Mrs. Alving. And then?

Oswald. At first I thought it was nothing but the headaches I always used to be so much troubled with while I was growing.

Mrs. Alving. Yes, yes—

Oswald. But it wasn't; I soon saw that. I couldn't work any longer. I would try and start some big new picture; but it seemed as if all my faculties had forsaken me, as if all my strength were paralysed. I couldn't manage to collect my thoughts; my head seemed to swim —everything went round and round. It was a horrible feeling! At last I sent for a doctor—and from him I learnt the truth.

Mrs. Alving. In what way, do you mean?

Oswald. He was one of the best doctors there. He made me describe what I felt, and then he began to ask me a whole heap of questions which seemed to me to have nothing to do with the matter. I couldn't see what he was driving at—

Mrs. Alving. Well?

Oswald. At last he said: "You have had the canker of disease in you practically from your birth"—the actual word he used was *"ver-moulu."*

MRS. ALVING [*anxiously*]. What did he mean by that?

OSWALD. I couldn't understand, either—and I asked him for a clearer explanation. And then the old cynic said—[*clenching his fist.*] Oh!—

MRS. ALVING. What did he say?

OSWALD. He said: "The sins of the fathers are visited on the children."

MRS. ALVING [*getting up slowly*]. The sins of the fathers—!

OSWALD. I nearly struck him in the face—

MRS. ALVING [*walking across the room*]. The sins of the fathers—!

OSWALD [*smiling sadly*]. Yes, just imagine! Naturally I assured him that what he thought was impossible. But do you think he paid any heed to me? No, he persisted in his opinion; and it was only when I got out your letters and translated to him all the passages that referred to my father—

MRS. ALVING. Well, and then?

OSWALD. Well, then of course he had to admit that he was on the wrong tack; and then I learnt the truth—the incomprehensible truth! I ought to have had nothing to do with the joyous happy life I had lived with my comrades. It had been too much for my strength. So it was my own fault!

MRS. ALVING. No, no, Oswald! Don't believe that!

OSWALD. There was no other explanation of it possible, he said. That is the most horrible part of it. My whole life incurably ruined—just because of my own imprudence. All that I wanted to do in the world—not to dare to think of it any more—not to be *able* to think of it! Oh! if only I could live my life over again—if only I could undo what I have done!

[*Throws himself on his face on the couch.* MRS. ALVING *wrings her hands and walks up and down silently fighting with herself.*]

OSWALD [*looks up after a while, raising himself on his elbows*]. If only it had been something I had inherited—something I could not help. But, instead of that, to have disgracefully, stupidly, thoughtlessly thrown away one's happiness, one's health, everything in the world—one's future, one's life—

MRS. ALVING. No, no, my darling boy; that is impossible! [*Bending over him.*] Things are not so desperate as you think.

OSWALD. Ah, you don't know—. [*Springs up.*] And to think, mother, that I should bring all this sorrow upon you! Many a time I have almost wished and hoped that you really did not care so very much for me.

MRS. ALVING.   I, Oswald? My only son! All that I have in the world! The only thing I care about!

OSWALD [*taking hold of her hands and kissing them*].   Yes, yes, I know that is so. When I am at home I know that is true. And that is one of the hardest parts of it to me. But now you know all about it; and now we won't talk any more about it to-day. I can't stand thinking about it long at a time. [*Walks across the room.*] Let me have something to drink, mother!

MRS. ALVING.   To drink? What do you want?

OSWALD.   Oh, anything you like. I suppose you have got some punch in the house.

MRS. ALVING.   Yes, but my dear Oswald—!

OSWALD.   Don't tell me I mustn't, mother. Do be nice! I must have something to drown these gnawing thoughts. [*Goes into the conservatory.*] And how—how gloomy it is here! [MRS. ALVING *rings the bell.*] And this incessant rain. It may go on week after week— a whole month. Never a ray of sunshine. I don't remember ever having seen the sun shine once when I have been at home.

MRS. ALVING.   Oswald—you are thinking of going away from me!

OSWALD.   Hm!—[*sighs deeply*]. I am not thinking about anything. I *can't* think about anything! [*in a low voice.*] I have to let that alone.

REGINA [*coming from the dining-room*].   Did you ring, ma'am?

MRS. ALVING.   Yes, let us have the lamp in.

REGINA.   In a moment, ma'am; it is all ready lit.

[*Goes out.*]

MRS. ALVING [*going up to* OSWALD].   Oswald, don't keep anything back from me.

OSWALD.   I don't, mother. [*Goes to the table.*] It seems to me I have told you a good lot.

[REGINA *brings the lamp and puts it upon the table.*]

MRS. ALVING.   Regina, you might bring us a small bottle of champagne.

REGINA.   Yes, ma'am.                    [*Goes out.*]

OSWALD [*taking hold of his mother's face*].   That's right. I knew my mother wouldn't let her son go thirsty.

MRS. ALVING. My poor dear boy, how could I refuse you anything now?

OSWALD [*eagerly*]. Is that true, mother? Do you mean it?

MRS. ALVING. Mean what?

OSWALD. That you couldn't deny me anything?

MRS. ALVING. My dear Oswald—

OSWALD. Hush!

[REGINA *brings in a tray with a small bottle of champagne and two glasses, which she puts on the table.*]

REGINA. Shall I open the bottle?

OSWALD. No, thank you, I will do it.

[REGINA *goes out.*]

MRS. ALVING [*sitting down at the table*]. What did you mean, when you asked if I could refuse you nothing?

OSWALD [*busy opening the bottle*]. Let us have a glass first—or two. [*He draws the cork, fills one glass and is going to fill the other.*]

MRS. ALVING [*holding her hand over the second glass*]. No, thanks— not for me.

OSWALD. Oh, well, for me then!

[*He empties his glass, fills it again and empties it; then sits down at the table.*]

MRS. ALVING [*expectantly*]. Now, tell me.

OSWALD [*without looking at her*]. Tell me this; I thought you and Mr. Manders seemed so strange—so quiet—at dinner.

MRS. ALVING. Did you notice that?

OSWALD. Yes. Ahem! [*After a short pause.*] Tell me—What do you think of Regina?

MRS. ALVING. What do I think of her?

OSWALD. Yes, isn't she splendid!

MRS. ALVING. Dear Oswald, you don't know her as well as I do—

OSWALD. What of that?

MRS. ALVING. Regina was too long at home, unfortunately. I ought to have taken her under my charge sooner.

OSWALD. Yes, but isn't she splendid to look at, mother?

[*Fills his glass.*]

MRS. ALVING. Regina has many serious faults—

OSWALD. Yes, but what of that?

[*Drinks.*]

MRS. ALVING. But I am fond of her, all the same; and I have made myself responsible for her. I wouldn't for the world she should come to any harm.

OSWALD [*jumping up*]. Mother, Regina is my only hope of salvation!

MRS. ALVING [*getting up*]. What do you mean?

OSWALD. I can't go on bearing all this agony of mind alone.

MRS. ALVING. Haven't you your mother to help you to bear it?

OSWALD. Yes, I thought so; that was why I came home to you. But it is no use; I see that it isn't. I cannot spend my life here.

MRS. ALVING. Oswald!

OSWALD. I must live a different sort of life, mother; so I shall have to go away from you. I don't want you watching it.

MRS. ALVING. My unhappy boy! But, Oswald, as long as you are ill like this—

OSWALD. If it was only a matter of feeling ill, I would stay with you, mother. You are the best friend I have in the world.

MRS. ALVING. Yes, I am that, Oswald, am I not?

OSWALD [*walking restlessly about*]. But all this torment—the regret, the remorse—and the deadly fear. Oh—this horrible fear!

MRS. ALVING [*following him*]. Fear? Fear of what? What do you mean?

OSWALD. Oh, don't ask me any more about it. I don't know what it is. I can't put it into words. [MRS. ALVING *crosses the room and rings the bell.*] What do you want?

MRS. ALVING. I want my boy to be happy, that's what I want. He mustn't brood over anything. [*To* REGINA, *who has come to the door.*] More champagne—a large bottle.

OSWALD. Mother!

MRS. ALVING. Do you think we country people don't know how to live?

OSWALD. Isn't she splendid to look at? What a figure! And the picture of health!

MRS. ALVING [*sitting down at the table*]. Sit down, Oswald, and let us have a quiet talk.

OSWALD [*sitting down*]. You don't know, mother, that I owe Regina a little reparation.

MRS. ALVING. You!

OSWALD. Oh, it was only a little thoughtlessness—call it what you like. Something quite innocent, anyway. The last time I was home—

MRS. ALVING. Yes?

OSWALD. —she used often to ask me questions about Paris, and I told her one thing and another about the life there. And I remember saying one day: "Wouldn't you like to go there yourself?"

MRS. ALVING. Well?

OSWALD. I saw her blush, and she said: "Yes, I should like to very much." "All right," I said, "I daresay it might be managed"—or something of that sort.

MRS. ALVING. And then?

OSWALD. I naturally had forgotten all about it; but the day before yesterday I happened to ask her if she was glad I was to be so long at home—

MRS. ALVING. Well?

OSWALD. —and she looked so queerly at me, and asked: "But what is to become of my trip to Paris?"

MRS. ALVING. Her trip!

OSWALD. And then I got it out of her that she had taken the thing seriously, and had been thinking about me all the time, and had set herself to learn French—

MRS. ALVING. So that was why—

OSWALD. Mother—when I saw this fine, splendid, handsome girl standing there in front of me—I had never paid any attention to her before then—but now, when she stood there as if with open arms ready for me to take her to myself—

MRS. ALVING. Oswald!

OSWALD. —then I realised that my salvation lay in her, for I saw the joy of life in her.

MRS. ALVING [*starting back*]. The joy of life—? Is there salvation in that?

REGINA [*coming in from the dining-room with a bottle of champagne*]. Excuse me for being so long; but I had to go to the cellar.

[*Puts the bottle down on the table.*]

OSWALD. Bring another glass, too.

REGINA [*looking at him in astonishment*]. The mistress's glass is there, sir.

OSWALD. Yes, but fetch one for yourself, Regina. [REGINA *starts, and gives a quick shy glance at* MRS. ALVING.] Well?

REGINA [*in a low and hesitating voice*]. Do you wish me to, ma'am?

MRS. ALVING. Fetch the glass, Regina.

[REGINA *goes into the dining-room.*]

OSWALD [*looking after her*]. Have you noticed how well she walks? —so firmly and confidently!

MRS. ALVING. It cannot be, Oswald.

OSWALD. It is settled. You must see that. It is no use forbidding it. [REGINA *comes in with a glass, which she holds in her hand.*] Sit down, Regina.

[REGINA *looks questioningly at* MRS. ALVING.]

MRS. ALVING. Sit down. [REGINA *sits down on a chair near the dining-room door, still holding the glass in her hand.*] Oswald, what was it you were saying about the joy of life?

OSWALD. Ah, mother—the joy of life! You don't know very much about that at home here. I shall never realise it here.

MRS. ALVING. Not even when you are with me?

OSWALD. Never at home. But you can't understand that.

MRS. ALVING. Yes, indeed I almost think I do understand you—now.

OSWALD. That—and the joy of work. They are really the same thing at bottom. But you don't know anything about that either.

MRS. ALVING. Perhaps you are right. Tell me some more about it, Oswald.

OSWALD. Well, all I mean is that here people are brought up to believe that work is a curse and a punishment for sin, and that life is a state of wretchedness and that the sooner we can get out of it the better.

MRS. ALVING. A vale of tears, yes. And we quite conscientiously make it so.

OSWALD. But the people over there will have none of that. There is no one there who really believes doctrines of that kind any longer. Over there the mere fact of being alive is thought to be a matter for exultant happiness. Mother, have you noticed that everything I have painted has turned upon the joy of life?—always upon the joy of life, unfailingly. There is light there, and sunshine, and a holiday feeling—and people's faces beaming with happiness. That is why I am afraid to stay at home here with you.

MRS. ALVING. Afraid? What are you afraid of here, with me?

OSWALD. I am afraid that all these feelings that are so strong in me would degenerate into something ugly here.

MRS. ALVING [*looking steadily at him*]. Do you think that is what would happen?

OSWALD. I am certain it would. Even if one lived the same life at home here, as over there—it would never really be the same life.

MRS. ALVING [*who has listened anxiously to him, gets up with a thoughtful expression and says:*]  Now I see clearly how it all happened.

OSWALD.  What do you see?

MRS. ALVING.  I see it now for the first time. And now I can speak.

OSWALD [*getting up*].  Mother, I don't understand you.

REGINA [*who has got up also*].  Perhaps I had better go.

MRS. ALVING.  No, stay here. Now I can speak. Now, my son, you shall know the whole truth. Oswald! Regina!

OSWALD.  Hush!—here is the parson—

[MANDERS *comes in by the hall door.*]

MANDERS.  Well, my friends, we have been spending an edifying time over there.

OSWALD.  So have we.

MANDERS.  Engstrand must have help with his Sailors' Home. Regina must go home with him and give him her assistance.

REGINA.  No, thank you, Mr. Manders.

MANDERS [*perceiving her for the first time*].  What—? you in here?—and with a wineglass in your hand!

REGINA [*putting down the glass hastily*].  I beg your pardon—!

OSWALD.  Regina is going away with me, Mr. Manders.

MANDERS.  Going away! With you!

OSWALD.  Yes, as my wife—if she insists on that.

MANDERS.  But, good heavens—!

REGINA.  It is not my fault, Mr. Manders.

OSWALD.  Or else she stays here if I stay.

REGINA [*involuntarily*].  Here!

MANDERS.  I am amazed at you, Mrs. Alving.

MRS. ALVING.  Neither of those things will happen, for now I can speak openly.

MANDERS.  But you won't do that! No, no, no!

MRS. ALVING.  Yes, I can and I will. And without destroying any one's ideals.

OSWALD.  Mother, what is it that is being concealed from me?

REGINA [*listening*].  Mrs. Alving! Listen! They are shouting outside.

[*Goes into the conservatory and looks out.*]

OSWALD [*going to the window on the left*].  What can be the matter?

Where does that glare come from?

REGINA [*calls out*]. The Orphanage is on fire!

MRS. ALVING [*going to the window*]. On fire?

MANDERS. On fire? Impossible. I was there just a moment ago.

OSWALD. Where is my hat? Oh, never mind that. Father's Orphanage—!

> [*Runs out through the garden door.*]

MRS. ALVING. My shawl, Regina! The whole place is in flames.

MANDERS. How terrible! Mrs. Alving, that fire is a judgment on this house of sin!

MRS. ALVING. Quite so. Come, Regina.

> [*She and* REGINA *hurry out.*]

MANDERS [*clasping his hands*]. And no insurance!

> [*Follows them out.*]

## ACT III

*The same scene. All the doors are standing open. The lamp is still burning on the table. It is dark outside, except for a faint glimmer of light seen through the windows at the back.* MRS. ALVING, *with a shawl over her head, is standing in the conservatory, looking out.* REGINA, *also wrapped in a shawl, is standing a little behind her.*

MRS. ALVING. Everything burnt—down to the ground.

REGINA. It is burning still in the basement.

MRS. ALVING. I can't think why Oswald doesn't come back. There is no chance of saving anything.

REGINA. Shall I go and take his hat to him?

MRS. ALVING. Hasn't he even got his hat?

REGINA [*pointing to the hall*]. No, there it is, hanging up.

MRS. ALVING. Never mind. He is sure to come back soon. I will go and see what he is doing.

> [*Goes out by the garden door.* MANDERS *comes in from the hall.*]

MANDERS. Isn't Mrs. Alving here?

REGINA. She has just this moment gone down into the garden.

MANDERS. I have never spent such a terrible night in my life.

REGINA. Isn't it a shocking misfortune, sir!

MANDERS. Oh, don't speak about it. I scarcely dare to think about it.

REGINA. But how can it have happened?

MANDERS. Don't ask me, Miss Engstrand! How should I know? Are you going to suggest too—? Isn't it enough that your father—?

REGINA. What has he done?

MANDERS. He has nearly driven me crazy.

ENGSTRAND [*coming in from the hall*]. Mr. Manders—!

MANDERS [*turning round with a start*]. Have you even followed me here!

ENGSTRAND. Yes, God help us all—! Great heavens! What a dreadful thing, your reverence!

MANDERS [*walking up and down*]. Oh dear, oh dear!

REGINA. What do you mean?

ENGSTRAND. Our little prayer-meeting was the cause of it all, don't you see? [*Aside, to* REGINA.] Now we've got the old fool, my girl. [*Aloud.*] And to think it is my fault that Mr. Manders should be the cause of such a thing!

MANDERS. I assure you, Engstrand—

ENGSTRAND. But there was no one else carrying a light there except you, sir.

MANDERS [*standing still*]. Yes, so you say. But I have no clear recollection of having had a light in my hand.

ENGSTRAND. But I saw quite distinctly your reverence take a candle and snuff it with your fingers and throw away the burning bit of wick among the shavings.

MANDERS. Did you see that?

ENGSTRAND. Yes, distinctly.

MANDERS. I can't understand it at all. It is never my habit to snuff a candle with my fingers.

ENGSTRAND. Yes, it wasn't like you to do that, sir. But who would have thought it could be such a dangerous thing to do?

MANDERS [*walking restlessly backwards and forwards*]. Oh, don't ask me!

ENGSTRAND [*following him about*]. And you hadn't insured it either, had you, sir?

MANDERS. No, no, no; you heard me say so.

ENGSTRAND. You hadn't insured it—and then went and set light to the whole place! Good Lord, what bad luck!

MANDERS [*wiping the perspiration from his forehead*]. You may well say so, Engstrand.

ENGSTRAND. And that it should happen to a charitable institution that would have been of service both to the town and the country, so to speak! The newspapers won't be very kind to your reverence, I expect.

MANDERS. No, that is just what I am thinking of. It is almost the worst part of the whole thing. The spiteful attacks and accusations— it is horrible to think of!

MRS. ALVING [*coming in from the garden*]. I can't get him away from the fire.

MANDERS. Oh, there you are, Mrs. Alving.

MRS. ALVING. You will escape having to make your inaugural address now, at all events, Mr. Manders.

MANDERS. Oh, I would so gladly have—

MRS. ALVING [*in a dull voice*]. It is just as well it has happened. This Orphanage would never have come to any good.

MANDERS. Don't you think so?

MRS. ALVING. Do you?

MANDERS. But it is none the less an extraordinary piece of ill luck.

MRS. ALVING. We will discuss it simply as a business matter.—Are you waiting for Mr. Manders, Engstrand?

ENGSTRAND [*at the hall door*]. Yes, I am.

MRS. ALVING. Sit down then, while you are waiting.

ENGSTRAND. Thank you, I would rather stand.

MRS. ALVING [*to* MANDERS]. I suppose you are going by the boat?

MANDERS. Yes. It goes in about an hour.

MRS. ALVING. Please take all the documents back with you. I don't want to hear another word about the matter. I have something else to think about now—

MANDERS. Mrs. Alving—

MRS. ALVING. Later on I will send you a power of attorney to deal with it exactly as you please.

MANDERS. I shall be most happy to undertake that. I am afraid the original intention of the bequest will have to be entirely altered now.

MRS. ALVING. Of course.

MANDERS. Provisionally, I should suggest this way of disposing of it. Make over the Solvik property to the parish. The land is undoubtedly not without a certain value; it will always be useful for some purpose or another. And as for the interest on the remaining capital that is on deposit in the bank, possibly I might make suitable use of that in support of some undertaking that promises to be of use to the town.

MRS. ALVING. Do exactly as you please. The whole thing is a matter of indifference to me now.

ENGSTRAND. You will think of my Sailors' Home, Mr. Manders?

MANDERS. Yes, certainly, that is a suggestion. But we must consider the matter carefully.

ENGSTRAND [*aside*]. Consider!—devil take it! Oh Lord.

MANDERS [*sighing*]. And unfortunately I can't tell how much longer I may have anything to do with the matter—whether public opinion may not force me to retire from it altogether. That depends entirely upon the result of the inquiry into the cause of the fire.

MRS. ALVING. What do you say?

MANDERS. And one cannot in any way reckon upon the result beforehand.

ENGSTRAND [*going nearer to him*]. Yes, indeed one can; because here stand I, Jacob Engstrand.

MANDERS. Quite so, but—

ENGSTRAND [*lowering his voice*]. And Jacob Engstrand isn't the man to desert a worthy benefactor in the hour of need, as the saying is.

MANDERS. Yes, but, my dear fellow—how—?

ENGSTRAND. You might say Jacob Engstrand is an angel of salvation, so to speak, your reverence.

MANDERS. No, no, I couldn't possibly accept that.

ENGSTRAND. That's how it will be, all the same. I know some one who has taken the blame for some one else on his shoulders before now, I do.

MANDERS. Jacob! [*Grasps his hand.*] You are one in a thousand! You shall have assistance in the matter of your Sailors' Home, you may rely upon that.

[ENGSTRAND *tries to thank him, but is prevented by emotion.*]

MANDERS [*hanging his wallet over his shoulder*]. Now we must be off. We will travel together.

ENGSTRAND [*by the dining-room door, says aside to* REGINA]. Come with me, you hussy! You shall be as cosy as the yolk in an egg!

REGINA [*tossing her head*]. *Merci!*

[*She goes out into the hall and brings back* MANDERS' *luggage.*]

MANDERS. Good-bye, Mrs. Alving! And may the spirit of order and of what is lawful speedily enter into this house.

Mrs. Alving.   Good-bye, Mr. Manders.

    [*She goes into the conservatory, as she sees* Oswald *coming in by the garden door.*]

Engstrand [*as he and* Regina *are helping* Manders *on with his coat*]. Good-bye, my child. And if anything should happen to you, you know where Jacob Engstrand is to be found. [*Lowering his voice.*] Little Harbour Street, ahem—! [*To* Mrs. Alving *and* Oswald.] And my house for poor seafaring men shall be called the "Alving Home," it shall. And, if I can carry out my own ideas about it, I shall make bold to hope that it may be worthy of bearing the late Mr. Alving's name.

Manders [*at the door*]. Ahem—ahem! Come along, my dear Engstrand. Good-bye—good-bye!

                [*He and* Engstrand *go out by the hall door.*]

Oswald [*going to the table*]. What house was he speaking about?

Mrs. Alving.   I believe it is some sort of a Home that he and Mr. Manders want to start.

Oswald.   It will be burnt up just like this one.

Mrs. Alving.   What makes you think that?

Oswald.   Everything will be burnt up; nothing will be left that is in memory of my father. Here am I being burnt up, too.

                [Regina *looks at him in alarm.*]

Mrs. Alving.   Oswald! You should not have stayed so long over there, my boy.

Oswald [*sitting down at the table*]. I almost believe you are right.

Mrs. Alving.   Let me dry your face, Oswald; you are all wet.

              [*Wipes his face with her handkerchief.*]

Oswald [*looking straight before him with no expression in his eyes*]. Thank you, mother.

Mrs. Alving.   And aren't you tired, Oswald? Don't you want to go to sleep?

Oswald [*uneasily*]. No, no—not to sleep! I never sleep; I only pretend to. [*Gloomily.*] That will come soon enough.

Mrs. Alving [*looking at him anxiously*]. Anyhow you are really ill, my darling boy.

Regina [*intently*]. Is Mr. Alving ill?

Oswald [*impatiently*]. And do shut all the doors! This deadly fear—

Mrs. Alving.   Shut the doors, Regina. [Regina *shuts the doors and remains standing by the hall door.* Mrs. Alving *takes off her shawl;*

REGINA *does the same.* MRS. ALVING *draws up a chair near to* OSWALD's *and sits down beside him.*] That's it! Now I will sit beside you—

OSWALD. Yes, do. And Regina must stay in here too. Regina must always be near me. You must give me a helping hand, you know, Regina. Won't you do that?

REGINA. I don't understand—

MRS. ALVING. A helping hand?

OSWALD. Yes—when there is need for it.

MRS. ALVING. Oswald, have you not your mother to give you a helping hand?

OSWALD. You? [*Smiles.*] No, mother, you will never give me the kind of helping hand I mean. [*Laughs grimly.*] You? Ha, ha! [*Looks gravely at her.*] After all, you have the best right. [*Impetuously.*] Why don't you call me by my Christian name, Regina? Why don't you say Oswald?

REGINA [*in a low voice*]. I did not think Mrs. Alving would like it.

MRS. ALVING. It will not be long before you have the right to do it. Sit down here now beside us, too. [REGINA *sits down quietly and hesitatingly at the other side of the table.*] And now, my poor tortured boy, I am going to take the burden off your mind—

OSWALD. You, mother?

MRS. ALVING. —all that you call remorse and regret and self-reproach.

OSWALD. And you think you can do that?

MRS. ALVING. Yes, now I can, Oswald. A little while ago you were talking about the joy of life, and what you said seemed to shed a new light upon everything in my whole life.

OSWALD [*shaking his head*]. I don't in the least understand what you mean.

MRS. ALVING. You should have known your father in his young days in the army. He was full of the joy of life, I can tell you.

OSWALD. Yes, I know.

MRS. ALVING. It gave me a holiday feeling only to look at him, full of irrepressible energy and exuberant spirits.

OSWALD. What then?

MRS. ALVING. Well, then this boy, full of the joy of life—for he was just like a boy, then—had to make his home in a second-rate town which had none of the joy of life to offer him, but only dissipations. He had to come out here and live an aimless life; he had only an official post. He had no work worth devoting his whole mind to; he had nothing more than official routine to attend to. He had not a single companion capable of appreciating what the joy of life meant; nothing but idlers and tipplers—

Oswald. Mother—!

Mrs. Alving. And so the inevitable happened!

Oswald. What was the inevitable?

Mrs. Alving. You said yourself this evening what would happen in your case if you stayed at home.

Oswald. Do you mean by that, that father—?

Mrs. Alving. Your poor father never found any outlet for the over-mastering joy of life that was in him. And I brought no holiday spirit into his home, either.

Oswald. You didn't either?

Mrs. Alving. I had been taught about duty, and the sort of thing that I believed in so long here. Everything seemed to turn upon duty— my duty, or his duty—and I am afraid I made your poor father's home unbearable to him, Oswald.

Oswald. Why did you never say anything about it to me in your letters?

Mrs. Alving. I never looked at it as a thing I could speak of to you, who were his son.

Oswald. What way did you look at it, then?

Mrs. Alving. I only saw the one fact, that your father was a lost man before ever you were born.

Oswald [*in a choking voice*]. Ah—!

[*He gets up and goes to the window.*]

Mrs. Alving. And then I had the one thought in my mind, day and night, that Regina in fact had as good a right in this house—as my own boy had.

Oswald [*turns round suddenly*]. Regina—?

Regina [*gets up and asks in choking tones*]. I—?

Mrs. Alving. Yes, now you both know it.

Oswald. Regina!

Regina [*to herself*]. So mother was one of that sort too.

Mrs. Alving. Your mother had many good qualities, Regina.

Regina. Yes, but she was one of that sort too, all the same, I have even thought so myself, sometimes, but—. Then, if you please, Mrs. Alving, may I have permission to leave at once?

MRS. ALVING.  Do you really wish to, Regina?

REGINA.  Yes, indeed, I certainly wish to.

MRS. ALVING.  Of course you shall do as you like, but—

OSWALD [*going to* REGINA].  Leave now? This is your home.

REGINA.  *Merci,* Mr. Alving—oh, of course I may say Oswald now, but that is not the way I thought it would become allowable.

MRS. ALVING.  Regina, I have not been open with you—

REGINA.  No, I can't say you have! If I had known Oswald was ill—. And now that there can never be anything serious between us—. No, I really can't stay here in the country and wear myself out looking after invalids.

OSWALD.  Not even for the sake of one who has so near a claim on you?

REGINA.  No, indeed I can't. A poor girl must make some use of her youth, otherwise she may easily find herself out in the cold before she knows where she is. And I have got the joy of life in me, too, Mrs. Alving!

MRS. ALVING.  Yes, unfortunately; but don't throw yourself away, Regina.

REGINA.  Oh, what's going to happen will happen. If Oswald takes after his father, it is just as likely I take after my mother, I expect.—May I ask, Mrs. Alving, whether Mr. Manders knows this about me?

MRS. ALVING.  Mr. Manders knows everything.

REGINA [*putting on her shawl*].  Oh, well then, the best thing I can do is to get away by the boat as soon as I can. Mr. Manders is such a nice gentleman to deal with; and it certainly seems to me that I have just as much right to some of that money as he—as that horrid carpenter.

MRS. ALVING.  You are quite welcome to it, Regina.

REGINA [*looking at her fixedly*].  You might as well have brought me up like a gentleman's daughter; it would have been more suitable. [*Tosses her head.*] Oh, well—never mind! [*With a bitter glance at the unopened bottle.*] I daresay some day I shall be drinking champagne with gentlefolk, after all.

MRS. ALVING.  If ever you need a home, Regina, come to me.

REGINA.  No, thank you, Mrs. Alving. Mr. Manders takes an interest in me, I know. And if things should go very badly with me, I know one house at any rate where I shall feel at home.

MRS. ALVING.  Where is that?

REGINA. In the "Alving Home."

MRS. ALVING. Regina—I can see quite well—you are going to your ruin!

REGINA. Pooh!—good-bye.

[*She bows to them and goes out through the hall.*]

OSWALD [*standing by the window and looking out*]. Has she gone?

MRS. ALVING. Yes.

OSWALD [*muttering to himself*]. I think it's all wrong.

MRS. ALVING [*going up to him from behind and putting her hands on his shoulders*]. Oswald, my dear boy—has it been a great shock to you?

OSWALD [*turning his face towards her*]. All this about father, do you mean?

MRS. ALVING. Yes, about your unhappy father. I am so afraid it may have been too much for you.

OSWALD. What makes you think that? Naturally it has taken me entirely by surprise; but, after all, I don't know that it matters much to me.

MRS. ALVING [*drawing back her hands*]. Doesn't matter!—that your father's life was such a terrible failure!

OSWALD. Of course I can feel sympathy for him, just as I would for anyone else, but—

MRS. ALVING. No more than that! For your own father!

OSWALD [*impatiently*]. Father—father! I never knew anything of my father. I don't remember anything else about him except that he once made me sick.

MRS. ALVING. It is dreadful to think of!—But surely a child should feel some affection for his father, whatever happens?

OSWALD. When the child has nothing to thank his father for? When he has never known him? Do you really cling to that antiquated superstition—you, who are so broadminded in other things?

MRS. ALVING. You call it nothing but a superstition!

OSWALD. Yes, and you can see that for yourself quite well, mother. It is one of those beliefs that are put into circulation in the world, and—

MRS. ALVING. Ghosts of beliefs!

OSWALD [*walking across the room*]. Yes, you might call them ghosts.

MRS. ALVING [*with an outburst of feeling*]. Oswald—then you don't love me either.

OSWALD. You I know, at any rate—

Mrs. Alving.   You know me, yes; but is that all?

Oswald.   And I know how fond you are of me, and I ought to be grateful to you for that. Besides, you can be so tremendously useful to me, now that I am ill.

Mrs. Alving.   Yes, can't I, Oswald! I could almost bless your illness, as it has driven you home to me. For I see quite well that you are not my very own yet; you must be won.

Oswald [*impatiently*].   Yes, yes, yes; all that is just a way of talking. You must remember I am a sick man, mother. I can't concern myself much with anyone else; I have enough to do, thinking about myself.

Mrs. Alving [*gently*].   I will be very good and patient.

Oswald.   And cheerful too, mother!

Mrs. Alving.   Yes, my dear boy, you are quite right. [*Goes up to him.*] Now have I taken away all your remorse and self-reproach?

Oswald.   Yes, you have done that. But who will take away the fear?

Mrs. Alving.   The fear?

Oswald [*crossing the room*].   Regina would have done it for one kind word.

Mrs. Alving.   I don't understand you. What fear do you mean—and what has Regina to do with it?

Oswald.   Is it very late, mother?

Mrs. Alving.   It is early morning. [*Looks out through the conservatory windows.*] The dawn is breaking already on the heights. And the sky is clear, Oswald. In a little while you will see the sun.

Oswald.   I am glad of that. After all, there may be many things yet for me to be glad of and to live for—

Mrs. Alving.   I should hope so!

Oswald.   Even if I am not able to work—

Mrs. Alving.   You will soon find you are able to work again now, my dear boy. You have no longer all those painful depressing thoughts to brood over.

Oswald.   No, it is a good thing that you have been able to rid me of those fancies. If only, now, I could overcome this one thing—. [*Sits down on the couch.*] Let us have a little chat, mother.

Mrs. Alving.   Yes, let us.

[*Pushes an armchair near to the couch and sits down beside him.*]

Oswald.   The sun is rising—and you know all about it; so I don't feel the fear any longer.

Mrs. Alving.   I know all about what?

OSWALD [*without listening to her*]. Mother, isn't it the case that you said this evening there was nothing in the world you would not do for me if I asked you?

MRS. ALVING. Yes, certainly I said so.

OSWALD. And will you be as good as your word, mother?

MRS. ALVING. You may rely upon that, my own dear boy. I have nothing else to live for, but you.

OSWALD. Yes, yes; well, listen to me, mother. You are very strong-minded, I know. I want you to sit quite quiet when you hear what I am going to tell you.

MRS. ALVING. But what is this dreadful thing—?

OSWALD. You mustn't scream. Do you hear? Will you promise me that? We are going to sit and talk it over quite quietly. Will you promise me that, mother?

MRS. ALVING. Yes, yes, I promise—only tell me what it is.

OSWALD. Well, then, you must know that this fatigue of mine—and my not being able to think about my work—all that is not really the illness itself—

MRS. ALVING. What is the illness itself?

OSWALD. What I am suffering from is hereditary; it—[*touches his forehead, and speaks very quietly*]—it lies here.

MRS. ALVING [*almost speechless*]. Oswald! no—no!

OSWALD. Don't scream; I can't stand it. Yes, I tell you, it lies here, waiting. And any time, any moment, it may break out.

MRS. ALVING. How horrible—!

OSWALD. Do keep quiet. That is the state I am in—

MRS. ALVING [*springing up*]. It isn't true, Oswald! It is impossible! It can't be that!

OSWALD. I had one attack while I was abroad. It passed off quickly. But when I learnt the condition I had been in, then this dreadful haunting fear took possession of me.

MRS. ALVING. That was the fear, then—

OSWALD. Yes, it is so indescribably horrible, you know. If only it had been an ordinary mortal disease—. I am not so much afraid of dying; though, of course, I should like to live as long as I can.

MRS. ALVING. Yes, yes, Oswald, you must!

OSWALD. But this is so appallingly horrible. To become like a helpless child again—to have to be fed, to have to be—. Oh, it's unspeakable!

Mrs. Alving. My child has his mother to tend him.

Oswald [*jumping up*]. No, never; that is just what I won't endure! I dare not think what it would mean to linger on like that for years —to get old and grey like that. And you might die before I did. [*Sits down in* Mrs. Alving's *chair.*] Because it doesn't necessarily have a fatal end quickly, the doctor said. He called it a kind of softening of the brain—or something of that sort. [*Smiles mournfully.*] I think that expression sounds so nice. It always makes me think of cherry-coloured velvet curtains—something that is soft to stroke.

Mrs. Alving [*with a scream*]. Oswald!

Oswald [*jumps up and walks about the room*]. And now you have taken Regina from me! If I had only had her. She would have given me a helping hand, I know.

Mrs. Alving [*going up to him*]. What do you mean, my darling boy? Is there any help in the world I would not be willing to give you?

Oswald. When I had recovered from the attack I had abroad, the doctor told me that when it recurred—and it will recur—there would be no more hope.

Mrs. Alving. And he was heartless enough to—

Oswald. I insisted on knowing. I told him I had arrangements to make—. [*Smiles cunningly.*] And so I had. [*Takes a small box from his inner breast-pocket.*] Mother, do you see this?

Mrs. Alving. What is it?

Oswald. Morphia powders.

Mrs. Alving [*looking at him in terror*]. Oswald—my boy!

Oswald. I have twelve of them saved up—

Mrs. Alving [*snatching at it*]. Give me the box, Oswald!

Oswald. Not yet, mother.

[*Puts it back in his pocket.*]

Mrs. Alving. I shall never get over this!

Oswald. You must. If I had Regina here now, I would have told her quietly how things stand with me—and asked her to give me this last helping hand. She would have helped me, I am certain.

Mrs. Alving. Never!

Oswald. If this horrible thing had come upon me and she had seen me lying helpless, like a baby, past help, past saving, past hope— with no chance of recovering—

Mrs. Alving. Never in the world would Regina have done it.

Oswald. Regina would have done it. Regina was so splendidly light-hearted. And she would very soon have tired of looking after an invalid like me.

Mrs. Alving. Then thank heaven Regina is not here!

Oswald. Well, now you have got to give me that helping hand, mother.

Mrs. Alving [*with a loud scream*]. I!

Oswald. Who has a better right than you?

Mrs. Alving. I? Your mother!

Oswald. Just for that reason.

Mrs. Alving. I, who gave you your life!

Oswald. I never asked you for life. And what kind of a life was it that you gave me? I don't want it! You shall take it back!

Mrs. Alving. Help! Help!

[*Runs into the hall.*]

Oswald [*following her*]. Don't leave me! Where are you going?

Mrs. Alving [*in the hall*]. To fetch the doctor to you, Oswald! Let me out!

Oswald [*going into the hall*]. You shan't go out. And no one shall come in.

[*Turns the key in the lock.*]

Mrs. Alving [*coming in again*]. Oswald! Oswald!—my child!

Oswald [*following her*]. Have you a mother's heart—and can bear to see me suffering this unspeakable terror?

Mrs. Alving [*controlling herself, after a moment's silence*]. There is my hand in it.

Oswald. Will you—?

Mrs. Alving. If it becomes necessary. But it shan't become necessary. No, no—it is impossible it should!

Oswald. Let us hope so. And let us live together as long as we can. Thank you, mother.

[*He sits down in the armchair, which* Mrs. Alving *had moved beside the couch. Day is breaking; the lamp is still burning on the table.*]

Mrs. Alving [*coming cautiously nearer*]. Do you feel calmer now?

Oswald. Yes.

Mrs. Alving [*bending over him*]. It has only been a dreadful fancy of yours, Oswald. Nothing but fancy. All this upset has been bad for you. But now you will get some rest, at home with your own mother, my darling boy. You shall have everything you want, just as you did when you were a little child.—There, now. The attack is over. You see how easily it passed off! I knew it would.—And look, Oswald, what a lovely day we are going to have? Brilliant sunshine. Now you will be able to see your home properly.

[*She goes to the table and puts out the lamp. It is sunrise. The glaciers and peaks in the distance are seen bathed in bright morning light.*]

OSWALD [*who has been sitting motionless in the armchair, with his back to the scene outside, suddenly says:*] Mother, give me the sun.

MRS. ALVING [*standing at the table, and looking at him in amazement*]. What do you say?

OSWALD [*repeats in a dull, toneless voice*]. The sun—the sun.

MRS. ALVING [*going up to him*]. Oswald, what is the matter with you? [OSWALD *seems to shrink up in the chair; all his muscles relax; his face loses its expression, and his eyes stare stupidly.* MRS. ALVING *is trembling with terror.*] What is it! [*Screams.*] Oswald! What is the matter with you! [*Throws herself on her knees beside him and shakes him.*] Oswald! Oswald! Look at me! Don't you know me!

OSWALD [*in an expressionless voice, as before*]. The sun—the sun.

MRS. ALVING [*jumps up despairingly, beats her head with her hands, and screams*]. I can't bear it! [*Whispers as though paralysed with fear.*] I can't bear it! Never! [*Suddenly.*] Where has he got it? [*Passes her hand quickly over his coat.*] Here! [*Draws back a little way and cries:*] No, no, no!—Yes!—no, no!

[*She stands a few steps from him, her hands thrust into her hair, and stares at him in speechless terror.*]

OSWALD [*sitting motionless, as before*]. The sun—the sun.

# The Cherry Orchard

## ANTON CHEKHOV

### CHARACTERS

LUBOV ANDREYEVNA RANEVSKAYA, *a landowner*
ANYA, *her seventeen-year-old daughter*
VARYA, *her adopted daughter, twenty-two years old*
LEONID ANDREYEVICH GAYEV, MME. RANEVSKAYA'S *brother*
YERMOLAY ALEXEYEVICH LOPAHIN, *a merchant*
PYOTR SERGEYEVICH TROFIMOV, *a student*
SIMEONOV-PISHCHIK, *a landowner*
CHARLOTTA IVANOVNA, *a governess*
SEMYON YEPIHODOV, *a clerk*
DUNYASHA, *a maid*
FIRS (*pronounced* fierce), *a man-servant, aged eighty-seven*
YASHA, *a young valet*
*A Tramp*
*Stationmaster, Post Office Clerk, Guests, Servants*

*The action takes place on* MME. RANEVSKAYA'S *estate.*

## ACT I

*A room that is still called the nursery. One of the doors leads into
Anya's room. Dawn, the sun will soon rise. It is May, the cherry
trees are in blossom, but it is cold in the orchard; there is a morning*

355

*frost. The windows are shut. Enter* DUNYASHA *with a candle, and* LOPAHIN *with a book in his hand.*

LOPAHIN. The train is in, thank God. What time is it?

DUNYASHA. Nearly two. [*Puts out the candle*] It's light already.

LOPAHIN. How late is the train, anyway? Two hours at least. [*Yawns and stretches*] I'm a fine one! What a fool I've made of myself! I came here on purpose to meet them at the station, and then I went and overslept. I fell asleep in my chair. How annoying! You might have waked me. . . .

DUNYASHA. I thought you'd left. [*Listens*] I think they're coming!

LOPAHIN [*listens*]. No, they've got to get the luggage, and one thing and another . . . [*Pause*] Lubov Andreyevna spent five years abroad, I don't know what she's like now. . . . She's a fine person—lighthearted, simple. I remember when I was a boy of fifteen, my poor father—he had a shop here in the village then—punched me in the face with his fist and made my nose bleed. We'd come into the yard, I don't know what for, and he'd had a drop too much. Lubov Andreyevna, I remember her as if it were yesterday—she was still young and so slim—led me to the wash-basin, in this very room . . . in the nursery. "Don't cry, little peasant," she said, "it'll heal in time for your wedding. . . ." [*Pause*] Little peasant . . . my father was a peasant, it's true, and here I am in a white waistcoat and yellow shoes. A pig in a pastry shop, you might say. It's true I'm rich, I've got a lot of money. . . . But when you look at it closely, I'm a peasant through and through. [*Pages the book*] Here I've been reading this book and I didn't understand a word of it. . . . I was reading it and fell asleep. . . . [*Pause*]

DUNYASHA. And the dogs were awake all night, they feel that their masters are coming.

LOPAHIN. Dunyasha, why are you so—

DUNYASHA. My hands are trembling. I'm going to faint.

LOPAHIN. You're too soft, Dunyasha. You dress like a lady, and look at the way you do your hair. That's not right. One should remember one's place.

[*Enter* YEPIHODOV *with a bouquet; he wears a jacket and highly polished boots that squeak badly. He drops the bouquet as he comes in*]

YEPIHODOV [*picking up the bouquet*]. Here, the gardener sent these, said you're to put them in the dining room.

[*Hands the bouquet to* DUNYASHA]

LOPAHIN.   And bring me some *kvass*.

DUNYASHA.   Yes, sir.

[*Exits*]

YEPIHODOV.   There's a frost this morning—three degrees below—and yet the cherries are all in blossom. I cannot approve of our climate. [*Sighs*] I cannot. Our climate does not activate properly. And, Yermolay Alexeyevich, allow me to make a further remark. The other day I bought myself a pair of boots, and I make bold to assure you, they squeak so that it is really intolerable. What should I grease them with?

LOPAHIN.   Oh, get out! I'm fed up with you.

YEPIHODOV.   Every day I meet with misfortune. And I don't complain, I've got used to it, I even smile.

[DUNYASHA *enters, hands* LOPAHIN *the kvass*]

YEPIHODOV.   I am leaving. [*Stumbles against a chair, which falls over*] There! [*Triumphantly, as it were*] There again, you see what sort of circumstance, pardon the expression. . . . It is absolutely phenomenal!

[*Exits*]

DUNYASHA.   You know, Yermolay Alexeyevich, I must tell you, Yepihodov has proposed to me.

LOPAHIN.   Ah!

DUNYASHA.   I simply don't know . . . he's a quiet man, but sometimes when he starts talking, you can't make out what he means. He speaks nicely—and it's touching—but you can't understand it. I sort of like him though, and he is crazy about me. He's an unlucky man . . . every day something happens to him. They tease him about it here . . . they call him, Two-and-Twenty Troubles.

LOPAHIN [*listening*].   There! I think they're coming.

DUNYASHA.   They *are* coming! What's the matter with me? I feel cold all over.

LOPAHIN.   They really are coming. Let's go and meet them. Will she recognize me? We haven't seen each other for five years.

DUNYASHA [*in a flutter*].   I'm going to faint this minute. . . . Oh, I'm going to faint!

[*Two carriages are heard driving up to the house.* LOPAHIN *and* DUNYASHA *go out quickly. The stage is left empty. There is a noise in the adjoining room.* FIRS, *who had driven to the station to meet* LUBOV ANDREYEVNA RANEVSKAYA, *crosses the stage hurriedly, leaning on a stick. He is wearing an old-fashioned livery and a tall hat. He mutters to himself indistinctly. The hubbub off-stage increases.* A VOICE: "Come, let's go this way." *Enter* LUBOV ANDREYEVNA, ANYA, *and* CHARLOTTA IVANOVNA, *with a pet dog on a leash, all in traveling dresses;* VARYA, *wearing a coat and kerchief;* GAYEV, SIMEONOV-PISHCHIK, LOPAHIN, DUNYASHA *with a bag and an umbrella, servants with luggage. All walk across the room*]

ANYA. Let's go this way. Do you remember what room this is, mamma?

MME. RANEVSKAYA [*joyfully, through her tears*]. The nursery!

VARYA. How cold it is! My hands are numb. [*To* MME. RANEVSKAYA] Your rooms are just the same as they were, mamma, the white one and the violet.

MME. RANEVSKAYA. The nursery! My darling, lovely room! I slept here when I was a child. . . . [*Cries*] And here I am, like a child again! [*Kisses her brother and* VARYA, *and then her brother again*] Varya's just the same as ever, like a nun. And I recognized Dunyasha. [*Kisses* DUNYASHA]

GAYEV. The train was two hours late. What do you think of that? What a way to manage things!

CHARLOTTA [*to* PISHCHIK]. My dog eats nuts, too.

PISHCHIK [*in amazement*]. You don't say so!

[*All go out, except* ANYA *and* DUNYASHA]

DUNYASHA. We've been waiting for you for hours.

[*Takes* ANYA's *hat and coat*]

ANYA. I didn't sleep on the train for four nights and now I'm frozen. . . .

DUNYASHA. It was Lent when you left; there was snow and frost, and now. . . . My darling! [*Laughs and kisses her*] I have been waiting for you, my sweet, my darling! But I must tell you something . . . I can't put it off another minute. . . .

ANYA [*listlessly*]. What now?

DUNYASHA. The clerk, Yepihodov, proposed to me, just after Easter.

ANYA. There you are, at it again. . . . [*Straightening her hair*] I've lost all my hairpins. . . .          [*She is staggering with exhaustion*]

DUNYASHA. Really, I don't know what to think. He loves me—he loves me so!

ANYA [*looking towards the door of her room, tenderly*]. My own room, my windows, just as though I'd never been away. I'm home! Tomorrow morning I'll get up and run into the orchard. Oh, if I could only get some sleep. I didn't close my eyes during the whole journey—I was so anxious.

DUNYASHA. Pyotr Sergeyevich came the day before yesterday.

ANYA [*joyfully*]. Petya!

DUNYASHA. He's asleep in the bath-house. He has settled there. He said he was afraid of being in the way. [*Looks at her watch*] I should wake him, but Miss Varya told me not to. "Don't you wake him," she said.

[*Enter* VARYA *with a bunch of keys at her belt*]

VARYA. Dunyasha, coffee, and be quick. . . . Mamma's asking for coffee.

DUNYASHA. In a minute.

[*Exits*]

VARYA. Well, thank God, you've come. You're home again. [*Fondling* ANYA] My darling is here again. My pretty one is back.

ANYA. Oh, what I've been through!

VARYA. I can imagine.

ANYA. When we left, it was Holy Week, it was cold then, and all the way Charlotta chattered and did her tricks. Why did you have to saddle me with Charlotta?

VARYA. You couldn't have traveled all alone, darling—at seventeen!

ANYA. We got to Paris, it was cold there, snowing. My French is dreadful. Mamma lived on the fifth floor; I went up there, and found all kinds of Frenchmen, ladies, an old priest with a book. The place was full of tobacco smoke, and so bleak. Suddenly I felt sorry for mamma, so sorry, I took her head in my arms and hugged her and couldn't let go of her. Afterwards mamma kept fondling me and crying. . . .

VARYA [*through tears*]. Don't speak of it . . . don't.

ANYA. She had already sold her villa at Mentone, she had nothing left, nothing. I hadn't a kopeck left either, we had only just enough to get home. And mamma wouldn't understand! When we had dinner at the stations, she always ordered the most expensive dishes, and tipped the waiters a whole ruble. Charlotta, too. And Yasha kept ordering, too—it was simply awful. You know Yasha's mamma's footman now, we brought him here with us.

VARYA. Yes, I've seen the blackguard.

ANYA. Well, tell me—have you paid the interest?

VARYA. How could we?

ANYA. Good heavens, good heavens!

VARYA. In August the estate will be put up for sale.

ANYA. My God!

[LOPAHIN *peeps in at the door and bleats*]

LOPAHIN. Meh-h-h.

[*Disappears*]

VARYA [*through tears*]. What I couldn't do to him!

[*Shakes her fist threateningly*]

ANYA [*embracing* VARYA, *gently*]. Varya, has he proposed to you? [VARYA *shakes her head*] But he loves you. Why don't you come to an understanding? What are you waiting for?

VARYA. Oh, I don't think anything will ever come of it. He's too busy, he has no time for me . . . pays no attention to me. I've washed my hands of him—I can't bear the sight of him. They all talk about our getting married, they all congratulate me—and all the time there's really nothing to it—it's all like a dream. [*In another tone*] You have a new brooch—like a bee.

ANYA [*sadly*]. Mamma bought it. [*She goes into her own room and speaks gaily like a child*] And you know, in Paris I went up in a balloon.

VARYA. My darling's home, my pretty one is back! [DUNYASHA *returns with the coffee-pot and prepares coffee*. VARYA *stands at the door of* ANYA's *room*] All day long, darling, as I go about the house, I keep dreaming. If only we could marry you off to a rich man, I should feel at ease. Then I would go into a convent, and afterwards to Kiev, to Moscow. . . . I would spend my life going from one holy place to another. . . . I'd go on and on. . . . What a blessing that would be!

ANYA. The birds are singing in the orchard. What time is it?

VARYA. It must be after two. Time you were asleep, darling. [*Goes into* ANYA's *room*] What a blessing that would be!

[YASHA *enters with a plaid and a traveling bag, crosses the stage*]

YASHA [*finically*]. May I pass this way, please?

DUNYASHA. A person could hardly recognize you, Yasha. Your stay abroad has certainly done wonders for you.

YASHA. Hm-m. . . and who are you?

DUNYASHA. When you went away I was that high—[*Indicating with her hand*] I'm Dunyasha—Fyodor Kozoyedev's daughter. Don't you remember?

YASHA. Hm! What a peach! [*He looks round and embraces her. She cries out and drops a saucer.* YASHA *leaves quickly*]

VARYA [*in the doorway, in a tone of annoyance*]. What's going on here?

DUNYASHA [*through tears*]. I've broken a saucer.

VARYA. Well, that's good luck.

ANYA [*coming out of her room*]. We ought to warn mamma that Petya's here.

VARYA. I left orders not to wake him.

ANYA [*musingly*]. Six years ago father died. A month later brother Grisha was drowned in the river. . . . Such a pretty little boy he was—only seven. It was more than mamma could bear, so she went away, went away without looking back. . . . [*Shudders*] How well I understand her, if she only knew! [*Pauses*] And Petya Trofimov was Grisha's tutor, he may remind her of it all. . . .

[*Enter* FIRS, *wearing a jacket and a white waistcoat. He goes up to the coffee-pot*]

FIRS [*anxiously*]. The mistress will have her coffee here. [*Puts on white gloves*] Is the coffee ready? [*Sternly, to* DUNYASHA] Here, you! And where's the cream?

DUNYASHA. Oh, my God!

[*Exits quickly*]

FIRS [*fussing over the coffee-pot*]. Hah! the addlehead! [*Mutters to himself*] Home from Paris. And the old master used to go to Paris too . . . by carriage. [*Laughs*]

VARYA. What is it, Firs?

FIRS. What is your pleasure, Miss? [*Joyfully*] My mistress has come home, and I've seen her at last! Now I can die.

[*Weeps with joy*]

[*Enter* MME. RANEVSKAYA, GAYEV, *and* SIMEONOV-PISHCHIK. *The latter is wearing a tight-waisted, pleated coat of fine cloth, and full trousers.* GAYEV, *as he comes in, goes through the motions of a billiard player with his arms and body*]

MME. RANEVSKAYA. Let's see, how does it go? Yellow ball in the corner! Bank shot in the side pocket!

GAYEV. I'll tip it in the corner! There was a time, sister, when you and I used to sleep in this very room, and now I'm fifty-one, strange as it may seem.

LOPAHIN. Yes, time flies.

GAYEV. Who?

LOPAHIN. I say, time flies.

GAYEV. It smells of patchouli here.

ANYA. I'm going to bed. Good night, mamma.

[*Kisses her mother*]

MME. RANEVSKAYA. My darling child! [*Kisses her hands*] Are you happy to be home? I can't come to my senses.

ANYA. Good night, uncle.

GAYEV [*kissing her face and hands*]. God bless you, how like your mother you are! [*To his sister*] At her age, Luba, you were just like her.

[ANYA *shakes hands with* LOPAHIN *and* PISHCHIK, *then goes out, shutting the door behind her*]

MME. RANEVSKAYA. She's very tired.

PISHCHIK. Well, it was a long journey.

VARYA [*to* LOPAHIN *and* PISHCHIK]. How about it, gentlemen? It's past two o'clock—isn't it time for you to go?

MME. RANEVSKAYA [*laughs*]. You're just the same as ever, Varya. [*Draws her close and kisses her*] I'll have my coffee and then we'll all go. [FIRS *puts a small cushion under her feet*] Thank you, my dear, I've got used to coffee. I drink it day and night. Thanks, my dear old man.

[*Kisses him*]

VARYA. I'd better see if all the luggage has been brought in.

[*Exits*]

MME. RANEVSKAYA. Can it really be I sitting here? [*Laughs*] I feel like dancing, waving my arms about. [*Covers her face with her hands*] But maybe I am dreaming! God knows I love my country, I love it tenderly; I couldn't look out of the window in the train, I kept crying so. [*Through tears*] But I must have my coffee. Thank you, Firs, thank you, dear old man. I'm so happy that you're still alive.

FIRS. Day before yesterday.

GAYEV. He's hard of hearing.

LOPAHIN. I must go soon, I'm leaving for Kharkov about five o'clock. How annoying! I'd like to have a good look at you, talk to you. . . . You're just as splendid as ever.

PISHCHIK [*breathing heavily*]. She's even better-looking. . . . Dressed in the latest Paris fashion. . . . Perish my carriage and all its four wheels. . . .

LOPAHIN. Your brother, Leonid Andreyevich, says I'm a vulgarian and an exploiter. But it's all the same to me—let him talk. I only want you to trust me as you used to. I want you to look at me with your touching, wonderful eyes, as you used to. Dear God! My father was a serf of your father's and grandfather's, but you, you yourself, did so much for me once . . . so much . . . that I've forgotten all about that; I love you as though you were my sister—even more.

MME. RANEVSKAYA. I can't sit still, I simply can't. [*Jumps up and walks about in violent agitation*] This joy is too much for me. . . . Laugh at me, I'm silly! My own darling bookcase! My darling table!

[*Kisses it*]

GAYEV. While you were away, nurse died.

MME. RANEVSKAYA [*sits down and takes her coffee*]. Yes, God rest her soul; they wrote me about it.

GAYEV. And Anastasy is dead. Petrushka Kossoy has left me and has gone into town to work for the police inspector.

[*Takes a box of sweets out of his pocket and begins to suck one*]

PISHCHIK. My daughter Dashenka sends her regards.

LOPAHIN. I'd like to tell you something very pleasant—cheering. [*Glancing at his watch*] I am leaving directly. There isn't much time to talk. But I will put it in a few words. As you know, your cherry orchard is to be sold to pay your debts. The sale is to be on the twenty-second of August; but don't you worry, my dear, you may sleep in peace; there is a way out. Here is my plan. Give me your attention! Your estate is only fifteen miles from the town; the railway runs close by it; and if the cherry orchard and the land along the river bank were cut up into lots and these leased for summer cottages, you would have an income of at least 25,000 rubles a year out of it.

GAYEV. Excuse me. . . . What nonsense.

MME. RANEVSKAYA. I don't quite understand you, Yermolay Alexeyevich.

LOPAHIN. You will get an annual rent of at least ten rubles per acre, and if you advertise at once, I'll give you any guarantee you like that you won't have a square foot of ground left by autumn, all the lots will be snapped up. In short, congratulations, you're saved. The location is splendid—by that deep river. . . . Only, of course, the ground must be cleared . . . all the old buildings, for instance, must be torn down, and this house, too, which is useless, and, of course, the old cherry orchard must be cut down.

MME. RANEVSKAYA. Cut down? My dear, forgive me, but you don't know what you're talking about. If there's one thing that's interesting—indeed, remarkable—in the whole province, it's precisely our cherry orchard.

LOPAHIN. The only remarkable thing about this orchard is that it's a very large one. There's a crop of cherries every other year, and you can't do anything with them; no one buys them.

GAYEV. This orchard is even mentioned in the Encyclopedia.

LOPAHIN [glancing at his watch]. If we can't think of a way out, if we don't come to a decision, on the twenty-second of August the cherry orchard and the whole estate will be sold at auction. Make up your minds! There's no other way out—I swear. None, none.

FIRS. In the old days, forty or fifty years ago, the cherries were dried, soaked, pickled, and made into jam, and we used to—

GAYEV. Keep still, Firs.

FIRS. And the dried cherries would be shipped by the cartload. It meant a lot of money! And in those days the dried cherries were soft and juicy, sweet, fragrant. . . . They knew the way to do it, then.

MME. RANEVSKAYA. And why don't they do it that way now?

FIRS. They've forgotten. Nobody remembers it.

PISHCHIK. Just imagine!

LOPAHIN. There used to be only landowners and peasants in the country, but now these summer people have appeared on the scene. . . . All the towns, even the small ones, are surrounded by these summer cottages; and in another twenty years, no doubt, the summer population will have grown enormously. Now the summer resident only drinks tea on his porch, but maybe he'll take to working his acre, too, and then your cherry orchard will be a rich, happy, luxuriant place.

GAYEV [*indignantly*]. Poppycock!

[*Enter* VARYA *and* YASHA]

VARYA. There are two telegrams for you, mamma dear. [*Picks a key from the bunch at her belt and noisily opens an old-fashioned bookcase*] Here they are.

MME. RANEVSKAYA. They're from Paris. [*Tears them up without reading them*] I'm through with Paris.

GAYEV. Do you know, Luba, how old this bookcase is? Last week I pulled out the bottom drawer and there I found the date burnt in it. It was made exactly a hundred years ago. Think of that! We could celebrate its centenary. True, it's an inanimate object, but nevertheless, a bookcase. . . .

PISHCHIK [*amazed*]. A hundred years! Just imagine!

GAYEV. Yes. [*Tapping it*] That's something. . . . Dear, honored bookcase, hail to you who for more than a century have served the glorious ideals of goodness and justice! Your silent summons to fruitful toil has never weakened in all those hundred years [*through tears*], sustaining, through successive generations of our family, courage and faith in a better future, and fostering in us ideals of goodness and social consciousness. . . . [*Pauses*]

LOPAHIN. Yes. . . .

MME. RANEVSKAYA. You haven't changed a bit, Leonid.

GAYEV [*somewhat embarrassed*]. I'll play it off the red in the corner! Tip it in the side pocket!

LOPAHIN [*looking at his watch*]. Well, it's time for me to go. . . .

YASHA [*handing a pill box to* MME. RANEVSKAYA]. Perhaps you'll take your pills now.

PISHCHIK. One shouldn't take medicines, dearest lady, they do neither harm nor good. . . . Give them here, my valued friend. [*Takes the pill box, pours the pills into his palm, blows on them, puts them in his mouth, and washes them down with some kvass*] There!

MME. RANEVSKAYA [*frightened*]. You must be mad!

PISHCHIK. I've taken all the pills.

LOPAHIN. What a glutton!

[*All laugh*]

Firs. The gentleman visited us in Easter week, ate half a bucket of pickles, he did. . . . [*Mumbles*]

Mme. Ranevskaya. What's he saying?

Varya. He's been mumbling like that for the last three years—we're used to it.

Yasha. His declining years!

[Charlotta Ivanovna, *very thin, tightly laced, dressed in white, a lorgnette at her waist, crosses the stage*]

Lopahin. Forgive me, Charlotta Ivanovna, I've not had time to greet you.

[*Tries to kiss her hand*]

Charlotta [*pulling away her hand*]. If I let you kiss my hand, you'll be wanting to kiss my elbow next, and then my shoulder.

Lopahin. I've no luck today. [*All laugh*] Charlotta Ivanovna, show us a trick.

Mme. Ranevskaya. Yes, Charlotta, do a trick for us.

Charlotta. I don't see the need. I want to sleep.

[*Exits*]

Lopahin. In three weeks we'll meet again. [*Kisses* Mme. Ranevskaya's *hand*] Good-by till then. Time's up. [*To* Gayev] Bye-bye. [*Kisses* Pishchik] Bye-bye. [*Shakes hands with* Varya, *then with* Firs *and* Yasha] I hate to leave. [*To* Mme. Ranevskaya] If you make up your mind about the cottages, let me know; I'll get you a loan of 50,000 rubles. Think it over seriously.

Varya [*crossly*]. Will you never go!

Lopahin. I'm going, I'm going.

[*Exits*]

Gayev. The vulgarian. But, excuse me . . . Varya's going to marry him, he's Varya's fiancé.

Varya. You talk too much, uncle dear.

Mme. Ranevskaya. Well, Varya, it would make me happy. He's a good man.

Pishchik. Yes, one must admit, he's a most estimable man. And my Dashenka . . . she too says that . . . she says . . . lots of things. [*Snores; but wakes up at once*] All the same, my valued friend, could you oblige me . . . with a loan of 240 rubles? I must pay the interest on the mortgage tomorrow.

Varya [*alarmed*]. We can't, we can't!

MME. RANEVSKAYA. I really haven't any money.

PISHCHIK. It'll turn up. [*Laughs*] I never lose hope, I thought everything was lost, that I was done for, when lo and behold, the railway ran through my land . . . and I was paid for it. . . . And something else will turn up again, if not today, then tomorrow . . . Dashenka will win two hundred thousand . . . she's got a lottery ticket.

MME. RANEVSKAYA. I've had my coffee, now let's go to bed.

FIRS [*brushes off* GAYEV: *admonishingly*]. You've got the wrong trousers on again. What am I to do with you?

VARYA [*softly*]. Anya's asleep. [*Gently opens the window*] The sun's up now, it's not a bit cold. Look, mamma dear, what wonderful trees. And heavens, what air! The starlings are singing!

GAYEV [*opens the other window*]. The orchard is all white. You've not forgotten it? Luba? That's the long alley that runs straight, straight as an arrow; how it shines on moonlight nights, do you remember? You've not forgotten?

MME. RANEVSKAYA [*looking out of the window into the orchard*]. Oh, my childhood, my innocent childhood. I used to sleep in this nursery —I used to look out into the orchard, happiness waked with me every morning, the orchard was just the same then . . . nothing has changed. [*Laughs with joy*] All, all white! Oh, my orchard! After the dark, rainy autumn and the cold winter, you are young again, and full of happiness, the heavenly angels have not left you. . . . If I could free my chest and my shoulders from this rock that weighs on me, if I could only forget the past!

GAYEV. Yes, and the orchard will be sold to pay our debts, strange as it may seem. . . .

MME. RANEVSKAYA. Look! There is our poor mother walking in the orchard . . . all in white . . . [*Laughs with joy*] It is she!

GAYEV. Where?

VARYA. What are you saying, mamma dear!

MME. RANEVSKAYA. There's no one there, I just imagined it. To the right, where the path turns towards the arbor, there's a little white tree, leaning over, that looks like a woman. . . .

[TROFIMOV *enters, wearing a shabby student's uniform and spectacles*]

MME. RANEVSKAYA. What an amazing orchard! White masses of blossom, the blue sky. . . .

TROFIMOV. Lubov Andreyevna! [*She looks round at him*] I just want to pay my respects to you, then I'll leave at once. [*Kisses her hand ardently*] I was told to wait until morning, but I hadn't the patience. . . .

[MME. RANEVSKAYA *looks at him perplexed*]

VARYA [*through tears*]. This is Petya Trofimov.

TROFIMOV. Petya Trofimov, formerly your Grisha's tutor. . . . Can I have changed so much?

[MME. RANEVSKAYA *embraces him and weeps quietly*]

GAYEV [*embarrassed*]. Don't, don't, Luba.

VARYA [*crying*]. I told you, Petya, to wait until tomorrow.

MME. RANEVSKAYA. My Grisha . . . my little boy . . . Grisha . . . my son.

VARYA. What can one do, mamma dear, it's God's will.

TROFIMOV [*softly, through tears*]. There . . . there.

MME. RANEVSKAYA [*weeping quietly*]. My little boy was lost . . . drowned. Why? Why, my friend? [*More quietly*] Anya's asleep in there, and here I am talking so loudly . . . making all this noise. . . . But tell me, Petya, why do you look so badly? Why have you aged so?

TROFIMOV. A mangy master, a peasant woman in the train called me.

MME. RANEVSKAYA. You were just a boy then, a dear little student, and now your hair's thin—and you're wearing glasses! Is it possible you're still a student?

[*Goes towards the door*]

TROFIMOV. I suppose I'm a perpetual student.

MME. RANEVSKAYA [*kisses her brother, then* VARYA]. Now, go to bed. . . . You have aged, too, Leonid.

PISHCHIK [*follows her*]. So now we turn in. Oh, my gout! I'm staying the night here. . . . Lubov Andreyevna, my angel, tomorrow morning. . . . I do need 240 rubles.

GAYEV. He keeps at it.

PISHCHIK. I'll pay it back, dear . . . it's a trifling sum.

MME. RANEVSKAYA. All right, Leonid will give it to you. Give it to him, Leonid.

GAYEV. Me give it to him! That's a good one!

MME. RANEVSKAYA. It can't be helped. Give it to him! He needs it. He'll pay it back.

[MME. RANEVSKAYA, TROFIMOV, PISHCHIK, *and* FIRS *go out;* GAYEV, VARYA, *and* YASHA *remain*]

GAYEV.   Sister hasn't got out of the habit of throwing money around. [*to* YASHA]. Go away, my good fellow, you smell of the barnyard.

YASHA [*with a grin*].   And you, Leonid Andreyevich, are just the same as ever.

GAYEV.   Who? [*to* VARYA] What did he say?

VARYA [*to* YASHA].   Your mother's come from the village; she's been sitting in the servants' room since yesterday, waiting to see you.

YASHA.   Botheration!

VARYA.   You should be ashamed of yourself!

YASHA.   She's all I needed! She could have come tomorrow.

[*Exits*]

VARYA.   Mamma is just the same as ever; she hasn't changed a bit. If she had her own way, she'd keep nothing for herself.

GAYEV.   Yes. . . . [*Pauses*] If a great many remedies are offered for some disease, it means it is incurable; I keep thinking and racking my brains; I have many remedies, ever so many, and that really means none. It would be fine if we came in for a legacy; it would be fine if we married off our Anya to a very rich man; or we might go to Yaroslavl and try our luck with our aunt, the Countess. She's very, very rich, you know. . . .

VARYA [*weeping*].   If only God would help us!

GAYEV.   Stop bawling. Aunt's very rich, but she doesn't like us. In the first place, sister married a lawyer who was no nobleman. . . . [ANYA *appears in the doorway*] She married beneath her, and it can't be said that her behavior has been very exemplary. She's good, kind, sweet, and I love her, but no matter what extenuating circumstances you may adduce, there's no denying that she has no morals. You sense it in her least gesture.

VARYA [*in a whisper*].   Anya's in the doorway.

GAYEV.   Who? [*Pauses*] It's queer, something got into my right eye— my eyes are going back on me. . . . And on Thursday, when I was in the circuit court—

[*Enter* ANYA]

VARYA.   Why aren't you asleep, Anya?

ANYA.   I can't get to sleep, I just can't.

GAYEV.   My little pet! [*Kisses* ANYA's *face and hands*] My child!

[*Weeps*] You are not my niece, you're my angel! You're everything to me. Believe me, believe—

ANYA. I believe you, uncle. Everyone loves you and respects you . . . but, uncle dear, you must keep still. . . . You must. What were you saying just now about my mother? Your own sister? What made you say that?

GAYEV. Yes, yes. . . . [*Covers his face with her hand*] Really, that was awful! Good God! Heaven help me! Just now I made a speech to the bookcase . . . so stupid! And only after I was through, I saw how stupid it was.

VARYA. It's true, uncle dear, you ought to keep still. Just don't talk, that's all.

ANYA. If you could only keep still, it would make things easier for you too.

GAYEV. I'll keep still. [*Kisses* ANYA's *and* VARYA's *hands*] I will. But now about business. On Thursday I was in court; well, there were a number of us there, and we began talking of one thing and another, and this and that, and do you know, I believe it will be possible to raise a loan on a promissory note, to pay the interest at the bank.

VARYA. If only God would help us!

GAYEV. On Tuesday I'll go and see about it again. [*To* VARYA] Stop bawling. [*To* ANYA] Your mamma will talk to Lopahin, and he, of course, will not refuse her . . . and as soon as you're rested, you'll go to Yaroslavl to the Countess, your great-aunt. So we'll be working in three directions at once, and the thing is in the bag. We'll pay the interest—I'm sure of it. [*Puts a candy in his mouth*] I swear on my honor, I swear by anything you like, the estate shan't be sold. [*Excitedly*] I swear by my own happiness! Here's my hand on it, you can call me a swindler and a scoundrel if I let it come to an auction! I swear by my whole being.

ANYA [*relieved and quite happy again*]. How good you are, uncle, and how clever! [*Embraces him*] Now I'm at peace, quite at peace, I'm happy.

[*Enter* FIRS]

FIRS [*reproachfully*]. Leonid Andreyevich, have you no fear of God? When are you going to bed?

GAYEV. Directly, directly. Go away, Firs. I'll . . . yes, I will undress myself. Now, children, 'nightie-'nightie. We'll consider details to-morrow, but now go to sleep. [*Kisses* ANYA *and* VARYA] I am a man of the 'Eighties; they have nothing good to say of that period nowadays. Nevertheless, in the course of my life I have suffered not a little for my convictions. It's not for nothing that the peasant loves me; one should know the peasant; one should know from which—

ANYA. There you go again, uncle.

VARYA. Uncle dear, be quiet.

FIRS [*angrily*]. Leonid Andreyevich!

GAYEV. I'm coming, I'm coming! Go to bed! Double bank shot in the side pocket! Here goes a clean shot. . . .

[*Exits,* FIRS *hobbling after him*]

ANYA. I am at peace now. I don't want to go to Yaroslavl—I don't like my great-aunt, but still, I am at peace, thanks to uncle.

[*Sits down*]

VARYA. We must get some sleep. I'm going now. While you were away something unpleasant happened. In the old servants' quarters there are only the old people, as you know: Yefim, Polya, Yevstigney, and Karp, too. They began letting all sorts of rascals in to spend the night. . . . I didn't say anything. Then I heard they'd been spreading a report that I gave them nothing but dried peas to eat—out of stinginess, you know . . . and it was all Yevstigney's doing. . . . All right, I thought, if that's how it is, I thought, just wait. I sent for Yevstigney. . . . [*Yawns*] He comes. . . . "How's this, Yevstigney?" I say, "You fool . . ." [*Looking at* ANYA] Anichka! [*Pauses*] She's asleep. [*Puts her arm around* ANYA] Come to your little bed. . . . Come . . . [*Leads her*] My darling has fallen asleep. . . . Come.

[*They go out. Far away beyond the orchard a shepherd is piping.* TROFIMOV *crosses the stage and, seeing* VARYA *and* ANYA, *stands still*]

VARYA. Sh! She's asleep . . . asleep . . . Come, darling.

ANYA [*softly, half-asleep*]. I'm so tired. Those bells . . . uncle . . . dear. . . . Mamma and uncle. . . .

VARYA. Come, my precious, come along.

[*They go into* ANYA's *room*]

TROFIMOV [*with emotion*]. My sunshine, my spring!

## ACT II

*A meadow. An old, long-abandoned, lopsided little chapel; near it, a well, large slabs, which had apparently once served as tombstones, and an old bench. In the background, the road to the Gayev estate. To one side poplars loom darkly, where the cherry orchard begins. In the distance a row of telegraph poles, and far off, on the horizon, the faint outline of a large city which is seen only in fine, clear weather. The sun will soon be setting.* CHARLOTTA, YASHA, *and* DUNYASHA *are seated on the bench.* YEPIHODOV *stands near and plays a guitar. All are pensive.* CHARLOTTA *wears an old peaked cap. She has taken a gun from her shoulder and is straightening the buckle on the strap.*

CHARLOTTA [*musingly*]. I haven't a real passport, I don't know how old I am, and I always feel that I am very young. When I was a little girl, my father and mother used to go from fair to fair and give performances, very good ones. And I used to do the *salto mortale,* and all sorts of other tricks. And when papa and mamma died, a German lady adopted me and began to educate me. Very good. I grew up and became a governess. But where I come from and who I am, I don't know. . . . Who were my parents? Perhaps they weren't even married. . . . I don't know. . . . [*Takes a cucumber out of her pocket and eats it*] I don't know a thing. [*Pause*] One wants so much to talk, and there isn't anyone to talk to. . . . I haven't anybody.

YEPIHODOV [*plays the guitar and sings*]. "What care I for the jarring world? What's friend or foe to me? . . ." How agreeable it is to play the mandolin.

DUNYASHA. That's a guitar, not a mandolin.

[Looks in a hand mirror and powders her face]

YEPIHODOV. To a madman in love it's a mandolin. [*Sings*] "Would that the heart were warmed by the fire of mutual love!"

[YASHA joins in]

CHARLOTTA. How abominably these people sing. Pfui! Like jackals!

DUNYASHA [*to* YASHA]. How wonderful it must be though to have stayed abroad!

YASHA. Ah, yes, of course, I cannot but agree with you there.

[Yawns and lights a cigar]

YEPIHODOV. Naturally. Abroad, everything has long since achieved full perplexion.

YASHA. That goes without saying.

YEPIHODOV. I'm a cultivated man, I read all kinds of remarkable books. And yet I can never make out what direction I should take, what is it that I want, properly speaking. Should I live, or should I shoot myself, properly speaking? Nevertheless, I always carry a revolver about me. . . . Here it is. . . .

*[Shows revolver]*

CHARLOTTA. I've finished. I'm going. *[Puts the gun over her shoulder]* You are a very clever man, Yepihodov, and a very terrible one; women must be crazy about you. Br-r-r! *[Starts to go]* These clever men are all so stupid; there's no one for me to talk to . . . always alone, alone, I haven't a soul . . . and who I am, and why I am, nobody knows.

*[Exits unhurriedly]*

YEPIHODOV. Properly speaking and letting other subjects alone, I must say regarding myself, among other things, that fate treats me mercilessly, like a storm treats a small boat. If I am mistaken, let us say, why then do I wake up this morning, and there on my chest is a spider of enormous dimensions . . . like this. . . . *[indicates with both hands]* Again, I take up a pitcher of kvass to have a drink, and in it there is something unseemly to the highest degree, something like a cockroach. *[Pause]* Have you read Buckle? *[Pause]* I wish to have a word with you, Avdotya Fyodorovna, if I may trouble you.

DUNYASHA. Well, go ahead.

YEPIHODOV. I wish to speak with you alone. *[Sighs]*

DUNYASHA *[embarrassed]*. Very well. Only first bring me my little cape. You'll find it near the wardrobe. It's rather damp here.

YEPIHODOV. Certainly, ma'am; I will fetch it, ma'am. Now I know what to do with my revolver.

*[Takes the guitar and goes off playing it]*

YASHA. Two-and-Twenty Troubles! An awful fool, between you and me. *[Yawns]*

DUNYASHA. I hope to God he doesn't shoot himself! *[Pause]* I've become so nervous, I'm always fretting. I was still a little girl when I was taken into the big house, I am quite unused to the simple life now, and my hands are white, as white as a lady's. I've become so soft, so delicate, so refined, I'm afraid of everything. It's so terrifying; and if you deceive me, Yasha, I don't know what will happen to my nerves.

[YASHA *kisses her*]

YASHA. You're a peach! Of course, a girl should never forget herself; and what I dislike more than anything is when a girl don't behave properly.

DUNYASHA. I've fallen passionately in love with you; you're educated —you have something to say about everything.

[*Pause*]

YASHA [*yawns*]. Yes, ma'am. Now the way I look at it, if a girl loves someone, it means she is immoral. [*Pause*] It's agreeable smoking a cigar in the fresh air. [*Listens*] Someone's coming this way. . . . It's our madam and the others. [DUNYASHA *embraces him impulsively*] You go home, as though you'd been to the river to bathe; go by the little path, or else they'll run into you and suspect me of having arranged to meet you here. I can't stand that sort of thing.

DUNYASHA [*coughing softly*]. Your cigar's made my head ache.

[*Exits.* YASHA *remains standing near the chapel. Enter* MME. RANEVSKAYA, GAYEV, *and* LOPAHIN]

LOPAHIN. You must make up your mind once and for all—there's no time to lose. It's quite a simple question, you know. Do you agree to lease your land for summer cottages or not? Answer in one word, yes or no; only one word!

MME. RANEVSKAYA. Who's been smoking such abominable cigars here?

[*Sits down*]

GAYEV. Now that the railway line is so near, it's made things very convenient. [*Sits down*] Here we've been able to have lunch in town. Yellow ball in the side pocket! I feel like going into the house and playing just one game.

MME. RANEVSKAYA. You can do that later.

LOPAHIN. Only one word! [*Imploringly*] Do give me an answer!

GAYEV [*yawning*]. Who?

MME. RANEVSKAYA [*looks into her purse*]. Yesterday I had a lot of money and now my purse is almost empty. My poor Varya tries to economize by feeding us just milk soup; in the kitchen the old people get nothing but dried peas to eat, while I squander money thoughtlessly. [*Drops the purse, scattering gold pieces*] You see there they go. . . .

[*Shows vexation*]

YASHA. Allow me—I'll pick them up.

[*Picks up the money*]

MME. RANEVSKAYA. Be so kind, Yasha. And why did I go to lunch in town? That nasty restaurant, with its music and the tablecloth smelling of soap. . . . Why drink so much, Leonid? Why eat so much? Why talk so much? Today again you talked a lot, and all so inappropriately about the 'Seventies, about the decadents. And to whom? Talking to waiters about decadents!

LOPAHIN. Yes.

GAYEV [*waving his hand*]. I'm incorrigible; that's obvious. [*Irritably, to* YASHA] Why do you keep dancing about in front of me?

YASHA [*laughs*]. I can't hear your voice without laughing—

GAYEV. Either he or I—

MME. RANEVSKAYA. Go away, Yasha; run along.

YASHA [*handing* MME. RANEVSKAYA *her purse*]. I'm going, at once. [*Hardly able to suppress his laughter*] This minute.

[*Exits*]

LOPAHIN. That rich man, Deriganov, wants to buy your estate. They say he's coming to the auction himself.

MME. RANEVSKAYA. Where did you hear that?

LOPAHIN. That's what they are saying in town.

GAYEV. Our aunt in Yaroslavl has promised to help; but when she will send the money, and how much, no one knows.

LOPAHIN. How much will she send? A hundred thousand? Two hundred?

MME. RANEVSKAYA. Oh, well, ten or fifteen thousand; and we'll have to be grateful for that.

LOPAHIN. Forgive me, but such frivolous people as you are, so queer and unbusinesslike—I never met in my life. One tells you in plain language that your estate is up for sale, and you don't seem to take it in.

MME. RANEVSKAYA. What are we to do? Tell us what to do.

LOPAHIN. I do tell you, every day; every day I say the same thing! You must do it and as soon as possible—right away. The auction is close at hand. Please understand! Once you've decided to have the cottages, you can raise as much money as you like, and you're saved.

MME. RANEVSKAYA. Cottages—summer people—forgive me, but it's all so vulgar.

GAYEV. I agree with you absolutely.

LOPAHIN. I shall either burst into tears or scream or faint! I can't stand it! You've worn me out! [*To* GAYEV] You're an old woman!

GAYEV. Who?

LOPAHIN. An old woman!

[*Gets up to go*]

MME. RANEVSKAYA [*alarmed*]. No, don't go! Please stay, I beg you, my dear. Perhaps we shall think of something.

LOPAHIN. What is there to think of?

MME. RANEVSKAYA. Don't go, I beg you. With you here it's more cheerful anyway. [*Pause*] I keep expecting something to happen, it's as though the house were going to crash about our ears.

GAYEV [*in deep thought*]. Bank shot in the corner. . . . Three cushions in the side pocket. . . .

MME. RANEVSKAYA. We have been great sinners. . . .

LOPAHIN. What sins could you have committed?

GAYEV [*putting a candy in his mouth*]. They say I've eaten up my fortune in candy! [*Laughs*]

MME. RANEVSKAYA. Oh, my sins! I've squandered money away recklessly, like a lunatic, and I married a man who made nothing but debts. My husband drank himself to death on champagne, he was a terrific drinker. And then, to my sorrow, I fell in love with another man, and I lived with him. And just then—that was my first punishment—a blow on the head: my little boy was drowned here in the river. And I went abroad, went away forever . . . never to come back, never to see this river again . . . I closed my eyes and ran, out of my mind. . . . But he followed me, pitiless, brutal. I bought a villa near Mentone, because he fell ill there; and for three years, day and night, I knew no peace, no rest. The sick man wore me out, he sucked my soul dry. Then last year, when the villa was sold to pay my debts, I went to Paris, and there he robbed me, abandoned me, took up with another woman, I tried to poison myself—it was stupid, so shameful—and then suddenly I felt drawn back to Russia, back to my own country, to my little girl. [*Wipes her tears away*] Lord, Lord! Be merciful, forgive me my sins—don't punish me any more! [*Takes a telegram out of her pocket*] This came today from Paris—he begs me to forgive him, implores me to go back. . . . [*Tears up the telegram*] Do I hear music? [*Listens*]

GAYEV. That's our famous Jewish band, you remember? Four violins, a flute, and a double bass.

MME. RANEVSKAYA. Does it still exist? We ought to send for them some evening and have a party.

LOPAHIN [*listens*]. I don't hear anything. [*Hums softly*] "The Germans for a fee will Frenchify a Russian." [*Laughs*] I saw a play at the theater yesterday—awfully funny.

MME. RANEVSKAYA. There was probably nothing funny about it. You shouldn't go to see plays, you should look at yourselves more often. How drab your lives are—how full of unnecessary talk.

LOPAHIN. That's true; come to think of it, we do live like fools. [*Pause*] My pop was a peasant, an idiot; he understood nothing, never taught me anything, all he did was beat me when he was drunk, and always with a stick. Fundamentally, I'm just the same kind of blockhead and idiot. I was never taught anything—I have a terrible handwriting, I write so that I feel ashamed before people, like a pig.

MME. RANEVSKAYA. You should get married, my friend.

LOPAHIN. Yes . . . that's true.

MME. RANEVSKAYA. To our Varya, she's a good girl.

LOPAHIN. Yes.

MME. RANEVSKAYA. She's a girl who comes of simple people, she works all day long; and above all, she loves you. Besides, you've liked her for a long time now.

LOPAHIN. Well, I've nothing against it. She's a good girl.

[*Pause*]

GAYEV. I've been offered a place in the bank—6,000 a year. Have you heard?

MME. RANEVSKAYA. You're not up to it. Stay where you are.

[FIRS *enters, carrying an overcoat*]

FIRS [*to* GAYEV]. Please put this on, sir, it's damp.

GAYEV [*putting it on*]. I'm fed up with you, brother.

FIRS. Never mind. This morning you drove off without saying a word.

[*Looks him over*]

MME. RANEVSKAYA. How you've aged, Firs.

FIRS. I beg your pardon?

LOPAHIN. The lady says you've aged.

FIRS. I've lived a long time; they were arranging my wedding and your papa wasn't born yet. [*Laughs*] When freedom came I was already head footman. I wouldn't consent to be set free then; I stayed on with the master. . . . [*Pause*] I remember they were all very happy, but why they were happy, they didn't know themselves.

LOPAHIN. It was fine in the old days! At least there was flogging!

FIRS [*not hearing*]. Of course. The peasants kept to the masters, the masters kept to the peasants; but now they've all gone their own ways, and there's no making out anything.

GAYEV. Be quiet, Firs. I must go to town tomorrow. They've promised to introduce me to a general who might let us have a loan.

LOPAHIN. Nothing will come of that. You won't even be able to pay the interest, you can be certain of that.

MME. RANEVSKAYA. He's raving, there isn't any general.

[*Enter* TROFIMOV, ANYA, *and* VARYA]

GAYEV. Here come our young people.

ANYA. There's mamma, on the bench.

MME. RANEVSKAYA [*tenderly*]. Come here, come along, my darlings. [*Embraces* ANYA *and* VARYA] If you only knew how I love you both! Sit beside me—there, like that.

[*All sit down*]

LOPAHIN. Our perpetual student is always with the young ladies.

TROFIMOV. That's not any of your business.

LOPAHIN. He'll soon be fifty, and he's still a student!

TROFIMOV. Stop your silly jokes.

LOPAHIN. What are you so cross about, you queer bird?

TROFIMOV. Oh, leave me alone.

LOPAHIN [*laughs*]. Allow me to ask you, what do you think of me?

TROFIMOV. What I think of you, Yermolay Alexeyevich, is this: you are a rich man who will soon be a millionaire. Well, just as a beast of prey, which devours everything that comes in its way, is necessary for the process of metabolism to go on, so you too are necessary.

[*All laugh*]

VARYA. Better tell us something about the planets, Petya.

MME. RANEVSKAYA. No, let's go on with yesterday's conversation.

TROFIMOV. What was it about?

GAYEV. About man's pride.

TROFIMOV. Yesterday we talked a long time, but we came to no conclusion. There is something mystical about man's pride in your sense of the word. Perhaps you're right, from your own point of view. But if you reason simply, without going into subtleties, then what call is there for pride? Is there any sense in it, if man is so poor a thing physiologically, and if, in the great majority of cases, he is coarse, stupid, and profoundly unhappy? We should stop admiring ourselves. We should work, and that's all.

GAYEV. You die, anyway.

TROFIMOV. Who knows? And what does it mean—to die? Perhaps man has a hundred senses, and at his death only the five we know perish, while the other ninety-five remain alive.

MME. RANEVSKAYA. How clever you are, Petya!

LOPAHIN [*ironically*]. Awfully clever!

TROFIMOV. Mankind goes forward, developing its powers. Everything that is now unattainable for it will one day come within man's reach and be clear to him; only we must work, helping with all our might those who seek the truth. Here among us in Russia only the very few work as yet. The great majority of the intelligentsia, as far as I can see, seek nothing, do nothing, are totally unfit for work of any kind. They call themselves the intelligentsia, yet they are uncivil to their servants, treat the peasants like animals, are poor students, never read anything serious, do absolutely nothing at all, only talk about science, and have little appreciation of the arts. They are all solemn, have grim faces, they all philosophize and talk of weighty matters. And meanwhile the vast majority of us, ninety-nine out of a hundred, live like savages. At the least provocation—a punch in the jaw, and curses. They eat disgustingly, sleep in filth and stuffiness, bedbugs everywhere, stench and damp and moral slovenliness. And obviously, the only purpose of all our fine talk is to hoodwink ourselves and others. Show me where the public nurseries are that we've heard so much about, and the libraries. We read about them in novels, but in reality they don't exist, there is nothing but dirt, vulgarity, and Asiatic backwardness. I don't like very solemn faces, I'm afraid of them, I'm afraid of serious conversations. We'd do better to keep quiet for a while.

LOPAHIN. Do you know, I get up at five o'clock in the morning, and I work from morning till night; and I'm always handling money, my own and other people's, and I see what people around me are really like. You've only to start doing anything to see how few honest, decent people there are. Sometimes when I lie awake at night, I think: "Oh, Lord, thou hast given us immense forests, boundless fields, the widest horizons, and living in their midst, we ourselves ought really to be giants."

MME. RANEVSKAYA.   Now you want giants! They're only good in fairy tales; otherwise they're frightening.

[YEPIHODOV *crosses the stage at the rear, playing the guitar*]

MME. RANEVSKAYA [*pensively*].   There goes Yepihodov.

ANYA [*pensively*].   There goes Yepihodov.

GAYEV.   Ladies and gentlemen, the sun has set.

TROFIMOV.   Yes.

GAYEV [*in a low voice, declaiming as it were*].   Oh, Nature, wondrous Nature, you shine with eternal radiance, beautiful and indifferent! You, whom we call our mother, unite within yourself life and death! You animate and destroy!

VARYA [*pleadingly*].   Uncle dear!

ANYA.   Uncle, again!

TROFIMOV.   You'd better bank the yellow ball in the side pocket.

GAYEV.   I'm silent, I'm silent. . . .

[*All sit plunged in thought. Stillness reigns. Only* FIRS's *muttering is audible. Suddenly a distant sound is heard, coming from the sky as it were, the sound of a snapping string, mournfully dying away*]

MME. RANEVSKAYA.   What was that?

LOPAHIN.   I don't know. Somewhere far away, in the pits, a bucket's broken loose; but somewhere very far away.

GAYEV.   Or it might be some sort of bird, perhaps a heron.

TROFIMOV.   Or an owl. . . .

MME. RANEVSKAYA [*shudders*].   It's weird, somehow.

[*Pause*]

FIRS.   Before the calamity the same thing happened—the owl screeched, and the samovar hummed all the time.

GAYEV.   Before what calamity?

FIRS.   Before the Freedom.[1]

[*Pause*]

MME. RANEVSKAYA.   Come, my friends, let's be going. It's getting dark. [*To* ANYA] You have tears in your eyes. What is it, my little one? [*Embraces her*]

---

[1] The emancipation of the serfs, proclaimed in 1861.

ANYA. I don't know, mamma; it's nothing.

TROFIMOV. Somebody's coming.

[*A Tramp appears, wearing a shabby white cap and an overcoat. He is slightly drunk*]

TRAMP. Allow me to inquire, will this short-cut take me to the station?

GAYEV. It will. Just follow that road.

TRAMP. My heartfelt thanks. [*Coughing*] The weather is glorious. [*Recites*] "My brother, my suffering brother. . . . Go down to the Volga! Whose groans . . . ?" [*To* VARYA] Mademoiselle, won't you spare 30 kopecks for a hungry Russian?

[VARYA, *frightened, cries out*]

LOPAHIN [*angrily*]. Even panhandling has its proprieties.

MME. RANEVSKAYA [*scared*]. Here, take this. [*Fumbles in her purse*] I haven't any silver . . . never mind, here's a gold piece.

TRAMP. My heartfelt thanks.

[*Exits. Laughter*]

VARYA [*frightened*]. I'm leaving, I'm leaving . . . Oh, mamma dear, at home the servants have nothing to eat, and you gave him a gold piece!

MME. RANEVSKAYA. What are you going to do with me? I'm such a fool. When we get home, I'll give you everything I have. Yermolay Alexeyevich, you'll lend me some more. . . .

LOPAHIN. Yes, ma'am.

MME. RANEVSKAYA. Come, ladies and gentlemen, it's time to be going. Oh! Varya, we've settled all about your marriage. Congratulations!

VARYA [*through tears*]. Really, mamma, that's not a joking matter.

LOPAHIN. "Aurelia, get thee to a nunnery, go. . . ."

GAYEV. And do you know, my hands are trembling: I haven't played billiards in a long time.

LOPAHIN. "Aurelia, nymph, in your orisons, remember me!"

MME. RANEVSKAYA. Let's go, it's almost suppertime.

VARYA. He frightened me! My heart's pounding.

LOPAHIN. Let me remind you, ladies and gentlemen, on the 22nd of August the cherry orchard will be up for sale. Think about that! Think!

[*All except* TROFIMOV *and* ANYA *go out*]

ANYA [*laughs*]. I'm grateful to that tramp, he frightened Varya and so we're alone.

TROFIMOV.  Varya's afraid we'll fall in love with each other all of a sudden. She hasn't left us alone for days. Her narrow mind can't grasp that we're above love. To avoid the petty and illusory, everything that prevents us from being free and happy—that is the goal and meaning of our life. Forward! Do not fall behind, friends!

ANYA [*strikes her hands together*].  How well you speak! [*Pause*] It's wonderful here today.

TROFIMOV.  Yes, the weather's glorious.

ANYA.  What have you done to me, Petya? Why don't I love the cherry orchard as I used to? I loved it so tenderly. It seemed to me there was no spot on earth lovelier than our orchard.

TROFIMOV.  All Russia is our orchard. Our land is vast and beautiful, there are many wonderful places in it. [*Pause*] Think of it, Anya, your grandfather, your great-grandfather and all your ancestors were serf-owners, owners of living souls, and aren't human beings looking at you from every tree in the orchard, from every leaf, from every trunk? Don't you hear voices? Oh, it's terrifying! Your orchard is a fearful place, and when you pass through it in the evening or at night, the old bark on the trees gleams faintly, and the cherry trees seem to be dreaming of things that happened a hundred, two hundred years ago and to be tormented by painful visions. What is there to say? We're at least two hundred years behind, we've really achieved nothing yet, we have no definite attitude to the past, we only philosophize, complain of the blues, or drink vodka. It's all so clear: in order to live in the present, we should first redeem our past, finish with it, and we can expiate it only by suffering, only by extraordinary, unceasing labor. Realize that, Anya.

ANYA.  The house in which we live has long ceased to be our own, and I will leave it, I give you my word.

TROFIMOV.  If you have the keys, fling them into the well and go away. Be free as the wind.

ANYA [*in ecstasy*].  How well you put that!

TROFIMOV.  Believe me, Anya, believe me! I'm not yet thirty, I'm young, I'm still a student—but I've already suffered so much. In winter I'm hungry, sick, harassed, poor as a beggar, and where hasn't Fate driven me? Where haven't I been? And yet always, every moment of the day and night, my soul is filled with inexplicable premonitions. . . . I have a premonition of happiness, Anya. . . . I see it already!

ANYA [*pensively*]. The moon is rising.

[YEPIHODOV *is heard playing the same mournful tune on the guitar. The moon rises. Somewhere near the poplars* VARYA *is looking for* ANYA *and calling* "Anya, where are you?"]

TROFIMOV. Yes, the moon is rising. [*Pause*] There it is, happiness, it's approaching, it's coming nearer and nearer, I can already hear its footsteps. And if we don't see it, if we don't know it, what does it matter? Others will!

VARYA'S *voice*. "Anya! Where are you?"

TROFIMOV. That Varya again! [*Angrily*] It's revolting!

ANYA. Never mind, let's go down to the river. It's lovely there.

TROFIMOV. Come on.

[*They go*]

VARYA'S *voice*. "Anya! Anya!"

## ACT III

*A drawing-room separated by an arch from a ballroom. Evening. Chandelier burning. The Jewish band is heard playing in the anteroom. In the ballroom they are dancing the* Grand Rond. PISHCHIK *is heard calling,* "Promenade à une paire." PISHCHIK *and* CHARLOTTA, TROFIMOV *and* MME. RANEVSKAYA, ANYA *and the* Post Office Clerk, VARYA *and the* Station-master, *and others, enter the drawing-room in couples.* DUNYASHA *is in the last couple.* VARYA *weeps quietly, wiping her tears as she dances. All parade through drawing-room.* PISHCHIK *calling* "Grand rond, balancez!" *and* "Les cavaliers à genoux et remerciez vos dames!" FIRS *wearing a dress-coat, brings in soda-water on a tray.* PISHCHIK *and* TROFIMOV *enter the drawing-room.*

PISHCHIK. I'm a full-blooded man; I've already had two strokes. Dancing's hard work for me; but as they say, "If you run with the pack, you can bark or not, but at least wag your tail." Still, I'm as strong as a horse. My late lamented father, who would have his joke, God rest his soul, used to say, talking about our origin, that the ancient line of the Simeonov-Pishchiks was descended from the very horse that Caligula had made a senator. [*Sits down*] But the trouble is, I have no money. A hungry dog believes in nothing but meat. [*Snores and wakes up at once*] It's the same with me—I can think of nothing but money.

TROFIMOV. You know, there *is* something equine about your figure.

PISHCHIK. Well, a horse is a fine animal—one can sell a horse.

[*Sound of billiards being played in an adjoining room.* VARYA *appears in the archway*]

TROFIMOV [*teasing her*]. Madam Lopahina! Madam Lopahina!

VARYA [*angrily*]. Mangy master!

TROFIMOV. Yes, I am a mangy master and I'm proud of it.

VARYA [*reflecting bitterly*]. Here we've hired musicians, and what shall we pay them with?

[*Exits*]

TROFIMOV [*to* PISHCHIK]. If the energy you have spent during your lifetime looking for money to pay interest had gone into something else, in the end you could have turned the world upside down.

PISHCHIK. Nietzsche, the philosopher, the greatest, most famous of men, that colossal intellect, says in his works, that it is permissible to forge banknotes.

TROFIMOV. Have you read Nietzsche?

PISHCHIK. Well . . . Dashenka told me. . . . And now I've got to the point where forging banknotes is about the only way out for me. . . . The day after tomorrow I have to pay 310 rubles—I already have 130. . . . [*Feels in his pockets. In alarm*] The money's gone! I've lost my money! [*Through tears*] Where's my money? [*Joyfully*] Here it is! Inside the lining . . . I'm all in a sweat. . . .

[*Enter* MME. RANEVSKAYA *and* CHARLOTTA]

MME. RANEVSKAYA [*hums the "Lezginka"*]. Why isn't Leonid back yet? What is he doing in town? [*To* DUNYASHA] Dunyasha, offer the musicians tea.

TROFIMOV. The auction hasn't taken place, most likely.

MME. RANEVSKAYA. It's the wrong time to have the band, and the wrong time to give a dance. Well, never mind.

[*Sits down and hums softly*]

CHARLOTTA. Shuffle the pack now. That's right. Give it here, my dear Mr. Pishchik. *Ein, zwei, drei!* Now look for it—it's in your side pocket.

PISHCHIK [*taking the card out of his pocket*]. The eight of spades! Perfectly right! Just imagine!

CHARLOTTA [*holding pack of cards in her hands. To* TROFIMOV]. Quickly, name the top card.

TROFIMOV. Well, let's see—the queen of spades.

CHARLOTTA. Right! [*To* PISHCHIK] Now name the top card.

PISHCHIK. The ace of hearts.

CHARLOTTA. Right! [*Claps her hands and the pack of cards disappears*] Ah, what lovely weather it is today! [*A mysterious feminine voice which seems to come from under the floor, answers her*]. "Oh, yes, it's magnificent weather, madam."

CHARLOTTA. You are my best ideal.

VOICE. "And I find you pleasing too, madam."

STATIONMASTER [*applauding*]. The lady ventriloquist, bravo!

PISHCHIK [*amazed*]. Just imagine! Enchanting Charlotta Ivanovna, I'm simply in love with you.

CHARLOTTA. In love? [*Shrugs her shoulders*] Are you capable of love? *Guter Mensch, aber schlechter Musikant!*

TROFIMOV [*claps* PISHCHIK *on the shoulder*]. You old horse, you!

CHARLOTTA. Attention please! One more trick! [*Takes a plaid from a chair*] Here is a very good plaid; I want to sell it. [*Shaking it out*] Does anyone want to buy it?

PISHCHIK [*in amazement*]. Just imagine!

CHARLOTTA. *Ein, zwei, drei!*

[*Raises the plaid quickly, behind it stands* ANYA. *She curtsies, runs to her mother, embraces her, and runs back into the ballroom amidst general enthusiasm*]

MME. RANEVSKAYA [*applauds*]. Bravo! Bravo!

CHARLOTTA. Now again! *Ein, zwei, drei!*

[*Lifts the plaid; behind it stands* VARYA *bowing*]

PISHCHIK [*running after her*]. The rascal! What a woman, what a woman!

[*Exits*]

MME. RANEVSKAYA. And Leonid still isn't here. What is he doing in town so long? I don't understand. It must be all over by now. Either the estate has been sold, or the auction hasn't taken place. Why keep us in suspense so long?

VARYA [*trying to console her*]. Uncle's bought it, I feel sure of that.

TROFIMOV [*mockingly*]. Oh, yes!

VARYA. Great-aunt sent him an authorization to buy it in her name, and to transfer the debt. She's doing it for Anya's sake. And I'm sure that God will help us, and uncle will buy it.

MME. RANEVSKAYA. Great-aunt sent fifteen thousand to buy the estate in her name, she doesn't trust us, but that's not even enough to pay the interest. [*Covers her face with her hands*] Today my fate will be decided, my fate—

TROFIMOV [*teasing* VARYA]. Madam Lopahina!

VARYA [*angrily*]. Perpetual student! Twice already you've been expelled from the university.

MME. RANEVSKAYA. Why are you so cross, Varya? He's teasing you about Lopahin. Well, what of it? If you want to marry Lopahin, go ahead. He's a good man, and interesting; if you don't want to, don't. Nobody's compelling you, my pet!

VARYA. Frankly, mamma dear, I take this thing seriously; he's a good man and I like him.

MME. RANEVSKAYA. All right then, marry him. I don't know what you're waiting for.

VARYA. But, mamma, I can't propose to him myself. For the last two years everyone's been talking to me about him—talking. But he either keeps silent, or else cracks jokes. I understand; he's growing rich, he's absorbed in business—he has no time for me. If I had money, even a little, say, 100 rubles, I'd throw everything up and go far away—I'd go into a nunnery.

TROFIMOV. What a blessing. . . .

VARYA. A student ought to be intelligent. [*Softly, with tears in her voice*] How homely you've grown, Petya! How old you look! [*To* MME. RANEVSKAYA, *with dry eyes*] But I can't live without work, mamma dear; I must keep busy every minute.

[*Enter* YASHA]

YASHA [*hardly restraining his laughter*]. Yepihodov has broken a billiard cue.

[*Exits*]

VARYA. Why is Yepihodov here? Who allowed him to play billiards? I don't understand these people!

[*Exits*]

MME. RANEVSKAYA. Don't tease her, Petya. She's unhappy enough without that.

TROFIMOV. She bustles so—and meddles in other people's business. All summer long she's given Anya and me no peace. She's afraid of a love-affair between us. What business is it of hers? Besides, I've given no grounds for it, and I'm far from such vulgarity. We are above love.

MME. RANEVSKAYA. And I suppose I'm beneath love? [*Anxiously*] What can be keeping Leonid? If I only knew whether the estate has been sold or not. Such a calamity seems so incredible to me that I don't know what to think—I feel lost. . . . I could scream. . . . I could do something stupid. . . . Save me, Petya, tell me something, talk to me!

TROFIMOV. Whether the estate is sold today or not, isn't it all one? That's all done with long ago—there's no turning back, the path is overgrown. Calm yourself, my dear. You mustn't deceive yourself. For once in your life you must face the truth.

MME. RANEVSKAYA. What truth? You can see the truth, you can tell it from falsehood, but I seem to have lost my eyesight, I see nothing. You settle every great problem so boldly, but tell me, my dear boy, isn't it because you're young, because you don't yet know what one of your problems means in terms of suffering? You look ahead fearlessly, but isn't it because you don't see and don't expect anything dreadful, because life is still hidden from your young eyes? You're bolder, more honest, more profound than we are, but think hard, show just a bit of magnanimity, spare me. After all, I was born here, my father and mother lived here, and my grandfather; I love this house. Without the cherry orchard, my life has no meaning for me, and if it really must be sold, then sell me with the orchard. [*Embraces* TROFIMOV, *kisses him on the forehead*] My son was drowned here. [*Weeps*] Pity me, you good, kind fellow!

TROFIMOV. You know, I feel for you with all my heart.

MME. RANEVSKAYA. But that should have been said differently, so differently! [*Takes out her handkerchief—a telegram falls on the floor*] My heart is so heavy today—you can't imagine! The noise here upsets me—my inmost being trembles at every sound—I'm shaking all over. But I can't go into my own room; I'm afraid to be alone. Don't condemn me, Petya. . . . I love you as though you were one of us, I would gladly let you marry Anya—I swear I would —only, my dear boy, you must study—you must take your degree— you do nothing, you let yourself be tossed by Fate from place to place—it's so strange. It's true, isn't it? And you should do something about your beard, to make it grow somehow! [*Laughs*] You're so funny!

TROFIMOV [*picks up the telegram*]. I've no wish to be a dandy.

MME. RANEVSKAYA. That's a telegram from Paris. I get one every day.

One yesterday and one today. That savage is ill again—he's in trouble again. He begs forgiveness, implores me to go to him, and really I ought to go to Paris to be near him. Your face is stern, Petya; but what is there to do, my dear boy? What am I to do? He's ill, he's alone and unhappy, and who is to look after him, who is to keep him from doing the wrong thing, who is to give him his medicine on time? And why hide it or keep still about it—I love him! That's clear. I love him, love him! He's a millstone round my neck, he'll drag me to the bottom, but I love that stone, I can't live without it. [*Presses* TROFIMOV's *hand*] Don't think badly of me, Petya, and don't say anything, don't say. . . .

TROFIMOV [*through tears*]. Forgive me my frankness in heaven's name; but, you know, he robbed you!

MME. RANEVSKAYA. No, no, no, you mustn't say such things! [*Covers her ears*]

TROFIMOV. But he's a scoundrel! You're the only one who doesn't know it. He's a petty scoundrel—a nonentity!

MME. RANEVSKAYA [*controlling her anger*]. You are twenty-six or twenty-seven years old, but you're still a schoolboy.

TROFIMOV. That may be.

MME. RANEVSKAYA. You should be a man at your age. You should understand people who love—and ought to be in love yourself. You ought to fall in love! [*Angrily*] Yes, yes! And it's not purity in you, it's prudishness, you're simply a queer fish, a comical freak!

TROFIMOV [*horrified*]. What is she saying?

MME. RANEVSKAYA. "I am above love!" You're not above love, but simply, as our Firs says, you're an addlehead. At your age not to have a mistress!

TROFIMOV [*horrified*]. This is frightful! What is she saying! [*Goes rapidly into the ballroom, clutching his head*] It's frightful—I can't stand it, I won't stay! [*Exits, but returns at once*] All is over between us!

[*Exits into anteroom*]

MME. RANEVSKAYA [*shouts after him*]. Petya! Wait! You absurd fellow, I was joking. Petya!

[*Sound of somebody running quickly downstairs and suddenly falling down with a crash.* ANYA *and* VARYA *scream. Sound of laughter a moment later*]

MME. RANEVSKAYA.   What's happened?

[ANYA *runs in*]

ANYA [*laughing*].   Petya's fallen downstairs!

[*Runs out*]

MME. RANEVSKAYA.   What a queer bird that Petya is!

[Stationmaster, *standing in the middle of the ballroom, recites Alexey Tolstoy's "Magdalene," to which all listen, but after a few lines, the sound of a waltz is heard from the anteroom and the reading breaks off. All dance.* TROFIMOV, ANYA, VARYA, *and* MME. RANEVSKAYA *enter from the anteroom*]

MME. RANEVSKAYA.   Petya, you pure soul, please forgive me. . . . Let's dance.

[*Dances with* PETYA. ANYA *and* VARYA *dance.* FIRS *enters, puts his stick down by the side door.* YASHA *enters from the drawing-room and watches the dancers*]

YASHA.   Well, grandfather?

FIRS.   I'm not feeling well. In the old days it was generals, barons, and admirals that were dancing at our balls, and now we have to send for the Post Office Clerk and the Stationmaster, and even they aren't too glad to come. I feel kind of shaky. The old master that's gone, their grandfather, dosed everyone with sealing-wax, whatever ailed 'em. I've been taking sealing-wax every day for twenty years or more. Perhaps that's what's kept me alive.

YASHA.   I'm fed up with you, grandpop. [*Yawns*] It's time you croaked.

FIRS.   Oh, you addlehead! [*Mumbles*]

[TROFIMOV *and* MME. RANEVSKAYA *dance from the ballroom into the drawing-room*]

MME. RANEVSKAYA.   *Merci*. I'll sit down a while. [*Sits down*] I'm tired.

[*Enter* ANYA]

ANYA [*excitedly*].   There was a man in the kitchen just now who said the cherry orchard was sold today.

MME. RANEVSKAYA.   Sold to whom?

ANYA.   He didn't say. He's gone.

[*Dances off with* TROFIMOV]

YASHA.   It was some old man gabbing, a stranger.

FIRS.   And Leonid Andreyevich isn't back yet, he hasn't come. And he's wearing his lightweight between-season overcoat; like enough, he'll catch cold. Ah, when they're young they're green.

Mme. Ranevskaya. This is killing me. Go, Yasha, find out to whom it has been sold.

Yasha. But the old man left long ago. [*Laughs*]

Mme. Ranevskaya. What are you laughing at? What are you pleased about?

Yasha. That Yepihodov is such a funny one. A funny fellow, Two-and-Twenty Troubles!

Mme. Ranevskaya. Firs, if the estate is sold, where will you go?

Firs. I'll go where you tell me.

Mme. Ranevskaya. Why do you look like that? Are you ill? You ought to go to bed.

Firs. Yes! [*With a snigger*] Me go to bed, and who's to hand things round? Who's to see to things? I'm the only one in the whole house.

Yasha [*to* Mme. Ranevskaya]. Lubov Andreyevna, allow me to ask a favor of you, be so kind! If you go back to Paris, take me with you, I beg you. It's positively impossible for me to stay here. [*Looking around; sotto voce*] What's the use of talking? You see for yourself, it's an uncivilized country, the people have no morals, and then the boredom! The food in the kitchen's revolting, and besides there's this Firs wanders about mumbling all sorts of inappropriate words. Take me with you, be so kind!

[*Enter* Pishchik]

Pishchik. May I have the pleasure of a waltz with you, charming lady? [Mme. Ranevskaya *accepts*] All the same, enchanting lady, you must let me have 180 rubles. . . . You must let me have [*dancing*] just one hundred and eighty rubles.

[*They pass into the ballroom*]

Yasha [*hums softly*]. "Oh, wilt thou understand the tumult in my soul?"

[*In the ballroom a figure in a gray top hat and checked trousers is jumping about and waving its arms; shouts:* "Bravo, Charlotta Ivanovna!"]

Dunyasha [*stopping to powder her face; to* Firs]. The young miss has ordered me to dance. There are so many gentlemen and not enough ladies. But dancing makes me dizzy, my heart begins to beat fast, Firs Nikolayevich. The Post Office Clerk said something to me just now that quite took my breath away.

[*Music stops*]

FIRS. What did he say?

DUNYASHA. "You're like a flower," he said.

YASHA [*yawns*]. What ignorance.

[*Exits*]

DUNYASHA. "Like a flower!" I'm such a delicate girl. I simply adore pretty speeches.

FIRS. You'll come to a bad end.

[*Enter* YEPIHODOV]

YEPIHODOV [*to* DUNYASHA]. You have no wish to see me, Avdotya Fyodorovna . . . as though I was some sort of insect. [*Sighs*] Ah, life!

DUNYASHA. What is it you want?

YEPIHODOV. Indubitably you may be right. [*Sighs*] But of course, if one looks at it from the point of view, if I may be allowed to say so, and apologizing for my frankness, you have completely reduced me to a state of mind. I know my fate. Every day some calamity befalls me, and I grew used to it long ago, so that I look upon my fate with a smile. You gave me your word, and though I—

DUNYASHA. Let's talk about it later, please. But just now leave me alone, I am daydreaming. [*Plays with a fan*]

YEPIHODOV. A misfortune befalls me every day; and if I may be allowed to say so, I merely smile, I even laugh.

[*Enter* VARYA]

VARYA [*to* YEPIHODOV]. Are you still here? What an impertinent fellow you are really! Run along, Dunyasha. [*To* YEPIHODOV] Either you're playing billiards and breaking a cue, or you're wandering about the drawing-room as though you were a guest.

YEPIHODOV. You cannot, permit me to remark, penalize me.

VARYA. I'm not penalizing you; I'm just telling you. You merely wander from place to place, and don't do your work. We keep you as a clerk, but Heaven knows what for.

YEPIHODOV [*offended*]. Whether I work or whether I walk, whether I eat or whether I play billiards, is a matter to be discussed only by persons of understanding and of mature years.

VARYA [*enraged*]. You dare say that to me—you dare? You mean to say I've no understanding? Get out of here at once! This minute!

YEPIHODOV [*scared*]. I beg you to express yourself delicately.

VARYA [*beside herself*]. Clear out this minute! Out with you! [YEPI-

HODOV *goes towards the door,* VARYA *following*] Two-and-Twenty
Troubles! Get out—don't let me set eyes on you!

> [*Exit* YEPIHODOV. *His voice is heard behind the door:* "I shall
> lodge a complaint against you!"]

VARYA.  Oh, you're coming back? [*She seizes the stick left near door
by* FIRS] Well, come then . . . come . . . I'll show you. . . . Ah,
you're coming? You're coming? . . . Come . . .

> [*Swings the stick just as* LOPAHIN *enters*]

LOPAHIN.  Thank you kindly.

VARYA [*angrily and mockingly*].  I'm sorry.

LOPAHIN.  It's nothing. Thank you kindly for your charming reception.

VARYA.  Don't mention it. [*Walks away, looks back and asks softly*]
I didn't hurt you, did I?

LOPAHIN.  Oh, no, not at all. I shall have a large bump, though.

> [*Voices from the ballroom:* "Lopahin is here! Lopahin!"]
> [*Enter* PISHCHIK]

PISHCHIK.  My eyes do see, my ears do hear! [*Kisses* LOPAHIN]

LOPAHIN.  You smell of cognac, my dear friend. And we've been
celebrating here, too.

> [*Enter* MME. RANEVSKAYA]

MME. RANEVSKAYA.  Is that you, Yermolay Alexeyevich? What kept
you so long? Where's Leonid?

LOPAHIN.  Leonid Andreyevich arrived with me. He's coming.

MME. RANEVSKAYA.  Well, what happened? Did the sale take place?
Speak!

LOPAHIN [*embarrassed, fearful of revealing his joy*].  The sale was
over at four o'clock. We missed the train—had to wait till half past
nine. [*Sighing heavily*] Ugh. I'm a little dizzy.

> [*Enter* GAYEV. *In his right hand he holds parcels, with his left he
> is wiping away his tears*]

MME. RANEVSKAYA.  Well, Leonid? What news? [*Impatiently, through
tears*] Be quick, for God's sake!

GAYEV [*not answering, simply waves his hand. Weeping, to* FIRS].
Here, take these; anchovies, Kerch herrings . . . I haven't eaten all
day. What I've been through! [*The click of billiard balls comes
through the open door. The expression changes; he no longer
weeps*] I'm terribly tired. Firs, help me change.

> [*Exits, followed by* FIRS]

PISHCHIK.  How about the sale? Tell us what happened.

MME. RANEVSKAYA.  Is the cherry orchard sold?

LOPAHIN.  Sold.

MME. RANEVSKAYA.  Who bought it?

LOPAHIN.  I bought it.

[*Pause.* MME. RANEVSKAYA *is overcome. She would fall to the floor, were it not for the chair and table near which she stands.* VARYA *takes the keys from her belt, flings them on the floor in the middle of the drawing-room and goes out*]

LOPAHIN.  I bought it. Wait a bit, ladies and gentlemen, please, my head is swimming, I can't talk. [*Laughs*] We got to the auction and Deriganov was there already. Leonid Andreyevich had only 15,000 and straight off Deriganov bid 30,000 over and above the mortgage. I saw how the land lay, got into the fight, bid 40,000. He bid 45,000. I bid fifty-five. He kept adding five thousands, I ten. Well . . . it came to an end. I bid ninety above the mortgage and the estate was knocked down to me. Now the cherry orchard's mine! Mine! [*Laughs uproariously*] Lord! God in Heaven! The cherry orchard's mine! Tell me that I'm drunk—out of my mind—that it's all a dream. [*Stamps his feet*] Don't laugh at me! If my father and my grandfather could rise from their graves and see all that has happened—how their Yermolay, who used to be flogged, their half-literate Yermolay, who used to run about barefoot in winter, how that very Yermolay has bought the most magnificent estate in the world. I bought the estate where my father and grandfather were slaves, where they weren't even allowed to enter the kitchen. I'm asleep—it's only a dream—I only imagine it. . . . It's the fruit of your imagination, wrapped in the darkness of the unknown! [*Picks up the keys, smiling genially*] She threw down the keys, wants to show she's no longer mistress here. [*Jingles keys*] Well, no matter. [*The band is heard tuning up*] Hey, musicians! Strike up! I want to hear you! Come, everybody, and see how Yermolay Lopahin will lay the ax to the cherry orchard and how the trees will fall to the ground. We will build summer cottages there, and our grandsons and great-grandsons will see a new life here. Music! Strike up!

[*The band starts to play.* MME. RANEVSKAYA *has sunk into a chair and is weeping bitterly*]

LOPAHIN [*reproachfully*].  Why, why didn't you listen to me? My dear friend, my poor friend, you can't bring it back now. [*Tearfully*]

Oh, if only this were over quickly! Oh, if only our wretched, disordered life were changed!

PISHCHIK [*takes him by the arm; sotto voce*]. She's crying. Let's go into the ballroom. Let her be alone. Come.

[*Takes his arm and leads him into the ballroom*]

LOPAHIN. What's the matter? Musicians, play so I can hear you! Let me have things the way I want them. [*Ironically*] Here comes the new master, the owner of the cherry orchard. [*Accidentally he trips over a little table, almost upsetting the candelabra*] I can pay for everything.

[*Exits with* PISHCHIK. MME. RANEVSKAYA, *alone, sits huddled up, weeping bitterly. Music plays softly. Enter* ANYA *and* TROFIMOV *quickly.* ANYA *goes to her mother and falls on her knees before her.* TROFIMOV *stands in the doorway*]

ANYA. Mamma, mamma, you're crying! Dear, kind, good mamma, my precious, I love you, I bless you! The cherry orchard is sold, it's gone, that's true, quite true. But don't cry, mamma, life is still before you, you still have your kind, pure heart. Let us go, let us go away from here, darling. We will plant a new orchard, even more luxuriant than this one. You will see it, you will understand, and like the sun at evening, joy—deep, tranquil joy—will sink into your soul, and you will smile, mamma. Come, darling, let us go.

## ACT IV

*Scene as in Act I. No window curtains or pictures, only a little furniture, piled up in a corner, as if for sale. A sense of emptiness. Near the outer door and at the back, suitcases, bundles, etc., are piled up. A door is open on the left and the voices of* VARYA *and* ANYA *are heard.* LOPAHIN *stands waiting.* YASHA *holds a tray with glasses full of champagne.* YEPIHODOV *in the anteroom is tying up a box. Behind the scene a hum of voices: peasants have come to say good-by. Voice of* GAYEV: "*Thanks, brothers, thank you.*"

YASHA. The country folk have come to say good-by. In my opinion, Yermolay Alexeyevich, they are kindly souls, but there's nothing in their heads.

[*The hum dies away. Enter* MME. RANEVSKAYA *and* GAYEV. *She is not crying, but is pale, her face twitches and she cannot speak*]

GAYEV. You gave them your purse, Luba. That won't do! That won't do!

MME. RANEVSKAYA. I couldn't help it! I couldn't!

[*They go out*]

LOPAHIN [*calls after them*]. Please, I beg you, have a glass at parting. I didn't think of bringing any champagne from town and at the station I could find only one bottle. Please, won't you? [*Pause*] What's the matter, ladies and gentlemen, don't you want any? [*Moves away from the door*] If I'd known, I wouldn't have bought it. Well, then I won't drink any, either. [YASHA *carefully sets the tray down on a chair*] At least you have a glass, Yasha.

YASHA. Here's to the travelers! And good luck to those that stay! [*Drinks*] This champagne isn't the real stuff, I can assure you.

LOPAHIN. Eight rubles a bottle. [*Pause*] It's devilishly cold here.

YASHA. They didn't light the stoves today—it wasn't worth it, since we're leaving. [*Laughs*]

LOPAHIN. Why are you laughing?

YASHA. It's just that I'm pleased.

LOPAHIN. It's October, yet it's as still and sunny as though it were summer. Good weather for building. [*Looks at his watch, and speaks off*] Bear in mind, ladies and gentlemen, the train goes in forty-seven minutes, so you ought to start for the station in twenty minutes. Better hurry up!

[*Enter* TROFIMOV *wearing an overcoat*]

TROFIMOV. I think it's time to start. The carriages are at the door. The devil only knows what's become of my rubbers; they've disappeared. [*Calling off*] Anya! My rubbers are gone. I can't find them.

LOPAHIN. I've got to go to Kharkov. I'll take the same train you do. I'll spend the winter in Kharkov. I've been hanging round here with you, till I'm worn out with loafing. I can't live without work—I don't know what to do with my hands, they dangle as if they didn't belong to me.

TROFIMOV. Well, we'll soon be gone, then you can go on with your useful labors again.

LOPAHIN. Have a glass.

TROFIMOV. No, I won't.

LOPAHIN. So you're going to Moscow now?

TROFIMOV.  Yes, I'll see them into town, and tomorrow I'll go on to Moscow.

LOPAHIN.  Well, I'll wager the professors aren't giving any lectures, they're waiting for you to come.

TROFIMOV.  That's none of your business.

LOPAHIN.  Just how many years have you been at the university?

TROFIMOV.  Can't you think of something new? Your joke's stale and flat. [*Looking for his rubbers*] We'll probably never see each other again, so allow me to give you a piece of advice at parting: don't wave your hands about! Get out of the habit. And another thing: building bungalows, figuring that summer residents will eventually become small farmers, figuring like that is just another form of waving your hands about. . . . Never mind, I love you anyway; you have fine, delicate fingers, like an artist; you have a fine, delicate soul.

LOPAHIN [*embracing him*].  Good-by, my dear fellow. Thank you for everything. Let me give you some money for the journey, if you need it.

TROFIMOV.  What for? I don't need it.

LOPAHIN.  But you haven't any.

TROFIMOV.  Yes, I have, thank you. I got some money for a translation—here it is in my pocket. [*Anxiously*] But where are my rubbers?

VARYA [*from the next room*].  Here! Take the nasty things. [*Flings a pair of rubbers onto the stage*]

TROFIMOV.  What are you so cross about, Varya? Hm . . . and these are not my rubbers.

LOPAHIN.  I sowed three thousand acres of poppies in the spring, and now I've made 40,000 on them, clear profit; and when my poppies were in bloom, what a picture it was! So, as I say, I made 40,000; and I am offering you a loan because I can afford it. Why turn up your nose at it? I'm a peasant—I speak bluntly.

TROFIMOV.  Your father was a peasant, mine was a druggist—that proves absolutely nothing whatever. [LOPAHIN *takes out his wallet*] Don't, put that away! If you were to offer me two hundred thousand I wouldn't take it. I'm a free man. And everything that all of you, rich and poor alike, value so highly and hold so dear, hasn't the slightest power over me. It's like so much fluff floating in the air. I can get on without you, I can pass you by, I'm strong and proud.

Mankind is moving towards the highest truth, towards the highest happiness possible on earth, and I am in the front ranks.

LOPAHIN. Will you get there?

TROFIMOV. I will. [*Pause*] I will get there, or I will show others the way to get there.

[*The sound of axes chopping down trees is heard in the distance*]

LOPAHIN. Well, good-by, my dear fellow. It's time to leave. We turn up our noses at one another, but life goes on just the same. When I'm working hard, without resting, my mind is easier, and it seems to me that I too know why I exist. But how many people are there in Russia, brother, who exist nobody knows why? Well, it doesn't matter. That's not what makes the wheels go round. They say Leonid Andreyevich has taken a position in the bank, 6,000 rubles a year. Only, of course, he won't stick to it, he's too lazy. . . .

ANYA [*in the doorway*]. Mamma begs you not to start cutting down the cherry trees until she's gone.

TROFIMOV. Really, you should have more tact!

[*Exits*]

LOPAHIN. Right away—right away! Those men. . . .

[*Exits*]

ANYA. Has Firs been taken to the hospital?

YASHA. I told them this morning. They must have taken him.

ANYA [*to YEPIHODOV who crosses the room*]. Yepihodov, please find out if Firs has been taken to the hospital.

YASHA [*offended*]. I told Yegor this morning. Why ask a dozen times?

YEPIHODOV. The aged Firs, in my definitive opinion, is beyond mending. It's time he was gathered to his fathers. And I can only envy him. [*Puts a suitcase down on a hat-box and crushes it*] There now, of course. I knew it!

[*Exits*]

YASHA [*mockingly*]. Two-and-Twenty Troubles!

VARYA [*through the door*]. Has Firs been taken to the hospital?

ANYA. Yes.

VARYA. Then why wasn't the note for the doctor taken too?

ANYA. Oh! Then someone must take it to him.

[*Exits*]

VARYA [*from adjoining room*]. Where's Yasha? Tell him his mother's come and wants to say good-by.

YASHA [*waves his hand*].   She tries my patience.

  [DUNYASHA *has been occupied with the luggage. Seeing* YASHA *alone, she goes up to him*]

DUNYASHA.   You might just give me one little look, Yasha. You're going away. . . . You're leaving me. . . . [*Weeps and throws herself on his neck*]

YASHA.   What's there to cry about? [*Drinks champagne*] In six days I shall be in Paris again. Tomorrow we get into an express train and off we go, that's the last you'll see of us. . . . I can scarcely believe it. *Vive la France!* It don't suit me here, I just can't live here. That's all there is to it. I'm fed up with the ignorance here, I've had enough of it. [*Drinks champagne*] What's there to cry about? Behave yourself properly, and you'll have no cause to cry.

DUNYASHA [*powders her face, looking in pocket mirror*].   Do send me a letter from Paris. You know I loved you, Yasha, how I loved you! I'm a delicate creature, Yasha.

YASHA.   Somebody's coming! [*Busies himself with the luggage; hums softly*]

  [*Enter* MME. RANEVSKAYA, GAYEV, ANYA, *and* CHARLOTTA]

GAYEV.   We ought to be leaving. We haven't much time. [*Looks at* YASHA] Who smells of herring?

MME. RANEVSKAYA.   In about ten minutes we should be getting into the carriages. [*Looks around the room*] Good-by, dear old home, good-by, grandfather. Winter will pass, spring will come, you will no longer be here, they will have torn you down. How much these walls have seen! [*Kisses* ANYA *warmly*] My treasure, how radiant you look! Your eyes are sparkling like diamonds. Are you glad? Very?

ANYA [*gaily*].   Very glad. A new life is beginning, mamma.

GAYEV.   Well, really, everything is all right now. Before the cherry orchard was sold, we all fretted and suffered; but afterwards, when the question was settled finally and irrevocably, we all calmed down, and even felt quite cheerful. I'm a bank employee now, a financier. The yellow ball in the side pocket! And anyhow, you are looking better, Luba, there's no doubt of that.

MME. RANEVSKAYA.   Yes, my nerves are better, that's true. [*She is handed her hat and coat*] I sleep well. Carry out my things, Yasha. It's time. [*To* ANYA] We shall soon see each other again, my little girl. I'm going to Paris, I'll live there on the money your great-aunt sent us to buy the estate with—long live Auntie! But that money won't last long.

ANYA. You'll come back soon, soon, mamma, won't you? Meanwhile I'll study, I'll pass my high school examination, and then I'll go to work and help you. We'll read all kinds of books together, mamma, won't we? [*Kisses her mother's hands*] We'll read in the autumn evenings, we'll read lots of books, and a new wonderful world will open up before us. [*Falls into a revery*] Mamma, do come back.

MME. RANEVSKAYA. I will come back, my precious.

>[*Embraces her daughter. Enter* LOPAHIN *and* CHARLOTTA *who is humming softly*]

GAYEV. Charlotta's happy: she's singing.

CHARLOTTA [*picks up a bundle and holds it like a baby in swaddling-clothes*]. Bye, baby, bye. [*A baby is heard crying* "Wah! Wah!"] Hush, hush, my pet, my little one. "Wah! Wah!" I'm so sorry for you! [*Throws the bundle down*] You will find me a position, won't you? I can't go on like this.

LOPAHIN. We'll find one for you, Charlotta Ivanovna, don't worry.

GAYEV. Everyone's leaving us. Varya's going away. We've suddenly become of no use.

CHARLOTTA. There's no place for me to live in town, I must go away. [*Hums*]

>[*Enter* PISHCHIK]

LOPAHIN. There's nature's masterpiece!

PISHCHIK [*gasping*]. Oh . . . let me get my breath . . . I'm in agony. . . . Esteemed friends . . . Give me a drink of water. . . .

GAYEV. Wants some money, I suppose. No, thank you . . . I'll keep out of harm's way.

>[*Exits*]

PISHCHIK. It's a long while since I've been to see you, most charming lady. [*To* LOPAHIN] So you are here . . . glad to see you, you intellectual giant. . . . There. . . . [*Gives* LOPAHIN *money*] Here's 400 rubles, and I still owe you 840.

LOPAHIN [*shrugging his shoulders in bewilderment*]. I must be dreaming. . . . Where did you get it?

PISHCHIK. Wait a minute. . . . It's hot. . . . A most extraordinary event! Some Englishmen came to my place and found some sort of white clay on my land. . . . [*To* MME. RANEVSKAYA] And 400 for you . . . most lovely . . . most wonderful. . . . [*Hands her the money*] The rest later. [*Drinks water*] A young man in the train was telling me just now that a great philosopher recommends jumping off roofs. "Jump!" says he; "that's the long and the short of it!" [*In amazement*] Just imagine! Some more water!

LOPAHIN. What Englishmen?

PISHCHIK. I leased them the tract with the clay on it for twenty-four years. . . . And now, forgive me, I can't stay. . . . I must be dashing on. . . . I'm going over to Znoikov . . . to Kardamanov . . . I owe them all money. . . . [*Drinks water*] Good-by, everybody . . . I'll look in on Thursday. . . .

MME. RANEVSKAYA. We're just moving into town; and tomorrow I go abroad.

PISHCHIK [*upset*]. What? Why into town? That's why the furniture is like that . . . and the suitcases. . . . Well, never mind! [*Through tears*] Never mind. . . . Men of colossal intellect, these Englishmen. . . . Never mind. . . . Be happy. God will come to your help. . . . Never mind. . . . Everything in this world comes to an end. [*Kisses* MME. RANEVSKAYA's *hand*] If the rumor reaches you that it's all up with me, remember this old . . . horse, and say: Once there lived a certain . . . Simeonov-Pishchik . . . the kingdom of Heaven be his. . . . Glorious weather! . . . Yes. . . . [*Exits, in great confusion, but at once returns and says in the doorway*] My daughter Dashenka sends her regards.

[*Exit*]

MME. RANEVSKAYA. Now we can go. I leave with two cares weighing on me. The first is poor old Firs. [*Glancing at her watch*] We still have about five minutes.

ANYA. Mamma, Firs has already been taken to the hospital. Yasha sent him there this morning.

MME. RANEVSKAYA. My other worry is Varya. She's used to getting up early and working; and now, with no work to do, she is like a fish out of water. She has grown thin and pale, and keeps crying, poor soul. [*Pause*] You know this very well, Yermolay Alexeyevich; I dreamed of seeing her married to you, and it looked as though that's how it would be. [*Whispers to* ANYA, *who nods to* CHARLOTTA *and both go out*] She loves you. You find her attractive. I don't know, I don't know why it is you seem to avoid each other; I can't understand it.

LOPAHIN. To tell you the truth, I don't understand it myself. It's all a puzzle. If there's still time, I'm ready now, at once. Let's settle it straight off, and have done with it! Without you, I feel I'll never be able to propose.

MME. RANEVSKAYA. That's splendid. After all, it will only take a minute. I'll call her at once. . . .

LOPAHIN. And luckily, here's champagne too. [*Looks at the glasses*] Empty! Somebody's drunk it all. [YASHA *coughs*] That's what you might call guzzling. . . .

MME. RANEVSKAYA [*animatedly*]. Excellent! We'll go and leave you alone. Yasha, *allez!* I'll call her. [*At the door*] Varya, leave everything and come here. Come!

[*Exits with* YASHA]

LOPAHIN [*looking at his watch*]. Yes. . . .
[*Pause. Behind the door, smothered laughter and whispering; at last, enter* VARYA]

VARYA [*looking over the luggage in leisurely fashion*]. Strange, I can't find it. . . .

LOPAHIN. What are you looking for?

VARYA. Packed it myself, and I don't remember. . . .

[*Pause*]

LOPAHIN. Where are you going now, Varya?

VARYA. I? To the Ragulins'. I've arranged to take charge there—as housekeeper, if you like.

LOPAHIN. At Yashnevo? About fifty miles from here. [*Pause*] Well, life in this house is ended!

VARYA [*examining luggage*]. Where is it? Perhaps I put it in the chest. Yes, life in this house is ended. . . . There will be no more of it.

LOPAHIN. And I'm just off to Kharkov—by this next train. I've a lot to do there. I'm leaving Yepihodov here. . . . I've taken him on.

VARYA. Oh!

LOPAHIN. Last year at this time it was snowing, if you remember, but now it's sunny and there's no wind. It's cold, though. . . . It must be three below.

VARYA. I didn't look. [*Pause*] And besides, our thermometer's broken.
[*Pause. Voice from the yard:* "Yermolay Alexeyevich!"]

LOPAHIN [*as if he had been waiting for the call*]. This minute!
[*Exits quickly.* VARYA *sits on the floor and sobs quietly, her head on a bundle of clothes. Enter* MME. RANEVSKAYA *cautiously*]

Mme. Ranevskaya. Well? [*Pause*] We must be going.

Varya [*wiping her eyes*]. Yes, it's time, mamma dear. I'll be able to get to the Ragulins' today, if only we don't miss the train.

Mme. Ranevskaya [*at the door*]. Anya, put your things on.

[*Enter* Anya, Gayev, Charlotta. Gayev *wears a heavy overcoat with a hood. Enter servants and coachmen.* Yepihodov *bustles about the luggage*]

Mme. Ranevskaya. Now we can start on our journey.

Anya [*joyfully*]. On our journey!

Gayev. My friends, my dear, cherished friends, leaving this house forever, can I be silent? Can I at leave-taking refrain from giving utterance to those emotions that now fill my being?

Anya [*imploringly*]. Uncle!

Varya. Uncle, uncle dear, don't.

Gayev [*forlornly*]. I'll bank the yellow in the side pocket. . . . I'll be silent. . . .

[*Enter* Trofimov, *then* Lopahin]

Trofimov. Well, ladies and gentlemen, it's time to leave.

Lopahin. Yepihodov, my coat.

Mme. Ranevskaya. I'll sit down just a minute. It seems as though I'd never before seen what the walls of this house were like, the ceilings, and now I look at them hungrily, with such tender affection.

Gayev. I remember when I was six years old sitting on that window sill on Whitsunday, watching my father going to church.

Mme. Ranevskaya. Has everything been taken?

Lopahin. I think so. [*Putting on his overcoat*] Yepihodov, see that everything's in order.

Yepihodov [*in a husky voice*]. You needn't worry, Yermolay Alexeyevich.

Lopahin. What's the matter with your voice?

Yepihodov. I just had a drink of water. I must have swallowed something.

Yasha [*contemptuously*]. What ignorance!

Mme. Ranevskaya. When we're gone, not a soul will be left here.

Lopahin. Until the spring.

[Varya *pulls an umbrella out of a bundle, as though about to hit someone with it.* Lopahin *pretends to be frightened*]

Varya. Come, come, I had no such idea!

TROFIMOV. Ladies and gentlemen, let's get into the carriages—it's time. The train will be in directly.

VARYA. Petya, there they are, your rubbers, by that trunk. [*Tearfully*] And what dirty old things they are!

TROFIMOV [*puts on rubbers*]. Let's go, ladies and gentlemen.

GAYEV [*greatly upset, afraid of breaking down*]. The train . . . the station. . . . Three cushions in the side pocket, I'll bank this one in the corner. . . .

MME. RANEVSKAYA. Let's go.

LOPAHIN. Are we all here? No one in there? [*Locks the side door on the left*] There are some things stored here, better lock up. Let us go!

ANYA. Good-by, old house! Good-by, old life!

TROFIMOV. Hail to you, new life!

[*Exit with* ANYA. VARYA *looks round the room and goes out slowly.* YASHA *and* CHARLOTTA *with her dog go out*]

LOPAHIN. And so, until the spring. Go along, friends. . . . 'Bye-'bye!
[*Exits*]

[MME. RANEVSKAYA *and* GAYEV *remain alone. As thought they had been waiting for this, they throw themselves on each other's necks, and break into subdued, restrained sobs, afraid of being overheard*]

GAYEV [*in despair*]. My sister! My sister!

MME. RANEVSKAYA. Oh, my orchard—my dear, sweet, beautiful orchard! My life, my youth, my happiness—good-by! Good-by!

[*Voice of* ANYA, *gay and summoning:* "Mamma!" *Voice of* TROFIMOV, *gay and excited:* "Halloo!"]

MME. RANEVSKAYA. One last look at the walls, at the windows. . . . Our poor mother loved to walk about this room. . . .

GAYEV. My sister, my sister!

[*Voice of* ANYA: "Mamma!" *Voice of* TROFIMOV: "Halloo!"]

MME. RANEVSKAYA. We're coming.

[*They go out. The stage is empty. The sound of doors being locked, of carriages driving away. Then silence. In the stillness is heard the muffled sound of the ax striking a tree, a mournful, lonely sound.*

[*Footsteps are heard.* FIRS *appears in the doorway on the right. He is dressed as usual in a jacket and white waistcoat and wears slippers. He is ill.*]

FIRS [*goes to the door, tries the handle*]. Locked! They've gone. . . .
[*Sits down on the sofa*] They've forgotten me. . . . Never mind.
. . . I'll sit here a bit. . . . I'll wager Leonid Andreyevich hasn't put
his fur coat on, he's gone off in his light overcoat. . . . [*Sighs
anxiously*] I didn't keep an eye on him. . . . Ah, when they're
young, they're green. . . . [*Mumbles something indistinguishable*]
Life has gone by as if I had never lived. [*Lies down*] I'll lie down a
while. . . . There's no strength left in you, old fellow; nothing is
left, nothing. Ah, you addlehead!

[*Lies motionless. A distant sound is heard coming from the sky
as it were, the sound of a snapping string mournfully dying away.
All is still again, and nothing is heard but the strokes of the ax
against a tree far away in the orchard*]

# Poetry

William Shakespeare · John Donne

George Herbert · Henry Vaughan

Andrew Marvel · William Wordsworth

John Keats · Walt Whitman

Matthew Arnold · Emily Dickinson

A. E. Housman · William Butler Yeats

Robert Frost · T. S. Eliot

Archibald MacLeish · W. H. Auden

Dylan Thomas · Theodore Roethke

# WILLIAM SHAKESPEARE

## Sonnets

### XVIII

Shall I compare thee to a summer's day?
Thou art more lovely and more temperate:
Rough winds do shake the darling buds of May,
And summer's lease hath all too short a date:
Sometime too hot the eye of heaven shines,      5
And often is his gold complexion dimm'd;
And every fair from fair sometime declines,
By chance, or nature's changing course, untrimm'd;
But thy eternal summer shall not fade
Nor lose possession of that fair thou ow'st,      10
Nor shall Death brag thou wand'rest in his shade
When in eternal lines[1] to time thou grow'st:
    So long as men can breathe or eyes can see,
    So long lives this, and this gives life to thee.

### XXX

When to the sessions of sweet silent thought
I summon up remembrance of things past,
I sigh the lack of many a thing I sought
And with old woes new wail my dear time's waste;
Then can I drown an eye unus'd to flow,      5
For precious friends hid in death's dateless night,
And weep afresh love's long since cancell'd woe,
And moan th' expense of many a vanish'd sight;
Then can I grieve at grievances foregone,
And heavily from woe to woe tell o'er      10
The sad account of fore-bemoaned moan,

[1] *eternal lines:* these verses.

Which I new pay as if not paid before:
> But if the while I think on thee, dear friend,
> All losses are restor'd and sorrows end.


## LXXIII

That time of year thou mayst in me behold
When yellow leaves, or none, or few, do hang
Upon those boughs which shake against the cold,
Bare ruin'd choirs, where late the sweet birds sang:
In me thou see'st the twilight of such day                 5
As after sunset fadeth in the west;
Which by and by black night doth take away,
Death's second self,[2] that seals up all in rest:
In me thou see'st the glowing of such fire,
That on the ashes of his[3] youth doth lie,               10
As the death-bed whereon it must expire,
Consum'd with that which it was nourish'd by.
> This thou perceiv'st, which makes thy love more strong,
> To love that well which thou must leave ere long.


## CXVI

Let me not to the marriage of true minds
Admit impediments. Love is not love
Which alters when it alteration finds,
Or bends with the remover[4] to remove:
O no! it is an ever fixed mark,[5]                         5
That looks on tempests and is never shaken;
It is the star to every wandering bark,
Whose worth's unknown, although his height be taken.
Love's not Time's fool,[6] though rosy lips and cheeks
Within his bending sickle's compass come;                 10

[2] *Death's second self:*  sleep.
[3] *his:*  its.
[4] *bends with the remover:*  changes with the plotting of another person.
[5] *mark:*  beacon.
[6] *fool:*  plaything.

Love alters not with his brief hours and weeks,
But bears it out even to the edge of doom:
    If this be error and upon me proved,
    I never writ, nor no man ever loved.

# JOHN DONNE

## Song

Go and catch a falling star,
   Get with child a mandrake[1] root,
Tell me where all past years are,
   Or who cleft the devil's foot,
Teach me to hear mermaids singing,         5
   Or to keep off envy's stinging,
       And find
       What wind
Serves to advance an honest mind.

If thou be'st born to strange sights,       10
   Things invisible to see,
Ride ten thousand days and nights,
   Till age snow white hairs on thee,
Thou, when thou return'st, wilt tell me
   All strange wonders that befell thee,     15
       And swear
       Nowhere
Lives a woman true, and fair.

If thou find'st one, let me know;
   Such a pilgrimage were sweet.       20
Yet do not; I would not go,

[1] *mandrake:* an herb which, when eaten, supposedly promotes conception: its forked root resembles the human shape.

Though at next door we might meet.
Though she were true when you met her,
And last till you write your letter,
     Yet she                                                                    25
     Will be
False, ere I come, to two or three.

# The Sun Rising

    Busy old fool, unruly sun,
      Why dost thou thus
Through windows and through curtains call on us?
Must to thy motions lovers' seasons run?
    Saucy pedantic wretch, go chide                                        5
    Late schoolboys and sour prentices,
  Go tell court-huntsmen that the king will ride,
  Call country ants to harvest offices;
Love, all alike, no season knows, nor clime,
Nor hours, days, months, which are the rags of time.                       10

    Thy beams, so reverend, and strong
      Why shouldst thou think?
I could eclipse and cloud them with a wink,
But that I would not lose her sight so long;
    If her eyes have not blinded thine,                                 15
    Look, and tomorrow late tell me
  Whether both the Indias of spice and mine[2]
  Be where thou left'st them, or lie here with me.
Ask for those kings whom thou saw'st yesterday,
And thou shalt hear, all here in one bed lay.                              20

    She is all states, and all princes I;
      Nothing else is.
Princes do but play us; compared to this,
All honor's mimic, all wealth alchemy.

[2] *mine:*   mines of precious stones.

Thou, sun, art half as happy as we,                    25
   In that the world's contracted thus;
  Thine age asks ease, and since thy duties be
  To warm the world, that's done in warming us.
Shine here to us, and thou art everywhere;
This bed thy center is, these walls thy sphere.        30

# Holy Sonnets

## X

Death, be not proud, though some have callèd thee
Mighty and dreadful, for thou art not so;
For those whom thou think'st thou dost overthrow
Die not, poor Death, nor yet canst thou kill me.
From rest and sleep, which but thy pictures be,        5
Much pleasure, then from thee much more must flow,
And soonest our best men with thee do go,
Rest of their bones and souls' delivery.
Thou art slave to fate, chance, kings, and desperate men,
And dost with poison, war, and sickness dwell,         10
And poppy, or charms can make us sleep as well,
And better than thy stroke; why swell'st thou then?
One short sleep past, we wake eternally,
And Death shall be no more; Death, thou shalt die.

## XIV

Batter my heart, three-personed God; for You
As yet but knock, breathe, shine, and seek to mend;
That I may rise, and stand, o'erthrow me, and bend
Your force, to break, blow, burn, and make me new.
I, like an usurped town to another due,                5
Labor to admit You, but oh! to no end;
Reason, Your viceroy in me, me should defend,
But is captived and proves weak or untrue.
Yet dearly I love You, and would be lovèd fain,
But am betrothed unto Your enemy.                      10

Divorce me, untie, or break that knot again,
Take me to You, imprison me, for I
Except You enthrall me, never shall be free;
Nor ever chaste, except You ravish me.

# GEORGE HERBERT

## The Pulley[1]

When God at first made man,
Having a glass of blessings standing by,
"Let us," said He, "pour on him all we can.
Let the world's riches, which dispersèd lie,
    Contract into a span."                                    5

So strength first made a way;
Then beauty flowed, then wisdom, honor, pleasure.
When almost all was out, God made a stay,
Perceiving that, alone of all His treasure,
    Rest in the bottom lay.                                    10

"For if I should," said He,
"Bestow this jewel also on My creature,
He would adore My gifts instead of Me
And rest in nature, not the God of nature;
    So both should losers be.                                    15

"Yet let him keep the rest,
But keep them with repining restlessness.
Let him be rich and weary, that at last,
If goodness lead him not, yet weariness
    May toss him to My breast."                                    20

[1] Emblem of restlessness.

# HENRY VAUGHAN

# The World

I saw eternity the other night
Like a great ring[1] of pure and endless light,
   All calm as it was bright;
And round beneath it, time, in hours, days, years,
   Driven by the spheres,                                                    5
Like a vast shadow moved, in which the world
   And all her train were hurled.
The doting lover in his quaintest strain
   Did there complain;
Near him, his lute, his fancy, and his flights,                                   10
   Wit's sour delights,
With gloves and knots,[2] the silly snares of pleasure,
   Yet his dear treasure,
All scattered lay, while he his eyes did pour
   Upon a flower.                                                             15

The darksome statesman, hung with weights and woe,
Like a thick midnight fog, moved there so slow
   He did not stay nor go;
Condemning thoughts, like mad eclipses, scowl
   Upon his soul,                                                             20
And crowds of crying witnesses without
   Pursued him with one shout.
Yet digged the mole, and lest his ways be found,
   Worked under ground,
Where he did clutch his prey. But one did see                                     25
   That policy:
Churches and altars fed him; perjuries

---

[1] *ring:* *primum mobile* in Ptolemaic cosmology.
[2] *knots:* love knots.

Were gnats and flies;[3]
It rained about him blood and tears; but he
   Drank them as free.[4]                                              30

The fearful miser on a heap of rust
Sat pining all his life there, did scarce trust
   His own hands with the dust;
Yet would not place one piece[5] above, but lives
   In fear of thieves.                                              35
Thousands there were as frantic as himself,
   And hugged each one his pelf:
The downright epicure placed heaven in sense,
   And scorned pretense;
While others, slipped into a wide excess,                          40
   Said little less;
The weaker sort, slight trivial wares enslave,
   Who think them brave;[6]
And poor, despisèd Truth sat counting by[7]
   Their victory.                                                  45

Yet some, who all this while did weep and sing,
And sing and weep, soared up into the ring;
   But most would use no wing.
"O fools!" said I, "thus to prefer dark night
   Before true light!                                              50
To live in grots and caves, and hate the day
   Because it shows the way,
The way which from this dead and dark abode
   Leads up to God;
A way where you might tread the sun and be                         55
   More bright than he!"
But, as I did their madness so discuss,
   One whispered thus:
"This ring[8] the Bridegroom did for none provide,
   But for His bride."                                             60

---

[3] *gnats and flies:* i.e., of little importance.
[4] *free:* freely.
[5] *piece:* coin.
[6] *brave:* costly.
[7] *counting by:* observing.
[8] *Bridegroom . . . bride:* see *Revelation* 21:9.

# ANDREW MARVELL

## To His Coy Mistress

Had we but world enough, and time,
This coyness, Lady, were no crime.
We would sit down, and think which way
To walk, and pass our long love's day.
Thou by the Indian Ganges' side                                5
Shouldst rubies find; I by the tide
Of Humber[1] would complain. I would
Love you ten years before the Flood,
And you should, if you please, refuse
Till the conversion of the Jews.                               10
My vegetable[2] love should grow
Vaster than empires and more slow;
An hundred years should go to praise
Thine eyes, and on thy forehead gaze;
Two hundred to adore each breast,                              15
But thirty thousand to the rest;
An age at least to every part,
And the last age should show your heart.
For, Lady, you deserve this state,
Nor would I love at lower rate.                                20
    But at my back I always hear
Time's wingèd chariot hurrying near;
And yonder all before us lie
Deserts of vast eternity.
Thy beauty shall no more be found,                             25
Nor, in thy marble vault, shall sound
My echoing song; then worms shall try
That long-preserved virginity,

[1] *Humber:* river in England.
[2] *vegetable:* growing.

And your quaint honor turn to dust,
And into ashes all my lust:                    30
The grave's a fine and private place,
But none, I think, do there embrace.
   Now therefore, while the youthful hue
Sits on thy skin like morning lew,[3]
And while thy willing soul transpires[4]        35
At every pore with instant fires,
Now let us sport us while we may,
And now, like amorous birds of prey,
Rather at once our time devour
Than languish in his slow-chapped[5] power.    40
Let us roll all our strength and all
Our sweetness up into one ball,
And tear our pleasures with rough strife
Thorough the iron gates of life;
Thus, though we cannot make our sun        45
Stand still, yet we will make him run.

[3] *lew:*    warmth.
[4] *transpires:*    emerges.
[5] *chapped:*    jawed.

# WILLIAM WORDSWORTH

# Tintern Abbey[1]

Five years have past; five summers, with the length
Of five long winters! and again I hear
These waters, rolling from their mountain-springs
With a soft inland murmur.—Once again
Do I behold these steep and lofty cliffs,         5
That on a wild secluded scene impress
Thoughts of more deep seclusion; and connect

[1] A beautiful ruin by the river Wye in Southwest England.

The landscape with the quiet of the sky.
The day is come when I again repose
Here, under this dark sycamore, and view        10
These plots of cottage-ground, these orchard-tufts,
Which at this season, with their unripe fruits,
Are clad in one green hue, and lose themselves
'Mid groves and copses. Once again I see
These hedge-rows, hardly hedge-rows, little lines        15
Of sportive wood run wild: these pastoral farms,
Green to the very door; and wreaths of smoke
Sent up, in silence, from among the trees!
With some uncertain notice, as might seem
Of vagrant dwellers in the houseless woods,        20
Or of some hermit's cave, where by his fire
The hermit sits alone.
                     These beauteous forms,
Through a long absence, have not been to me
As is a landscape to blind man's eye:        25
But oft, in lonely rooms, and 'mid the din
Of towns and cities, I have owed to them
In hours of weariness, sensations sweet,
Felt in the blood, and felt along the heart;
And passing even into my purer mind,        30
With tranquil restoration:—feelings too
Of unremembered pleasure: such, perhaps,
As have no slight or trivial influence
On that best portion of a good man's life,
His little, nameless, unremembered acts        35
Of kindness and of love. Nor less, I trust,
To them I may have owed another gift,
Of aspect more sublime; that blessed mood,
In which the burthen of the mystery,
In which the heavy and the weary weight        40
Of all this unintelligible world,
Is lightened;—that serene and blessed mood,
In which the affections gently lead us on,—
Until, the breath of this corporeal frame
And even the motion of our human blood        45
Almost suspended, we are laid asleep

In body, and become a living soul:
While with an eye made quiet by the power
Of harmony, and the deep power of joy,
We see into the life of things.                              50
                         If this
Be but a vain belief, yet, oh! how oft—
In darkness and amid the many shapes
Of joyless daylight; when the fretful stir
Unprofitable, and the fever of the world,                   55
Have hung upon the beatings of my heart—
How oft, in spirit, have I turned to thee,
O sylvan Wye! thou wander thro' the woods,
How often has my spirit turned to thee!

  And now, with gleams of half-extinguished thought,        60
With many recognitions dim and faint,
And somewhat of a sad perplexity,
The picture of the mind revives again:
While here I stand, not only with the sense
Of present pleasure, but with pleasing thoughts             65
That in this moment there is life and food
For future years. And so I dare to hope,
Though changed, no doubt, from what I was when first
I came among these hills; when like a roe
I bounded o'er the mountains, by the sides                  70
Of the deep rivers, and the lonely streams,
Wherever nature led: more like a man
Flying from something that he dreads, than one
Who sought the thing he loved. For nature then
(The coarser pleasures of my boyish days,                   75
And their glad animal movements all gone by)
To me was all in all.—I cannot paint
What then I was. The sounding cataract
Haunted me like a passion: the tall rock,
The mountain, and the deep and gloomy wood,                 80
Their colours and their forms, were then to me
An appetite; a feeling and a love,
That had no need of a remoter charm,
By thought supplied, nor any interest

Unborrowed from the eye.—That time is past,     85
And all its aching joys are now no more,
And all its dizzy raptures. Not for this
Faint I, nor mourn nor murmur; other gifts
Have followed; for such loss, I would believe,
Abundant recompense. For I have learned     90
To look on nature, not as in the hour
Of thoughtless youth; but hearing oftentimes
The still, sad music of humanity,
Nor harsh nor grating, though of ample power
To chasten and subdue. And I have felt     95
A presence that disturbs me with the joy
Of elevated thoughts; a sense sublime
Of something far more deeply interfused,
Whose dwelling is the light of setting suns,
And the round ocean and the living air,     100
And the blue sky, and in the mind of man:
A motion and a spirit, that impels
All thinking things, all objects of all thought,
And rolls through all things. Therefore am I still
A lover of the meadows and the woods,     105
And mountains; and of all that we behold
From this green earth; of all the mighty world
Of eye, and ear,—both what they half create,
And what perceive; well pleased to recognise
In nature and the language of the sense,     110
The anchor of my purest thoughts, the nurse,
The guide, the guardian of my heart, and soul
Of all my moral being.
                    Nor perchance,
If I were not thus taught, should I the more     115
Suffer my genial spirits to decay:
For thou art with me here upon the banks
Of this fair river; thou my dearest friend,
My dear, dear friend; and in thy voice I catch
The language of my former heart, and read     120
My former pleasures in the shooting lights
Of thy wild eyes. Oh! yet a little while
May I behold in thee what I was once,

My dear, dear sister! and this prayer I make,
Knowing that Nature never did betray                          125
The heart that loved her; 'tis her privilege,
Through all the years of this our life, to lead
From joy to joy: for she can so inform
The mind that is within us, so impress
With quietness and beauty, and so feed                        130
With lofty thoughts, that neither evil tongues,
Rash judgments, nor the sneers of selfish men,
Nor greetings where no kindness is, nor all
The dreary intercourse of daily life,
Shall e'er prevail against us, or disturb                     135
Our cheerful faith, that all which we behold
Is full of blessings. Therefore let the moon
Shine on thee in thy solitary walk;
And let the misty mountain-winds be free
To blow against thee: and, in after years,                    140
When these wild ecstasies shall be matured
Into a sober pleasure; when thy mind
Shall be a mansion for all lovely forms,
Thy memory be as a dwelling-place
For all sweet sounds and harmonies; oh! then,                 145
If solitude, or fear, or pain, or grief,
Should be thy portion, with what healing thoughts
Of tender joy wilt thou remember me,
And these my exhortations! Nor, perchance—
If I should be where I no more can hear                        150
Thy voice, nor catch from thy wild eyes these gleams
Of past existence—wilt thou then forget
That on the banks of this delightful stream
We stood together; and that I, so long
A worshipper of Nature, hither came                            155
Unwearied in that service: rather say
With warmer love—oh! with far deeper zeal
Of holier love. Nor wilt thou then forget,
That after many wanderings, many years
Of absence, these steep woods and lofty cliffs,               160
And this green pastoral landscape, were to me
More dear, both for themselves and for thy sake!

# Composed upon Westminster Bridge, September 3, 1803

Earth has not anything to show more fair:
Dull would he be of soul who could pass by
A sight so touching in its majesty:
This City now doth, like a garment, wear
The beauty of the morning; silent, bare,     5
Ships, towers, domes, theatres, and temples lie
Open unto the fields, and to the sky;
All bright and glittering in the smokeless air.
Never did sun more beautifully steep
In his first splendour, valley, rock, or hill;     10
Ne'er saw I, never felt, a calm so deep!
The river glideth at his own sweet will:
Dear God! the very houses seem asleep;
And all that mighty heart is lying still!

# It Is a Beauteous Evening, Calm and Free

It is a beauteous evening, calm and free,
The holy time is quiet as a Nun
Breathless with adoration; the broad sun
Is sinking down in its tranquillity;
The gentleness of heaven broods o'er the Sea:     5
Listen! the mighty Being is awake,
And doth with his eternal motion make
A sound like thunder—everlastingly.
Dear Child![2] dear Girl; that walkest with me here,[3]
If thou appear untouched by solemn thought,     10
Thy nature is not therefore less divine:
Thou liest in Abraham's bosom all the year;
And worship'st at the temple's inner shrine,
God being with thee when we know it not.

[2] *Dear Child:* Wordsworth's daughter.
[3] *here:* Calais Beach.

# London, 1802

Milton! thou shouldst be living at this hour:
England hath need of thee: she is a fen
Of stagnant waters: altar, sword, and pen,
Fireside, the heroic wealth of hall and bower,
Have forfeited their ancient English dower          5
Of inward happiness. We are selfish men;
Oh! raise us up, return to us again;
And give us manners, virtue, freedom, power.
Thy soul was like a star, and dwelt apart;
Thou hadst a voice whose sound was like the sea:     10
Pure as the naked heavens, majestic, free,
So didst thou travel on life's common way,
In cheerful godliness; and yet thy heart
The lowliest duties on herself did lay.

# The World Is Too Much With Us;
# Late and Soon

The world is too much with us; late and soon,
Getting and spending, we lay waste our powers:
Little we see in Nature that is ours;
We have given our hearts away, a sordid boon!
This sea that bares her bosom to the moon;           5
The winds that will be howling at all hours,
And are up-gathered now like sleeping flowers;
For this, for everything, we are out of tune;
It moves us not.—Great God! I'd rather be
A Pagan suckled in a creed outworn;                  10
So might I, standing on this pleasant lea,
Have glimpses that would make me less forlorn;
Have sight of Proteus rising from the sea;
Or hear old Triton blow his wreathèd horn.

# JOHN KEATS

## On First Looking into Chapman's[1] Homer

Much have I travelled in the realms of gold,
And many goodly states and kingdoms seen;
Round many western islands have I been
Which bards in fealty to Apollo hold.
Oft of one wide expanse had I been told                     5
That deep-browed Homer ruled as his demesne;[2]
Yet did I never breathe its pure serene
Till I heard Chapman speak out loud and bold:
Then felt I like some watcher of the skies
When a new planet swims into his ken;                      10
Or like stout Cortez[3] when with eagle eyes
He stared at the Pacific—and all his men
Looked at each other with a wild surmise—
Silent, upon a peak in Darien.[4]

## Ode on Melancholy

No, no! go not to Lethe,[5] neither twist
   Wolf's-bane,[6] tight-rooted, for its poisonous wine;
Nor suffer thy pale forehead to be kiss'd
   By nightshade,[7] ruby grape of Proserpine;
Make not your rosary of yew-berries,[8]                     5

[1] George Chapman, Elizabethan translator of Homer.
[2] *demesne:*  domain.
[3] Balboa, not Cortez, discovered the Pacific in 1513.
[4] *Darien:*  Panama.
[5] *Lethe:*  river of forgetfulness.
[6] *Wolf's-bane:*  a poisonous plant.
[7] *nightshade:*  a poisonous plant.
[8] *yew:*  a tree associated with mourning.

Nor let the beetle,[9] nor the death-moth[10] be
    Your mournful Psyche,[11] nor the downy owl
A partner in your sorrow's mysteries;
    For shade to shade will come too drowsily,
        And drown the wakeful anguish of the soul.      10

But when the melancholy fit shall fall
    Sudden from heaven like a weeping cloud,
That fosters the droop-headed flowers all,
    And hides the green hill in an April shroud;
Then glut thy sorrow on a morning rose,      15
    Or on the rainbow of the salt sand-wave,
        Or on the wealth of globèd peonies;

Or if thy mistress some rich anger shows,
    Emprison her soft hand, and let her rave,
        And feed deep, deep upon her peerless eyes.      20
She dwells with Beauty—Beauty that must die;
    And Joy, whose hand is ever at his lips
Bidding adieu; and aching Pleasure nigh,
    Turning to poison while the bee-mouth sips:
Ay, in the very temple of Delight      25
    Veiled Melancholy has her sovran shrine,
        Though seen of none save him whose strenuous tongue
Can burst Joy's grape against his palate fine;
His soul shall taste the sadness of her might,
        And be among her cloudy trophies hung.      30

# Ode on a Grecian Urn

Thou still unravished bride of quietness,
    Thou foster-child of silence and slow time,
Sylvan historian, who canst thus express
    A flowery tale more sweetly than our rhyme:

[9] *beetle:* In Egypt, a symbol of resurrection.
[10] *death-moth:* a moth whose markings resemble a human skull.
[11] *Psyche:* soul, symbolized by the butterfly.

What leaf-fringed legend haunts about thy shape          5
  Of deities or mortals, or of both,
    In Tempe or the dales of Arcady?
    What men or gods are these? What maidens loth?
What mad pursuit? What struggle to escape?
    What pipes and timbrels? What wild ecstasy?          10

Heard melodies are sweet, but those unheard
  Are sweeter; therefore, ye soft pipes, play on;
Not to the sensual ear, but, more endeared,
  Pipe to the spirit ditties of no tone:
Fair youth, beneath the trees, thou canst not leave          15
  Thy song, nor ever can those trees be bare;
    Bold Lover, never, never canst thou kiss,
Though winning near the goal—yet, do not grieve;
    She cannot fade, though thou hast not thy bliss,
  For ever wilt thou love, and she be fair!          20

Ah, happy, happy boughs! that cannot shed
  Your leaves, nor ever bid the Spring adieu;
And, happy melodist, unwearièd,
  For ever piping songs for ever new;
More happy love! more happy, happy love!          25
  For ever warm and still to be enjoyed,
    For ever panting, and for ever young;
All breathing human passion far above,
  That leaves a heart high-sorrowful and cloyed,
    A burning forehead, and a parching tongue.          30

Who are these coming to the sacrifice?
  To what green altar, O mysterious priest,
Lead'st thou that heifer lowing at the skies,
  And all her silken flanks with garlands drest?
What little town by river or sea shore,          35
  Or mountain-built with peaceful citadel,
    Is emptied of this folk, this pious morn?
And, little town, thy streets for evermore
  Will silent be; and not a soul to tell
    Why thou art desolate, can e'er return.          40

O Attic shape! Fair attitude! with brede[12]
Of marble men and maidens overwrought,
With forest branches and the trodden weed;
    Thou, silent form, dost tease us out of thought
As doth eternity: Cold Pastoral!                   45
    When old age shall this generation waste,
      Thou shalt remain, in midst of other woe
Than ours, a friend to man, to whom thou say'st,
Beauty is truth, truth beauty—that is all
    Ye know on earth, and all ye need to know.     50

# Ode to a Nightingale

My heart aches, and a drowsy numbness pains
    My sense, as though of hemlock[13] I had drunk,
Or emptied some dull opiate to the drains
    One minute past, and Lethe-wards[14] had sunk:
'Tis not through envy of thy happy lot,            5
    But being too happy in thine happiness,—
      That thou, light-wingèd Dryad of the trees,
        In some melodious plot
Of beechen green, and shadows numberless,
    Singest of summer in full-throated ease.     10

O, for a draught of vintage! that hath been
    Cool'd a long age in the deep-delvèd earth,
Tasting of Flora and the country green,
    Dance, and Provençal song, and sunburnt mirth!
O for a beaker full of the warm South,          15
    Full of the true, the blushful Hippocrene,[15]
      With beaded bubbles winking at the brim,
        And purple-stainèd mouth;
That I might drink, and leave the world unseen,
    And with thee fade away into the forest dim:     20

---

[12] *brede:* embroidery.
[13] *hemlock:* poison.
[14] *Lethe:* river of forgetfulness.
[15] *Hippocrene:* a fountain on Mt. Helicon in Greece.

Fade far away, dissolve, and quite forget
 What thou among the leaves hast never known,
The weariness, the fever, and the fret
 Here, where men sit and hear each other groan;
Where palsy shakes a few, sad, last gray hairs,     25
  Where youth grows pale, and spectre-thin, and dies;
   Where but to think is to be full of sorrow
    And leaden-eyed despairs,
  Where Beauty cannot keep her lustrous eyes,
   Or new Love pine at them beyond tomorrow.   30

Away! away! for I will fly to thee,
 Not charioted by Bacchus and his pards,[16]
But on the viewless wings of Poesy,
 Though the dull brain perplexes and retards:
Already with thee! tender is the night,      35
  And haply the Queen-Moon is on her throne,
   Clustered around by all her starry fays;
    But here there is no light,
  Save what from heaven is with the breezes blown
   Through verdurous glooms and winding mossy ways.  40

I cannot see what flowers are at my feet,
 Nor what soft incense hangs upon the boughs,
But, in embalmèd[17] darkness, guess each sweet
 Wherewith the seasonable month endows
The grass, the thicket, and the fruit-tree wild;    45
  White hawthorn, and the pastoral eglantine;
   Fast fading violets covered up in leaves;
    And mid-May's eldest child,
  The coming musk-rose, full of dewy wine,
   The murmurous haunt of flies on summer eves.   50

Darkling I listen; and for many a time
 I have been half in love with easeful Death,
Called him soft names in many a musèd rhyme,
 To take into the air my quiet breath;

---

[16] *pards:* leopards.
[17] *embalmèd:* balmy, sweet-smelling.

Now more than ever seems it rich to die,                          55
  To cease upon the midnight with no pain,
    While thou art pouring forth thy soul abroad
      In such an ecstasy!
  Still wouldst thou sing, and I have ears in vain—
    To thy high requiem become a sod.                            60

Thou wast not born for death, immortal Bird!
  No hungry generations tread thee down;
The voice I hear this passing night was heard
  In ancient days by emperor and clown:
Perhaps the self-same song that found a path                     65
  Through the sad heart of Ruth,[18] when, sick for home,
    She stood in tears amid the alien corn;
      The same that oft-times hath
  Charmed magic casements, opening on the foam
    Of perilous seas, in faery lands forlorn.                    70

Forlorn! the very word is like a bell
  To toll me back from thee to my sole self!
Adieu! the fancy cannot cheat so well
  As she is famed to do, deceiving elf.
Adieu! adieu! thy plaintive anthem fades                         75
  Past the near meadows, over the still stream,
    Up the hill-side; and now 'tis buried deep
      In the next valley-glades:
  Was it a vision, or a waking dream?
    Fled is that music:—Do I wake or sleep?                      80

# To Autumn

Season of mists and mellow fruitfulness,
  Close bosom-friend of the maturing sun;
Conspiring with him how to load and bless
  With fruit the vines that round the thatch-eves run;
To bend with apples the mossed cottage-trees,                     5

[18] See *Ruth*, 2.

And fill all fruit with ripeness to the core;
   To swell the gourd, and plump the hazel shells
With a sweet kernel; to set budding more,
   And still more, later flowers for the bees,
   Until they think warm days will never cease,     10
      For Summer has o'er-brimmed their clammy cells.

Who hath not seen thee oft amid thy store?
   Sometimes whoever seeks abroad may find
Thee sitting careless on a granary floor,
   Thy hair soft-lifted by the winnowing wind;     15
Or on a half-reaped furrow sound asleep,
   Drowsed with the fume of poppies, while thy hook
      Spares the next swath and all its twinèd flowers:
And sometimes like a gleaner thou dost keep
   Steady thy laden head across a brook;     20
   Or by a cider-press, with patient look,
      Thou watchest the last oozings hours by hours.

Where are the songs of Spring? Ay, where are they?
   Think not of them, thou hast thy music too,—
While barrèd clouds bloom the soft-dying day,     25
   And touch the stubble-plains with rosy hue;
Then in a wailful choir the small gnats mourn
   Among the river sallows,[19] borne aloft
      Or sinking as the light wind lives or dies;
And full-grown lambs loud bleat from hilly bourn;[20]     30
   Hedge-crickets sing; and now with treble soft
   The red-breast whistles from a garden-croft;
      And gathering swallows twitter in the skies.

---

[19] *swallows:* willows.
[20] *bourn:* boundry.

# WALT WHITMAN

## Out of the Cradle Endlessly Rocking

Out of the cradle endlessly rocking,
Out of the mocking-bird's throat, the musical shuttle,
Out of the Ninth-month midnight,
Over the sterile sands and the fields beyond, where the child leaving
    his bed wander'd alone, bareheaded, barefoot,
Down from the shower'd halo,                                              5
Up from the mystic play of shadows twining and twisting as if they
    were alive,
Out from the patches of briers and blackberries,
From the memories of the bird that chanted to me,
From your memories sad brother, from the fitful risings and fallings
    I heard,
From under that yellow half-moon late-risen and swollen as if with
    tears,                                                              10
From those beginning notes of yearning and love there in the mist,
From the thousand responses of my heart never to cease,
From the myriad thence-arous'd words,
From the word stronger and more delicious than any,
From such as now they start the scene revisiting,                        15
As a flock, twittering, rising, or overhead passing,
Borne hither, ere all eludes me, hurriedly,
A man, yet by these tears a little boy again,
Throwing myself on the sand, confronting the waves,
I, chanter of pains and joys, uniter of here and hereafter,              20
Taking all hints to use them, but swiftly leaping beyond them,
A reminiscence sing.

Once Paumanok,[1]
When the lilac-scent was in the air and Fifth-month grass was grow-
    ing,

[1] *Paumanok:*   Indian name for Long Island.

Up this seashore in some briers,                                    25
Two feather'd guests from Alabama, two together,
And their nest, and four light-green eggs spotted with brown,
And every day the he-bird to and fro near at hand,
And every day the she-bird crouch'd on her nest, silent, with bright
    eyes,
And every day I, a curious boy, never too close, never disturbing
    them,                                    30
Cautiously peering, absorbing, translating.

*Shine! shine! shine!*
*Pour down your warmth, great sun!*
*While we bask, we two together.*

*Two together!*                                    35
*Winds blow south, or winds blow north,*
*Day come white, or night come black,*
*Home, or rivers and mountains from home,*
*Singing all time, minding no time,*
*While we two keep together.*                                    40

Till of a sudden,
May-be kill'd, unknown to her mate,
One forenoon the she-bird crouch'd not on the nest,
Nor return'd that afternoon, nor the next,
Nor ever appear'd again.                                    45

And thenceforward all summer in the sound of the sea,
And at night under the full of the moon in calmer weather,
Over the hoarse surging of the sea,
Or flitting from brier to brier by day,
I saw, I heard at intervals the remaining one, the he-bird,                                    50
The solitary guest from Alabama.

*Blow! blow! blow!*
*Blow up sea-winds along Paumanok's shore;*
*I wait and I wait till you blow my mate to me.*

Yes, when the stars glisten'd,                                    55
All night long on the prong of a moss-scallop'd stake,

Down almost amid the slapping waves,
Sat the lone singer wonderful causing tears.

He call'd on his mate,
He pour'd forth the meanings which I of all men know.                    60

Yes my brother I know,
The rest might not, but I have treasur'd every note,
For more than once dimly down to the beach gliding,
Silent, avoiding the moonbeams, blending myself with the shadows,
Recalling now the obscure shapes, the echoes, the sounds and sights
    after their sorts,                                                    65
The white arms out in the breakers tirelessly tossing,
I, with bare feet, a child, the wind wafting my hair,
Listen'd long and long.

Listen'd to keep, to sing, now translating the notes,
Following you my brother.                                                 70

*Soothe! soothe! soothe!*
*Close on its wave soothes the wave behind,*
*And again another behind embracing and lapping, every one close,*
*But my love soothes not me, not me.*

*Low hangs the moon, it rose late,*                                       75
*It is lagging—O I think it is heavy with love, with love.*

*O madly the sea pushes upon the land,*
*With love, with love.*

*O night! do I not see my love fluttering out among the breakers?*
*What is that little black thing I see there in the white?*              80

*Loud! loud! loud!*
*Loud I call to you, my love!*

*High and clear I shoot my voice over the waves,*
*Surely you must know who is here, is here,*
*You must know whom I am, my love.*                                      85

*Low-hanging moon!*
*What is that dusky spot in your brown yellow?*
*O it is the shape, the shape of my mate!*
*O moon do not keep her from me any longer.*

*Land! land! O land!* 90
*Whichever way I turn, O I think you could give me my mate back*
   *again if you only would,*
*For I am almost sure I see her dimly whichever way I look.*

*O rising stars!*
*Perhaps the one I want so much will rise, will rise with some of you.*

*O throat! O trembling throat!* 95
*Sound clearer through the atmosphere!*
*Pierce the woods, the earth,*
*Somewhere listening to catch you must be the one I want.*

*Shake out carols!*
*Solitary here, the night's carols!* 100
*Carols of lonesome love! death's carols!*
*Carols under that lagging, yellow, waning moon!*
*O under that moon where she droops almost down into the sea!*
*O reckless despairing carols.*

*But soft! sink low!* 105
*Soft! let me just murmur,*
*And do you wait a moment you husky-nois'd sea,*
*For somewhere I believe I heard my mate responding to me,*
*So faint, I must be still, be still to listen,*
*But not altogether still, for then she might not come immediately to*
   *me.* 110

*Hither my love!*
*Here I am! here!*
*With this just-sustain'd note I announce myself to you,*
*This gentle call is for you my love, for you.*

*Do not be decoy'd elsewhere,* 115

*That is the whistle of the wind, it is not my voice,*
*That is the fluttering, the fluttering of the spray,*
*Those are the shadows of leaves.*

*O darkness! O in vain!*
*O I am very sick and sorrowful.*                                    120

*O brown halo in the sky near the moon, drooping upon the sea!*
*O troubled reflection in the sea!*
*O throat! O throbbing heart!*
*And I singing uselessly, uselessly all the night.*

*O past! O happy life! O songs of joy!*                             125
*In the air, in the woods, over fields,*
*Loved! loved! loved! loved! loved!*
*But my mate no more, no more with me!*
*We two together no more.*

The aria sinking,                                                   130
All else continuing, the stars shining,
The winds blowing, the notes of the bird continuous echoing,
With angry moans the fierce old mother incessantly moaning,
On the sands of Paumanok's shore gray and rustling,
The yellow half-moon enlarged, sagging down, drooping, the face of
the sea almost touching,                                            135
The boy ecstatic, with his bare feet the waves, with his hair the atmos-
phere dallying,
The love in the heart long pent, now loose, now at last tumultuously
bursting,
The aria's meaning, the ears, the soul, swiftly depositing,
The strange tears down the cheeks coursing,
The colloquy there, the trio, each uttering,                        140
The undertone, the savage old mother incessantly crying,
To the boy's soul's questions sullenly timing, some drown'd secret
hissing,
To the outsetting bard.

Demon or bird! (said the boy's soul,)
Is it indeed toward your mate you sing? or is it really to me?       145

For I, that was a child, my tongue's use sleeping, now I have heard
     you,
Now in a moment I know what I am for, I awake,
And already a thousand singers, a thousand songs, clearer, louder and
     more sorrowful than yours,
A thousand warbling echoes have started to life within me, never to
     die.

O you singer solitary, singing by yourself, projecting me,                150
O solitary me listening, never more shall I cease perpetuating you,
Never more shall I escape, never more the reverberations,
Never more the cries of unsatisfied love be absent from me,
Never again leave me to be the peaceful child I was before what there
     in the night,
By the sea under the yellow and sagging moon,                             155
The messenger there arous'd, the fire, the sweet hell within,
The unknown want, the destiny of me.

O give me the clew! (it lurks in the night here somewhere,)
O if I am to have so much, let me have more!

A word then, (for I will conquer it,)                                     160
The word final, superior to all,
Subtle, sent up—what is it?—I listen;
Are you whispering it, and have been all the time, you sea waves?
Is that it from your liquid rims and wet sands?

Whereto answering, the sea,                                               165
Delaying not, hurrying not,
Whisper'd me through the night, and very plainly before daybreak,
Lisp'd to me the low and delicious word death,
And again death, death, death, death,
Hissing melodious, neither like the bird nor like my arous'd child's
     heart,                                                               170
But edging near as privately for me rustling at my feet,
Creeping thence steadily up to my ears and laving me softly all over,
Death, death, death, death, death.

Which I do not forget,

But fuse the song of my dusky demon and brother,                    175
That he sang to me in the moonlight on Paumanok's gray beach,
With the thousand responsive songs at random,
My own songs awaked from that hour,
And with them the key, the word up from the waves,
The word of the sweetest song and all songs,                       180
That strong and delicious word which, creeping to my feet,
(Or like some old crone rocking the cradle, swathed in sweet gar-
    ments, bending aside,)
The sea whisper'd me.


# A March in the Ranks Hard-Prest, and the Road Unknown

A march in the ranks hard-prest, and the road unknown,
A route through a heavy wood with muffled steps in the darkness,
Our army foil'd with loss severe, and the sullen remnant retreating,
Till after midnight glimmer upon us the lights of a dim-lighted build-
    ing,
We come to an open space in the woods, and halt by the dim-lighted
    building,                                                        5
'Tis a large old church at the crossing roads, now an impromptu
    hospital,
Entering but for a minute I see a sight beyond all the pictures and
    poems ever made,
Shadows of deepest, deepest black, just lit by moving candles and
    lamps,
And by one great pitchy torch stationary with wild red flame and
    clouds of smoke,
By these, crowds, groups of forms vaguely I see on the floor, some in
    the pews laid down,                                             10
At my feet more distinctly a soldier, a mere lad, in danger of bleeding
    to death, (he is shot in the abdomen,)
I stanch the blood temporarily, (the youngster's face is white as a lily,)
Then before I depart I sweep my eyes o'er the scene fain to absorb
    it all,

Faces, varieties, postures beyond description, most in obscurity, some
    of them dead,
Surgeons operating, attendants holding lights, the smell of ether, the
    odor of blood,                                                                   15
The crowd, O the crowd of the bloody forms, the yard outside also
    fill'd,
Some on the bare ground, some on planks or stretchers, some in the
    death-spasm sweating,
An occasional scream or cry, the doctor's shouted orders or calls,
The glisten of the little steel instruments catching the glint of the
    torches,
These I resume as I chant, I see again the forms, I smell the odor,   20
Then hear outside the orders given, *Fall in, my men, fall in;*
But first I bend to the dying lad, his eyes open, a half-smile gives he
    me,
Then the eyes close, calmly close, and I speed forth to the darkness,
Resuming, marching, ever in darkness marching, on in the ranks.
The unknown road still marching.                                                 25

# MATTHEW ARNOLD

## Requiescat

Strew on her roses, roses,
    And never a spray of yew![1]
In quiet she reposes:
    Ah! would that I did too!

Her mirth the world required:                                                        5
    She bathed it in smiles of glee.
But her heart was tired, tired,
    And now they let her be.

[1] *yew:* a tree associated with mourning.

Her life was turning, turning,
   In mazes of heat and sound.          10
But for peace her soul was yearning,
   And now peace laps her round.

Her cabin'd,[2] ample spirit,
   It flutter'd and fail'd for breath.
To-night it doth inherit               15
   The vasty hall of death.

# Dover Beach

The sea is calm to-night.
The tide is full, the moon lies fair
Upon the straits;—on the French coast, the light
Gleams, and is gone; the cliffs of England stand,
Glimmering and vast, out in the tranquil bay.     5
Come to the window, sweet is the night air!
Only, from the lone line of spray
Where the sea meets the moon-blanch'd land,
Listen! you hear the grating roar
Of pebbles which the waves draw back, and fling,     10
At their return, up the high strand,
Begin, and cease, and then again begin,
With tremulous cadence slow, and bring
The eternal note of sadness in.

Sophocles[3] long ago              15
Heard it on the Ægæn, and it brought
Into his mind the turbid ebb and flow
Of human misery; we
Find also in the sound a thought,
Hearing it by this distant northern sea.     20

---

[2] *cabin'd:*   confined (by its mortality).
[3] *Sophocles:*   Greek dramatist.

The Sea of Faith
Was once, too, at the full, and round earth's shore
Lay like the folds of a bright girdle furl'd.
But now I only hear
Its melancholy, long, withdrawing roar,            25
Retreating, to the breath
Of the night-wind down the vast edges drear
And naked shingles of the world.

Ah, love, let us be true
To one another! for the world, which seems          30
To lie before us like a land of dreams,
So various, so beautiful, so new,
Hath really neither joy, nor love, nor light,
Nor certitude, nor peace, nor help for pain;
And we are here as on a darkling plain              35
Swept with confused alarms of struggle and flight,
Where ignorant armies clash by night.

# EMILY DICKINSON

# Success Is Counted Sweetest

Success is counted sweetest
By those who ne'er succeed.
To comprehend a nectar
Requires sorest need.

Not one of all the purple Host                       5
Who took the Flag today
Can tell the definition
**So clear** of Victory

As he defeated—dying—
On whose forbidden ear      10
The distant strains of triumph
Burst agonized and clear!


# Safe in Their Alabaster Chambers —

Safe in their Alabaster Chambers—
Untouched by Morning
And untouched by Noon—
Sleep the meek members of the Resurrection—
Rafter of satin,      5
And Roof of stone.

Light laughs the breeze
In her Castle above them—
Babbles the Bee in a stolid Ear,
Pipe the Sweet Birds in ignorant cadence—      10
Ah, what sagacity perished here!

*version of 1859*


Safe in their Alabaster Chambers—
Untouched by Morning—
And untouched by Noon—
Lie the meek members of the Resurrection—
Rafter of Satin—and Roof of Stone!      5

Grand go the Years—in the Crescent—above them—
Worlds scoop their Arcs—
And Firmaments—row—
Diadems—drop—and Doges—surrender—
Soundless as dots—on a Disc of Snow—      10

*version of 1861*

# I Like a Look of Agony

I like a look of Agony,
Because I know it's true—
Men do not sham Convulsion,
Nor simulate, a Throe—

The Eyes glaze once—and that is Death—                    5
Impossible to feign
The Beads upon the Forehead
By homely Anguish strung.

# Because I Could Not Stop for Death—

Because I could not stop for Death—
He kindly stopped for me—
The Carriage held but just Ourselves—
And Immortality.

We slowly drove—He knew no haste                          5
And I had put away
My labor and my leisure too,
For his Civility—

We passed the School, where Children strove
At Recess—in the Ring—                                    10
We passed the Fields of Gazing Grain—
We passed the Setting Sun—

Or rather—He passed Us—
The Dews drew quivering and chill—
For only Gossamer, my Gown—                               15
My Tippet[1]—only Tulle[2]—

---

[1] *Tippet:*   scarf.
[2] *Tulle:*   a thin fine net.

We paused before a House that seemed
A Swelling of the Ground—
The Roof was scarcely visible—
The Cornice—in the Ground—                    20

Since then—'tis Centuries—and yet
Feels shorter than the Day
I first surmised the Horses Heads
Were toward Eternity—

# A Narrow Fellow in the Grass

A narrow Fellow in the Grass
Occasionally rides—
You may have met Him—did you not
His notice sudden is—

The Grass divides as with a Comb—          5
A spotted shaft is seen—
And then it closes at your feet
And opens further on—

He likes a Boggy Acre
A Floor too cool for Corn—                    10
Yet when a Boy, and Barefoot—
I more than once at Noon
Have passed, I thought, a Whip lash
Unbraiding in the Sun
When stooping to secure it                    15
It wrinkled, and was gone—

Several of Nature's People
I know, and they know me—
I feel for them a transport
Of cordiality—                                20

But never met this Fellow
Attended, or alone
Without a tighter breathing
And Zero at the Bone—

# The Bustle in a House

The Bustle in a House
The Morning after Death
Is solemnest of industries
Enacted upon Earth—

The Sweeping up the Heart                                    5
And putting Love away
We shall not want to use again
Until Eternity.

# Immortal Is an Ample Word

Immortal is an ample word
When what we need is by
But when it leaves us for a time
'Tis a necessity.

Of Heaven above the firmest proof                            5
We fundamental know
Except for its[1] marauding Hand
It had been Heaven below.

# Apparently with No Surprise

Apparently with no surprise
To any happy Flower
The Frost beheads it at its[1] play—
In accidental power—

---

[1] *its:*   original spelling, *it's.*

The blonde Assassin passes on—                                        5
The Sun proceeds unmoved
To measure off another Day
For an Approving God.


# A. E. HOUSMAN


## Loveliest of Trees

Loveliest of trees, the cherry now
Is hung with bloom along the bough,
And stands about the woodland ride,
Wearing white for Eastertide.

Now, of my threescore years and ten,                                  5
Twenty will not come again,
And take from seventy springs a score,
It only leaves me fifty more.

And since to look at things in bloom
Fifty springs are little room,                                       10
About the woodlands I will go
To see the cherry hung with snow.


## With Rue My Heart Is Laden

With rue my heart is laden
     For golden friends I had,
For many a rose-lipt maiden
     And many a lightfoot lad.

By brooks too broad for leaping                          5
   The lightfoot boys are laid;
The rose-lipt girls are sleeping
   In fields where roses fade.

# Terence, This Is Stupid Stuff

'Terence, this is stupid stuff:
You eat your victuals fast enough;
There can't be much amiss, 'tis clear,
To see the rate you drink your beer.
But oh, good Lord, the verse you make,                   5
It gives a chap the belly-ache.
The cow, the old cow, she is dead;
It sleeps well, the horned head:
We poor lads, 'tis our turn now
To hear such tunes as killed the cow.                    10
Pretty friendship 'tis to rhyme
Your friends to death before their time
Moping melancholy mad:
Come, pipe a tune to dance to, lad.'

   Why, if 'tis dancing you would be,                15
There's brisker pipes than poetry.
Say for what were hop-yards meant,
Or why was Burton[1] built on Trent?
Oh many a peer of England brews
Livelier liquor than the Muse,                           20
And malt does more than Milton can
To justify God's ways to man.
Ale, man, ale's the stuff to drink
For fellows whom it hurts to think:
Look into the pewter pot                                 25
To see the world as the world's not.
And faith 'tis pleasant till 'tis past:
The mischief is that 'twill not last.
Oh I have been to Ludlow fair
And left my necktie God knows where,                     30

---

[1] *Burton:* English town famous for its breweries.

And carried halfway home, or near,
Pints and quarts of Ludlow beer:
Then the world seemed none so bad,
And I myself a sterling lad;
And down in lovely muck I've lain,                    35
Happy till I woke again.
Then I saw the morning sky:
Heigho, the tale was all a lie;
The world it was the old world yet,
I was I, my things were wet,                          40
And nothing now remained to do
But begin the game anew.

Therefore, since the world has still
Much good, but much less good than ill,
And while the sun and moon endure                     45
Luck's a chance but trouble's sure,
I'd face it as a wise man would,
And train for ill and not for good.
'Tis true, the stuff I bring for sale
Is not so brisk a brew as ale:                        50
Out of a stem that scored the hand
I wrung it in a weary land.
But take it: if the smack is sour,
The better for the embittered hour;
It should do good to heart and head                   55
When your soul is in my soul's stead;
And I will friend you, if I may,
In the dark and cloudy day.

There was a king reigned in the East:
There, when kings will sit to feast,                  60
They get their fill before they think
With poisoned meat and poisoned drink.
He gathered all that springs to birth
From the many-venomed earth;
First a little, thence to more,                       65
He sampled all her killing store;
And easy, smiling, seasoned sound,

Sate the king when healths went round.
They put arsenic in his meat
And stared aghast to watch him eat;                                70
They poured strychnine in his cup
And shook to see him drink it up:
They shook, they stared as white's their shirt:
Them it was their poison hurt.
—I tell the tale that I heard told.                               75
Mithridates,[2] he died old.


# The Chestnut Casts His Flambeaux

The chestnut casts his flambeaux, and the flowers
    Stream from the hawthorn on the wind away,
The doors clap to, the pane is blind with showers.
    Pass me the can, lad; there's an end of May.

There's one spoilt spring to scant our mortal lot,
    One season ruined of our little store.                     5
May will be fine next year as like as not:
    Oh ay, but then we shall be twenty-four.

We for a certainty are not the first
    Have sat in taverns while the tempest hurled              10
Their hopeful plans to emptiness, and cursed
    Whatever brute and blackguard made the world.

It is in truth iniquity on high
    To cheat our sentenced souls of aught they crave,
And mar the merriment as you and I                                15
    Fare on our long fool's-errand to the grave.

Iniquity it is; but pass the can.
    My lad, no pair of kings our mothers bore;
Our only portion is the estate of man:
    We want the moon, but we shall get no more.               20

2 *Mithridates:* king of ancient Pontus in Asia Minor.

If here to-day the cloud of thunder lours
   To-morrow it will hie on far behests;
The flesh will grieve on other bones than ours
   Soon, and the soul will mourn in other breasts.

The troubles of our proud and angry dust     25
   Are from eternity and shall not fail.
Bear them we can, and if we can we must.
   Shoulder the sky, my lad, and drink your ale.


# WILLIAM BUTLER YEATS


## The Lake Isle of Innisfree

I will arise and go now, and go to Innisfree,
And a small cabin build there, of clay and wattles made:
Nine bean rows will I have there, a hive for the honey bee,
   And live alone in the bee-loud glade.

And I shall have some peace there, for peace comes dropping slow,   5
Dropping from the veils of the morning to where the cricket sings;
There midnight's all a glimmer, and noon a purple glow,
   And evening full of the linnet's wings.

I will arise and go now, for always night and day
I hear lake water lapping with low sounds by the shore;    10
While I stand on the roadway, or on the pavements gray,
   I hear it in the deep heart's core.

# The Magi

Now as at all times I can see in the mind's eye,
In their stiff, painted clothes, the pale unsatisfied ones
Appear and disappear in the blue depth of the sky
With all their ancient faces like rain-beaten stones,
And all their helms of silver hovering side by side,          5
And all their eyes still fixed, hoping to find once more,
Being by Calvary's turbulence unsatisfied,
The uncontrollable mystery on the bestial floor.

# The Second Coming

Turning and turning in the widening gyre
The falcon cannot hear the falconer;
Things fall apart; the centre cannot hold;
Mere anarchy is loosed upon the world,
The blood-dimmed tide is loosed, and everywhere          5
The ceremony of innocence is drowned;
The best lack all conviction, while the worst
Are full of passionate intensity.

Surely some revelation is at hand;
Surely the Second Coming is at hand.          10
The Second Coming! Hardly are those words out
When a vast image out of *Spiritus Mundi*[1]
Troubles my sight: somewhere in sands of the desert
A shape with lion body and the head of a man,
A gaze blank and pitiless as the sun,          15
Is moving its slow thighs, while all about it
Reel shadows of the indignant desert birds.
The darkness drops again; but now I know

[1] *Spiritus Mundi:*   world-spirit or collective imagination.

That twenty centuries of stony sleep
Were vexed to nightmare by a rocking cradle,                    20
And what rough beast,[2] its hour come round at last,
Slouches towards Bethlehem to be born?


# Leda[3] and the Swan[4]

A sudden blow: the great wings beating still
Above the staggering girl, her thighs caressed
By the dark webs, her nape caught in his bill,
He holds her helpless breast upon his breast.

How can those terrified vague fingers push                     5
The feathered glory from her loosening thighs?
And how can body, laid in that white rush,
But feel the strange heart beating where it lies?

A shudder in the loins engenders[5] there
The broken wall, the burning roof and tower                    10
And Agamemnon[6] dead.
                           Being so caught up,
So mastered by the brute blood of the air,
Did she put on his knowledge with his power
Before the indifferent beak could let her drop?


---

2 *rough beast:*  the Antichrist (see *I John* 2:18) establishing the title's irony.

3 *Leda:*  wife of Tyndareus, king of Sparta.

4 *The Swan:*  disguise of Zeus when he made love to Leda.

5 *engenders:*  born of this union were Castor and Pollux, gods of war; line 10: destruction of Troy.

6 *Agamemnon:*  slain upon his return from the Trojan War by Clytemnestra and Aegisthus.

# Sailing to Byzantium

## I

That is no country for old men. The young
In one another's arms, birds in the trees
—Those dying generations—at their song,
The salmon-falls, the mackerel-crowded seas,
Fish, flesh, or fowl, commend all summer long          5
Whatever is begotten, born, and dies.
Caught in that sensual music all neglect
Monuments of unageing intellect.

## II

An aged man is but a paltry thing,
A tattered coat upon a stick, unless          10
Soul clap its hands and sing, and louder sing
For every tatter in its mortal dress,
Nor is there singing school but studying
Monuments of its own magnificence;
And therefore I have sailed the seas and come          15
To the holy city of Byzantium.[7]

## III

O sages standing in God's holy fire
As in the gold mosaic of a wall,
Come from the holy fire, perne[8] in a gyre,
And be the singing-masters of my soul.          20
Consume my heart away; sick with desire
And fastened to a dying animal
It knows not what it is; and gather me
Into the artifice of eternity.

[7] *the holy city of Byzantium:* capital of the Roman Empire after 330 A.D. and, literally, the Holy City of the Eastern Church; later called Constantinople, now Istanbul. Byzantium epitomized for Yeats man's highest achievement in art and religion.
[8] *perne:* revolve.

## IV

Once out of nature I shall never take                                                    25
My bodily form from any natural thing,
But such a form as Grecian goldsmiths make[9]
Of hammered gold and gold enamelling
To keep a drowsy Emperor awake;
Or set upon a golden bough to sing                                                       30
To lords and ladies of Byzantium
Of what is past, or passing, or to come.

[9] Artifical birds sang from golden trees in Emperor's garden.

# ROBERT FROST

# Reluctance

Out through the fields and the woods
    And over the walls I have wended;
I have climbed the hills of view
    And looked at the world, and descended;
I have come by the highway home,                                                          5
    And lo, it is ended.

The leaves are all dead on the ground,
    Save those that the oak is keeping
To ravel them one by one
    And let them go scraping and creeping                                                 10
Out over the crusted snow,
    When others are sleeping.

And the dead leaves lie huddled and still,
    No longer blown hither and thither;
The last lone aster is gone;                                                              15
    The flowers of the witch-hazel wither;

The heart is still aching to seek,
  But the feet question "Whither?"

Ah, when to the heart of man
  Was it ever less than a treason                    20
To go with the drift of things,
  To yield with a grace to reason,
And bow and accept the end
  Of a love or a season?


# After Apple-Picking

My long two-pointed ladder's sticking through a tree
Toward heaven still,
And there's a barrel that I didn't fill
Beside it, and there may be two or three
Apples I didn't pick upon some bough.                 5
But I am done with apple-picking now.
Essence of winter sleep is on the night,
The scent of apples: I am drowsing off.
I cannot rub the strangeness from my sight
I got from looking through a pane of glass            10
I skimmed this morning from the drinking trough
And held against the world of hoary grass.
It melted, and I let it fall and break.
But I was well
Upon my way to sleep before it fell,                  15
And I could tell
What form my dreaming was about to take.
Magnified apples appear and disappear,
Stem end and blossom end,
And every fleck of russet showing clear.              20
My instep arch not only keeps the ache,
It keeps the pressure of a ladder-round.
I feel the ladder sway as the boughs bend.
And I keep hearing from the cellar bin
The rumbling sound                                    25

Of load on load of apples coming in.
For I have had too much
Of apple-picking: I am overtired
Of the great harvest I myself desired.
There were ten thousand thousand fruit to touch,      30
Cherish in hand, lift down, and not let fall.
For all
That struck the earth,
No matter if not bruised or spiked with stubble,
Went surely to the cider-apple heap      35
As of no worth.
One can see what will trouble
This sleep of mine, whatever sleep it is.
Were he not gone,
The woodchuck could say whether it's like his      40
Long sleep, as I describe its coming on,
Or just some human sleep.

# "Out, Out —"

The buzz saw snarled and rattled in the yard
And made dust and dropped stove-length sticks of wood,
Sweet-scented stuff when the breeze drew across it.
And from there those that lifted eyes could count
Five mountain ranges one behind the other      5
Under the sunset far into Vermont.
And the saw snarled and rattled, snarled and rattled,
As it ran light, or had to bear a load.
And nothing happened: day was all but done.
Call it a day, I wish they might have said      10
To please the boy by giving him the half hour
That a boy counts so much when saved from work.
His sister stood beside them in her apron
To tell them "Supper." At the word, the saw,
As if to prove saws knew what supper meant,      15
Leaped out at the boy's hand, or seemed to leap—
He must have given the hand. However it was,

Neither refused the meeting. But the hand!
The boy's first outcry was a rueful laugh,
As he swung toward them holding up the hand                    20
Half in appeal, but half as if to keep
The life from spilling. Then the boy saw all—
Since he was old enough to know, big boy
Doing a man's work, though a child at heart—
He saw all spoiled. "Don't let him cut my hand off—           25
The doctor, when he comes. Don't let him, sister!"
So. But the hand was gone already.
The doctor put him in the dark of ether.
He lay and puffed his lips out with his breath.
And then—the watcher at his pulse took fright.                30
No one believed. They listened at his heart.
Little—less—nothing!—and that ended it.
No more to build on there. And they, since they
Were not the one dead, turned to their affairs.

# Fire and Ice

Some say the world will end in fire,
Some say in ice.
From what I've tasted of desire
I hold with those who favor fire.
But if it had to perish twice,                                 5
I think I know enough of hate
To say that for destruction ice
Is also great
And would suffice.

# Stopping by Woods on a Snowy Evening

Whose woods these are I think I know.
His house is in the village though;
He will not see me stopping here
To watch his woods fill up with snow.

My little horse must think it queer          5
To stop without a farmhouse near
Between the woods and frozen lake
The darkest evening of the year.

He gives his harness bells a shake
To ask if there is some mistake.          10
The only other sound's the sweep
Of easy wind and downy flake.

The woods are lovely, dark and deep,
But I have promises to keep,
And miles to go before I sleep,          15
And miles to go before I sleep.

# Desert Places

Snow falling and night falling fast, oh, fast
In a field I looked into going past,
And the ground almost covered smooth in snow,
But a few weeds and stubble showing last.

The woods around it have it—it is theirs.          5
All animals are smothered in their lairs.
I am too absent-spirited to count;
The loneliness includes me unawares.

And lonely as it is that loneliness
Will be more lonely ere it will be less—                          10
A blanker whiteness of benighted snow
With no expression, nothing to express.

They cannot scare me with their empty spaces
Between stars—on stars where no human race is.
I have it in me so much nearer home                               15
To scare myself with my own desert places.


# T. S. ELIOT


# The Love Song of
# J. Alfred Prufrock

*S'io credesse che mia risposta fosse*
*A persona che mai tornasse al mondo,*
*Questa fiamma staria senza piu scosse.*
*Ma perciocche giammai di questo fondo*
*Non torno vivo alcun, s'i'odo il vero,*
*Senza tema d'infamia ti rispondo.*[1]

Let us go then, you and I,
When the evening is spread out against the sky
Like a patient etherised upon a table;
Let us go, through certain half-deserted streets,
The muttering retreats                                            5
Of restless nights in one-night cheap hotels
And sawdust restaurants with oyster-shells:
Streets that follow like a tedious argument

[1] Epigraph from Dante's *Inferno*, Canto 27: "If I thought my answer were/to one who ever could return to the world,/this flame should shake no more./But since none from this depth/ever did return alive, if what I hear be true,/without fear of infamy I answer thee "

Of insidious intent
To lead you to an overwhelming question . . .    10
Oh, do not ask, "What is it?"
Let us go and make our visit.

In the room the women come and go
Talking of Michelangelo.

The yellow fog that rubs its back upon the window-panes,    15
The yellow smoke that rubs its muzzle on the window-panes
Licked its tongue into the corners of the evening,
Lingered upon the pools that stand in drains,
Let fall upon its back the soot that falls from chimneys,
Slipped by the terrace, made a sudden leap,    20
And seeing that it was a soft October night,
Curled once about the house, and fell asleep.

And indeed there will be time
For the yellow smoke that slides along the street,
Rubbing its back upon the window-panes;    25
There will be time, there will be time
To prepare a face to meet the faces that you meet;
There will be time to murder and create,
And time for all the works and days of hands
That lift and drop a question on your plate;    30
Time for you and time for me,
And time yet for a hundred indecisions,
And for a hundred visions and revisions,
Before the taking of a toast and tea.

In the room the women come and go    35
Talking of Michelangelo.

And indeed there will be time
To wonder, "Do I dare?" and, "Do I dare?"
Time to turn back and descend the stair,
With a bald spot in the middle of my hair—    40
[They will say: "How his hair is growing thin!"]
My morning coat, my collar mounting firmly to the chin,

My necktie rich and modest, but asserted by a simple pin—
[They will say: "But how his arms and legs are thin!"]
Do I dare                                                          45
Disturb the universe?
In a minute there is time
For decisions and revisions which a minute will reverse.

For I have known them all already, known them all:—
Have known the evenings, mornings, afternoons,                      50
I have measured out my life with coffee spoons;
I know the voices dying with a dying fall
Beneath the music from a farther room.
   So how should I presume?

And I have known the eyes already, known them all—                  55
The eyes that fix you in a formulated phrase,
And when I am formulated, sprawling on a pin,
When I am pinned and wriggling on the wall,
Then how should I begin
To spit out all the butt-ends of my days and ways?                  60
   And how should I presume?

And I have known the arms already, known them all—
Arms that are braceleted and white and bare
[But in the lamplight, downed with light brown hair!]
Is it perfume from a dress                                          65
That makes me so digress?
Arms that lie along a table, or wrap about a shawl.
   And should I then presume?
   And how should I begin?

     .  .  .  .  .  .  .  .  .
Shall I say, I have gone at dusk through narrow streets              70
And watched the smoke that rises from the pipes
Of lonely men in shirt-sleeves, leaning out of windows? . . .

I should have been a pair of ragged claws
Scuttling across the floors of silent seas.

     .  .  .  .  .  .  .  .  .
And the afternoon, the evening, sleeps so peacefully!               75

Smoothed by long fingers,
Asleep . . . tired . . . or it malingers,
Stretched on the floor, here beside you and me.
Should I, after tea and cakes and ices,
Have the strength to force the moment to its crisis?                    80
But though I have wept and fasted, wept and prayed,
Though I have seen my head [grown slightly bald] brought in upon
    a platter,
I am no prophet[2]—and here's no great matter;
I have seen the moment of my greatness flicker,
And I have seen the eternal Footman hold my coat, and snicker,      85
And in short, I was afraid.

And would it have been worth it, after all,
After the cups, the marmalade, the tea,
Among the porcelain, among some talk of you and me,
Would it have been worth while,                                        90
To have bitten off the matter with a smile,
To have squeezed the universe into a ball
To roll it toward some overwhelming question,
To say: "I am Lazarus,[3] come from the dead,
Come back to tell you all, I shall tell you all"—                      95
If one, settling a pillow by her head,
    Should say: "That is not what I meant at all.
    That is not it, at all."

And would it have been worth it, after all,
Would it have been worth while,                                       100
After the sunsets and the dooryards and the sprinkled streets,
After the novels, after the teacups, after the skirts that trail along the
    floor—
And this, and so much more?—
It is impossible to say just what I mean!
But as if a magic lantern threw the nerves in patterns on a screen:   105
Would it have been worth while
If one, settling a pillow or throwing off a shawl,

[2] See *Matthew* 14:3–11.
[3] See *John* 11.

And turning toward the window, should say:
  "That is not it at all,
  That is not what I meant, at all."                110

    . . . . . . . . . . .

No! I am not Prince Hamlet, nor was meant to be;
Am an attendant lord, one that will do
To swell a progress,[4] start a scene or two,
Advise the prince; no doubt, an easy tool,
Deferential, glad to be of use,                115
Politic, cautious, and meticulous;
Full of high sentence, but a bit obtuse;
At times, indeed, almost ridiculous—
Almost, at times, the Fool.

I grow old . . . I grow old . . .                120
I shall wear the bottoms of my trousers rolled.[5]

Shall I part my hair behind? Do I dare to eat a peach?
I shall wear white flannel trousers, and walk upon the beach.
I have heard the mermaids singing, each to each.

I do not think that they will sing to me.                125

I have seen them riding seaward on the waves
Combing the white hair of the waves blown back
When the wind blows the water white and black.

We have lingered in the chambers of the sea
By sea-girls wreathed with seaweed red and brown                130
Till human voices wake us, and we drown.

[4] *swell a progress:*   increase a prince's retinue on a journey.
[5] *rolled:*   cuffed.

# ARCHIBALD MacLEISH

## Ars Poetica

A poem should be palpable and mute
As a globed fruit,

Dumb
As old medallions to the thumb,

Silent as the sleeve-worn stone                                    5
Of casement ledges where the moss has grown—

A poem should be wordless
As the flight of birds.

     .    .    .    .    .

A poem should be motionless in time
As the moon climbs,                                                10

Leaving, as the moon releases
Twig by twig the night-entangled trees,

Leaving, as the moon behind the winter leaves,
Memory by memory the mind—

A poem should be motionless in time                                15
As the moon climbs.

     .    .    .    .    .

A poem should be equal to:
Not true.

For all the history of grief
An empty doorway and a maple leaf.                                 20

For love
The leaning grasses and two lights above the sea—

A poem should not mean
But be.

# W. H. AUDEN

## Musée des Beaux Arts

About suffering they were never wrong,
The Old Masters: how well they understood
Its human position; how it takes place
While someone else is eating or opening a window or just walking
    dully along;
How, when the aged are reverently, passionately waiting        5
For the miraculous birth, there always must be
Children who did not specially want it to happen, skating
On a pond at the edge of the wood:
They never forgot
That even the dreadful martyrdom must run its course        10
Anyhow in a corner, some untidy spot
Where the dogs go on with their doggy life and the torturer's horse
Scratches its innocent behind on a tree.


In Brueghel's *Icarus*,[1] for instance: how everything turns away
Quite leisurely from the disaster; the ploughman may        15
Have heard the splash, the forsaken cry,
But for him it was not an important failure; the sun shone
As it had to on the white legs disappearing into the green
Water; and the expensive delicate ship that must have seen
Something amazing, a boy falling out of the sky,        20
Had somewhere to get to and sailed calmly on.

---

[1] *Brueghel*: Pieter Brueghel, a sixteenth-century Flemish painter. *Icarus*: the painting is entitled "The Fall of Icarus" and depicts Icarus plunging into the sea, the wax on his wings having melted from his having soared too near the sun.

# September 1, 1939[2]

I sit in one of the dives
On Fifty-Second Street
Uncertain and afraid
As the clever hopes expire
Of a low dishonest decade:　　　　　　　　　　　5
Waves of anger and fear
Circulate over the bright
And darkened lands of the earth,
Obsessing our private lives;
The unmentionable odour of death　　　　　　　10
Offends the September night.

Accurate scholarship can
Unearth the whole offence[3]
From Luther until now
That has driven a culture mad,　　　　　　　　15
Find what occurred at Linz,[4]
What huge imago made
A psychopathic god:[5]
I and the public know
What all schoolchildren learn,　　　　　　　　20
Those to whom evil is done
Do evil in return.

Exiled Thucydides[6] knew
All that a speech can say
About Democracy,　　　　　　　　　　　　　25
And what dictators do,
The elderly rubbish they talk
To an apathetic grave;

[2] The day Germany invaded Poland to begin World War II.

[3] *the whole offence:*  the doctrine of state rather than individual supremacy.

[4] *Linz:*  city in which the treaty was signed (March 13, 1938) annexing Austria to Germany.

[5] allusion to Hitler's paranoia.

[6] See Thucydides' *The Peloponnesian War*, Bk. III, chs. 82–83.

Analysed all in his book,
The enlightenment driven away, 30
The habit-forming pain,
Mismanagement and grief:
We must suffer them all again.

Into this neutral air
Where blind skyscrapers use 35
Their full height to proclaim
The strength of Collective Man,
Each language pours its vain
Competitive excuse:
But who can live for long 40
In an euphoric dream;
Out of the mirror they stare,
Imperialism's face
And the international wrong.

Faces along the bar 45
Cling to their average day:
The lights must never go out,
The music must always play,
All the conventions conspire
To make this fort assume 50
The furniture of home;
Lest we should see where we are,
Lost in a haunted wood,
Children afraid of the night
Who have never been happy or good. 55

The windiest militant trash
Important Persons shout
Is not so crude as our wish:
What mad Nijinsky wrote
About Diaghilev[7] 60
Is true of the normal heart;
For the error bred in the bone

[7] See *The Diary of Vaslav Nijinsky* (1936) and the claim (p. 27) that Diaghilev sought only the love of others, not universal love.

Of each woman and each man
Craves what it cannot have,
Not universal love                                           65
But to be loved alone.


From the conservative dark
Into the ethical life
The dense commuters come,
Repeating their morning vow;                                 70
"I *will* be true to the wife,
I'll concentrate more on my work,"
And helpless governors wake
To resume their compulsory game:
Who can release them now,                                    75
Who can reach the deaf,
Who can speak for the dumb?

Defenceless under the night
Our world in stupor lies;
Yet, dotted everywhere,                                      80
Ironic points of light
Flash out wherever the Just
Exchange their messages:
May I, composed like them
Of Eros[8] and of dust,                                      85
Beleaguered by the same
Negation and despair,
Show an affirming flame.

---

[8] *Eros:*   god of love.

# DYLAN THOMAS

# The Force that Through the Green Fuse Drives the Flower

The force that through the green fuse drives the flower
Drives my green age; that blasts the roots of trees
Is my destroyer.
And I am dumb[1] to tell the crooked rose
My youth is bent by the same wintry fever.                    5

The force that drives the water through the rocks
Drives my red blood; that dries the mouthing streams
Turns mine to wax.
And I am dumb to mouth unto my veins
How at the mountain spring the same mouth sucks.        10

The hand that whirls the water in the pool
Stirs the quicksand; that ropes the blowing wind
Hauls my shroud sail.
And I am dumb to tell the hanging man
How of my clay is made the hangman's lime.               15

The lips of time leech to the fountain head;
Love drips and gathers, but the fallen blood
Shall calm her sores.
And I am dumb to tell a weather's wind
How time has ticked a heaven round the stars.            20

And I am dumb to tell the lover's tomb
How at my sheet goes the same crooked worm.

[1] *dumb:* speechless.

# A Refusal to Mourn the Death, by Fire, of a Child in London

Never until the mankind making
Bird beast and flower
Fathering and all humbling darkness
Tells with silence the last light breaking
And the still hour                          5
Is come of the sea tumbling in harness

And I must enter again the round
Zion of the water bead
And the synagogue of the ear of corn
Shall I let pray the shadow of a sound                10
Or sow my salt seed
In the least valley of sackcloth to mourn

The majesty and burning of the child's death.
I shall not murder
The mankind of her going with a grave truth        15
Nor blaspheme down the stations of the breath
With any further
Elegy of innocence and youth.

Deep with the first dead lies London's daughter,
Robed in the long friends,                           20
The grains beyond age, the dark veins of her mother,
Secret by the unmourning water
Of the riding Thames.
After the first death, there is no other.

# Do Not Go Gentle into That Good Night

Do not go gentle into that good night,
Old age should burn and rave at close of day;
Rage, rage against the dying of the light.

Though wise men at their end know dark is right,
Because their words had forked no lightning they          5
Do not go gentle into that good night.

Good men, the last wave by, crying how bright
Their frail deeds might have danced in a green bay,
Rage, rage against the dying of the light.

Wild men who caught and sang the sun in flight,          10
And learn, too late, they grieved it on its way,
Do not go gentle into that good night.

Grave men, near death, who see with blinding sight
Blind eyes could blaze like meteors and be gay,
Rage, rage against the dying of the light.          15

And you, my father, there on the sad height,
Curse, bless, me now with your fierce tears, I pray.
Do not go gentle into that good night.
Rage, rage against the dying of the light.

# And Death Shall Have No Dominion

And death shall have no dominion.
Dead men naked they shall be one
With the man in the wind and the west moon;
When their bones are picked clean and the clean bones gone,
They shall have stars at elbow and foot;          5
Though they go mad they shall be sane,

Though they sink through the sea they shall rise again;
Though lovers be lost love shall not;
And death shall have no dominion.

And death shall have no dominion.      10
Under the windings of the sea
They lying long shall not die windily;
Twisting on racks when sinews give way,
Strapped to a wheel, yet they shall not break;
Faith in their hands shall snap in two,      15
And the unicorn evils run them through;
Split all ends up they shan't crack;
And death shall have no dominion.

And death shall have no dominion.
No more may gulls cry at their ears      20
Or waves break loud on the seashores;
Where blew a flower may a flower no more
Lift its head to the blows of the rain;
Though they be mad and dead as nails,
Heads of the characters hammer through daisies;      25
Break in the sun till the sun breaks down,
And death shall have no dominion.

# THEODORE ROETHKE

## Open House

My secrets cry aloud.
I have no need for tongue.
My heart keeps open house,
My doors are widely swung.
An epic of the eyes      5
My love, with no disguise.

My truths are all foreknown,
This anguish self-revealed.
I'm naked to the bone,
With nakedness my shield.                              10
Myself is what I wear:
I keep the spirit spare.

The anger will endure,
The deed will speak the truth
In language strict and pure.                           15
I stop the lying mouth:
Rage warps my clearest cry
To witless agony.

# Dolor

I have known the inexorable sadness of pencils,
Neat in their boxes, dolor of pad and paper-weight,
All the misery of manila folders and mucilage,
Desolation in immaculate public places,
Lonely reception room, lavatory, switchboard,         5
The unalterable pathos of basin and pitcher,
Ritual of multigraph, paper-clip, comma,
Endless duplication of lives and objects.
And I have seen dust from the walls of institutions,
Finer than flour, alive, more dangerous than silica,  10
Sift, almost invisible, through long afternoons of tedium,
Dropping a fine film on nails and delicate eyebrows,
Glazing the pale hair, the duplicate gray standard faces.

# Biographical Notes

ANDERSON, SHERWOOD (1876–1941), the son of an unsuccessful sign painter, was born in Camden, Ohio. More interested in horse racing than in school, he only finished the elementary grades before going to work among laborers and hangers-on at livery stables and race tracks. After brief military service during the Spanish-American War, he joined an advertising firm in Chicago and later became manager of a paint factory in Ohio. Deeply impressionable and introspective, he abruptly left his business one day never again to return to it. He went immediately to Chicago and began his writing career. It included associations, both in this country and abroad, with the literary elite of his day, and culminated in his writing more than a dozen separate works of fiction, poetry, and autobiography. Best known is *Winesburg, Ohio* (1919), a deeply psychoanalytical work of fiction dealing with small-town people (he called them "grotesques") in the Middle West. His rebellion against conventional literary style and themes influenced many subsequent writers, most notably William Faulkner. He died in 1941 in Panama from complications that resulted from his having swallowed a toothpick sliver.

ARNOLD, MATTHEW (1822–1888), was the son of Thomas Arnold, famous Headmaster of Rugby. Soon after his graduation from Oxford, he was appointed inspector of schools, a position he held from 1851 until nearly the end of his life. His duties required extensive travel in England and on the Continent, and on one occasion in 1883 he toured the United States. Though not a prolific poet, he was elected professor of poetry at Oxford in 1857, a title he retained for 10 years. Among all his poetry, "Dover Beach" ranks as one of the finest of the Victorian period. Of concern to scholars are his erudite works of literary criticism and cultural philosophy, the best known entitled *Essays in Criticism, First Series* (1865) and *Culture and Anarchy* (1869).

AUDEN, W(YSTAN) H(UGH) (1907–    ), was born in York, England, but in 1939 came to the United States where he gained American citizenship. Educated at Oxford and associated with such younger poets as Stephen Spender, Louis MacNeice, and Christopher Isherwood, he published his first poetry in 1930 and another volume of poetry in 1935. In 1935 he married Erika Mann, daughter of Thomas Mann, the greatest German novelist of the century. After crystallizing many of his social and political ideas while serving as an ambulance driver in the Spanish Civil War, he collaborated with Isherwood in the plays *The Ascent of F.6* (1936), *On the Frontier* (1938), and *Journey to a War* (1939). Still an active writer he has also written a critical work entitled *The Enchafèd Flood* (1950) and two books on Kierkegaard.

CHEEVER, JOHN (1912–    ), was born in Quincy, Massachusetts, attended Thayer Academy in Braintree, and served with an infantry division in World War II. The common theme of his stories, most of them appearing in *The New Yorker,* is the surreptitious discontent and immorality among affluent suburbanites. A collection of his stories appeared in 1954 entitled *The Enormous Radio, and Other Stories.* For his *The Wapshot Chronicle* he received the National Book Award in 1958.

CHEKHOV, ANTON (1860–1904), the son of a grocery shop owner, studied medicine at Moscow University, at the same time helping to support his parents by writing humorous sketches and stories for periodicals. After his graduation in 1884 he took up the practice of medicine, though his own health was already impaired by hard work and oncoming tuberculosis. He continued writing fiction, much of it reflecting Tolstoy's ideas about morality and nonresistance to evil. His greatest success came in later years as a dramatist. *Uncle Vanya* (1899) and *The Three Sisters* (1901) were followed by *Cherry Orchard* (1904), unquestionably his finest work, in which external action is almost nonexistent but the elusive states of mind assume a powerful reality.

CONRAD, JOSEPH (1857–1924), insisted he was Polish, though he was born in the Ukraine. When he became a British subject in 1886 he shortened his name from Jozef Teodor Konrad Nalecz Korzeniowski. In addition to his native language which was Polish, he spoke and wrote fluent French and became one of the all-time masters of English. After serving a short time with the French merchant marine, he started a 20-year career in the English merchant service in 1878, rising from a common sailor to first mate (1883) and master (1886). When he left the sea in 1894 to devote full time to writing, he had so thoroughly mastered English that his subsequent novels and stories were said to resemble the polished style of Henry James and Robert Louis Stevenson. From his intimate knowledge of the sea and, one needs to add, of human nature, he began a brilliant series of tales which included *Almayer's Folly* (1895), *The Nigger of the 'Narcissus'* (1897), *Lord Jim* (1900), *Heart of Darkness* (1902), *Youth* (short stories; 1902), *Typhoon* (short stories; 1903), *Nostromo* (1904), and *The Secret Agent* (1907). In these works, many of them full of magnificent word-painting, he probed with rare subtlety beneath youthful illusions and found in the human heart dark loneliness and evil.

CRANE, STEPHEN (1871–1900), lived less than 29 years, but in that short time brought American literary realism to full bloom. The fourteenth child of a Methodist clergyman, he studied a year at Lafayette College and another year at Syracuse University. His interest in journalism took him to New York where, at the age of 20, he started writing articles for the New York *Tribune* and *Herald* about his slumming in the Bowery. In 1893 he borrowed enough money to publish *Maggie: A Girl of the Streets,* his first literary piece of genuine distinction. Desperate from poverty and ill health, he borrowed money from William Dean Howells to have *The Red Badge of Courage* typed. This novel, published in 1894, is a masterful description of the cavernous fears deep within Henry Fleming, a soldier in the Civil War. After publishing two collections, one of poetry called *The Black Riders* (1895) and the other of Civil War stories entitled *The Little Regiment* (1896), he went to Cuba as a correspondent. His experiences of being shipwrecked enroute are told in "The Open Boat," the title story of another collection published in 1898. After a stint as war correspondent on the Greco-Turkish front, he married and lived for a short time in England. He died of tuberculosis.

DICKINSON, EMILY (1830–1886), and Walt Whitman are now considered America's two greatest nineteenth century poets. Yet one can hardly imagine two more dissimilar careers. In contrast to Whitman's uneducated family, active public life, and seemingly unrestrained and even bombastic expression, Emily Dickinson's father was a distinguished lawyer and legislator and she spent most of her years in the small town of Amherst, Massachusetts, writing more than 1500 incredibly condensed little poems and seeing only three of them published during her lifetime. Obviously her life has puzzled biographers and critics; only recently have definitive editions of her letters and poems, edited by Thomas H. Johnson, and complete biographical data, edited by Jay Leyda, been available.

DONNE, JOHN (1572–1631), the son of a wealthy London merchant, gained a reputation during his younger years as a swashbuckling rake in the world of wit and fashion. After attending both Oxford and Cambridge but taking a degree from neither university, he studied law at the Inns of Court, and took part in two naval expeditions in 1596 and 1597. Sojourning in Europe, marrying, and writing lyrical gems about love, collected posthumously in *Songs and Sonnets* (1633), led to a painful spiritual struggle with himself which resulted in his taking holy orders in the Anglican Church. During this inner turmoil, between 1607 and 1615, he wrote most of his religious verse including the twenty-six "holy" *Sonnets*. Six years after his ordination in 1615, he was appointed Dean of St. Paul's in London, and achieved a widespread reputation as an intensely passionate and clarion preacher.

ELIOT, T(HOMAS) S(TEARNS) (1888–    ), like Henry James, left the country of his birth to become a British citizen. He was born in St. Louis, Missouri, and educated at Harvard, the Sorbonne, and Oxford. His early poem "The Love Song of J. Alfred Prufrock" (1917) marked the beginning of a literary career which, by 1922 with the publication of "The Waste Land," has remained foremost among all twentieth century poets. Retaining his complex elliptical style, he infused *Ash Wednesday* (1930) and the *Four Quartets* (1943) with a deeply religious, Anglo-Catholic spirit. In addition to poetry, such plays as *Murder in the Cathedral* (1935) and *Cocktail Party* (1949) and such critical works as *The Sacred Wood* (1920) all have contributed to his monumental reputation.

FAULKNER, WILLIAM (1897–    ), left New Albany, Mississippi, early in his childhood and grew up forty miles away in Oxford, his home almost uninterruptedly ever since. As a member of the Canadian Flying Corps he served with the R.A.F. in France during the First World War. When he returned home he attended the University of Mississippi for one year. He lived for awhile in New Orleans, sharing an apartment with Sherwood Anderson, and in 1925 took a walking tour of Europe. Back in Oxford, isolated from the clamor of the times, he wrote *Soldier's Pay* (1926) and *Mosquitoes* (1927) and then began writing a southern saga unmatched for its virtuosity and extravagance. The saga unfolds in fictional Yoknapatawpha County—"William Faulkner sole owner and proprietor," as he described it. In more than a dozen novels placed in Yoknapatawpha County, he intricately wove together such themes as violence, degeneration, heroism, and endurance. Of these novels, his most famous are *The Sound and the Fury* (1929), *Light in August* (1932), *Absalom, Absalom!* (1936), *The Hamlet* (1940), *Intruder in the Dust* (1948), and *The Fable* (1954). In 1949 he won the Nobel Prize for literature.

FROST, ROBERT (1875–    ), though born in San Francisco, has traditionally been considered the poet of New England. Educated at Dartmouth and Harvard, he worked in a textile mill, taught school in New Hampshire, and even tried his hand at shoemaking. Finding no publisher for his poetry, he lived in England for a short time where he published *A Boy's Will* (1913) and *North of Boston* (1914), his first volumes of verse. In 1916 he joined the English faculty at Amherst where he taught, with brief leaves of absence, until 1938. Always direct and lucid, his writing has counterbalanced much modern poetry which is often characterized by its radical unconventionality frequently leading to obscurity. For his many volumes of poetry, collected into the *Complete Poems* (1949), he has received four Pulitzer Prizes and the gold medal of the National Institute of Arts and Letters.

HAWTHORNE, NATHANIEL (1804–1864), was born in Salem, Massachusetts, a town made infamous by the witchcraft trials of 1692 in which Hawthorne's great-grandfather was one of the three judges. After he was graduated from Bowdoin College, he returned to Salem where he wrote *Fanshawe* (1828) and many short stories, all published anonymously. His literary success was first established with the publication, under his own name, of *Twice-Told Tales* (1837)—stories which had earlier appeared in magazines. In 1839 he worked at the Boston Custom House, but resigned after two years to live at Brook Farm, a utopian experiment which disillusioned him after only six months. He married Sophia Peabody in 1842 and settled in the Old Manse in Concord where, amid an idyllic setting with his young bride, he wrote perhaps his most somber if not terrifying stories including "Young Goodman Brown," collected and published in *Mosses from an Old Manse* (1846). Financially hard-pressed, he took a job as Surveyor of the Port of Salem in 1846, but he quit in 1849 to start writing *The Scarlet Letter,* published the next year. After a move to Lenox, Massachusetts, in 1851, where he met Herman Melville and wrote *The House of the Seven Gables;* then another move to West Newton where he wrote *The Blithedale Romance* (1852); and still another move back to Concord where he wrote a biography of Franklin Pierce—he sailed with his family in 1853 to Liverpool, England, to serve as an American consul. He left in 1857 for the warmer climate of Italy, remaining there two years and writing *The Marble Faun* (1860). He returned to the United States in 1860 and lived in Concord until his death four years later.

HERBERT, GEORGE (1593–1633), was born into an aristocratic family at Montgomery Castle, Wales. He was educated by his mother, whom he fondly characterizes in his poetic *Parentalia,* his only published volume during his lifetime. After his graduation from Cambridge in 1613, he stayed on until 1626 when he was ordained deacon in Lincoln Cathedral. Four years later he was ordained as an Anglican priest and assigned to the rectory of Fulston St. Peter's in Wiltshire, where he became one of the most sought-after preachers in England. Izaak Walton called him "holy Herbert," and because of his profoundly metaphysical poetry he was referred to as "God's troubadour." Published after his death, his collection of sacred poems entitled *The Temple: Sacred Poems and Private Ejaculations* (1633) contains, in 129 poems, the record of his spiritual experiences.

HOUSMAN, A(LFRED) E(DWARD) (1859–1936), born at Fockbury in Worcestershire County, England, was graduated from Oxford in 1881 and took a position the following year in the Patent Office in London. A classical scholar while at Oxford, he continued to devote his spare time to Latin and Greek studies. Ten years later, in 1892, he was offered a Latin professorship at University College, London, where he stayed until 1911. In that year he was chosen from among England's best scholars to go to Cambridge as professor of Latin. Erudite, withdrawn, and single, he spent his remaining years at the University. His most famous collection of poems, *A Shropshire Lad* (1896), was followed by *Last Poems* (1922) and *More Poems* (1936). His poems show classical restraint and concentration. They center on a single theme: the brevity and tragedy of life.

IBSEN, HENRIK (1828–1906), is recognized today as the father of modern drama. Born in Skien, Norway, and accustomed to poverty and loneliness, he made his way to Oslo where his first play, *Catiline,* was published in 1850. There and in Bergen he studied dramaturgy, and in 1857 became Director of The Norwegian Theater in Oslo. Overworked and unhappy, he resigned in 1862 to have the leisure to write. Up to this time he had written nine plays, none of them successful; now one masterpiece followed another. *Brand* (1866) and *Peer Gynt* (1867) preceded *A Doll's House* (1879) and *Ghosts* (1881), the last two of such startlingly new realism that the public was outraged. *An Enemy of the People* (1882) re-established his reputation with his audiences, who missed the irony of his comedy. *The Wild Duck* (1884) and *Rosmersholm* (1886) contain exquisite poetry and deep soundings into the unconscious mind. *Hedda Gabler* (1890), a profound character study, and *The Master Builder* (1892), ironic and pessimistic, concluded his creative work. Shortly afterward, he suffered a paralytic stroke which disabled him until his death.

JAMES, HENRY (1843–1916), born in New York City, was a member of one of America's most illustrious families. His father, Henry James, Sr., wrote several books on Swedenborgian theology and his brother, William, was a brilliant professor and the foremost philosopher of Pragmatism. Of great inherited wealth, the family frequently traveled in Europe where Henry received much of his formal education. From 1865 he devoted himself to literature, and while in Boston he wrote stories for *Nation, Atlantic Monthly, Galaxy,* and other magazines. A most crucial decision, he took up permanent residence in England in 1876, becoming a naturalized British citizen in 1915. During his long and impressive career, he published scores of novels, stories, and plays. Toward the end of his career he rose to meteoric height, writing in heated succession his three most intricate and subtle novels: *The Wings of the Dove* (1902), *The Ambassadors* (1903), and *The Golden Bowl* (1904). These novels established him as one of the great psychological novelists of the present century. Shortly before his death he was awarded the British Order of Merit.

JOYCE, JAMES (1882–1941), more than any writer of our century, experimented with the craft of fiction and, as a result, created one of the most controversial novels of all time. In a stream-of-consciousness style, *Ulysses* (1922) deals with the events and countless psychological entanglements of a middle-class Dubliner and his wife during a single day. Full of blasphemy and obscenity the book was banned for many years in the United States and England, but it has since been acclaimed by both critics and artists as a vastly monumental work. In *Finnegans Wake* (1939), recording the subconscious mind in sleep, he extended his ambitious experiments in writing fiction to the point that he lost all but his most persevering readers. Born and educated in Dublin, he sensitively reacted to the poverty and squalor of the large city and to the pathos in the lives of its inhabitants. From this background he wrote *Dubliners* (1914), a collection of exquisite short stories. Two years later he wrote his first novel, *A Portrait of the Artist as a Young Man*, describing with incredible artistry the inner torments of Stephen Dedalus attempting to free himself from the inhibiting loyalties of family, church, and nation.

KAFKA, FRANZ (1883–1924), remains a literary enigma; certainly he is among the most neurotic of artists—and one of the most penetrating interpreters of neurosis. Scholars still puzzle over his weird tales. He was born in Prague of Jewish parentage and in 1906 received his degree in law at the German University in Prague. To his father's satisfaction, he obtained a position in an accident-insurance company. Caught between wanting to please his father, who was a forceful and thoroughly bourgeois businessman, and wanting to write fiction, he spent years of torment ineffectually doing both. Filled with guilt and wild discontent, he wrote in 1912 his famous story "The Judgment," which explores this terrible struggle between father and son. This story marks the beginning of his brief literary career, madly dedicated to the existential problems of man lonely and guilt-ridden in a neutral universe. In addition to several short stories—"The Metamorphosis," "In the Penal Colony," "The Hunger Artist" among his most famous—he also wrote three posthumously published novels: *The Trial* (1925), *The Castle* (1926), and *Amerika* (1927). He died at the age of 41 of tuberculosis.

KEATS, JOHN (1795–1821), greatest of the so-called second generation of Romantic poets, grew up in London where his father managed a livery stable. After his father's death in 1804 and his mother's in 1810, the four children were subjected to the haphazard care of guardians. Keats was apprenticed to a surgeon and passed his examinations before the Court of Apothecaries in 1816. Vastly more interested in poetry than chemistry, he showed one of his first poems—"On First Looking into Chapman's Homer" —to Leigh Hunt who promptly published it in his London newspaper in 1815. His first modest collection entitled *Poems* (1817) received abusive criticism and he was hailed as merely a "Cockney" rhymer. Alone on the Isle of Wight and deeply hurt from these reviews, he wrote *Endymion* which was published in 1818, the same year he developed tuberculosis. He went to live at Hampstead where he fell in love with Fanny Brawne, a 17-year-old coquette who understood nothing of her lover's anguish until after his death. During a flush of creative energy late in 1818, he wrote his most delicately beautiful poetry including his Odes "To a Nightingale," "On a Grecian Urn," "On Melancholy," and "To Autumn." In February, 1820, he realized his illness was fatal. In September he went to Italy with Joseph Severn and died in Rome the following February.

LAWRENCE, D(AVID) H(ERBERT) (1885–1930), was born in Nottingham, England, the son of a coal miner who would have been satisfied with his rugged life had it not been for his wife's complaints. Resentful toward her social inferiority, she insisted that her children get some education and leave the working-class life. David attended the University of Nottingham and taught school for a short time, but his over-ruling interest was in literature. In rapid order he wrote *The White Peacock* (1911), *The Tres-passers* (1912), and *Sons and Lovers* (1913) which is his best book. After marrying Frieda von Richthofen, wife of Ernest Weekly who was one of his university teachers, he boldly explored the problems of successful mating in *The Rainbow* (1915). Embittered by the public's suppression of this novel, he wrote as a more explicit sequel *Women in Love* which no publisher accepted till 1921. So, thoroughly hostile toward social hypocrisy, with its scientific education and pursuit of wealth, he left England permanently, hoping to rediscover the deep sources of imagination and spontaneity which modern civilization had blighted. First to Italy, then Australia, Mexico, and southwestern United States—he wandered continually looking for cultures in which one's emotional life could harmonize with social life. Expressive of these anxieties are several novels written during this time, most notably *Aaron's Rod* (1922), *Kangaroo* (1923), and the mystical *The Plumed Serpent* (1926). His strongest repudiation of emotionless, mechanized civilization was *Lady Chatterley's Lover* (1929), written in Italy where he died a year later of tuberculosis.

MacLEISH, ARCHIBALD (1892–    ), attended Yale and the Harvard Law School. After serving in the field artillery during World War I he practiced law in Boston for three years. In 1923 he left the legal profession to begin a long and fruitful career in teaching and writing. His early volumes of verse include *Tower of Ivory* (1917), *Streets of the Moon* (1926), and *The Hamlet of A. MacLeish* (1928). His recent poetic drama entitled *J.B.* (1958) has had a long run on Broadway and throughout the country. In addition to his literary achievements—for which he has received the Bollingen Prize, the National Book Award, and the Pulitzer Prize twice—he has been Boylston Professor of Rhetoric and Oratory at Harvard since 1949. He has also served as an editor of *Fortune,* as Librarian of Congress, and as an Assistant Secretary of State.

MARVELL, ANDREW (1621–1678), the son of an Anglican clergyman, was born at Winestead, Yorkshire, England. He spent most of his life at Cambridge University after his graduation in 1638. Few of his love lyrics were published during his life, though "To His Coy Mistress" has since become one of the best known in English lyric poetry. His contemporary fame as a writer came with his sharp satires against Charles II and his government. After his death from an accidental overdose of opiates, the main substance of his poetry was posthumously published in 1681.

MELVILLE, HERMAN (1819–1891), one of the literary giants of all time, was born in New York City and, when only 17, ran away to sea, leaving his widowed and destitute mother with seven other children. When he returned the following year (he had sailed to England), he looked far and wide for employment but found little except school teaching jobs at Pittsfield and East Albany. With a "damp, drizzly November" in his soul, he signed aboard the whaler *Acushnet* in 1841 and sailed for the south seas. In 1845 he was back home, ready to begin an incredibly prolific period of creative work: ten books in eleven years. His first books—*Typee* (1846) and *Omoo* (1847)—made him widely popular as a man who had lived among exotic savages. *Mardi* (1849) puzzled its readers, who could not understand why he had veered from the plot to devote over half the book to seemingly incoherent philosophy and exasperating satire. He returned to more conventional writing in *Redburn* (1849) and in *White Jacket* (1850). His masterpiece, *Moby Dick* (1851), dedicated to Nathaniel Hawthorne whose vision of blackness reinforced his own, was not popular, and *Pierre: or the Ambiguities* (1852) in its intense treatment of guilt alienated his readers even further. In 1855 he published *Israel Potter,* followed by *The Piazza Tales* in 1856, *The Confidence Man* in 1857, and three volumes of verse. From 1866 to 1885 he worked as a U.S. customs inspector on the New York docks. Just before his death in 1891 he wrote one of his greatest short stories, "Billy Budd," published posthumously in 1924.

POE, EDGAR ALLAN (1809–1849), orphaned in 1811, was taken from Boston, the city of his birth, to the home of John Allan, a merchant living in Richmond, Virginia. Quarreling often with his foster father, he left home in 1826 after completing only one term at the University of Virginia. In Boston he published *Tamerlane and Other Poems* (1827). But constantly in debt, he enlisted the same year in the U.S. Army, serving two years before procuring an appointment at West Point. Rebellious and unhappy, Poe deliberately neglected his duties and was dismissed in 1831. Earlier he had published *Al Aaraff, Tamerlane, and Minor Poems* (1829) in Baltimore, and after his West Point fiasco he published *Poems by Edgar A. Poe* (1831) in New York. His foster father dead and Mrs. Allan deserted, he moved into the house of Mrs. Clemm and her daughter and, in 1836, married the 13-year-old Virginia who died 11 years later from tuberculosis. During his erratic career he served as editor of several magazines including the *Southern Literary Messenger* in Richmond, *Burton's Gentleman's Magazine* (in which "The Fall of the House of Usher" first appeared) and *Graham's Magazine* in Philadelphia, and the *Broadway Journal* in New York. Constantly tortured by precarious physical and mental health, he irregularly contributed stories and poems to numerous periodicals. He published collections of them in such works as *Tales of the Grotesque and Arabesque* (1840) and *The Raven and Other Poems* (1845). Found beaten and intoxicated in a gutter, he was taken to a Baltimore hospital where, five days later, he died at the age of 40.

ROETHKE, THEODORE (1908–    ), was born in Saginaw, Michigan, and educated at the University of Michigan and Harvard. Before coming to his present teaching post at the University of Washington, he taught English at Lafayette College, Pennsylvania State College, and Bennington College. For his several volumes of poetry he has received both the Pulitzer Prize and the National Book Award.

SARTRE, JEAN-PAUL (1905–    ), is the most famous modern existentialist. Born in Paris, he finished his formal education in Berlin where he studied the writings of Husserl, Heidegger, and Kierkegaard—all philosophical existentialists. In his first novel, *Nausea* (1938), he probed into the meaning of existence, finding nothing except reasons for nausea. He continued in "The Wall," published the following year, to explore the meaning of life which lacked essence. During World War II he was taken prisoner on the Maginot Line and repatriated nine months later. *The Flies* (1942) and *No Exit* (1944) established him as a bold and skillful playwright, and his long philosophical work entitled *Being and Nothingness* (1943) made him the leading spokesman of atheistic existentialism. In fiction, drama, and philosophy, he has continued to represent French intellectualism in its most brilliant and fluent aspects.

SHAKESPEARE, WILLIAM (1564–1616), probably the greatest writer of all time, was born in Stratford-upon-Avon and, 52 years later, died in the same city. He married Anne Hathaway, who bore him three children. Most of his literary life was spent in London where, from 1594 on, he was associated exclusively with the Lord Chamberlain's Company which later became the King's Company; financially well off, it built the Globe Theater in 1599. From 1590 to 1600 he wrote his main chronicle plays, romances, and comedies. After 1600 his titanic plays appeared: *Hamlet* (1602), *Othello* (1604), *Macbeth* (1606), *King Lear* (1607), *Coriolanus* (1609). Of several volumes of poetry, his *Sonnets* (1609) are the best known. During a period of "reposeful contemplation" he wrote *Cymbeline* (1610), *The Tempest* (1611), and *The Winter's Tale* (1611), preceding his return to the city of his birth.

THOMAS, DYLAN (1914–1953), born in Swansea, Wales, served as an anti-aircraft gunner during World War II and also read his poetry over the BBC. Contained in his poetry are the acute contrasts between the romantic lyricism about nature and the agonized horror about war, death, and meaninglessness. His poetry was brought together in his *Collected Poems* (1953), but he is also remembered for such works as his play *Under Milk Wood* (1954) and his sprightly, anecdotal autobiography entitled *Portrait of the Artist as a Young Dog* (1940). Frequently reading his poetry to public audiences, he was well known on many American college campuses. Some critics believe his last four years of extensive touring and public readings wasted his creative energy. His tragic death in New York City resulted from acute alcoholism.

TOLSTOY, LEO (1828–1910), despite the fact that he came from a background of aristocratic landowners, was chiefly interested in the primitive living conditions and simplicity of the Russian peasants. He described the Cossack settlers in his first novel, *The Cossacks,* written in 1854 and published nine years later. He traveled extensively in Russia and Europe, returning to his estate each time with a greater respect for the serfs. On his estate he started a school for peasant children whom he paternally taught. In 1862 he was married and in that same year started writing his great novel *War and Peace* which he finished nine years later. After more years of work he completed *Anna Karenina* in 1877. Deeply moral in his search for the meaning of life, found he said in the Sermon on the Mount, he wrote several more haunting masterpieces: *The Death of Iván Ilych* (1884), *The Kreutzer Sonata* (1889), and his last great novel *The Resurrection* (1899).

VAUGHAN, HENRY (1622–1695), a British mystic poet, was known as "the Silurist" because he was born in South Wales, home of the ancient Silures who inhabited southern Wales. First a student of law in London, then of medicine, he returned to Wales to live and practice among his own people. After a prolonged illness his heightened spiritual awareness led to his writing the deeply moving sacred poetry in *Silex Scintillans* (1650). His mystical poetry immediately linked him with the work of George Herbert, another metaphysical poet. Two centuries later scholars noticed similarities in Vaughan's mysticism and love of nature with these same qualities in Wordsworth's poetry.

WHITMAN, WALT(ER) (1819–1892), was born in Huntington, Long Island, New York. Four years later his parents, with their nine children, moved to Brooklyn, where his father, a carpenter, built and sold houses and where Walt, after leaving school in 1830, first worked as office boy and printer's assistant to help supplement his father's meager earnings. By 1841 he had become a full-time editor of newspapers both on Long Island and in New York City. His most important editorship, from 1846 to 1848, was for the Brooklyn *Eagle*. His gigantic contribution to American literature occurred in 1855, the publication date of his first edition of *Leaves of Grass* containing 12 untitled poems. This one major volume, enlarged and revised through ten subsequent editions, appeared in its final eleventh edition in 1892 and contained 383 titled poems. Few other American writers have been as controversial—as abused and as heralded—as Whitman. Several prose works including *Democratic Vistas* (1871) and *Specimen Days* (1883) reveal further dimensions to his enormous power of expression. Nothing he wrote, however, has the broad grandeur and poignancy of his poems such as "Song of Myself," "Out of the Cradle Endlessly Rocking," "When Lilacs Last in the Dooryard Bloom'd," "Crossing Brooklyn Ferry," "Passage to India," and poems in *Drum-Taps* including "A March in the Ranks Hard-Prest." In 1873, after a paralytic stroke which left him a semi-invalid, he moved to Camden, New Jersey, where he spent his remaining years.

WORDSWORTH, WILLIAM (1770–1850), and the Lake District of Cumberland recall England's greatest romantic poetry. Born in Cockermouth, he was dependent upon his uncles for his education after his mother died when he was eight, his father when he was 13. After leaving Cambridge in 1787, he went to France where his two great passions were the French Revolution and Annette Vallon whom he never married but whose daughter, Anne Caroline, was born from this relationship. Another important phase in his life was meeting Samuel Taylor Coleridge in 1794 and collaborating with him in *Lyrical Ballads* (1798). This slender volume of verse, including Wordsworth's "Tintern Abbey" and Coleridge's "The Rime of the Ancient Mariner," is highly important for its rebellion against the contorted and artificially stylized contemporary verse. In 1799 Wordsworth and his sister Dorothy settled at Dove Cottage by Grasmere where he and Coleridge worked on an enlarged edition of *Lyrical Ballads* (1800). During the next three years Wordsworth reached the pinnacle of his creative work. He wrote much poetry after this period, but it was anti-climactic. With Mary Hutchinson, whom he married in 1802, he spent his remaining years in the Lake District. He became Poet Laureate of England in 1843, long after his best poetry had been written.

YEATS, WILLIAM BUTLER (1865–1939), who was born near Dublin, enjoyed as a child the west country of Ireland, especially the lakes of Sligo, which inspired his early poem "The Lake Isle of Innisfree." As the leading poet of the Irish Literary Revival, he was determined to create a literature purely Irish. To this end, he studied Irish folk tales before publishing his first poem of importance, *The Wanderings of Oisin* (1889). With the same nationalistic spirit he collaborated with Isabella Augusta, Lady Gregory, in founding the Irish National Theatre Society in 1899. For two decades he loved Maud Gonne, but he was finally rejected in marriage by both her and her daughter Iseult. In 1917 he married Georgie Hyde-Lees. His poetry in later years was inspired by occult and prophetic depths, manifested with tremendous splendor in such poems as "The Magi" and "Sailing to Byzantium." His pronouncements of gloom and destruction assume an eerie power in "The Second Coming" and "Leda and the Swan." For his numerous plays, published essays, criticisms, and volumes of verse, he was awarded the Nobel Prize for literature in 1923.

# Index of Authors and Titles